THE CONGRESSMAN
His Work as He Sees It

THE CONGRESSMAN

His Work as He Sees It

by

Charles L. Clapp

THE BROOKINGS INSTITUTION

Washington, D. C.

© 1963 by

THE BROOKINGS INSTITUTION

Published December 1963

Library of Congress Catalog Card Number 63-23202

THE BROOKINGS INSTITUTION is an independent organization devoted to nonpartisan research, education, and publication in economics, government, foreign policy, and the social sciences generally. Its principal purposes are to aid in the development of sound public policies and to promote public understanding of issues of national importance.

The Institution was founded December 8, 1927, to merge the activities of the Institute for Government Research, founded in 1916, the Institute of Economics, founded in 1922, and the Robert Brookings Graduate School of Economics and Government, founded in 1924.

The general administration of the Institution is the responsibility of a self-perpetuating Board of Trustees. The Trustees are likewise charged with maintaining the independence of the staff and fostering the most favorable conditions for creative research and education. The immediate direction of the policies, program, and staff of the Institution is vested in the President, assisted by the division directors and an advisory council, chosen from the professional staff of the Institution.

In publishing a study, the Institution presents it as a competent treatment of a subject worthy of public consideration. The interpretations and conclusions in such publications are those of the author or authors and do not purport to represent the views of the other staff members, officers, or trustees of the Brookings Institution.

Foreword

Building on successful experience with the conference technique as an aid to research, the Brookings Institution organized a Round Table Conference on Congress in the spring of 1959.[1] The purpose of the Round Table was to encourage a group of congressmen to discuss Congress and their life in it fully and frankly in an atmosphere of intellectual inquiry, and thus to provide a revealing and realistic view of one of the most interesting and important institutions in democratic government, the House of Representatives. The House had been comparatively neglected by researchers, and it was hoped that a study based on first-hand testimony of thoughtful members would contribute to a better understanding of the House and of the problems of the congressman. It was hoped also that the ideas presented would stimulate further investigation of issues touched on only lightly in this book. The Round Table participants are identified and the procedures followed are outlined in the Introduction to the study.

Charles L. Clapp, then of the Governmental Studies staff, served as executive secretary, and had the principal part in organizing the conference and preparing the agenda. George A. Graham, Director of Governmental Studies at the Brookings Institution, served as conference chairman. Mr. Clapp subsequently prepared this book from the recorded discussions, from additional interviews, and from other relevant materials. A political scientist with teaching and governmental experience, he had worked in both the House and the Senate, in the offices of members of Congress, and for congressional committees before joining the Brookings staff. He has now returned to Capitol Hill where he is Legislative Assistant to Senator Leverett Saltonstall of Massachusetts. The Brookings Institution is indebted to him for the skill with which he has brought the material together and prepared the manuscript.

The Institution and the author wish to record their indebtedness to the

[1] For an account of two previous conferences see: *The Job of the Federal Executive* by Marver H. Bernstein (1958) and *The Business Representative in Washington* by Paul W. Cherington and Ralph L. Gillen (1962).

participants for their contribution to the volume and for reviewing the manuscript, and for offering constructive suggestions. They are grateful also to Laurin Henry of the Brookings staff, Professor Ralph Huitt of the University of Wisconsin, and Professor H. D. Price of Syracuse University, who served as an Advisory Committee to review the manuscript, and to Evelyn Breck who edited it. Adele Garrett prepared the index.

The Round Table was financed by a grant from the McKinsey Foundation for Management Research, Inc., for which the Institution expresses its grateful appreciation.

The opinions and interpretations contained in this publication are those of the participants or the author and do not purport to represent the views of the trustees, officers, or other staff members of the Brookings Institution, the Advisory Committee, or the McKinsey Foundation.

Robert D. Calkins
President

October 1963
The Brookings Institution
1775 Massachusetts Avenue, N.W.
Washington 36, D. C.

Contents

Introduction

THIS IS A BOOK ABOUT the congressman and the Congress, written essentially from the congressman's point of view. Its purpose is to help inform the public about the responsibilities and difficulties of members of the House and the ways in which representatives meet them. For, as one congressman observed, constituents tend to be poor employers: few understand the nature of the jobs they distribute biennially.

There is relatively little in the literature that focuses directly and with understanding on the congressman and his problems. As a result, although a satisfactory impression of the formal organization of the Congress can readily be obtained, the system as it actually functions tends to remain a mystery to the public and even to many serious students of the subject. Testimony of congressmen regarding their role and functions and about the legislative process itself is valuable but it is fragmentary. Additional information from the members themselves would provide a more realistic appreciation of Congress in action.

In approaching the subject, it was decided, therefore, to draw heavily on the experiences and views of a cross section of able House members (by means of both individual interview and group discussion) and to produce a volume that would emphasize their perspective. To provide greater depth to the study, the author examined articles and books written by members of Congress and others and undertook further research on certain issues.

The Brookings Round Table

At the core of the study was the Brookings Institution Round Table Conference on Congress, which was divided into two panels, one composed of nineteen Democratic members of the House of Representatives, the other consisting of seventeen Republican members.[1]

---

[1] Initially there were eighteen representatives in each panel. Following the first session of the Democratic round table, one congressman, who had indicated earlier he would be unable to participate, expressed an interest in attending and was invited to do so. One Republican panelist found it impossible to attend any of the early sessions and withdrew.

Each group met separately at eight dinner meetings during the first six months of 1959. The decision to have them meet separately was reached after consultation with representatives of both parties. Everyone consulted agreed that a full and frank discussion would be materially promoted by such a separation; some warned that joint sessions could be disastrous if candor was a goal. A by-product of the separate sessions was the discovery that each group exaggerated somewhat the resources and strength of the opposition.

To focus the discussion, the author prepared an agenda for each meeting, forwarding it to panelists in advance. Democratic and Republican groups received the same agenda. A stenographic record was made of the proceedings, but participants were assured it was confidential and would not be made available to nonparticipants. While the essence of the statements was to be maintained, it was understood that remarks would be edited and condensed where necessary. A final meeting was held in the spring of 1963 to review the manuscript to which all conference participants and their spouses were invited. Everyone present agreed that the round table sessions had been reported faithfully, and no objections were raised to the interview material and other source material used to supplement them.

Participants. The thirty-six congressional participants represented all geographic sections of the country and were drawn from middle and junior groups in Congress in terms of seniority. Senior members of the House were deliberately excluded on the ground that they might dominate the sessions and yet might be less inclined to be expansive than colleagues with somewhat less service; this decision was not without its disadvantages, of course. Five freshmen members were included, and four panelists were in their sixth terms in the House. Conferees were selected primarily on the basis of interest, competence, and standing among their colleagues. The desirability of including members representing various kinds of constituencies and reflecting different ideological points of view was kept in mind. Eighteen of the twenty standing committees of the House were represented.

The participants would not be regarded as "average" congressmen. As a group they were above the average in terms of effectiveness and ability. In selecting them, Brookings solicited advice from many members of Congress and from individuals close to Congress; there was considerable similarity among lists of suggestions obtained in this manner. The response to the Brookings invitation was excellent. Very few legislators declined; and, with one or two exceptions, participants were conscientious in attending sessions despite busy schedules.

Discussions. Attendance and interest held up very well in both groups. For most discussions about three-fourths of the conferees were present. The discussion was never dull, and sometimes was spirited and even heated. All conferees participated fully and frankly, and participants did not hesitate to express disagreement with, or reservations about, the observations and assertions of colleagues. The quality of discussion was exceptionally high in both groups. Neither group could fairly be said to have been superior. There were, inevitably, slight differences in approach. There was somewhat more levity in the Democratic group than in the Republican one, and it was a little more difficult to keep the Democrats within the confines of the agenda. The Republicans adhered somewhat more closely to the matter at hand.

It was evident that those invited appreciated the opportunity to sit down together to discuss systematically common problems and various aspects of the House. Indeed, the meetings served to underscore the fact that too few opportunities are available to congressmen to evaluate their experience in a serious, detached manner.

After several sessions, it was clear, too, that the participants regarded the conference as a learning experience: they learned much from one another about phases of congressional activity on which they previously lacked information, and they got from each other new insights into problems on which they had regarded themselves as well informed. They also gained new perspectives about the problems of colleagues whose districts and situations differed significantly from theirs. Congressional districts, of course, differ markedly, as do congressmen, and solutions to problems arising out of one district or viewed from one vantage point might not be suitable for application in other circumstances, discussants emphasized. Participants clearly gained ideas from colleagues, which they could and would put to good use, and increased the breadth of their understanding regarding many procedural matters. At times, however, though they might marvel at the success of an associate in meeting a particular problem, they believed his solution would not be effective in their own situation.

At the conclusion of the round table meetings one participant said:

It was most stimulating to participate. Each of us learned a great deal from the discussions. We do not often have the opportunity to devote an extended period to joint discussion of these various problems. As one result we all gained a better insight into the problems faced by some of our fellow congressmen in their own states and districts.

Added another Congressman: "We were privileged to be chosen to be the guinea pigs. It was a rich, rewarding and educational experience of a high order." Wrote another participant: "The sessions were very helpful to me. As a matter of fact, in my ten and a half years in Congress I have not enjoyed any series of meetings so much as I did these."

The focus of the round table discussions was on the job of the congressman and the environment within which he functions. It is understandable, probably inevitable, that in such discussions the difficulties and weaknesses of the system should receive the most attention. Some concern was expressed in both groups that the record would appear basically negative rather than positive, illuminating weaknesses rather than strengths, thereby appearing to lend support to critics of the House and its membership. In fact, however, the legislators believe that, on balance, the House is an effective institution.

Within the alert and intelligent group assembled at Brookings, there was much affection for the House and a conviction that it has been too long in the shadow of the Senate. Among the strengths of the House mentioned most frequently were the careful scrutiny given to legislative proposals; the generally high calibre of the membership and the salutary effects of specialization; the "representativeness" of the House: the close relationship existing between member and constituency; and the successful evolution of workable procedures facilitating the operation of a large, unwieldy body.

Although conference participants believed many criticisms of the House to be unfair and based on misunderstanding or misconceptions, there was no attempt to whitewash Congress. Panelists clearly were aware that there are many flaws in the system, some of which they believe to be serious. Although they regret that the House has not devoted sufficient attention to seeking remedies for its failings, they stressed that the pressures of congressional responsibilities are so great and correction of some of the deficiencies poses such problems that it is understandable that matters of direct and immediate concern take precedence. Defects in procedure tend to receive serious attention only when some crisis thrusts special focus on them.

Interviews

Approximately fifty interviews were taken by the author following the completion of the round table sessions, most of them during the last weeks of the first session of the Eighty-sixth Congress. These were scheduled to complete certain gaps in the conference record and to clarify and supplement other parts of it. About twenty of the interviewees were round table participants, a like number were other members of the House (mostly freshmen), and the remainder were employees of congressional committees or of House members. Cooperation was excellent. The observations of individuals interviewed are interspersed throughout the volume in the same way as the discussions recorded in the round table sessions, minimizing the possibility of identifying what was said by any individual.

The combination of group discussion and individual interviews worked well. The group situation seemed to trigger responses and insights that might never have been brought out in the interviews. It facilitated the gathering of certain kinds of information, and it faced participants with the prospect of being challenged about their views by colleagues, thus placing special emphasis on accuracy. The exchange was beneficial, too, in serving as something of an educational experience for members and in demonstrating vividly the difference in member reactions to the same situations.

Yet the individual interview possessed advantages, too. On certain sensitive issues, for example, some conference participants were privately more forthright, sometimes taking the initiative in raising these matters. Sharing the common experience of the conference sessions with the interviewer may have promoted this tendency. The interviews also broadened the base of congressional opinion, which contributed to the study and permitted fuller exposition by members of points of special interest to them.

This volume does not, of course, pretend to point up all the strengths and weaknesses of the House or to suggest solutions to all of the problems that plague that legislative body. Quite apart from the fact that all Congresses have their own special qualities, depending on events and personalities, most of the comments recorded here were made when one political party controlled Congress and the other the Executive.

Congressional Wives Luncheon

Before the round table sessions were concluded, a luncheon meeting was organized to which the wives of all conference participants were invited. The luncheon grew out of a belief that the story would be incomplete without proper recognition of the role and attitudes of the wives with respect to their husbands' work and of their insights into the special problems that confront congressional families. Twenty-one wives attended the three-hour bipartisan meeting, which added new dimensions to the total picture. The record of the meeting was supplemented by individual discussions with several of the participants, letters received from invitees unable to attend the luncheon, personal knowledge of the activities and attitudes of other congressional wives in connection with politics, and conversations with round table participants regarding the role of their wives in their work.

List of Participants

The following members of Congress participated in the round table sessions:

The Honorable Perkins Bass	(New Hampshire)
The Honorable John F. Baldwin	(California)
The Honorable Richard Bolling	(Missouri)
The Honorable John Brademas	(Indiana)
The Honorable Marguerite Stitt Church	(Illinois)
The Honorable Frank M. Coffin	(Maine)
The Honorable Silvio O. Conte	(Massachusetts)
The Honorable Thomas B. Curtis	(Missouri)
The Honorable Ed Edmondson	(Oklahoma)
The Honorable Carl Elliott	(Alabama)
The Honorable Gerald R. Ford, Jr.	(Michigan)
The Honorable Peter Frelinghuysen, Jr.	(New Jersey)
The Honorable Robert P. Griffin	(Michigan)

The Honorable Byron L. Johnson — (Colorado)
The Honorable Charles Raper Jonas — (North Carolina)
The Honorable Richard E. Lankford — (Maryland)
The Honorable John V. Lindsay — (New York)
The Honorable George S. McGovern — (South Dakota)
The Honorable Lee Metcalf — (Montana)
The Honorable John E. Moss — (California)
The Honorable Richard H. Poff — (Virginia)
The Honorable Albert H. Quie — (Minnesota)
The Honorable James M. Quigley — (Pennsylvania)
The Honorable Henry S. Reuss — (Wisconsin)
The Honorable John J. Rhodes — (Arizona)
The Honorable Paul C. Rogers — (Florida)
The Honorable Alfred E. Santangelo — (New York)
The Honorable Fred Schwengel — (Iowa)
The Honorable Frank E. Smith — (Mississippi)
The Honorable Keith Thomson — (Wyoming)
The Honorable Stewart L. Udall — (Arizona)
The Honorable Al Ullman — (Oregon)
The Honorable Jessica Weis — (New York)
The Honorable Bob Wilson — (California)
The Honorable James C. Wright, Jr. — (Texas)
The Honorable Sidney R. Yates — (Illinois)

I

The Member and His Colleagues

A NEW MEMBER of the House of Representatives finds himself in a body where, in recent years, the average age at the beginning of each Congress has been around fifty-two, where slightly more than half of the membership are lawyers, nearly one-third have backgrounds in business or banking, another 10 percent have been teachers, and about the same percentage have been engaged in farming. Approximately three-fifths have served in the armed forces. The number of women House members reached a peak of fifteen in the Eighty-seventh Congress, dropping back to eleven in the Eighty-eighth.

When a member begins to get acquainted with his colleagues and with the House itself, he finds that the members are very much individuals, on the whole able, with varied strengths and interests, like himself anxious to succeed, but all compelled to function more or less in accordance with traditional rules of the game established over the years. The system gives little advantage to newcomers, innovators, independents, men in a hurry, or those who are not prepared to work.

Introducing the Freshman to Congress

Following his election to the House of Representatives a new member is forwarded a pamphlet entitled "Information for Representatives Elect." This document tells him of the procedure to be followed in the allocation of office suites, and supplies information regarding his salary and the congressional retirement system, as well as the clerk hire allotment at his disposal and how it may be distributed. It also sets forth the allowances available to him for travel, stationery, telephone and telegrams, stamps, and his district office. Yet it provides no guidance regarding the most important problems which immediately concern him: how to obtain a choice committee assignment, how to organize a superior staff, or what

8

to do about housing. Nor is it helpful in suggesting what is expected of him as a new member of the House, what he can anticipate congressional life to be like, and how he can become an effective, respected member.

Unfortunately, there is no other official communication that covers these matters. Except for congratulatory letters from the party leadership and his new colleagues, and a rather formal note about organization from the party leaders, there is little assistance from the Congress, unless a senior colleague or friend, anticipating his questions, proffers advice. He is left largely to his own devices, and though the experience of seeking solutions to his problems may be worthwhile, much valuable time is wasted. At the same time he may make serious errors that will delay his advancement.

The Initial Reaction. The new legislator comes to Congress with opinions about lobbyists, seniority, the calibre of his colleagues, and a host of other matters—many of them erroneous but firmly held nonetheless. He is likely to have held political or elective office previously and to have become interested in politics at an early age. Thus he is prone to regard himself as politically sophisticated, and qualified to move quickly into positions of responsibility.

The first term congressman often has been a member of a state legislature, and he may expect to be a full partner in the day-to-day operations of the legislative process, ignoring the substantial differences between the national and state legislative bodies. Representatives who state that congressional service has not been significantly different from their expectations (many proceed to demonstrate that it has indeed been much different) often cite prior state legislative experience as having prepared them fully for life in the House.

The value of tenure at the state level in facilitating adjustment to the congressional scene is easily exaggerated, however, as some former state legislators are careful to point out. The more accurate view is that such service "prepared me somewhat" or "provided a partial understanding of the legislative process and some idea of what to expect." The national and state legislative bodies "differ markedly." The state legislature is "much more informal and less complicated," the turnover is rapid, and there a newcomer is likely to "play an active role more quickly."

Some freshmen House members are difficult to persuade that the differences are important. In view of their backgrounds, adjustment may not be easy. A freshman finds he is entering a group with firmly established, though ostensibly informal, patterns of behavior, where he is expected to serve an apprenticeship. He has more to learn than he sometimes realizes. The rapidity with which he learns what must be done and what must be avoided can go far to determine his eventual success in the House.

Woodrow Wilson, writing in 1885, described the situation confronting the freshman House member in this way:

The newly-elected member always experiences great difficulty in adjusting his pre-conceived ideas of congressional life to the strange and unlooked for conditions by which he finds himself surrounded. No man, when chosen to the membership of a body possessing great powers and exalted prerogatives, likes to find his activity repressed and himself suppressed, by imperative rules and precedents which seem to have been framed for the deliberate purpose of making usefulness unattainable by individual members. Yet such the new member finds the rules and precedents of the House to be. It matters not to him, because it is not apparent on the face of things, that those rules and precedents have grown, not out of set purpose to curtail the privileges of new members as such, but out of the plain necessities of business; it remains the fact that he suffers under their curb.[1]

His description retains much relevance today although some members display little evidence of suffering, and others appear to adjust rapidly to the realities of life in the House. Yet initial distress at the inhibiting effects of the rules and precedents (if it is apparent) is but part of the consternation of the congressman in his first session as a national legislator. As has been suggested, he may be surprised to find how little formal effort is made to facilitate his assimilation within his new peer group.

Some influential House veterans recognize the long-range value of assisting new members; others seem only to take a casual interest in them. Although there is clear evidence that both parties are making increased and important use of the talents of freshmen and other relatively junior members, it is apparent that a number of the recent arrivals are not satisfied with their status or progress. They chafe under inferior committee assignments, and resent following the leadership of party col-

[1] *Congressional Government* (Houghton Mifflin Company, 1885), pp. 61–63.

leagues who, whether in committee or on the floor, seem less than articulate and alert. Some freshmen are impatient for recognition, and they feel ignored. Gradually, however, most of them come to accept the system, understand and even defend the reasons it is as it is, learn to appreciate the strengths of their colleagues, and begin to watch for the clues that indicate a man is on the way up. This state is achieved in no set time period, but most representatives are absorbed rather quickly.

The Influence of Folklore. Although junior members are being assimilated into the work of the House more easily and readily than formerly, the traditions and folklore of that body serve to impress on them the virtues of being patient and not being troublesome. They operate to restrain a freshman from exercising his impulse to plunge wholeheartedly into all aspects of House activity. He hears and notes the truisms that have gained nearly universal acceptance. Most of them have come to be regarded as emanating from some House "giant," often the late Speaker, Sam Rayburn. Thus advice such as "to get along, go along," and "a man is never defeated by the speech he didn't make" is passed along to the newcomer who is told that time will demonstrate its wisdom.

Some of the truisms, though they remain essentially accurate, have been modified by time. The old admonition that new members should observe but not participate in debate was swept aside long ago. Apprenticeship may still precede full partnership, but the increased volume and complexity of the problems with which the Congress is compelled to cope dictate more efficient use of the membership. Freshmen are now advised to defer speaking only until the moment arrives when they have something significant to say—indeed, colleagues counsel them not to wait too long—although they are cautioned to be sure they are well informed about their topic. They are also warned against speaking too often and on too many different subjects. Senior colleagues face a similar though somewhat more flexible stricture. Freshmen who ignore this advice—and some do—irritate their peers and are often the subject of sanctions. "He talks too much," is a description often heard in connection with a few members. At times these men cannot understand why they are passed over for assignments for which they are intellectually prepared. The blunt truth is that colleagues do not wish to see them get ahead or to work with them, despite their qualifications.

The Workload and Pressures. There is so much to be done and there are so many conflicting pressures that it is small wonder that a few representatives do not appear well informed about their jobs or current congressional activities. A large proportion seem amazingly versatile and accomplished.

Being a congressman is a full-time and exacting job. Freshmen who have served in state legislatures are often pleased to discover the wealth of research assistance available to them, in sharp contrast to that provided in the state capital. Their pleasure turns to chagrin, however, when they come to appreciate the workload and how little personal staff time is available for research activities. The two-year term promotes preoccupation with re-election, the committee work is often onerous and time consuming, yet the conscientious member desires to perform his duties well and to be recognized by his colleagues as an able legislator, a welcome addition to the House. In his anxiety to be so recognized, he seeks advice from many quarters—from colleagues on committees and in his state delegation, party leaders, veteran Hill staff, and other sources. And he does not seek in vain. Much advice is forthcoming.

A Lecture for Freshmen. The enterprising freshman member who wants to get ahead is told that the committee system is the core of the legislative process and that the best way to attract the favorable attention of his colleagues is to participate wholeheartedly in his committee work. There he should develop a specialty and concentrate on it, playing down other interests he may have that fall within the jurisdiction of other committees.

He is advised to spend as much time as possible on the House floor and in the cloakrooms, absorbing parliamentary procedure and observing the give and take which is such a fundamental part of the legislative process. He should participate in the activities of a variety of informal House groups and clubs, thereby expanding the number of his potential allies. Making friends with his colleagues is a most important activity indeed, and he should develop friendly relationships with committee and House staff and agency personnel as well. The resourceful beginner will learn that the cornerstones of success are, in fact, hard work and making friends.

The new member is counseled to resist the temptation to recruit an inexperienced staff from his district. One or more competent, experienced Capitol Hill professionals should be hired. He should try to organize the staff so as to permit himself time for reading and study. He should become familiar with the research facilities available to him and his office and learn how to make best use of them. For the first session at least, he should try to read the *Congressional Record* regularly. He should examine as many committee reports as possible and, in his field of special interest, obtain reports over a three- or four-year period, a valuable source of background information and ideas.

The junior member should defer to the elders of the House and the leadership, but not to the Senate or the executive. While he must not move precipitously, he need not hesitate to speak up when he has something to say. He is advised not to draw attention to himself by unusual dress or attitude—only senior members can successfully defy convention. When he receives his committee assignment, it will be wise to arrange for briefings at the appropriate executive agencies. This will help to make him an effective member early and will be favorably received by the executive.

While attending to all of these matters, he must not neglect his constituents. They should be carefully cultivated. Prompt attention should be given to mail from home, district newspapers should be read or scanned regularly, and press coverage of the legislator's office should be supplemented by his own releases publicizing his activities. He should undertake all sorts of projects designed to create a district image of him as an active legislator, informed and concerned about public problems and deeply interested in the opinions and welfare of those he represents.

Because so much of a legislator's time is spent in close association with colleagues, and because their cooperation is so often required if he is to succeed, freshman members are especially cautioned about intragroup relationships. Thus a brief discussion within the Democratic round table regarding "rules of the game" was primarily concerned with this subject:

The main rule of the game is "thou shalt not demagogue thy colleagues." We acknowledge that a person does a little bit of demagoguery with his people, but snow is for the folks.

*

There is another rule that you shouldn't do harm to a colleague if you can avoid it. You have to live with these people. You need their votes just as they need yours.

*

Another rule is the rule of convenience. Whatever is most convenient for the majority of the members will be respected. Along the same line is the idea that agreements made between leaders on both sides will be respected and followed. Once in awhile you run into individualists who will refuse to abide by an agreement but ordinarily people go along.

Personal Relationships and Reactions

Getting acquainted with one's colleagues is perhaps one of the most important and immediate tasks confronting a new member. The relationships that develop between individuals go far toward determining effectiveness in the House.

Developing Friendships with the Opposition. Members agree that it is much easier to become acquainted with party colleagues than political opponents. Friendships with the latter seem most likely to develop in informal rather than formal settings. Said one Republican:

> The system seems to prevent one's forming strong friendships on the other side of the aisle. Somehow we never seem to get down to that. Some people have mentioned the gym as a place where Democrats and Republicans can meet easily. I'd say the same thing about the golf course. That's one place where I get to know a lot of Democrats much better.

At a session of House Democrats, members discussed ways in which they came to know their colleagues. Of special concern was the difficulty in meeting Republicans. Participants emphasized the value of informal contacts such as the gym and playing cards provide. Working together in committee, especially on matters of mutual interest, was considered helpful in breaking down party barriers, but again the less formal committee situations were stressed, such as taking trips together on committee business. The friendships that develop between wives of members as they participate in community activities was also noted as leading to increased association between the members themselves.

> In the few months I have been here I have had almost no social intercourse with the Republicans. From watching the Senate in action you get the impression that those guys all get along pretty well with one another, regardless of party. In the House, people are pleasant, but you don't see much of them. I don't know more than a very few Republicans by sight.

*

_____'s reclamation project carried by just a few votes. One thing that broke the liberal and big city line against it was the fact that all the boys who played poker and gin rummy with him voted for it. And they took some of the rest of us with them. They said he wasn't going to be so difficult in the future.

*

A feeling of comraderie develops in the committees. You tend to go along with your fellow committee members on bills in which they are particularly interested. I find myself going along sometimes even with members on the other side, although for some that principle works in reverse: they irritate you so much that you are against anything they are for.

*

The trips we take with our Republican colleagues are a great help in leading to mutual understanding and cooperation, and the kinds of activities which enlist the support of the wives are important too. My attitude toward _____ is influenced by the fact that his wife works well with mine on a particular project.

One member summed up the most important advantage of the informal contact:

There aren't enough hours in the day to permit us to get to know all the members of the House and Senate. Any activity—social, political, religious, recreational, whatever it may be—that gives you a sense of common knowledge and affinity promotes cooperation, if there isn't some strong reason for going the other way.

Attitudes toward Colleagues. As illustrated in the discussion reported above, close association can have negative as well as positive effects on a member's future. He may antagonize colleagues, and his proposals as well as his own progress may suffer. Generally, however, the bonds are strong among members. Congressmen have shared many similar experiences, including exposure to the electorate, and together they face the continuing threat of defeat. They are plagued by many of the same problems and uncertainties, and they can understand, and forgive, temporary aberrations of colleagues. As Speaker Champ Clark once told his associates, "Men who fight together in this legislative body have a feeling approximating that of the soldiers feeling for each other."

Members are continuously evaluating the abilities of their associates, even as they share a general feeling of affinity and good will toward one another and display the courtesy and thoughtfulness to which colleagues are deemed entitled by virtue of their position. They are mindful of the statement of Speaker Rayburn that "the House is the greatest jury in the world when it comes to knowing its own membership," and they quote it often with endorsement. Their beliefs are echoed, too, in the words of another great Speaker of the House, "Uncle Joe" Cannon who said:

Nowhere else will you find such a ready appreciation of merit and character. In few gatherings of equal size is there so little jealousy and envy. The House must be considerate of the feelings of its members; there is a certain courtesy that has to be observed; a man may be voted a bore or shunned as a pest, and yet he must be accorded the rights to which he is entitled by virtue of being a representative of the people. On the other hand, a man may be universally popular, a good fellow, amusing, and yet with those engaging qualities never go far.

If their views regarding their colleagues have changed since they entered the House, the change has been in the direction of a greater appreciation of their abilities. In conversation the legislators may mention that the public image of the typical congressman is unfortunate: Representatives are of much higher calibre and far more dedicated than the public realizes. Respect for one another grows. Many members have undergone a change of attitude toward their peers similar to that reflected in the words of one of their more respected colleagues:

When I first came I was awed by the situation and by the people around me and I said, "What am I doing here in the company of these great men?" Then I began to see their weaknesses and I realized that many of them had clay feet. Pretty soon I was saying, "What's he doing here?" But in most cases I find upon longer association that each member possesses some trait which makes him desirable and valuable, and so my respect has been rekindled and regenerated. My present view is that most congressmen are pretty able people.

One quality the legislators believe is possessed by a large number of their associates is that of versatility. Even more impressive, in their eyes, is the collegial versatility that characterizes the House and constitutes one measure in which it is superior to its rival, the Senate. Stated one member at the conclusion of his first year in Congress:

The versatility of my colleagues is a source of amazement to me. There is always someone around here who's an expert on something you need to know. I dare say there is not one subject you could think of that doesn't have at least one member of the House particularly qualified to give you advice about.

Public disparagement of colleagues is strongly discouraged; it is not the way to play the game. Personal attacks are sharply censured, and members seldom invade the congressional districts of colleagues of another party to campaign against them. Democrats reacted strongly to the action of one House Republican in sending letters into the district of a Democratic colleague criticizing the latter for apparent inconsistencies between a stated position and a vote. The Republican was inaccurate and unfair, though in character, they said. Moreover, he had violated an unwritten rule of the House, and it was clear that somewhere along the route of his career he would be held accountable for it.

The tendency to maintain at least surface friendliness and to avoid personal controversy with colleagues constitutes a weakness of the House as well as a strength. If carried too far, it may result in condoning situations that need attention and reform. As one realistic member described the implications:

> One of the problems here is that of cronyism. All kinds of strange alliances develop and people just don't like to hurt one another. Part of the problem is that the men who might well bring about reform in our system are so much a part of the cronyism that you really cannot count on them. They are the kind who say, "yes, I agree with everything you say, something should be done, but so far as I am concerned. . . . "

The Image of the Opposition

There are important differences in the way House Democrats and Republicans look at themselves and at each other. Each legislator is judged separately by his colleagues, of course, and congressmen do not hesitate to express their esteem and respect for specific members on the other side of the aisle. Still, the group image of the opposition contrasts sharply (and unfavorably) with that which they ascribe to their allies.

The Democrats tend to see themselves as more articulate and gregarious than their Republican counterparts, less likely to take themselves too seriously, and possessing much greater breadth of interests and understanding. In their own image they are characteristically independent beings who resist attempts to subject them to party discipline, and they thoroughly enjoy politics.

In terms of issues, they think that they are pragmatic in contrast to the Republicans who are regarded as likely to be tightly bound by adherence to traditional outmoded concepts. Democrats believe they are more aware of, and concerned with, the needs of the American people. One Democrat put it this way:

> Republicans are apt to have theories of private enterprise, state-federal relationships and so on which they adhere to closely. Democrats are more pragmatic. They will see a need and try to meet it. When they are through, they may find it fits in with their general philosophy. The Republicans are more frustrated and rigid because they are philosophers in a narrow sense.

Unlike Democrats, Republicans are rather dour, possibly dull, lack a well-developed sense of humor, and don't really like people or politics. Without protest they take orders from party leaders. "Democrats are just nicer than Republicans," explained one Democratic leader with a smile. "Most Republican politicians don't like politics and most Democratic politicians—with a few exceptions—love it." "No matter how they try to hide it," added another Democrat, "Republicans just don't like people." Democrats often assert that representatives of the GOP are "stuffy" and unnecessarily formal. One member told his colleagues that this Republican attribute worked to the advantage of his party. Explained he, "In our campaign my opponent wore a vest everywhere and it became a symbol. You would be amazed how many people said, 'he is a nice fellow, but he wears a vest.'"

The Republican view of the contrasts between party representatives in Congress is much different. They view themselves as far more responsible than Democrats, much more concerned with principle, and less likely to endorse unsound schemes just for the special attraction they are considered to possess for voters. They proudly assert their greater devotion to individual initiative and decentralization of government. Said one moderate Republican:

> Republicans are more concerned with fiscal responsibility than the Democrats, many of whom are interested only in spending on the supposition that this will please more and more groups in the population. We Republicans are also more favorable to decentralization in government.

Republicans are convinced they are the true individualists, by nature incapable of being coerced into support of legislation they do not approve, whereas they regard the Democratic House group as containing "more captive members" owing "an obvious allegiance to strong special interests such as labor," and generally being more subservient to party leadership. Democrats, they assert, are far more likely to be products of political machines. Said one political veteran:

> In my state a Republican runs in a primary because he wants to but I don't think you could run and win in a Democratic primary if you didn't have the organization behind you. In other words theirs is a closely knit organization down here that goes right straight back into the precincts. There is a whip over your head as well as a loving wand.

Members of the GOP firmly believe that though their role is the proper one, it is a far more difficult one to perform. Explained one congressman:

> We Republicans have a more difficult job. One reason Democrats appear to be good speakers is that they are always promoting something. It is easier to be articulate and enthusiastic when you are advocating some new service. They tell people what they are going to do *for* them, we tell them what we are keeping the government from doing *to* them. Objecting to things and trying to stop excesses is a difficult position to be in.

When the question of articulateness was raised, an element of defensiveness was observable in the responses of some Republican members of the Eighty-sixth Congress. They worried a bit that the Democrats might be somewhat more articulate, though they often mentioned the point made above: Republicans operate under handicaps. They were careful, too, to distinguish between northern and southern Democrats. Their sometimes allies, the southern Democrats, it was conceded, seemed to have developed a special talent for speaking and general effectiveness that made them superior to any other group in Congress, including the Republicans. But the non-southern Democrats, Republicans insisted, were not better orators or more articulate than they. The large influx of young, aggressive, articulate Republicans in the succeeding Congresses, however, fully compensated for this alleged deficiency, according to GOP members. No longer are they defensive on this point.

Republicans do not agree that Democrats have a better sense of humor, are more imaginative, or better informed than they. A frequent response to such a suggestion is that "both parties cover the whole spectrum and you can't make a fair generalization on those grounds." They believe, too, that on balance congressional Republicans are more able and conscientious than Democrats, although once again they often specifically exempt the southerners from such a comparison. They are proud of the quality of the young Republicans entering the House and consider them superior to the junior members of the opposition.

Yet, as noted, although members of both parties are quick to depict their opposition in less favorable terms—"remarkably undistinguished" "some pretty substandard characters," "irresponsible"—than they use to describe their political associates, they do not hesitate to identify certain adversaries they think are outstanding. Generally, these are members whose views are not dissimilar from their own. But there are exceptions. Representatives may find it easier to recognize ability in allies, but they value the quality so highly that they can even appreciate it in militant opponents.

Moving Ahead in the House

While common experiences and House operating procedures—the eulogies, birthday greetings, method of indirect address preceded by flattering references, and the rules themselves—go far to sublimate differences and promote understanding and tolerance, the ambitious member recognizes that toleration is not respect. If he frequently flaunts custom and tradition, it will be difficult to achieve influence if that is his goal. If, of course, his seat in the House is but a stepping stone to higher ambition, he may deliberately choose to risk the displeasure of his associates there to advance those ambitions. In other circumstances, he is likely to be cautious. He knows some members have achieved a unique spot in the House by their very nonconformity and that they are not always without influence. But he is also aware that this status is a function of both time and personality. It is not an activity into which a knowledgeable man rushes.

A Basic Decision. Early in their careers, representatives often must choose between achieving a position of power and influence within the legislative body or seeking to affect public policy by issuing frequent pronouncements directed at a larger, more national audience. While it is theoretically possible to combine the two endeavors, perceptive observers of the House believe that the odds are heavily against it. To establish himself within the House requires that a new member be patient and unobtrusive during his first years there, delaying attainment of national stature until he has consolidated his position and gained the confidence of his colleagues. Some members find this an unreasonable and impossible restriction. They must speak up. By doing so, they risk losing the attention of their peers. As one legislator put it: "Some of the most able people will never get power here because they feel they should speak up." While, as has been noted, junior members should not consider themselves relegated to a role of enforced silence, House tradition, even in its modified more permissive form, dictates that they should proceed with caution in injecting themselves into debate, deferring participation until the subject matter offers an opportunity to impress one's colleagues. Certainly the newcomer should not attempt to speak on many diverse subjects. Warns one legislator:

> The very ingredients which make you a powerful House leader are the ones which keep you from being a public leader. It is analogous to the fable that when you go over the wall you are speared; when you go underneath you end up with the fair lady. The yappers just won't get to be leaders. Take _____ [a freshman] for example. He is a very able individual, but because he persists in getting on the floor and discussing the issues he'll never have any power around here. The structure of power in the House is based on quietude and getting along with the leadership. Freshmen who are vocal and want to exercise initiative and leadership are confined to the cellar, merely because they have been speaking too often.

Partisanship Amidst Consensus. Compromise and consensus are important in a body the size of the House where debate is sharply limited and informal procedures have developed to facilitate the consummation of business. Yet the member remains aware that he is operating within a political system and that it is within the framework of practical politics that consensus is achieved. Said one legislator:

> I recall a conversation with an elder in our church before I came to Congress. He said, "now that you are elected, I want you to forget all about politics and go back there to Congress and be a statesman." Those are fine sentiments and I endorse them. But that man forgot, and I think many people forget, that we are elected under a political system, and are part of it, and no matter what our goal is it must enter into what we do. Anything else would be completely unrealistic.

A strong sense of partisanship may, in fact, make it difficult for a congressman, especially a junior one, to adjust to the tendencies for accommodation and moderation which epitomize the activites of the legislative body. It may intensify his criticism of the party leadership. He may react sharply and angrily to the defeat or serious modification of proposals in which he is concerned, especially if he believes the leadership is not sufficiently aggressive in pursuing victory. Occasionally, he may even erupt in bitterness, as one first term member did:

I came here thinking this was for real, that this was the only parliament where democratic processes were at work. That is a myth, I find. You can't stand on the floor and inform people; they don't want to listen. The decision on the labor bill was actually made some months ago with the vote on another measure. . . . At that time the coalition of southern Democrats and Republicans was sealed for this legislation. If anybody thinks he is going to come down here to legislate he is crazy. When I first arrived and looked around the Capitol, the White House, and the Washington Monument, I had a lump in my throat and I felt pretty humble about being part of this great scene. But now all I see is skulduggery and shenanigans.

The Fascination of the Legislative Process. The member who achieves stature in the House is likely to be challenged and excited by the legislative process, interested in mastering its subtleties, and at least moderately successful in doing so. He appreciates the system, and though he is aware of some of its weaknesses and is willing to discuss them, or even join an effort to reform certain phases of the operation, his general reaction is one of acceptance. Indeed, he marvels at its effect. As one critic of certain aspects of the legislative process remarked admiringly:

Despite my criticisms, by and large it's amazing how good the system is. You can see the handiwork of many men working on our process, refining it, polishing it, improving it over the years, developing it into a system which is expedient and yet which still serves justice.

The more the challenged congressman probes into the complexities of the system, the more its intricacies and possibilities intrigue him. He regards himself as student rather than master of the process. Explained one representative, "Here, more than in any other situation in which I have found myself, things are not what they seem. There are subcurrents and subscenes which don't strike the naked eye, but which play important roles in determining the final outcome of legislation and all magnitudes of decisions." A freshman member expressed somewhat the same point:

Service in the state legislature led to an awareness of some of the processes of decision and maneuverings which take place. Still I was hardly prepared for what I have seen here. While we all know that much legislation is the result of pressure and behind the door activities, I found the extent of its deep roots surprising. What often seems to be a black or white decision actually is far from that. It is fascinating to try to find the bloc basis of legislation. The legislative process is rather like an iceberg. Only the top part, perhaps only the top quarter, of the legislation and the story behind it, shows. What is really important is usually below the surface. It is rather like bridge: the more you play the more you come to know about the game; yet there is always so much to learn. It is an endless process and a never completely satisfying one.

The Effective House Member

Considerable agreement is evident among House members regarding characteristics which tend to promote effectiveness in that body. Yet there are important areas of disagreement, and numerous exceptions are readily cited to practically every rule. Thus while most observers assert that the really effective House member should be a specialist above all, there is much dispute over whether the acknowledged specialist can extend his prestige beyond the area of his special competence and become an influential generalist. And students of the House will point to influential members who are not specialists at all. Again, if objectivity and reasonableness are considered by some to be basic to the effective member, one can name representatives who lack one or both of these qualities and yet are effective. While complete agreement is lacking, certain qualities do stand out.

Basic Ingredient for House "Type." A Democratic group adhered closely to the concept of the true House man as a specialist as it sought to define the House "type." There was no consensus, however, on how far the generalist could or should seek to extend his influence.

Basically I think the House type is an infighter, an operator. He is not a speaker; he may speak, but he does not speak frequently.

*

If you are going to take for the House type a man who makes a career of the House you could add the fact that he is primarily a worker, a specialist, and a craftsman—someone who will concentrate his energies in a particular field and gain prestige and influence in that. A senator, on the other hand, is more inclined to be an actor on a broad stage and to have a concept of politics that leads him to take a broad role in a much bigger field of activity.

*

A man can build his reputation as a specialist and eventually become enormously powerful as a generalist. The prestige as a specialist can carry him over into other fields. But he can destroy that effectiveness if he tries to be too much of a generalist. There is a tendency among House members to listen to a man when he belongs to the committee which considered the bill up for discussion, whereas a man who may have just as deep an interest in the subject and may be as well versed in it but who is not a member of the committee will encounter more resistance.

*

If he does speak when he is not on the committee concerned with the legislation, the subject matter should relate to a matter of vital importance to his district. Even if a man is exceptionally able there is resentment if he seeks to be an expert on a matter not related to his district or his committee work. _____ was one of the most able speakers on almost any subject that came up, and he usually spoke on every subject before us. Yet members resented the fact that he was in on every discussion.

A Republican discussion dealing with participation in debate revealed a similar division of opinion:

The members who are most successful are those who pick a specialty or an area and become real experts in it. As a consequence, when they speak they are looked upon as authorities and are highly respected. Even though they may be an authority in only one field, their influence tends to spread into other areas.

*

A few of the people who don't participate in floor debate are influential, but most of them have negligible influence. The most effective people are those who confine their activity to bills that come from their own committees.

*

An exception is when a bill affects your geographic area; then you are expected to participate whether or not it concerns your committee. You are recognized as another kind of expert.

*

I don't think a fellow who is intelligent and works hard enough to be really knowledgeable in areas other than those relating to his committee would lose any stature by speaking on those issues. But because you have only so much time, you have little opportunity to develop expertise in other areas.

The structure of the House and the expectations and duties of members dictate reliance on the specialist; congressmen accomplish their business largely by relying on the judgments of others. In his role, though, the specialist must have qualities which commend him to the House. What are the qualities that a member seeks in those in whom he reposes his trust?

A Republican group, in discussing the question, identified several. In their view, to be of maximum effectiveness, a legislator should be regarded as well-informed, hard working, reasonable, responsible, objective, and dedicated. He should be identified as motivated by concern for the national rather than sectional interest, and preferably he should have taken occasional public stands in opposition to the parochial interests of his constituency. He should possess integrity, that "priceless ingredient," and honor his commitments. He should be a recognized authority on the subject to which he addresses himself. He should also respect House traditions and rules and be generally accommodating to his colleagues. Excerpts of the discussion follow:

> If I feel a member is really responsible and that he has demonstrated that over a period of time I am inclined to give a careful ear to what he has to say. If I think he sizes up the national interests properly I pay more attention to him when he goes into local interests. When I decide a man weighs factors very carefully and requires a position to stand up before he brings it around I am inclined to give it a lot of consideration.

*

> I certainly respect a man who stands to benefit from an action, yet stands up and opposes it. Then I listen very carefully when he gets up on other measures.

*

> _____ is a very effective chairman who seldom loses a fight on the floor. That is because he knows his bills as well as any chairman and he speaks well and has a manner about him that exudes confidence. I disagree with him frequently, but nevertheless I have the highest respect for his knowledge and ability.

*

> _____ is a good chairman too. He can sway me just with plain logic. He knows what he is saying and has the answer to every question.

*

> Integrity is a very important quality, a priceless ingredient. We have to rely so much on specialists and people we believe in. We couldn't get by if we didn't know we could depend on certain members who are experts and whose opinions we respect. I would hate to think that I had to read every line of testimony in order to get the proper position. Integrity crosses party lines. You rely on some of your Democratic colleagues equally; those who you know possess integrity.

> Also there is the question of a man's reasonableness. One man may come in and say something and everybody is taking after him; another says the same thing in a different manner and makes some progress. If certain members say

something on the floor, I am inclined to be opposed to it, even if I think the position has merit, just because they have been so unreasonable in their approach.

Unconventional Types. In the legislative system, as in other groups, there is a place for a few people who deviate sharply from the expected norms. Thus some congressmen successfully assume unusual roles with which they are commonly identified and in which they are accepted by their colleagues; other members seeking to establish themselves in similar roles may encounter difficulties, perhaps because the role has been preempted, perhaps because of their personality. The needler, comedian, summarizer, protector of the public purse, objector, technician, conscience of the legislative body—these and other identifiable types have sat in the Congress. Sometimes they have made their mark there, achieving real influence. Often their idiosyncrasies are ignored or condoned in the light of the generally constructive nature of the role they have created for themselves.

Legislators admire the skilled technicians within their ranks, and they are likely to exert important influence in the House. Yet one of the most powerful individuals within that body is a man who is not an authority in any substantive field. He is not a careful, informed, or especially diligent committee member. He seldom addresses the House, nor does he hold a formal position in the hierarchy of power. Yet throughout that body he is regarded as a force to be reckoned with, a good person to know and to have as an ally. His role is unique. Dean of his delegation, the major source of his power is his ability to deliver the votes of the members of his party from his state when these votes are important. A man of his word, he is interested in the advance of legislation important to his state; to gain support for such measures he often commits the delegation to causes in which they have no particular interest. Some of his colleagues discuss him:

The one speech I heard him make up until he assumed the deanship of his delegation was when John Rankin of Mississippi was on the floor and asked for an additional five minutes to go into one of his race baiting speeches. _____ got up and said, "I object." That was his speech. Yet the man has tremendous influence in the House; he is almost a unique phenomenon.

*

Much of his power rests with the fact he is on Ways and Means. Since that committee determines committee assignments, he is in a very important and strategic spot. He makes his deals with various groups as to which people he will support for certain spots. Naturally when the time comes that he wants something, he can make a request and people reciprocate.

One reason he is able to get a bill passed that nobody else with the possible exception of the Speaker could get passed is that time and time again he has delivered his delegation intact.

*

Whether he delivers or not, he says that he delivers, and people believe it.

*

Well, he either succeeds in getting the vote on the floor when he says he will, or he sees to it that those who are opposed are absent or pretty quiet about their opposition. The appearance is one of solidarity, even if some of the boys are back in the state when the vote comes up.

*

They also know he doesn't like anybody to be against him. That is important. He fights back. He claims to have purged personally a couple of Republicans who gave him trouble. And he clearly had a role in the departure of a Democrat from his area not too many years ago.

Irritating Behavior. While it is true that some men are effective who create special roles for themselves that diverge sharply from the norms, it is also true that other men—although able men—may not be excused by their colleagues for their aberrations. They lose whatever influence they may have had; they are ignored, ridiculed, treated with minimum courtesy, and tolerated at best. Their sponsorship of legislation, their advocacy of a cause, constitutes an initial handicap that is often difficult to surmount. Yet they persist in their activity pattern, seemingly oblivious to the reactions they stimulate. It is not always easy for legislators who can identify colleagues who are so regarded to explain precisely the cause for their inclusion in the "out" group. One representative while talking about the House said, "People feel like leaving when certain individuals get up to speak. Take _____. I respect his judgment but somehow he rubs me the wrong way. There are others also who have lost their effectiveness with the average congressman even though they may possess a great deal of information about a specific subject."

Inevitably, the discussion of effective colleagues turned to associates who have no standing in the House. "If we could just be certain that _____ or _____ would argue against our position we'd feel much more optimistic about the result," said one member.

Democrats discussed a colleague to whom most of them were favorably disposed. Considered well-informed on his subject by many of his associates, he arouses strong reactions in the House. His advocacy of legislation can be counted on to muster the support of the hard core of Democratic votes and to array the Republicans almost solidly against the measure. But he alienates the swing group, and therefore he is ineffective.

_____ probably knows more about his subject than any man in Congress. He has written more, has been sitting on the committee longer and has asked more questions, but he is not persuading anybody. A lot of people who can't answer him are content just to damn him. They have been so effective it is questionable whether he has any influence at all.

*

It is unquestionably true that the fact that he has his name on something is a disadvantage. Recently we sponsored a bill and worked hard on it. But there was a bloc of votes we should have been able to get that we couldn't get because he was the sponsor. The bill would have passed with someone else's name on it.

*

He has become so identified with one issue that whenever he speaks on it one thinks, "well, there he goes on that again. He thinks that is the only problem that confronts the people of the world." Those who are associated with him think he is an expert in his field; yet for most House members he isn't an expert.

*

It isn't most of the members. It is the 60 or so members of the "float" that moves this way or that on the basis of a personality who kill him.

Discussion next centered on several Republican members. First the contrast between two Republicans who serve as the sole GOP members of their delegations was noted; then the conversation moved on to other types.

A and B are two examples of a lone Republican in a delegation, yet they operate so differently. A gets along pretty well with his Democratic colleagues; he is helpful to them at times, and they are helpful to him on other occasions. He follows the rules. B is something quite different. He regards himself as the only purist in the House. Everybody else operates from demagogic motives. He is allowed to operate this way because that is what his party thinks he must do to survive. He cuts the throat of every Democrat he can in his delegation.

*

Some people have said essentially the same thing as he, and I have not been outraged in the slightest. But whenever this fellow gets up I find him personally offensive.

*

Let's talk about another type. What about _____?

*

Young fogies are more offensive than old fogies. If _____ were fifty years younger he would be offensive too. You can't really mind what anybody in his eighties does.

*

You mind when he sits there with the scythe and cuts time off, saying, "I will not permit anybody to speak longer than five minutes."

*

There is still another type, the guardian of the purse. Whether you agree with him or not, he makes a contribution. I enjoy him because he points out things which normally no one would ever find out about.

The First Election

It is readily apparent that many different types of people are elected to the national legislature. When one considers personality, physical appearance and bearing, and apparent grasp and enjoyment of practical politics, it is not difficult to understand why some members are successful at the polls. But when one applies the same tests to other legislators, the reasons for success are less readily apparent. This is not to say that those falling in the latter group are not effective legislators or unusually able individuals. They may be among the best in Congress. Yet, at first glance, they may not appear electable. In many legislators, a certain toughness and detachment, a single-mindedness of purpose, an ample measure of confidence, and a desire for recognition are apparent. In others, similar qualities are not observable. What then led individual representatives to seek election and what were the circumstances of their initial victories?

A sample of the House membership reveals that a sizable number discount the influence of the party organization in their victory; indeed, if active at all in the campaign, the organization frequently was arrayed against the victor. The incidence of apparent self-starters is not insignificant, and a goodly number, defeated in their first attempt to gain a congressional seat, returned to the fray and after one or more successive efforts were successful. Service in the state legislature is often the route by which a seat in Congress is attained; some members "inherit" their seats from a parent or spouse; and others go to Congress on retirement from their life work. A number are successful primarily because fortuitous circumstances projected them into a favorable position unanticipated by themselves or potential opponents when first they sought nomination or election. Some congressmen were initially reluctant to contest for their seats, others were undeniably eager to do so. The number of legislators who have deserted their first party preference or that of their parents, while not large, is nonetheless surprising.

The Role of the Organization. Most congressmen would agree with the observation of a colleague that "it is much harder to get in than to stay in." And they commonly associate the problem of getting in with the necessity for developing a personal organization and raising sufficient funds to wage an aggressive campaign, rather than with concern about obtaining the endorsement and support of the official organization.

An overwhelming majority of a sample of House members believed that opposition of the organization did not in itself represent a serious obstacle to success at the polls. They described it as weak, unable to dictate the party nominee in the face of spirited opposition. "I had to fight the organization to get in but it didn't amount to much." "We don't have any organization." "In most districts in our state, it is strictly an 'every man for himself' proposition." "I ran against the former county and state chairman and beat him 5–1, which shows how effective the organization is." "In my district the organization itself is of little consequence. I ran against an incumbent who had been here ten years. I guess what organization there was helped him, but it certainly wasn't decisive." "When I announced, it was entirely on my own; nobody asked me to run. I squeaked through the primary, but I didn't get any party support even then."

Of the few who testified that the organization was strong in their area ("in the metropolitan districts, the organization often determines everything"), some qualified their statements by adding that they had gained the congressional nomination at the expense of someone designated by the organization itself.

The organization is very important in my district and in most of the state. Every two years it designates the whole ticket. The party is a well behaved group, and we rarely have a primary fight or contest of any kind. I did not turn out to be the organization candidate, but normally it meets and announces the candidate.

*

The organization is strong throughout the state, but in my district I ran against it in the primary and won.

Occasionally, the party organization will develop an elaborate, and democratic, procedure to obtain its congressional candidate. One legislator describes his entry into the political arena:

Our state gained several congressional seats and a new district was put in the area in which I lived. The party set up a screening committee. I was invited to appear along with twelve other candidates at a meeting which cut the list to four. We appeared before a larger screening meeting of about two hundred and explained our backgrounds. I was selected by the group, ran, and was defeated the first time. The second time I ran, I defeated the incumbent.

Reasons for Running. Not all people who are elected to Congress are enthusiastic about making the initial race, although one member insists "no one here had his arm twisted to run."

Some candidates enter politics primarily to advance their professional careers by becoming better known rather than to pursue it as a career in itself; victory may be a secondary goal.

I ran for the state legislature because the Republicans had no candidate; I had been an independent up to that point. The Democratic incumbent had been in office sixteen years, and there was a good chance for a budding young lawyer to get some publicity. I ran against him and beat him.

A man intent on attaining another political office may be persuaded to seek a congressional seat instead by party officials who see in his candidacy an opportunity to gain the seat for their county:

I had to be talked into running for Congress. Not because I am that kind of person but because I had other ambitions. I was in the state legislature and had a private desire for the governor's chair sometime. Our congressman ran for the Senate and our county hadn't had a congressman for thirty years so the party leaders there decided it was about time we got one.

Not all successful candidates enter the fray with bright prospects for victory. Some who expect the party nominee to lose may reluctantly offer themselves as "sacrificial lambs" when it proves difficult for the party to find candidates:

We don't have any organization. We thought we had a chance to carry the state for our presidential nominee that year, though, and a group of us decided to get together to try to decide on a congressional candidate. When I returned from the meeting and told my family I had agreed to run, it was quite a blow to them. I never would have run, frankly, if I had thought I would be elected because it didn't suit me to come to Congress. I was very busy in my profession. I am a political accident.

*

When I got out of the service and set out my shingle I looked for the Republican party and it wasn't very easy to find. A small group got together and drafted a man to run for governor, and he won. He drafted me to run for attorney general. I didn't win, no one expected me to, but I ran a pretty good race. Next time they were looking for a congressional candidate. I told everybody I was through. I had a good practice and wanted to practice law. The state committee went out and got somebody, but at about that time the Young Republicans drafted me. How I ever beat my primary opponent I'll never know.

Some candidates have long been strongly motivated toward politics, perhaps toward a career in Congress:

I grew up in politics. My Dad was a district captain and my brother was a county leader. When I got out of law school I sought the assembly post against the organization, but withdrew when a friend got the organization designation. Later I moved to another district and got an opportunity to serve in the state senate. After eight years there I challenged the Democratic congressman in the primaries and beat him; I felt he was not a Democrat.

*

I decided I wanted to go to Congress when I was a high school sophomore. I started running about then and 15 years later I made it. I ran against an incumbent for the nomination, without much encouragement.

*

I ran for Congress in a district heavily favoring the other party, against an incumbent of two years who had kept his nose pretty clean. I had never run for political office or held any. I had two degrees in government, had always been interested in politics, and knew that sooner or later I'd get into it. I got in through the resources issue, organizing groups to educate them on various programs. When I ran for the nomination, I was competing with pros, but pros who didn't have a lot of guts and who weren't willing to run unless they had somebody put some money on the line. I was naive enough to get in ahead of them and file strictly on my own, without any promise of money. I lost the first time but ran the second time and won.

While some of the men most interested in politics have been successful without the support of powerful district leaders, the support of a key leader may also make the difference. Self confidence and "brass" may not be essential to political success, but they often provide the initial drive:

I went to see our national committeeman and asked him if I would get party support if I wanted to run for Congress two years later. He said that was two years away, that he thought they had a candidate for the race coming up but suggested I take a flier in the primary. Following his advice I went down to a small town and talked to the district chairman. I said, "I want to run for Congress and I think I can win." He said: "Well, let's go around and meet some folks" and we did. That night he drove me back to the city where he had a date with his old law school classmate, the national committeeman. The next day I went in to see the latter again and he looked up and smiled and said, "I hear you have been traveling around the countryside. Well, there are some people I want you to see." At that point I knew he had changed his mind about me. It was early in the game when nobody was thinking much about congressional politics. I just went around to see all the local leaders most of whom didn't care who the congressional candidate was. They didn't think our man would win, and the job had no patronage anyway. Thus I was able to get the party endorsement, though there was a great deal of resentment that I did. It was just a case where the guy who happened to be very powerful decided, "You are our boy."

Occasionally, men will move quickly into the top echelons of a weak party organization, revitalize it, and find that their success leads to demands that they seek elective office:

A couple of us [Democrats] have rather parallel careers in that we started out as party chairmen in states that had been predominantly Republican for a long period. I served in that capacity for about three years; when we got ready to run the machine was all oiled. We were in states where Democratic politics were more or less in a vacuum. In other states starting off as state chairman would be unheard of.

Perhaps two dozen legislators are former congressional assistants who won their seats following the departure of their bosses. Although other members of Congress move easily into a seat which has been held by a spouse or parent, some who are persuaded to make the race find the situation more complicated.

My predecessor and husband, who was serving his seventh term in the Congress, died suddenly while testifying before a House committee. His death occurred shortly before the April primary in which he was the only candidate named on the ballot for his party's nomination for Congress in the coming November election.

Under the laws of our state if a vacancy occurs after a nomination has been made by ballot, the vacancy is filled by the vote of the elected committeemen of the district. It was suggested that a write-in campaign be conducted to name another candidate in the April primary; in fact, an eminent and respected university professor sought to win the nomination by this method, without the support of the county leaders. Because, however, of the respect in which my husband had been held during his 16 years in the state legislature and his nearly 14 years in the Congress, he won the nomination by a large margin, approximately three weeks after his death. As a result of this, the choice for a party nominee in the November election was thrown into a special convention of the elected committeemen of the 13th district. At that time, I was the only person of my sex competing with 17 men who sought the nomination. I was nominated in June.

Getting "the breaks" is helpful in politics, particularly in the initial campaign for an office. For example, a candidate may be swept into office as a by-product of a smashing national victory by his party, or the seat may fall vacant after he has had time to prepare the way to inherit it:

When I ran, in 1948, nobody wanted the nomination. Truman was expected to lose. I thought I'd like to go to Congress and indicated an interest in the job to the ward committeeman. I had no political background, unlike some, and no burning ambition, unlike others. The ward committeeman decided the nomination should go to a person of German descent which eliminated me. Subsequently the organization's choice withdrew. That was eight weeks before the election, and they asked me whether I was still interested. I said yes and they let me run. Nobody thought the chances were bright, including me. Mr. Truman swept me into office. Since then I have managed to hang on.

*

A lot of us have had the ambition, but the timing is highly important. My predecessor started to retire in 1948. If he had done so, I might have run but I know I couldn't have won. Two years later I could win and did. That two years gave me the chance to make the contacts that counted.

7   The House Looks at the Senate

The House looks with some suspicion on the Senate and is particularly sensitive to references to the latter as "the upper body." To members of the House it is "the other body," and a somewhat overrated one. Fear of Senate domination explains in part the aversion of the House leadership (particularly former Speaker Rayburn) toward increased use of joint committees and leads House members of conference committees to fight hard for a compromise that cannot be regarded as a concession to the Senate. The struggle may even be evident in the selection of a conference meeting place. In 1962 House conferees on an appropriations bill refused to go to the Senate side of the Capitol to meet with Senate conferees. They also insisted that the appropriations conference chairmanship rotate between the House and the Senate; previously a senator had chaired these meetings. The Senate retaliated by demanding that half the appropriation bills originate in the Senate; the House had claimed the right to originate appropriation bills as well as revenue bills under Article I, Section 7, of the Constitution, which reads: "All bills for raising revenue shall originate in the House of Representatives, but the Senate may propose or concur with amendments, as on other bills." After a stalemate of several months a room in the center of the Capitol was made available and the conferees met. It was agreed that the House-Senate appropriations committee conferees would select their own chairman, thus settling the other point in controversy.

The House regards itself as the true representative of the people, more responsive to the needs and views of the citizenry than the more secure and smaller Senate. Congressmen believe that the Senate gets an inordinate amount of the publicity, but that it is in the House where the most thorough work is done. As one representative has written, "if the Senate has been the nation's great forum, the House has been its workshop." The House insists it does superior committee work, has better craftsmen, and specialists the Senate cannot match, and it asserts that only in the House has the term "legislator" any true meaning. It regards the Senate as too "clubbish" and too ready to support a senator's special projects regardless of the merits of the case. Evidence that the Senate recognizes areas of the House pre-eminence is eagerly sought and firmly proclaimed. Excerpts from a discussion point up alleged differences in information:

By and large we tend to respect the person who has special knowledge. I think this is the one quality that distinguishes the House type from the Senate type. In order for the House man to attain great influence he has to know his subject, and everybody has got to know he knows it. That isn't necessarily true in the Senate.

A sharp contrast is made between the outlook of senators and representatives:

There is no comparison in the way House and Senate members get inflated. Part of the explanation is the attention the Senate gets in the press; part of it is the huge buildup in staff they have, and the fact they are elected for six-year terms. The House member doesn't delude himself that the world is watching his every move. Every senator seems to feel his great sovereignty.

*

Many people come to the House with the thought that they are going somewhere else. There is an enormous drive among House members to go to the Senate, to become governor, and so on. I don't think that exists in the Senate to the same degree. That doesn't mean there isn't great professional pride in the House; there is. It simply establishes that greater publicity and pride exists in the Senate.

*

It is easy to understand the greater feeling of sovereignty in the Senate. Legislation is a much more personal kind of thing. One man can sit for a committee, hold a hearing, and, with a staff member, mark up a bill over there. Where can you do that in the House? Also, over there you can call the subcommittee and ask the chairman to add a half million dollars for this or that and you can't quite do that in the House.

*

There is no sense of power resulting from membership in the House, at least until you get to be a chairman. If anything, there is a sense of frustration at times.

To the last statement one of the most able members of the House entered a strong dissent. Said he:

That is the image but I don't think it is the reality. There are a great many people in the House who have substantially more real power than a great many senators. There is the difference between the image, the appearance, and the reality in terms of the legislative process, and in terms of the power of getting something done.

The Special Groups

Members of the House may belong to a number of unofficial House groups such as the organizations of entering freshmen of one party, various discussion groups, the Prayer Breakfast Group, and less formal social systems such as the "gym group." The influence on the views and voting habits of the legislators of participation in these organizations is difficult to measure accurately in concrete terms. But they *are* influential. The opportunities they provide for mingling informally with colleagues and getting to know them better, for sharing common experiences, for relaxing from the persisting strains of an arduous demanding job, constitute important socializing factors which are difficult to ignore in an assessment of influences on a congressman. As one member commented, "In this very large group which is the House, these smaller groups which rise and decline through the years are valuable for several reasons, psychological and social. They give a little more air of friendliness, support, and confidence to what is a rather strenuous life. And they are a vehicle for learning."

The "Classes." Perhaps the most numerous of these groups are the classes of entering freshmen, organized initially as the 86th Club, 87th Club, 88th Club, etc. to reflect the congress in which the members entered the House. Other groups with broader membership such as the Chowder & Marching, SOS, and Acorn units of Republicans are the outgrowth of these original classes. The Republicans are more disposed than the Democrats to activate such groups and to maintain them, perhaps in part because of the tendency for many of the members of the more recent Democratic groups to become absorbed in the Democratic Study Group.

These organizations seem to fulfill four primary functions. They are a means by which to facilitate the indoctrination of freshmen ("The Clubs serve an indoctrination mission. Their members are stray sheep lost in the wilderness who get together to find their way from the House Office Building over to the Capitol"); they serve an educational function, a means of keeping informed regarding legislation ("It is one way of keeping up with legislation; I couldn't begin to do it otherwise. You are meeting with people you have come to know and respect and you get their ideas about the bills being considered in their committees"); they provide a social outlet, a means for broadening the base of one's friendships; and they are useful in providing potential sources of assistance on legislation.

One Democrat discusses a group of which he was one of the leaders:

The 84th and 85th Clubs combined. Each spring we would have a successful series of meetings, lasting until about June. Last year they were concerned with defense matters. Very few of us were on the Armed Services Committee, and the sessions provided a means for learning a little bit more than we otherwise would know. Toward the end of the session, we would also have a social event, a means of getting out for an evening with colleagues. There are not many opportunities for that here, so it was very valuable. There is a place for this kind of organization socially, and it also provides a limited opportunity to exchange views and even to do lobbying on people who don't have any special reason to go in any particular direction on some legislation. You get so you can count on a few friends whether the matter on which you want help is a special order, a piece of legislation important to your district, or something on which you want your committee to show up well. It's true that in certain cases you can't get people to vote with you, but there are others on whom you can exert some influence on occasion.

Throughout congressional discussions of these groups, one point is stressed: Because of the common uncertainties and tensions associated with the job of congressmen, legislators are inclined to sympathize with one another's problems. Bonds of friendship and association, however casual, strengthen this natural inclination and provide the basis for supporting one another's endeavors. Activities that serve to promote a common bond are to be encouraged. The advantages of participation in the informal groups are stressed in the following discussion.

Members of the clubs that represent classes in Congress help one another in floor situations in particular. When there is an amendment affecting a man who came into Congress at the same time you did, there is a tendency to help him.

*

Isn't it the same spirit of fellowship which is present in any of these groups? In terms of the liberal Democrats, for example, I think there is a kind of informal fellowship of liberalism that provides emotional and intellectual support for the people who think of themselves in that group. I know, I feel it. It is more than just the formal meeting of a group of twenty, thirty, or fifty people. You can almost see it in the way people cluster around each other in the cloakrooms. There is a feeling of fellowship there that exerts a subtle pressure.

*

There is a natural tendency to want to be helpful to people you know well and whose problems you know well. I wouldn't be surprised to see this round table develop a certain spirit of mutual helpfulness just from having gotten to know each other better and our outlooks better.

There is some testimony—especially among Democrats—that organizations such as the 85th Club tend to outlive their usefulness rather quickly and that because of their diverse membership they are not particularly useful in influencing opinions with respect to substantive legislation. The ideological heterogeneity of the group may, in fact, limit the value of even discussing issues in the meetings. Thus two Democrats, the first a freshman member, tend to disparage the importance of these organizations:

> I don't think there is very much the 86th Club or any club like that can do. Membership varies so tremendously. Those who are automatically members of the 86th Club have no common bridge with which to approach problems and thus it becomes extremely difficult to arrive at any conclusions or to take any joint effective action.

*

> The clubs are not very significant or powerful. In the first year or two they serve a valuable purpose in bringing together people with common problems, but once congressmen form their friendships and get to know their way around, the clubs become less important.

Yet unquestionably the Republican groups have been successful and have fulfilled valuable functions beyond the social one. One of the more active of these groups meets twice weekly, once in the afternoon for a session that is largely though not entirely social, the other at a breakfast meeting where an outside speaker discusses a subject of interest. And, as noted, friendships formed in these endeavors may provide substantial advantages at some future time.

The Breakfast and Gym Groups. Two widely divergent groups that influence House members are the Prayer Breakfast Group and the informal "gym group," both of which are unusual in that they provide opportunities for the crossing of party lines; most nonofficial House groups are organized on a party basis.

Each body has a prayer breakfast group. The House group, a voluntary organization open to any member who cares to participate, meets weekly for breakfast and an hour of prayer and fellowship throughout the congressional session, with an average attendance of between thirty-five and forty. Legislators state that the bonds between members of this group are unusually strong and that they are often expressed in acts of legislative cooperation. Since 1955, a room has been set aside in the Capitol where members of Congress may pray and meditate. Normally used sparingly at the beginning of a session, the room is much frequented when critical, complex issues are before the House.

In discussing the importance of informal groups in the House, members of both parties frequently volunteer that the gym exerts a significant role in the development of friendships and alliances and eases the way for the accommodation of views and the passage of legislation.

Some of the advantages of the various kinds of nonofficial groups are mentioned in this excerpt from a discussion of Republican members:

> The clubs I know about have no influence on the voting habits of their members. But they are helpful in supplying information on legislation, attitudes, and so forth. I think they could be called influential from the standpoint of making friends out of colleagues and thus being able to get support for given legislation on a friendship basis rather than on solid argument, especially for measures that don't have international significance. Friendships make a difference with respect to private bills, for example.

*

> The House Prayer Breakfast Group cuts across party lines better than any group you have.

*

> The gymnasium group is about the most influential one in the House. That isn't a joke either. Actually a lot of work is done in the gym. You can accomplish a lot on an informal, casual basis. You can discuss informally things you don't want to call a man about. One important value of the gym is that it crosses party lines. You have an opportunity to get to know better the guys in the other party.

The Informational Groups. The primary purpose of the Democratic Study Group is to organize the liberal Democrats so they can become more effective in advancing a liberal program. Unlike other nonofficial groups it has a system of regional whips for alerting its members to group positions and to impending votes. Its name is somewhat misleading: To date the "study" aspect of its activities has clearly been subordinate to more practical political purposes.

There are, however, groups within the House that stress the quest for information. There are small breakfast groups that concern themselves almost entirely with issues; there are small evening seminar sessions; there are occasional conscious efforts by the Department of State and other executive branch agencies to provide systematic briefings for members of Congress. House members themselves may initiate such groups— partisan or nonpartisan—to gain knowledge not normally available to them. In 1959 a bipartisan House effort made possible a training session for new members of the House. This series of meetings was conducted again in 1963, this time under the sponsorship of the American Political Science Association. All of these activities, though of interest to representatives at all stages of seniority, draw most of their support from the younger, more junior members who feel especially deficient in the knowledge they deem essential to informed decision.

State Delegations. Observers of Congress have written with some surprise about the apparently positive influence exerted by state delegations on the votes and activities of individual members. Discussions with congressmen reveal the existence of widely divergent practices and influences, depending on the size of the delegation involved, its political division, and the personalities of the leading congressmen within the group. Provisions for regular meetings—generally confined to members of one party within one delegation but in some instances extending to the full delegation—are frequent, on a weekly, biweekly, or monthly basis. Breakfast, luncheon, late afternoon, and even dinner sessions may be scheduled. Promotion of good fellowship and camaraderie and the exchange of political gossip seem to be important goals of most such gatherings, with little conscious attempt to seek solidarity in voting, although many organized delegations regularly discuss the issues of the day. Whether by design or not these group discussions of legislative proposals often result in the subtle crystallization of group sentiment. As one Democrat expressed it in confirming a colleague's statement that even without prolonged discussions of proposals state party delegations were often united, "I think he is right in saying that members of his delegation will vote similarly on a lot of key issues without ever discussing them. There is a certain quality about the situation here so that when certain key people in the delegation go one way you have a 'clubby' idea you ought to go along too."

A member relates the practice prevalent in one of the larger Democratic delegations:

The Democrats in our delegation meet monthly for dinner to discuss the pros and cons of legislation. Generally our people vote alike, but it is not by formal agreement; our meetings may lead to this action, but we never have a caucus where we are bound. The fellow who is the expert in a field will give the benefit of his views. I have seen the delegation switch from one position to another based on the fervor of the argument of the person most informed about the issue. A fellow like _____ won't go along if he disagrees, even if the delegation strongly favors the position. I think there are about three who vote on certain issues on the basis of friendship, but otherwise the delegation is rather united. In the main we take the guidance of a senior man, but there is some independence; we don't have the same deference to a leader that exists in the _____ delegation. We have one member who goes to church to pray for guidance on difficult issues; the leadership can't do much with that vote.

Delegations do not bind members to vote with the majority. Certain delegations may even deliberately avoid carrying discussion of issues to any kind of showdown stage, aware of the existence of strongly divided opinions within the group. To avoid controversy, some groups organize their meetings as social gatherings with only incidental discussion of issues. A Texan tells about the situation in his delegation:

Except on a few issues, I don't think you would find the Texans all voting alike, nor do we usually even discuss legislation in our weekly meetings. Unless the issue is of special concern to the state, we frequently split almost directly down the middle. The Speaker [Rayburn] almost never attempts to influence any member against his own best judgment or conviction. There are some members of the delegation he just can't reach. Some members owe their allegiance to the southern coalition, others like to think for themselves. We do stick by our colleagues if someone is jumping on one of them—or Texas if people are jumping on Texas. Generally many of us incline to follow the judgment of the Texan on the given committee that has considered the bill, but that is not absolute.

One congressman who stated he did not believe the state delegations to be very powerful proceeded to reveal that in many ways his own delegation did indeed exert a centralizing force:

The state delegations are not very powerful. We used to meet together, though not too regularly, for informal discussions of issues with no attempt to bind members. There are few meetings of the delegation as a whole now, but we are a fairly close working group and by informal means we manage to cooperate closely. There are many phone calls between members, we sit together on the floor, things of that sort. We also work very closely with our senators.

In considering the possibilities for united action within a state delegation, the partisan division of the delegation may be an important factor. According to one Democratic leader, "the one-party character of a situation may not be essential, but it is very important. It makes things easier, because you don't look at the guy across the table as a potential enemy in another election." Although some delegations which are rather evenly divided politically function as units in matters related to advancement of the state's interests—in the 1950's California was a good example—normally where one party strongly dominates a delegation, greater accord and cooperation seems possible with respect to matters of statewide interest. A California Republican speaks of the remarkable degree of cooperation which has been maintained in his state's congressional contingent despite its large size and sharply divided political cast. This cooperation, one might speculate, may date from a tradition developed in earlier years when one party long strongly dominated the delegation.

Not only are the Republicans in our delegation organized as a unit, but the full delegation has an organization too. We don't have meetings at stated intervals, but every time a matter of importance to the state arises which is not partisan in nature, the full delegation meets to discuss it. It more often involves conduct or activities of the administrative agencies than questions of issues on the floor.

It may be true that California meetings are most often concerned with problems relating to administrative agencies as the congressman suggests, but it is also true that the delegation unites to see special recognition for the state, achieving an influence which other members find disturbing at times. One congressman from another large state indicated that increased cooperation among the members of his own delegation was directly attributable to concern about the results obtained by a united California delegation, results which threatened to affect adversely the economic interests of his state.

Personal rivalries within, as well as between, party delegations in a state naturally influence the nature of the organization. Difficult internal situations and the presence of independent, "loner" type legislators may impair seriously the effectiveness of a group and lead to a decision to hold few meetings. Two examples of such situations are referred to below, the first involving one of the largest state delegations, the second one of about eight members. Both refer to intraparty delegations.

We meet together as a delegation occasionally, but we don't do too much. We don't take formal stands on legislation although there is a discussion of current issues which are before the Congress. One problem is that we have so many prima donnas. Some of the young men dash in, see that their presence is noted, and dash out again. They're not particularly interested in sitting down and talking about these things. On the other hand, some of the older members are pretty cantankerous and inflexible and that creates a problem.

*

The delegation doesn't meet together very often and part of the reason for this is that we don't get along very well as a group. Cohesion is lacking, and there aren't very many close ties. Furthermore, we have been rather headless of late. The delegation dean has been ill much of the time so there have been few meetings. Prior to this year _____ was head, and he didn't like to call meetings at all. He was a pretty difficult, independent type, and when he did call us together, all he wanted to talk about was the fact that the party was not doing well by him in terms of patronage.

It is difficult to generalize about the status of congressmen who are the lone representatives of their party in a state delegation. Examples can be cited of instances where close cooperation and pleasant social relationships exist; in other situations there is serious antagonism. After colleagues had referred to states reflecting one category or the other, one man who was the sole member of his party in a small delegation said: "I am frank to admit there is almost no cooperation in our delegation between myself and the other members. There is a feeling of bitter tension most of the time." Another legislator whose four-man delegation was all of one party commented on the varying patterns observable in small state groups:

Let me say a word about the small state delegations. There are four members in ours. When we get together on matters of local concern we tend to unify very quickly. On other matters we exchange information, and the temptation is to go along unless you have a good reason not to. You haven't much strength in the small delegation, and there is no point in dissipating it. But in other small delegations, there are situations where the people even in the same party don't talk to each other, much less have meetings. There is no cooperation at all. There are others where informally on purely local matters, they will tend to coalesce, but there is no effort to cement the delegation. State delegations need strong senior members to provide a degree of coherence and leadership. Where that is lacking, as it sometimes is, particularly in the smaller states, you have almost no significance.

Finally, a word should be said about the role of delegation deans. While many of them do not appear to possess unusual influence within their groups as a result of the seniority that has thrust the deanship on them, it is true that the leadership and the whip organization occasionally find the deans a means by which to gauge delegation sentiment or to disseminate information or seek support from the group. It is true, too, that at least a few delegation deans are noted for their ability to deliver the votes of colleagues, accumulating IOU's which eventually may be called in. Delegations, by standing together, may increase their bargaining power substantially.

Congressional Reading

The lives of members of Congress unquestionably are changed as a result of their election and their service in the national legislature. Most of them travel more than they used to, have somewhat more prestige than formerly, and receive more invitations. Yet in other aspects of their lives, where one would expect precongressional habits to be modified sharply, no such change may occur. Reading habits appear to fall in this category.

At the same time that the diverse nature of the subject matter on which congressmen are required to legislate places a premium on the acquisition of information (both general and specific), the severe time pressures under which the representatives function and the wide range of their responsibilities restrict sharply the opportunities to become fully informed. The one serves as an incentive to reading; the other as a deterrent. To ascertain how members responded to these conflicting pressures, they were asked about their reading habits: how much reading they have time for and what kind of reading they do. The discussion was not limited to reading pursued in connection with the congressional job, and it was apparent that many legislators read primarily for relaxation rather than for information they could apply in their work. It is evident, too, that there is little discussion of books and articles between members of the House and little exchange of materials. As one representative expressed it:

I recently spoke at a college and a professor asked me what books had most influenced congressmen in the last year or two. I was embarrassed because I have no idea what my colleagues' reading habits are. I don't know either whether books as such are at all influential in shaping our attitudes towards our jobs or towards society as a whole. It is something we never discuss.

Lack of adequate time for reading was termed by one member "the greatest frustration of all," but there was only one expressed dissent when another panelist, at the conclusion of the discussion in the Democratic group, said: "Despite the varying testimony as to how much we read, it seems true that nobody has a real complaint that his duties prevent his reading pretty much what he would like to read." While the statement is too sweeping—some legislators *are* unable to read as much as they would like, and others, while less interested in reading, comment nonetheless that they *should* read more often—most House members would agree that they have no complaint on this score. Comments such as "I guess I'm better off so far as reading time is concerned than I was before I came to Congress" and "I have no complaints. I read a fair amount, easily a couple of books a month" are not uncommon among legislators.

There probably has been no appreciable decline in the amount of reading done by a legislator since going to the House, as compared with his previous practice. In fact, he is likely to read more than he used to, though the nature of his job may place greater reliance on articles, reports, editorials, and briefs than on books. A wider variety of subjects can be covered more quickly and in capsule form. As one Republican observed, "Books don't have anywhere near as much influence on members as magazines and newspapers. This job has not caused us to read less, but we have tended to concentrate on a different kind of reading." Books appear less significant than other written sources in shaping the outlook of congressmen with respect to issues of public policy.

The newspapers receive first priority in the allocation of reading time. Members want to keep up with the news. Important, too, is the desire to at least scan the newspapers of the home district for local items and perhaps for editorial opinion. These district-oriented publications normally are supplemented by one or more "national" newspapers such as the *New York Times, Wall Street Journal, Christian Science Monitor*, or one of the Washington papers. Beyond that, many members glance fairly regularly at one or more weekly news magazines such as *Newsweek*, *Time*, or *U. S. News and World Report*. Less frequently, periodicals of the *Harper's*, *Nation*, *Reporter*, and *New Republic* variety are examined.

A heavy volume of pamphlets, booklets, newsletters of various organizations, books, and official government publications is sent to congressional offices, the majority of them not having been requested by the member. These materials are examined on a selective basis. Some legislators see virtually none of them, the staff bringing to their employer's attention the few items which seem particularly relevant to his work or his interests. Other representatives sift the materials themselves. Whatever the method employed, few of these materials receive the serious attention of either the member or his staff. Certain national newspapers and periodicals (*Christian Science Monitor* and *U. S. News and World Report*, for example) are made available to members without charge, and there is evidence that these are read.

While many congressmen appear to follow no particular schedule of reading, others, despite their manifold duties, make a conscious effort to pursue their interests in more organized fashion. One member may spend a half day in his office every Saturday to go through the week's accumulation of materials or to engage in serious reading with the staff gone, the door locked, and the telephone permitted to ring unanswered. Another may set aside a month between sessions in which serious reading is the main object, important books of the year being deferred until that time.

I concentrate my serious reading in a month in the pre-legislative period, usually December, in which I do nothing but read and eat. Sometimes I read at the Library of Congress, sometimes at home. In addition to that policy, routinely I will scan, not read, ten or fifteen books a month, and read a half dozen or so light books to put myself to sleep.

Still another legislator may read an hour or two every morning, or before retiring in the evening. One member regularly saves reading materials for his trips home: "Our reading may have to be done in fits and starts, but I go back to the district nearly every weekend and read going and coming."

Relatively few members appear to attempt serious research; for that there is a heavy reliance on other sources, although legislators are often not happy that this is so. Lamented one former college professor, "When you speak of independent research, those days are gone—they are all behind me."

Many congressmen read primarily for relaxation, often deliberately selecting books that are not directly related to their work. A congress-woman discusses her reading policy:

> I read as an antidote or something that would enrich a background from the side. I think you can find plenty of time for that if you take it. I read a full hour and a half every morning before going to the office and at least an hour at night. But I don't go in for the kind of thing which is necessarily related to the subject I deal with all day. If you make a habit of reading it becomes as much a part of your life as going on the House floor and voting.

Whatever their reading tastes, some representatives have become highly dependent on reading. Said one who restricts himself to "serious" books, "You have to read. You can't do this job without keeping up on all kinds of things. I read periodicals primarily, but I try to read two or three books a month."

The volume and variety of books read by members of Congress show a wide range of interests. In the two Brookings panels, for example, the quota of books read ranged from none at all to a high of ten to twelve weekly. Some participants refused to read anything but "heavy" books; others consciously shunned those and read mystery stories, historical novels, and book club selections.

The following excerpts from comments by House members will illus-trate something of the divergent practices followed:

> I am probably the most illiterate person here. I don't read any books.

*

> In 1928 I started reading two books a week and haven't missed a week since. A good two-thirds of them have no connection with the legislative process.

*

> I refuse to comment on the quality, but I read ten to twelve books a week, with rare exceptions. I read about ten daily newspapers and skim all the weeklies in my district. I also read innumerable periodicals.

*

> We take two of those book of the month club deals, and I try to keep up with them. For the most part I read the who-done-its and things like that.

*

I am in the lower brackets here as a reader—three daily newspapers, about as many weekly periodicals, and probably two or three books a month. I have fairly prissy literate tastes, running towards the so-called great books and stiltedly anti-trash.

Only one member volunteered that he particularly enjoyed reading poetry. Said he:

I probably shouldn't admit this, but I enjoy reading poetry to my wife when she is working—ironing or something—because I get a bang out of her reaction to some of it. I don't think poetry helps me in my legislative duties at all, but I think it is relaxing just as I enjoy riding horseback.

Thus, although pressed by the many demands on their time, it is evident that congressmen do find time to read. The books they read are generally unrelated to their legislative responsibilities and constitute one means of "unwinding" from them. Indeed, representatives who do not spend much time reading are quick to observe that a change of pace is the primary motive for much congressional reading; they assert that, for themselves, golf, swimming, walking, or camping is preferable.

Election to the House begins a new experience with a new peer group as part of an institution which, though giving the appearance of informality and flexibility, actually functions subject to subtle disciplines and fairly rigid codes. Men and women of varying backgrounds whose interest in politics and manner of and reason for selection differ markedly find that membership entails far more than being assigned to a committee and voting on legislative issues. They need to be aware of the institutional norms, the folkways, and rituals that cannot be ignored, the existence and influence of subgroups, and facets of a power system that are not always readily discernible. The House has a sense of propriety, a mystique, a life of its own, which the successful member comes to understand and appreciate and with which he makes his peace. He grasps the special importance of personal relationships and becomes aware of the opportunities available to judge his colleagues and to be judged by them. He begins to be discriminating in his evaluation of colleagues, to be stimulated by the legislative body in which he finds himself, and to be intrigued by its complexities. In short, he becomes increasingly involved and committed to his role as a congressman.

II

The Congressman and His Constituents

THE SIGNIFICANT INCREASE in the impact of government on the daily lives of the population that has characterized the period since the early 1930's, has thrust increasing responsibilities on members of the Congress. Bewildered, sometimes engulfed, by their new relationship with government, citizens have turned to their representatives in Washington for assistance. One result has been the steady rise in the time which legislators allocate to performance of the "representative" function, often at the expense of activities commonly associated with the "legislative" role.

Constituent Demands

These new demands, along with the greater complexity of the legislative decisions the Congress is required to make, have added new dimensions to the congressional workload, altering significantly the more relaxed patterns of the past. As one congressman said of the job, "It is a bottomless pit. The only limits are a person's time, energy, and ability. The limits would be there whether or not we had constituent pressures." It is with considerable justification that legislators express resentment when they are charged with failing to earn their keep. Congressmen are busy people unable to cover completely the gamut of their responsibilities. They are frequently torn, by time pressures and also by the uncertainties of politics, between the many legitimate functions that seek their attention. Their primary function is to legislate, yet the clearly meritorious demands of constituents may severely limit their capacity to do so. The situation is complicated by the fact that the less legitimate requests from home may be far more important to success at the polls than careful scrutiny of legislation. These dilemmas are not easily resolved.

New congressmen are occasionally bewildered by the extent of citizen demand for personal services, and veteran members of Congress, though reconciled to it, confess they had not anticipated the volume. In distinguishing between his expectations about his role as a congressman and the reality, one veteran legislator remarked that "I thought I was going to be Daniel Webster and I found that most of my work consisted of personal work for constituents." Another experienced member reflected about the burdens imposed by the servicing of constituent requests:

It seems to me that the drains on a congressman's energy for administrative and "representative" duties are very considerable, even assuming he has a fine staff and is able to delegate intelligently. Most people in comparable positions in business and executive life would not put up with the interruptions of their thought processes that are a necessary price of entry to this arena. It won't do to say that under a properly organized executive branch all constituents will receive their just dues merely by applying to the executive. Until philosophers become kings you are going to need an outside needling force. I think everyone here would agree that but for us far greater injustices would occur. I honestly can see no way of changing the system. Outside intervention such as ours is needed and I see no appreciably better way of organizing the workload if we are to undertake it. I find it burdensome, but I am glad to do it.

Each legislator must face the problem of how best to distribute his efforts. Solutions vary with such factors as personal inclination, length of service, and the nature of the district represented, as well as with the traditional relationship that has existed between constituents and the congressional office. As politicians, congressmen are ever mindful of the necessity of maintaining strong ties with the voters. Many of them also derive a real sense of personal achievement, pride, and participation in moving forward substantive legislation. The fundamental task is to determine the proper subjects for their own attention, and those that should be delegated to their staff. District expectations based on past practices may impose some restrictions on new congressmen, but considerable flexibility exists.

Most congressional offices are more concerned with activities not strictly legislative in character than they are with legislative ones. In determining the distribution of the workload, representatives generally assign as much of the extra legislative work as possible to their staff. Even so, constituent-oriented activities usually occupy the major portion of their own time. In the words of one congressman highly regarded by his colleagues:

This life consists of preoccupation with the unimportant at the expense of the more important. My committee has been relatively active this year, but my committee responsibilities are not what occupy my time. It is taken up with the row over which of three good party members is going to get the nomination for postmaster in a town and what is going to happen to a party committeewoman if I can't get her a job as a part time postal employee. Not only do people write me, they phone me, come to see me, and get their friends to do so also.

Commented another member:

Unless you can keep constantly in contact with your people, serving them and letting them know what you are doing, you are in a bad way. My experience is that people don't care how I vote on foreign aid, federal aid to education, and all those big issues, but they are very much interested in whether I answer their letter and who is going to be the next rural mail carrier or the next postmaster. Those are the things that really count.

Increased seniority and added committee responsibilities may lead to increased preoccupation with legislative duties, but few members surrender even to trusted staff many of their more important "representative" functions. Becoming a legislative expert is a less certain avenue to re-election than other more constituent-oriented activities. Recognizing this, some members are reluctant to delegate determination of their fate to others. Their own beliefs regarding the importance of efficient execution of the nonlegislative aspects of their job are reinforced by personal knowledge of the electoral fate of former colleagues who failed to maintain close relationships with their district and who became indifferent or casual about courting the voters. One result is that even within the legislative realm tentative decisions are often tested against anticipated constituent reaction. Failure to withstand that test may not result in modification of the decision, but, at the very minimum, it is likely to lead to greater efforts to create a more favorable climate for it. The voter is king, and the legislator, beset by the uncertainty of tenure, tends, in determining how to spend his time, to move in the direction he believes most certain to ensure voter confidence in him as an effective representative. "It is true," commented one respected member, "that you are re-elected or defeated on the basis of what you do in the office rather than what you do on the floor. I didn't believe that when I first heard it, but I do now."

Congressmen do indeed believe that their constituents are less concerned with votes and major issues than with the more personal contacts between themselves and their representatives. This belief influences their activities: the constituent is assiduously cultivated, and new means of gaining his favor are constantly being sought. On that score one thoughtful legislator had this to say:

I am tremendously concerned about the amount of time congressmen spend in selling their wares to constituents. I sat at luncheon with a new member who was telling me about his newsletter and his difficulties in working up a mailing list. His major problem in his first five weeks in office was how he could write a catchy newsletter and whether he should engage a professional writer as he had been advised to do. The real question is whether it has become part of our existence to campaign not so much on whether or not we are doing a good job or representing the basic thinking of our people but rather simply to try to be a Luden's coughdrop to them. If they see the name often enough, they will buy it once more. I think that is one of our real problems.

Another member spoke frankly of the situation which faces the conscientious representative:

The main area in which you can create news while you are in Washington is in matters not related to floor activities, committee work, or the sponsorship or passage of legislation, but in other things you do such as needling the executive. The legislative and re-election functions are not really closely related. You can be a superb legislator and yet by neglecting the "how do I get known to the voter?" question you will be a superb ex-legislator. Conversely, you can be a great fellow with the voters and a mediocre legislator.

The result of this dichotomy is that, as suggested, it is not uncommon for members of the House to devote the major portion of their time and energy to the nonlegislative aspects of their job. The following discussion, which occurred shortly after the opening of a new Congress, reflects the surprise of a promising newcomer about allocation of his time. While the experience of the member who responded to his question is not typical, it illustrates that some members resist the pressure to assume extensive personal obligations with respect to the discharge of constituent work; most of his colleagues devote far more of their time to these matters.

To what extent, as you stay in Congress longer, is less of your time devoted to projects and more given over to thinking about what you vote on? My impression after six weeks is that about 98 percent of one's time is given to nonlegislative functions.

*

I think I am in disagreement with some people here who have been more effective in increasing their majorities than I have. After you get your office organized and have confidence in and know your staff, you can make a shift from the proportion of the time you put into office work in your first year or two here. In my first year I think I spent 105 percent of my time on my constituency and in my second year probably 95 percent and from then on about 10 percent because I had the good luck to get a staff that seems to function. I control my case work with my signature. I represent a regional office town in which I keep my top staff man. Much of my work is handled on the telephone by him. But even if there were no regional offices in my district and a man there to deal with them, I think much of my work would be handled by my staff. My staff spends 100 percent of its time on constituent matters. I spend 10 percent of my own time on constituent service and 90 percent on legislation.

*

That is not universal. There are many members who have been here a long time who still devote 90 percent of their time to case work.

The seeming preoccupation of many legislators and their staffs with the servicing of constituents has led many observers to assert that congressmen have become "errand boys" rather than legislators. While few participants in the legislative process would deny that much time is devoted to constituents' interests, many of them see no alternative. An experienced legislator and a freshman member expressed similar views:

When I first came here I was dumbfounded by the number of requests. I was inclined to think I didn't have time to take care of them, and that I would have no time for legislation. My first reaction was, "Why don't they contact the executive agencies or the proper department with which these problems are associated? Why should they expect me to take care of this for them?" Gradually I came to realize that each of these problems is very important to the person writing me, and that it is important for me to treat them as significant. Many people are baffled by our bureaucracy and don't know where to turn for help. Eventually somebody says, "Why don't you write your congressman?" and they do. I now realize that one of my most important functions is to help these people. If they are entitled to go through a door they cannot find, it is my job to locate that door so they can go through.

*

Much of the work that comes across a congressman's desk has absolutely no relationship to legislation. All of these case work problems probably could not easily be sent elsewhere. Certainly the people don't know where else to take them. But the fact is that having to deal with these matters takes vital time that a congressman should be devoting to government and requires him to do a lot of housekeeping things for constituents.

For some members the solution to the problem is one proposed some years ago: Divide representation of a district between two people one of whom would carry out the legislative function, the other the representative function. As one congressman commented:

> The least appealing aspect of my job is the service we have to perform for constituents. I don't know why the administrative agencies can't respond to these requests directly without the intervention of congressmen, although I recognize it is essential for us to be used as a final check on the action of the agency. Too much of our time and energy is diverted in that direction with the result that the opportunity for creative thinking in a legislative way is greatly lessened. It is too bad we don't have two members of Congress for each district, with one having the responsibility for handling constituent requests, the other being free to study legislation and to legislate.

Allowances and Services

The effectiveness of a member of Congress and his capacity to fulfill his responsibilities cannot be considered apart from the personnel and equipment provided to help him carry out his role. The size and quality of his staff and the manner in which it is organized, the auxiliary services to which he may turn for research and information, the mechanical equipment available to expedite and simplify his job, and the physical surroundings in which his organization functions all are relevant.

Though to many members these perquisites fall short of what is desirable or even necessary, to the outsider (who does not understand how busy the active congressional offices are), they usually appear impressive, sometimes excessive. The truth of the matter is that there are sharp differences in need between offices, and it is virtually impossible to establish a reasonable standard that will not restrict some members unduly and provide so much aid to other legislators that it cannot possibly be used efficiently.

Office Space. Many congressmen need larger quarters. A few House members are provided with three room suites, but the vast majority have only two rooms. Usually the congressman occupies one of these and his staff the other, although some legislators share their own office with their top assistant. A third House Office Building, scheduled to be completed by late 1964, and to be occupied in January 1965, will permit the enlargement of the suites in the two present buildings, thus alleviating what for many members is a serious space problem.

In addition to his Washington office each representative receives a maximum allowance of $1,200 annually for the rental of office space in his home district and $600 for official office expenses incurred outside the District of Columbia.[1] If space is available in a federal building, it is provided without charge to the congressman.

Staff Allowances. It is difficult to be precise about clerk-hire allowances because the system for computing salaries is cumbersome and misleading. Although there are occasional efforts to revise it so that it can be more readily understood by the public, most legislators seem content with maintaining the status quo.

Each member of the House is allowed close to $50,000 annually to hire up to nine assistants. A clerk-hire allowance of $20,500 "basic" is allocated to each member, which he may apply to the salaries of his employees, except that no employee may exceed a basic rate of $7,000. An extra employee and an additional allowance of $2,500 "basic" is provided representatives whose districts contain more than 500,000 people.[2] In 1963, only 91 congressmen were using their full allowance. Ten formulas representing post-1944 pay increase acts are then applied to the basic annual rate of the employee to determine his actual gross annual salary. The materials that follow illustrate the ten formulas, present some sample basic annual rates and the gross annual salaries they represent, and show how it is determined that a person awarded a basic salary of $3,000 is actually paid $7,255.93. The law also provides that the basic annual salary of a person listed on more than one congressional payroll may not exceed $2,000. As one House committee has observed, it is legally possible for one employee to appear on as many as

[1] As of March 31, 1963, 299 members were renting offices in their congressional districts, 5 of them having two offices under contract; 400 members were receiving expense allowances for office expenses incurred outside the District of Columbia.

[2] In 1963 one-fourth of the membership of the House qualified for the additional allowance. Only 14 of these members were using the full $23,000 "basic" allowance available to them. Another 51 were using between $20,501 and $22,999. Seventy-seven congressmen representing districts below 500,000 in population were expending their entire allowance of $20,500; 243 between $15,000 and $20,499; 46 between $10,000 and $14,999; and 4 less than $10,000.

400 payrolls at the basic salary of $5 annually on each; in such a case the gross salary of the individual would reach $350,000!

Formulas applied in 1963 to basic rate to reach gross annual salary were as follows:

1. 20% increase of first $1,200; 10% additional from $1,200 to $4,600; 5% further additional from $4,600 to $7,000.
2. After preceding, add an additional 14% or a flat $250 whichever is the greater, but this increase must not exceed 25%.
3. After applying preceding increases, add 10% (in lieu of overtime).
4. Add an additional increase of $330.
5. Add 5%.
6. Add an additional 10% but not more than $800 or less than $300 a year.
7. Add 7½%.
8. Add 10%.
9. Add 7½%.
10. Add 7%.

For example:

	$3,000.00	Basic per annum
	240.00	20% first $1,200 (par. 1)
	180.00	10% next $1,800 (par. 1)
	$3,420.00	
	478.80	14% additional (par. 2)
	$3,898.80	
	389.88	10% additional (par. 3)
	$4,288.68	
	330.00	additional (par. 4)
	$4,618.68	
	230.93	5% additional (par. 5)
	$4,849.61	
	484.96	10% additional (par. 6)
	$5,334.57	
	400.09	7½% additional (par. 7)
	$5,734.66	
	573.47	10% additional (par. 8)
	$6,308.13	
	473.11	7½% additional (par. 9)
	$6,781.24	
	474.69	7% additional (par. 10)
	$7,255.93	Total annual Gross Salary

BASIC ANNUAL RATE	GROSS ANNUAL SALARY
$ 5	$ 891.13
100	1,114.99
1,000	3,157.29
1,500	4,052.76
2,000	5,088.89
2,500	6,172.40
3,000	7,255.63
4,000	9,422.97
5,000	11,550.60
6,000	13,469.15
7,000	15,349.65

Stationery and Equipment. A member also receives a stationery allowance of $2,400 for each regular session. This may be withdrawn in cash or credited to his account with the stationery room. It permits the purchase of miscellaneous office supplies; the mimeographing, folding, inserting, and sealing of materials; the printing of newsletters, robotyping of letters, addressing of envelopes, and the acquisition of flags, books and other items, some of which are not related to the operation of a congressional office.[3] In 1962, more than half of the House found it necessary to make cash deposits to their stationery room accounts to supplement the $1,800 allowed. This led to a $600 increase in October 1963.

Each member is furnished, through the Clerk of the House, with electric and automatic typewriters, addressographs, duplicating machines, and dictaphones. The equipment, which remains the property of the House, cannot exceed a value of $2,500 at any one time, but in addition to the electric typewriters charged to the account, a member can obtain three additional electric typewriters on request.[4]

The Franking Privilege. Perhaps the most valuable service provided the legislator is the franking privilege, permitting him to send free in the mails any official communication. "Official" is interpreted very broadly though occasionally the Post Office Department has upheld the charges of

[3] A member could use the money as salary and report it as income. Any stationery allowance remaining is payable to a member when he leaves Congress or to his estate in the event of his death.

[4] When the Bureau of the Census estimates the population of a congressman's constituency to be 500,000 or more, he is entitled to an allowance of $3,000 for equipment and a fourth electric typewriter not charged against his account.

political opponents of incumbents that the latter have violated the law by distributing blatantly political newsletters under the frank.

To avoid possible embarrassment, some congressmen request a ruling on the eligibility of certain materials before sending them out. The Post Office Department reports that franked mail increased from 44.9 million pieces in 1955 to 63.4 million pieces in 1958, and 111 million pieces in 1962. In 1962, franked mail for all the lawmakers cost the government $4,867,374. The congressman also receives an allowance of $500 per calendar year for airmail and special delivery stamps.

In recent years, a divided House has engaged in a running battle with the Senate regarding use of the congressional franking privilege in connection with mail bearing no specific address but merely addressed to "occupant" and delivered on carrier routes. Once limited to rural areas, in 1961 the practice was extended to urban areas by the House. The Senate did not accord this privilege to its members and sought unsuccessfully to deny it to representatives. In 1962 it succeeded in eliminating the practice, at least temporarily, by inserting a provision in the legislative appropriation bill for fiscal 1963. But House-Senate jousting over the matter continued in 1963. Advocates of the House position argued that under the restriction members of Congress using the frank do not have privileges on a parity with private mailers on rural, star, or city routes or boxes, an "absurd situation."

Other Services. To facilitate their work, members formerly were permitted 6,000 minutes of long distance telephone time and 40,000 words of telegraphing annually. But demands for increase in telephone time and recognition that the telegram allowance was generous led to consolidation of the two services. Presently congressional offices are allowed 100,000 units of the two (in any combination) per Congress (two years). Each word in a telegram counts for one unit whereas each minute of long distance telephoning counts for five units. Despite an allowance increase to 90,000 units in the Eighty-seventh Congress, 20 per cent of the members had exceeded their units; thus the figure was raised again in 1963.

Other valuable services to congressmen include the Office of the Legislative Counsel (which drafts bills for the legislators and the committees on which they serve), the Legislative Reference Service of the Library of Congress, the Office of the Coordinator of Information (a source of answers to questions of congressional staffs), the Recording Studios (where transcriptions and tapes for radio and television use are made for members at cost), and the Folding Room (where materials may be sent for stuffing into envelopes, to be crated, etc.). Some government agencies such as the Veterans Administration and the Civil Service Commission maintain offices in the House office building to be more accessible to congressional offices. And some liaison groups such as the Army, Navy, and Air Force make frequent visits to the legislators' offices to seek to be of maximum assistance.

Each member of Congress is also allowed a quota of various government publications, including the *Congressional Record* (68 copies daily), the *Congressional Directory*, Agricultural yearbooks, *Infant Care* (most popular), and *Family Fare*. Publications are exchanged between offices depending on the demands of individual districts.

Staff Needs and Personnel Policy

Staff requirements vary appreciably among congressional offices. Wide disparity in the population of congressional districts (from about 180,000 to more than 950,000), the kind of district represented (urban centers or more sparsely populated farming communities, for example),[5] and the congressman's attitude toward encouraging constituent communication with his office are but a few of the many elements contributing to a determination of office needs. Many congressmen do not use all of their clerk-hire allowance, and few distribute it so as to achieve the maximum number of full-time employees.[6] Yet, until recently at least, a substantial number of legislators were sorely pressed for staff assistance.

A survey in 1958 by the Committee on House Administration revealed more support for the addition of an administrative assistant than for any other suggested reform. Some House members want two such assistants, one to run the office, the other to keep the congressman informed on

[5] For a recent review of apportionment issues, see Andrew Hacker, *Congressional Districting: The Issue of Equal Representation* (Brookings Institution, 1963).

[6] Figures provided to the Committee on House Administration showed that in 1963 there were 12 members employing 10 assistants, 67 employing 9, 90 employing 8, and 85 employing 7. There were 71 members employing 6 aides, 57 employing 5, 36 employing 4, and 17 employing 3. There were nearly 4,500 employees on the House side in 1963.

legislation. Considerable sentiment thus exists for creation of a position sufficiently attractive to permit recruitment of a skilled professional person. Commented one conservative Republican known for his reluctance to support additional expenditures for member convenience:

> Our offices are not equipped to do some things it is helpful to have done. I have a good man but I couldn't give him responsibility for the newsletter, nor is there anyone with the time and knowledge to do extensive research on important bills. We need more staff assistants. What I need is a legislative assistant. I'd like to go out and hire somebody capable for that job, probably someone with a legal background. But I can't do that and take care of the mail so I try to take care of the legislative work myself.

A party colleague added his support of the position:

> It is true that we just don't have much time to legislate around here . . . all this nonlegislative work which our office gets means that I don't get any help from anybody there on research or speeches or things like that. My staff is busy taking care of constituent matters, case work, and such things. My press man helps some on political speeches but not very much. It would be helpful to have someone who could assist me in carrying out my legislative role.

Most House offices probably do not have anyone with important responsibilities in connection with legislation. In fact, the main deficiency in staffing may be the absence of a qualified legislative assistant who can do research for the congressman and help him perform his legislative role more efficiently. Said one thoughtful legislator:

> I need a good legislative man very badly. Time after time we go on the floor, not knowing anything about the subjects to be discussed. It is hard to keep on the top of the whole operation, and having someone who could be of assistance in the legislative aspect of the job is very important. I think most members need such additional assistance and that they would know how to use it. I do agree with the Speaker that any provision for such a professional man should be drawn up so that the money could not be divided into small sums for additional secretaries. What Congress needs is professional assistance. I need research work going on all the time in a number of areas. If it could be done in depth I could propose something. I am hampered in carrying my work forward because of lack of proper staff.

The heavy volume of mail and the necessity of undertaking numerous large mailings to the district has forced many representatives to divide their clerk-hire allowance so as to get a maximum number of secretaries plus, possibly, someone to handle press releases and perhaps a newsletter.

As one member stated: "The need for professional assistance varies with the office. Some members wouldn't know how to use the help. Those of us who are active and wish to be more active have a real need." A well regarded congressman, though aware that many of his associates wanted a legislative assistant, thought the real need was for more secretarial assistance.

> It seems to me that we may be too belittling with respect to stenographers and that part of our office. If I had the space and the allowance, I would certainly like to have a bigger staff, but I think it would be appropriate for part of that additional staff to be stenographic in order to get the mail off. I went home this past weekend and got some complaints that letters were not answered or were answered very slowly. People take it for granted, I suppose, that you are going to vote intelligently on issues. But by and large if they write they want action. We've got to get the mail out.

The growing movement for a professional staff able to assist the congressman in the legislative realm was blocked, at least temporarily, by public reaction to disclosure of nepotism in congressional offices. Some staff aides who are related to their employers are outstanding, but the wisdom of some appointments is questionable. Reluctant in the circumstances to vote themselves a high salaried assistant, the House in the Eighty-seventh Congress added $2,500 to its "basic" clerk-hire allowance and increased the number permitted on staff by one.[7]

There are, of course, potential sources of staff assistance other than those recruited under clerk-hire allowances. Some senior congressmen, particularly committee chairmen, make frequent use of committee personnel to help them with their work; occasionally committee staff will even be housed in the congressman's office. This may enable the latter to employ more people at the district level or back in his district.

Another source of assistance is the rapidly increasing number of intern programs, which locate students and professional people in Hill offices for varying periods of time. The talents of college undergraduates and graduate students, law students and lawyers, newspapermen and teachers of political science are made available, often without cost to the congressman, sometimes at minimal cost. From some of these volunteers the member

---

[7] If the entire $2,500 were used to pay the salary of an additional staff member, the gross annual salary of the employee would be $6,172.40. But it might be added to the basic allowance of existing positions.

receives valuable assistance, enabling him to undertake activities that otherwise he would be forced to neglect. Other volunteers are of more dubious value. The temporary nature of their stay in the office limits the effectiveness of all volunteers. One congressman who lists the members of his staff on his stationery adds underneath the notation "and all the volunteers we can get," emphasizing the receptivity of some members to such assistance.

The House does not maintain a central personnel office, although traditionally there have been several persons to whom applicants were directed for advice and "leads" and whom employers have asked for suggestions. The United States Employment Service maintains an office to assist prospective employers and employees but, except at the beginning of each session, its success has fallen short of its goal.

Once it was customary for legislators to recruit their staffs entirely from their home districts; some continue to hire nearly all, if not all, of their aides from the home area. Increasingly, however, the complexity and volume of work in a congressional office have placed a premium on experience and expertise, and there has been a relaxation of the residence requirement. Secretaries move easily from one office to another, their new employer often representing another state, and perhaps another political party, from that of their former boss. Congressmen generally believe it is advantageous—both politically and personally—to have at least part of their staff from their own district (though some caution that it is more difficult to discharge someone from home), but professional competence is a more important criterion of selection than it used to be. Some legislators say they receive no job applications from constituents; some state that political organizations dictate staff selections to certain of their colleagues.

There is no clear pattern in office organization, particularly where the duties of the top assistant are concerned. Some first assistants perform little more than routine responsibilities; others are in every sense advisers and assistants. As one congressman said, "I think every office is run differently and shaped after the personality of the congressman. I know some of my friends run their offices totally and completely differently from the way I run mine, and I think probably that is the way it should be."

If there is no central personnel office, there also is no uniformity among salary scales. Congressmen determine their own staff salaries, and sharp differences between offices exist. Secretarial salaries may range from a little more than $3,000 to $12,000 or more; salaries of $7,500–$8,500 are not uncommon. The top assistant in one office may receive a gross salary of more than $15,000; the assistant in a neighboring office may do more work and receive approximately half that amount. On the whole, secretaries tend to be somewhat better paid than people doing comparable work elsewhere in the government. But they possess no job security (they may be fired at will), often carry a substantially heavier workload, receive no extra compensation for overtime (which may be required frequently), and have considerably less flexibility with respect to vacations.

In an operation of the scope of that of a congressional office, the quality of the staff can be important in determining success. In all but the least active offices, wide discretionary powers must necessarily be delegated to them. Congressional willingness to increase both staff size and the sums available for staff salaries reflect both an increasing volume of work and recognition that it is important to obtain talented personnel; congressmen usually approach cautiously legislation that will make them vulnerable to the charge that they are adding unnecessarily to their emoluments at the taxpayers' expense.

Members appear satisfied with their staff, with the exception noted elsewhere that under existing allowances they often cannot afford the luxury of allocating any appreciable staff time to consideration of legislation. Certainly the versatility of staff seems on the increase; the resourcefulness and skill of many Hill employees is outstanding.

Office Visitors

A congressional office is visited by many people. Representatives of interest groups, newspapermen, job seekers, colleagues and committee staff, agency liaison personnel, a few "regulars" whose business and claim to attention are not quite clear, students, tourists, constituents with problems—these are but a few of the groups to whom a congressman and his staff are exposed in any given week. Some seek access to the congressman; others expect to consult with staff. The staff soon learns which of the nonconstituents their employer wishes to see and which he desires to avoid. Some congressmen have their door open to everyone; others expect careful staff screening of prospective visitors. If they were willing to do so, a large proportion of the legislators could spend nearly every minute not spent in committee or on the floor in conversation with those seeking to talk with them.

The constituent is a special kind of visitor. Most congressional offices report that they have a considerable number of visitors from home. They are ordinarily welcomed cordially by the staff; memories of a pleasant reception in their congressman's office may last a long time. Staff urge constituents to sign the guest book (potential additions to the mailing list), furnish them with passes to House sessions, provide them with literature about things to do in Washington and a copy of the congressman's current newsletter or his questionnaire, and engage them in conversation about their home town. They may even offer to arrange special tours of the White House or the Federal Bureau of Investigation. Generally this expression of hospitality satisfies the visitor. Sometimes, however, he wants to see his congressman. There are congressmen who delight in meeting constituents and instruct staff to interrupt them should constituents arrive. Sometimes if they hear strangers in the outer office, they will come out to meet the guests. If they are not too busy, certain legislators may even conduct a tour of the Capitol for the benefit of the visitors, or they may send for a photographer and have a group picture taken. Often, of course, members are in committee or on the floor of the House rather than in their offices. A few, however, even encourage staff to suggest they be called off the floor.

Not all congressmen, however, are anxious to spend time with visitors, and even if they ordinarily are willing, it is not always convenient for them to do so. One freshman congressman explains why:

I had been coming here since 1936 to testify on different bills and thus I thought I had a very good idea of what went on in a congressional office. Every time I came I stopped in to see my congressman and senators and was under the impression that they had a lot of time to spare and that I was not inconveniencing them. I realize now how much I must have encroached on their time. A congressman is the busiest person on earth. He has to devote all of his waking hours to doing a good legislative job.

Unless they are unusually pressed for time, legislators normally will see any constituent who asks to see them, reluctant as they may be to do so; nonconstituents who do not know the member may find it more difficult to gain admittance. Where the constituent has a problem he wants to discuss, the staff is often instructed by the representative to seek to get the facts and act on them, referring only the most unusual cases to the congressman himself. If the visitor insists on talking with the legislator about the matter, and is successful in doing so, he often finds himself eventually directed back to the staff. A constituent's reluctance to deal with staff may be shortsighted. The staff will normally be required to carry through, and it is often more important that they be fully informed than the congressman. In discussing constituent visits one legislator stated that he seldom talked to them himself. The statement led to the following discussion among his colleagues:

That is fine for you. In my district, however, people will accept that attitude from a senator but not from the congressman. They reason: "Well, I know him well enough so that I can go in to see him personally." You have people who sit in your office for an hour waiting to see you over some trivial thing that could be taken care of in five minutes by a member of the staff. But they want to see the congressman.

*

It is a habit of the district, I think, and the tradition developed in the representation of the district. My own view is that you can play it any way you want to if you are prepared to make a sacrifice.

*

I think a lot of the problem comes from the image you build of yourself in the campaign. I always have said, "the door is open and you can see me anytime you want to." So it is my own fault.

District Offices

The majority of congressmen maintain district offices, many of which are staffed by part time help; a few have two or more located at different ends of the district. Few local offices appear to have important responsibilities. They provide an additional point of contact with constituents, prepare mailing lists, clip items from local newspapers to be forwarded to the congressman, and carry out other like activities. Members representing areas that are close to regional offices of government agencies may shift the responsibility for handling constituents' requests pertaining to those agencies to the local scene. Many, however, elect to handle such matters from the Washington office, apparently preferring the more direct supervision that is possible there. Tradition is sometimes a factor in determining the distribution of responsibilities. Although members believe that district habits can be changed and a new pattern of constituent behavior established, they note the difficulty of educating citizens to deal with their district offices, particularly when there has been no previous local office.

The discussion that follows reveals the variety of practices with respect to operations in the district, ranging from no district office at all to handling 80 percent of constituents' problems there.

I have found that nothing much can or should be done in my district office except to tell visitors "please write that to the congressman," or if they won't write, "fine, tell me about it and I will send him a memorandum on it." I make no effort to solve things at the district level.

*

I don't agree. My district office does about 80 percent of my constituent work on the telephone. Perhaps 20 percent of that 80 percent involves a Washington contact but _____ is a regional office city, and I have my top assistant there. He handles most of the constituent problems—the routine ones—on the phone with the agency people there. I admit that politically there are disadvantages because I stay in Washington and work on legislation and try to have an assistant congressman out there contacting the people. It may very well be that it will catch up with me, but certainly so far it has worked reasonably well.[8]

*

I probably take a middle ground. I have an experienced secretary in my home town office who handles a good volume of work with the Veterans Administration, Social Security, and the area office of the Bureau of Indian Affairs. In those three fields in particular, she can handle almost anything that comes along that can be resolved at a regional or area office level. If a problem has to come up to Washington, she sends it along.

*

We handle 100 percent of our case work in Washington although I have a district office. I have one of those widely spread out districts. I have a good man there whose main job is to keep on top of what is happening in the various communities and to report areas where there are problems. He renders an invaluable service to me and the district in doing so, but he doesn't take care of any case work.

*

I tried to set up a district office right in the center of my district, but it wouldn't take hold. Nobody would go there except on Saturday morning when I was there. They would rather come to Washington to see me. [A district near Washington.]

[8] This division of workload between district and Washington offices is unusual.

Congressmen representing large metropolitan areas close to Washington spend much of their time at home and form the core of the "Tuesday to Thursday" group in the House. They hold frequent office hours in the district listening to constituent requests and problems and servicing them without an exchange of correspondence. Their district offices assume special importance in their organization, and citizens are accustomed to going there for help. Although these congressmen appreciate the opportunity for direct contact with the people they represent, they are aware that definite disadvantages also are attached to the proximity of their districts to Washington: they are expected to go home regularly, and there is no escape from people with problems. Many of them resent the criticism of colleagues who charge that their frequent absences from Washington impede the passage of legislation. Two congressmen serving urban constituencies within a 250 mile radius of Washington speak of their plight:

I have two congressional offices in the district in addition to my Washington office. When Congress is out of session I spend Mondays and Thursdays in one of them and Tuesdays, Wednesdays, and Fridays in the other. When I get home during congressional sessions I spend every night and Saturday in one or the other of the offices. Sometimes I am even there on Sundays. People who criticize congressmen just don't recognize all the pressure they are under and all the types of work they have to do, or the long hours which are involved. Constituents are not particularly thoughtful when it comes to deciding when they should break in on their congressman. In my first two years in Congress I had 13,000 visits from constituents. You certainly are called on to carry out a wide variety of functions, including acting as people's legal counselor. When you realize you write about four letters on each problem, you realize how involved and time consuming the job can become. I get a lot of cases dealing with problems of housing and relocation. Unfortunately the people involved don't always relocate in my own congressional district. Thus sometimes I find myself helping people who are no longer going to be able to vote for me.

*

Case work takes a lot of time. When you are home you cannot even go to church in safety. Every time I go, there are thirty to forty people hiding behind automobiles just waiting to bump into me, always quite by accident. Each thinks his individual problem is the most important in the world. Problems of world peace and international tension pale into insignificance beside some personal problem of many constituents. People knock the Tuesday to Thursday group. I agree that it is a problem. I would be very happy if I didn't live so close to Washington. As it is, there is a 100 percent demand on my time. I go to my district on weekends and I hold office hours there every Friday evening, beginning at 8 o'clock and usually continuing until midnight. This life is no picnic no matter what some people think.

The Mail

The mail, delivered five times daily in the House, covers a wide variety of subjects some of them surprising topics for congressional action. The volume often runs to several hundred a day for most offices, particularly when pressure group efforts result in heavy correspondence on legislative matters;[9] some such communications are form letters or printed postcards to which a citizen need only affix his signature. There are many requests for free government publications and for bills and committee reports. The unemployed want assistance in getting jobs, the employed wish help in moving to better ones. There is "case" mail requesting assistance in constituent dealings with various government agencies. Some people want information regarding legislative proposals, others write to offer advice on these matters or to tell the congressman how world tensions can be relaxed; many protest government action; and some comment on votes and stands of the legislator.

The most effective letters are straightforward, give evidence that the correspondent is well informed about the subject matter, include reasons for taking the position expressed, and, preferably, relate the issue directly to the personal situation of the writer. Congressmen prefer that a letter treat only one subject, but their preference often is a selfish one. Such letters are easier to answer and are better adapted to the congressional practice of using a standard reply typed on the automatic typewriters for subjects on which correspondence is heavy. Many legislators are irritated when they are urged to work actively for passage or defeat of a measure which already has passed the House and on which they have taken a stand. Congressmen also observe that in the early stages of a bill's consideration it often is difficult to write a meaningful letter that will satisfy a constituent. They may hesitate to take a stand since committee or floor action may so alter a measure as to change their position. They may prefer to have the advantage of the hearings and report on the bill or at least know what the party stand will be.

Correspondence from students is increasing: teachers at all levels of in-

[9] In 1961 and again in 1962, the House post office handled nearly 23,000,000 pieces of incoming mail.

struction seem to be stimulating letters to members of Congress. At the grammar school level, pupils from all over the country write for information about the legislator's state or district; high school and college students want materials that will be useful in preparing for the annual debate topics (the Library of Congress anticipates the demand for such materials and prepares packets that can be forwarded to them) or in enabling them to "play" the member in mock student legislatures.

Some mail is obviously "pressure" mail; some reflects the view that the congressman is a sales representative for his constituents and has an obligation to plead their cause. Requests for donations are not uncommon. Some congressmen report that solicitors are not very understanding when they explain they receive many such requests and therefore find it necessary to limit their contributions sharply, however worthwhile the cause may be.

Unusual Requests. As might be expected, congressmen and their staffs are sometimes amazed at the kinds of things they are asked to do. They may be asked to make hotel or plane reservations, to match a constituent's draperies, or replace china. A congressman who was requested to perform the latter services noted that they seemed "a little outside the realm of a legislator's responsibility." He continued, "I don't mean to make fun of these people. I think it is very nice that they turn to us for assistance when they have a problem and feel that we represent them in so many ways. Naturally one must recognize it is their votes which help to return members of Congress, but even apart from that I think it is wonderful they expect us to help."

Another example of a request that constitutes an imposition on a congressional office is mentioned by a Republican, who passed it along to another branch of the government to which it should not have been sent either:

Not long ago I had a letter from a constituent who said she collected spoons from all over the world. She had read that Vice President Nixon was going to Russia to see Khrushchev, and she wanted me to phone him and ask him to bring back a spoon for her. Now I couldn't phone Nixon and ask him in the middle of all his important duties to get a spoon for that woman. Yet I had to do something. I wrote her and said I knew Nixon's time would be well occupied during his stay in Russia, and that I would hesitate to ask him to fulfill her request. At the same time, I told her I'd written to Ambassador Thomson in Moscow to ask him to select a spoon and send it to her. Fortunately, we are not required to deal with that sort of request every day, but I think you will agree that it is a somewhat strange one to make of a congressman.

The Tone of the Letters. Just as the subject matter of letters varies, so does the tone. The percentage of letters that are sharply critical of the congressman or could be regarded as abusive or threatening is small, but they succeed in irritating legislators nonetheless. Certainly they are not effective; if the writer expects to change a member's vote with that approach, he is nearly always disappointed. Some lawmakers take criticism philosophically and regard it as inevitable as one particularly industrious congressman does:

You've got to realize that for most people it is an event to write their congressman. They get pretty keyed up about things and sometimes they become discourteous. I get a number of letters like that, but I realize the atmosphere in which they were written. I always try to reply in a very nice and courteous manner. I've checked it out, and I find that the next letter I get from those people tends to be different in tone. If you treat them carefully and with respect you find they are impressed by it.

But to other legislators, vitriolic and unfair comments, which go beyond the issues and are in the nature of personal attacks on their intelligence and motivations, are inexcusable and cannot be ignored. Much as they try to react philosophically they cannot do so. They are angered. Statements of two hard-working legislators illustrate this point:

I don't mean to be thin skinned, but the thing that is most upsetting is the occasional snide or caustic letter which frequently reflects ignorance as well as spite. Demeaning the office as well as the officeholder seems to me to be going too far. There is no defense for it, but I guess it must be accepted as part of the job. I want to emphasize that differences of opinion are natural and don't distress me. It is the unfair tone that gets under my skin.

*

On the labor bill I got letters saying, "I support Landrum-Griffin and I'm watching you. I'll vote against you unless you support the bill." I replied and told them how complicated the problem was, that I was giving it my close attention, and after considering all of the evidence would vote my best judgment. Then I would receive another letter from them saying, "You cheap politician. By God, we'll get you the next time there is an election. You don't understand anything about public problems." They don't give you the benefit of the doubt for any thinking at all. That I guess is one of the things which bothers congressmen more than almost anything else—when you get letters which reveal the writer has a chip on his shoulder and is not really interested in your view if it isn't completely in line with his.

Another source of irritation results from the tendency of people to expect Congress to do the impossible. Said one representative, "I get letters instructing me to prevent Khrushchev's coming as though I had any power to determine a matter like that. It is almost as though these people will blame me once he comes."

On the other hand, some members are surprised that the mail does not contain more expressions of opinion. When opinions *are* expressed they are surprised at their moderation. At the conclusion of his first year in the House, a freshman reflected about the mail:

I'm a little surprised to find the mail so little expressive of views. I expected far more instructions than I've been getting. When people do tell me of their stands on legislation, they do so in such a kind and gentle manner that it surprises me. I expected their letters to be more demanding and forceful.

Sometimes members seek to test the knowledge of constituents who write them opposing the representative's view on specific legislation:

I don't appreciate pressure from people who don't know the facts, but who don't hesitate to give you their opinions. During a debate on labor legislation I received a good deal of mail and quite a few wires, so I picked up some letters at random and phoned the people to test their knowledge. I'd say, "I was much interested to hear from you and to get your views on the labor legislation. What can you tell me about the bill?" I soon discovered that most people had written me because they had been told to write or because they had gotten excited, without really knowing what the issues were. When I asked them what was in the committee bill which they didn't like, they couldn't tell me. When I asked them to compare the bills, they were unable to do that. Many of them had just received letters which they were to copy and forward. By contacting them directly, I was able to discover how much information they had. Since I always remained friendly, there was no opportunity for them to become angry with me. I think some of them even appreciated my phoning.

Handling the Mail. The general policy is that every communication must receive a reply. If a large volume of mail is received on a specific subject, a standard reply is prepared, and the letters are run off on the automatic typewriters. The clerk need only type in the name, address, and salutation, and press a button whereupon the text of the letter is typed automatically. Each letter appears as an original; it gives no indication of being a form letter.

Congressional offices often maintain a card file that contains a record of each letter received from a constituent and its general subject.[10] Occasionally if the writer seems to rate a spot in the "crackpot" file, a letter may go unanswered, but generally only after previous efforts to carry on reasonable correspondence have been unsuccessful. Normally, even sharp critics rate an answer; sometimes congressmen will go to extraordinary lengths to woo people who disagree with them. A courteous letter to the individual may be followed by a phone call when the congressman goes back to his district. Sometimes he phones from Washington. In some circumstances, the call may even be followed by a personal visit or a suggestion that the constituent appear at the congressman's district office the next time the representative is there. Some legislators regard criticism as a challenge. They are mindful, too, of the special impact of a "conversion." If the district is marginal politically, a number of such conversions may have important consequences. The thoughtful, reasoned letter impresses the member even though it may be in disagreement with his position; on some matters it may even influence his position. Writers of such communications are the objects of special attention.

Although the mail is regarded as important in revealing what constituents are thinking about and in providing occasional ideas for action, congressmen cannot read all the mail every day. ("The mail is heavy and the staff takes care of it.") They have not the time to do so, nor is it necessary. One assistant usually is responsible for examining the mail and dividing it among the staff for action, although another clerk may previously have set aside those communications that involve routine requests for government publications, newsletters, and things of that nature. The congressman may wish to see all significant case or legislative mail—it

---

[10] The card file serves several purposes. It may prove especially helpful when a member returns to his district and meets constituents:

"As we are driving along touring our district, my wife goes through the card file for the next town. She reads off the names and identifies the kind of correspondence we have had with the various individuals. When we get there, the names of those people are familiar and you can say, 'Oh, yes, you wrote me about public power, or you wrote me about a farm bill,' or something like that. We have a duplicate file. My Washington office files alphabetically and the field office by area."

may even be he who divides it among the staff—but more frequently only the complicated problems are referred to him along with letters from his personal friends. Those that are brought to his attention tend, in the first instance, to be provided for informational rather than action purposes. He controls staff disposition of the mail later at the point where his signature is required on the response to the constituent communication. (House members are less likely to authorize staff to sign the member's name on letters than are senators.) When a letter is given to him for signature, a record of previous correspondence is attached so that he will have the information necessary for judging the adequacy of the staff action.

If controversial problems are before the Congress, the legislator may request that all letters dealing with those matters be set aside for his examination so that he can better gauge district sentiment. Fearful that staff may become too casual in their treatment of the less complicated case mail, the congressman may, as a deterrent, stop by their desks occasionally to see how this work is being handled; this display of interest is regarded as having a salutary effect on staff attention to detail. Observed one congressman:

> Unless you retain a fairly direct interest in the so-called routine case work you may find the staff takes it too much in stride, without realizing that for the individual involved it is a matter of great importance. I sometimes find an irritated letter from a constituent saying, "Why haven't you been able to help me?" or "Why haven't I gotten an answer?" Had I known about those cases perhaps I would have been able to accelerate them more than the staff did. So I always find myself looking over their shoulder saying, "What is this case?" and asking them to put anything unusual on my desk.

Stimulating Correspondence. Although there are frequent complaints that the volume of mail is too heavy and that much of it is unnecessary or misdirected ("The vast majority of requests I get have merit, but they shouldn't come to me. People should not be writing me about many of these matters.") every one on Capitol Hill will tell you it is important. Once a congressman becomes accustomed to a heavy mail, he tends to worry if it drops off. So important does he regard mail to his success that he actively seeks it. The special mailings to particular groups, for example, constitute an important means by which legislators try to stimulate correspondence with residents of their districts. In closely contested districts, this device is often regarded as crucial to success at the polls.

Some members who complain about the heavy influx of mail from their districts have in fact aggressively encouraged it in this and other ways.

I wonder how many congressmen invite (unnecessary) mail by returning to their districts and going to each court house or prominent place and saying, "Now please bring your problems to me." Hasn't that become quite a campaign gimmick?

*

It is a corollary of being re-elected. An old time congressman told me the quickest way to get defeated is not to answer the mail or pay attention to constituents. They care less about your votes and attitudes than about whether you are interested in, and take care of, their individual problems.

Many congressional mass mailings are designed to get recipients to write to the congressman, and a large mailing list is a source of much pride. Once a constituent has communicated with his legislator, his name is placed on the mailing list for newsletters, questionnaires, agricultural bulletins, and other material. The lawmaker believes correspondence (unless the citizen is inflexibly unfriendly) is an effective means of gaining friends and support at the polls.

"Case" Mail. Probably the most important mail is the "case" mail, which touches on the relationship between the constituent and the government. Because of this, the expert case handler is much in demand in congressional offices. Denied a favorable ruling by the bureaucracy on a matter of direct concern to him, puzzled or irked by delays in obtaining a decision, confused by the administrative maze through which he is directed to proceed, or ignorant of whom to write, a constituent may turn to his congressman for help. These letters offer great potential for political benefit to the congressman since they affect the constituent personally. If the legislator can be of assistance, he may gain a firm ally; if he is indifferent, he may even lose votes.

Careful staff attention is directed, therefore, to case mail. A person who has a reasonable complaint or query is regarded as providing an opportunity rather than as adding an extra burden to an already busy office. The party affiliation of the individual even when known to be different from that of the congressman does not normally act as a deterrent to action. Some legislators have built their reputations and their majorities on a program of service to all constituents irrespective of party. Regularly, voters affiliated with the opposition in other contests lend strong support to the lawmaker whose intervention has helped them in their struggle with the bureaucracy.

Some mail seeks aid for causes of doubtful merit, but legislators believe that a substantial portion of the requests involve situations where congressional intervention is justified. As one thoughtful representative put it, "Usually it seems to me there has been a wrong against the person writing in, but I would think the writer often exaggerates the extent of the wrong." Said another:

Most people who write me have valid problems and feel that only their representative can help them get action. Now sometimes they are wrong in sending things to us or in thinking their case has merit, but they are sincere, and I think it is one of the functions of a congressman to do what he can for them. It really doesn't irritate or bother me.

As one would anticipate, there are occasions when the congressman is convinced that constituents seek preferential treatment rather than justice in turning to their representative. Commented one congressman:

Our biggest headache in terms of the volume of mail concerns the problems of servicemen or their families—their service regulations, retirement, and release procedures. We are frequently approached not as a last resort but just as one means by which to try to get preferential treatment.

Elsewhere[11] a group of federal executives are reported as believing that constituents often go to Congress with very minor complaints and problems, which could be handled more quickly and effectively if mailed directly to the agency. Members of both parties were invited to comment on that belief; in both groups there was an inclination to stress those instances where the constituent action had been the appropriate one, although some support was found for the position of the executives. Said one forthright Democrat:

The majority of cases in my district concern persons who have become so enmeshed in red tape that the only place they can go and hope to get any action is to a member of Congress. These cases usually represent the errors of the field offices. I have a district with many aliens and thus have many immigration problems. Rarely do I get a case that hasn't been worked over—misworked—by one of the nearby immigration service branches.

[11] See Marver H. Bernstein, *The Job of the Federal Executive* (Brookings Institution, 1958), Chap. 5.

The following discussion took place among Republican members:

One reason we get the mail is because people either have not been able to find out with whom they should deal or have been exposed to a lot of red tape. The federal government is entering into the lives of people more and more, and the agencies are not known to them or are not near. Thus they think of their congressman. One of the most rewarding things we do is rectifying some of the erroneous decisions or lack of attention from administrative agencies to the problems of individual constituents. In many instances the executive branch is wrong, and the only recourse the individual has is to come to a senator or member of the House.

*

One difference is that we have to have their votes to get elected and the bureaucrat doesn't need them.

*

Most of the people who write me about such problems write from the very town where there is a social security office and where offices of other government agencies are located. They don't even know those offices exist. We can't disregard these people.

That considerable executive branch time is taken up in congressional inquiries relating to problems of constituents is indisputable. In 1962–63, for example, the Air Force alone had 156 people engaged in activities associated with legislative affairs and liaison. Headed by a major general, the working force included 67 military personnel and 89 civilians. More than 5,500 contacts monthly were received from the Congress by the liaison section, and these did not include the contacts of the three House and two Senate liaison officers, the activities of the Investigative Division, which worked with committees, or those of the Legislative Division, which was concerned with preparation of materials in connection with Defense Department legislation. For the same period, the Department of Agriculture estimated that 30,992 man-hours were devoted to researching, developing, and supplying information to Congress; 13,477 letters and 43,201 telephone calls were received from congressional sources. At the same time, 219,828 congressional publication lists were distributed, and 4,721,413 copies of publications were forwarded for distribution by members of Congress. The Treasury Department reported that its liaison staff alone received 21,500 information requests, while the Post Office Department stated that its liaison section handled about 25,000 member and 5,000 committee requests during fiscal 1963 and estimated that other sections handled another 50,000. In calendar 1962, the State Department's liaison office received 18,576 letters and 12,303 telephone calls, allied offices getting another 13,250 calls. The liaison office of the Department of Health, Education, and Welfare sets 2,000 as the average number of calls coming to it monthly, only a fraction of the total number of congressional contacts made to the bureaus and departments. Some of the communications were undoubtedly of minor importance involving a single question of fact or an inquiry regarding status of a case, but many involved complicated matters. Whatever the purpose, it is clear that much executive staff time is spent dealing with the legislative branch.

When the question how often decisions are changed as a result of congressional intervention is considered, the feeling is strong that it is not the percentages which are important but the fact that occasionally an injustice is corrected. It helps, too, congressmen assert, to make bureaucrats aware that their actions are subject to review. Consider the following discussion of Democratic members:

> Perhaps in one out of ten instances you can do something. That one case is eminently worth the harassment you give the bureaucracy because it is a way of cutting across the veritable bureaucratic chain. It is worthwhile politically too.

*

> I'd put the figure higher than one in ten. I'd say somewhere between a fifth and a third.

*

> We are talking about two different things. One question is how many cases are worthy; we might think from a third to a half fitted in that category. The other is how many you can get the administrative agency to do something about; there I'd stick to the 10 percent.

*

> During the Second World War, I handled personnel and was on the other side of the fence. I feel very strongly that even if 90 percent of our endeavors don't bring any change, making the effort is worthwhile. In a vast personnel operation, the case ceases to involve humanity. Officials deal with it as they would a set of cards rather than people. Even if we were helpful in only 1 percent of the cases, it would be well worth the effort. Everybody puts the tough cases in the bottom drawers. Congress represents people by moving in and saying, "Bud, you look at this one; a congressman asked about it." It is a constant reminder that there is some surveillance other than at the next rung of the ladder.

Assisting constituents in their dealings with administrative agencies has rewards other than serving as a check on the actions of bureaucracy and gaining political support at home. The legislator becomes better informed about the operation of government programs in the process of his investigations. In the words of one congressman, "These situations give you the best picture of how administrative agencies are functioning, what they are doing and how they are meeting the problems of the people. Complaints about agency malfunctioning give me a better picture than I believe I could get from any other source." Added a colleague, "I agree. We had a very bad situation in the regional office of _____. It was only because of the volume of complaints that it was possible to pinpoint this problem and take steps to correct it."

Through his handling of complaints the congressman feels that he learns about laws that need revision and agencies that would benefit from reorganization. The mail, then, helps the legislator to carry out his legislative responsibilities as well as his representative function. In pointing up weaknesses in the executive branch, it contributes to the strengthening of the administrative process. "You should not underestimate the value of constituent work on the legislative process," one legislator warned his colleagues. "Don't you get a lot of your ideas about needed changes in the laws from the problems of your constituents? In processing a problem before the VA or a draft problem you gain your best insight as to how laws operate, and you discover where they might be changed."

Legislators are not always interested in using a case as a means of developing increased understanding of how the laws operate in a particular area of government activity, nor do they always feel they have time to follow up evidence they uncover of faulty application of existing law. They are not always generous, either, in their evaluation of bureaucrats. After one member had outlined a situation in which he felt the rights of a constituent had been arbitrarily and flagrantly abused, a colleague observed that the case provided the legislator with an opportunity to know the industry and its problems better and to introduce corrective legislation. The congressman replied: "I will not have time to follow that up. I will get the guy's contract and I will forget it. Obviously some bureaucrat just overstepped his authority. This happens every day."

Some congressmen attach such significance to the value of constituent mail relating to problems with government that they suggest it offers the best means of exercising oversight of the executive departments. In speaking of the problems involved in maintaining effective oversight one member said:

> I would emphasize that the best watchdogs we have are not the committees but our constituents who in their letters bring to our attention things which require looking into. We get plenty of warnings of real significance in our mail which are extremely helpful in assisting us to carry out our responsibilities.

The vast majority of instances of congressional intervention in behalf of constituents is undertaken by staff, the congressman usually not participating directly in the process in any way, except perhaps to sign a letter. Staff are trained to perform this function, and some are extremely knowledgeable. Many of them automatically proceed to investigate the facts in a case and the prospects for adjustment of a decision without prior consultation with their employer. "I wouldn't have time to do anything if I looked at them," said one member. "Nineteen times out of twenty," said another, "my staff can do better on these cases than I can. On technical matters dealing with the military services or pensions or veterans problems, I have a secretary who is persistent and follows through. We never resort to a letter until we have made our initial probe by phone, and she can get more accomplished on the phone than I can." A colleague commented, "She probably has set up a permanent personal liaison with people as members of my staff have done. There are certain people they call all the time, so they can do better than we can."

There is agreement that expression of congressional interest in a case improves the likelihood of an action favorable to the constituent. Congressmen admit, too, that personal intervention by the member at some point in the process (rather than having the staff handle the entire negotiation) is even more effective. "I think I have as competent an assistant as anyone as far as contacting the agencies is concerned," said one representative, "but occasionally I wonder whether in terms of a specific case we missed out on something because I failed to intervene personally." A colleague was more blunt:

> Your effectiveness in cases where you yourself pick up the phone and talk to a responsible official at the government agency concerned is a good deal higher than in those which get a routine handling in your office. If the official knows you have some personal knowledge of the case and are checking on it, you are more likely to get favorable action.

There is considerable feeling within the Congress that these activities in behalf of constituents not only are legitimate functions of the representative and his staff but are essential to ensure proper protection of the rights of individuals. Who but the representative, the argument goes, can intervene to ensure the average citizen just treatment at the hands of a huge, impersonalized bureaucracy. Buttressed by the power to legislate and to exercise influence over the operating budget of the agencies concerned, he and a few others have the means of compelling the bureaucracy to review ill considered actions or to cut through normal procedures to reach a decision.

There are potential dangers in this fact, of course, and many legislators are aware of them and disturbed by them. Even a routine expression of interest may prejudice a case. Requests for information originating in congressional offices receive special handling from government agencies and replies are expedited. A letter signed by a member of Congress requesting information about a specific case usually does not reveal the extent of the legislator's interest or involvement in the matter; it may be a routine inquiry, or it may reflect personal concern. Unclear regarding the true interest of the congressman but reluctant to chance antagonizing him, the agency may bend regulations as much as possible in determining final disposition of the case. An element of discretion often is present in these matters, and congressional intervention often means that whatever discretion exists will operate in behalf of the constituent. Special deference may be granted to the views of those members in a position to influence agency appropriations.

The following excerpts from the Democratic round table discussions show that congressmen are aware of their position, and at least some are concerned lest they go too far in pushing constituent causes.

I have only gone to bat on two cases in ten years, on a personal basis. The thing that worried me was that I was getting too much service. Too often a case that looked to me, as a former personnel officer, as one decided within regulations was given special treatment just because I had made a routine inquiry. Too often decisions were made in favor of my constituent that I didn't really think fit the personnel pattern. And that was without direct intervention. My own impression is that on a staff and letter basis we get about as good service as could possibly be expected.

*

That is beginning to change, though. Liaison has come to act as a complete buffer giving you just barely enough information to send on to the constituent unless you take enough interest to push something. They are perfecting the art of the perfunctory answer and on just a normal approach with a letter you often get shoved aside. I call myself, bypass the liaison and go directly to the man concerned, when I am really interested in something.

*

Or get the head man of the liaison group and say, "This I mean." When something does come along that is important, and they know it really means something to you, they will put out more effort. I have found this particularly true with the military.

*

It should be brought out that we do not personally go to bat for all the requests that come in. The first thing I always do is get a report from the agency. I won't go to bat for anyone until I have that. If it seems to me, after reading the report, that the agency decision is correct, that is as far as I will go. Personally my philosophy—and that of most congressmen, I think—is that you don't want special favors for your constituents, but you want to make sure they get the full benefit of the law.

*

You have oversimplified it. There is a lot of latitude in fair treatment under the law.

*

I find that under normal circumstances just the fact that you ask for a routine investigation is sufficient to get the job done. If an agency is at fault it will go to bat and help your constituent.

*

What you actually are saying is that it is a good thing the congressman does interfere and that it is a very valuable service. It keeps the agency on its toes.

A few congressmen are so active in behalf of constituents that they will appear before administrative agencies to testify in cases involving them, a practice that sometimes has aroused the ire of lawyers because of the special privileges that are accorded congressmen. Some legislators even appear as counsel for residents of their district before groups such as the Board of Veterans Appeals and speak with obvious satisfaction of their success. Said one:

Jere Cooper and I used to go before the Board of Veterans Appeals a lot, and I still do. The folks down there tell me I have been before them more than any other living member. But you know I get a great deal of satisfaction out of that; last year I won $8,800 for a man whose case had been turned down for many years.

Other members reported that they either regarded such activities as "above and beyond the call of duty" or performed such services only rarely. "Don't let my constituents hear about this," one man pleaded. But performing such services may not only be time-consuming; it may also be discouraging. Another congressman related his experience:

I have gone on occasion and have been an unpaid lawyer for people, perhaps two or three times in all. Uniformly I have been mildly successful and uniformly my man has been an ingrate and grumbled at the results, whereas in other kinds of activities for constituents you may make one quick phone call and have a pathetically grateful family and a bonded debtor forever.

Working for constituents is a tricky business. The payoff is often difficult to anticipate, members agree, and some activities requiring little effort that would be regarded as "minor league" by independent observers are among the most appreciated, often because they have such a direct impact on the constituent. On the other hand, the most routine kinds of aid may lead to trouble. Both points are evident in the following discussion:

I get my biggest assist from people I have been able to help on *little* things. I was born and reared on a farm where our mail box was a half mile from home, and because it seemed like every time it rained Dad sent me for the mail as a youngster, I have a feeling about people who have to go far to their mailboxes. I was helpful in getting inserted in post office regulations a provision that there be extensions granted for farmers in certain instances. A survey indicated I had 3,000 farmers in my district who had to go over half a mile for mail so I started a campaign. By the last election I had gotten 1,300 extensions. They think of me every time they go get that mail. I assisted with some Small Business Administration appointments and got myself in terrible trouble.

*

I got a call from London about two months ago. A lawyer and his wife from my district were there and the wife left her passport in a taxicab. They planned to go to the Continent the next day and couldn't without the passport. I told them I would do what I could, and as luck would have it I reached the duty officer in the Passport Division at the State Department. He sent a cable. When the lawyer got back home he said, "I went to the Embassy and they showed me a telegram signed 'Herter'[12] and I got my passport right away." He really was impressed.

*

Let me assure you, though, that helping people with passports does not always work to your advantage. Nine times out of ten it does, but I recall a routine request for help in getting a passport expedited. We got the man the passport, expedited the process, and next thing I learned he was one of thirteen men who

[12] Christian A. Herter, then Secretary of State.

had gone on to Moscow with one of those "Peace Forever" groups. I had more letters demanding to know why I helped a communist get over to Moscow—the incident occurred during the Korean War, and it was terrible.

*

How did it get publicized? I never publicize what I do on passports.

*

I don't either but the home addresses of the thirteen men were listed in the paper. A newspaperman got hold of the fellow over there and asked, "How did you get here?" My constituent said, "I wrote my congressman and he helped get the passport expedited."

As much as some members dislike requests that they assist constituents in their troubles with agencies of the government and as misdirected as they think some such solicitations of help are, they are reluctant to surrender the opportunities provided to bind themselves closer to the constituent and his vote. Two congressmen explain:

Before I came to Washington I used to think it might be nice if the individual states had administrative arms here that would take care of necessary liaison between citizens and the national government. But a congressman running for re-election is interested in building fences by providing personal services. The system is set to re-elect incumbents regardless of party, and incumbents wouldn't dream of giving any of this servicing function away to any subagency. As an elected member I feel the same way.

*

We talk about remedies. It is conceivable that a lot of the mail we get is so similar that it could be handled by a central office and never need come to us at all. But I think we would resist any move to have constituents' problems deferred to somebody else. It seems to be an aspect of our lives we appreciate even if it is only to build up a file of names for us to send out questionnaires to. It is part of the process of being in politics, it seems to me.

Conflict of Interests

Congressmen are sensitive to conflict of interest charges, and some are beset by doubts regarding their proper role in expressing interest in the awarding of government contracts or in pressing the case of constituents before government agencies. Federal laws relating to conflict of interest and corrupt practices offer only a partial guide to the problems they face.

Statutes are on the books that serve to restrict somewhat the law practice activities of lawyer members of Congress. There are provisions which make it a crime for congressmen to receive compensation for services before a government agency, to enter into contracts with the government, or to conspire to defraud it. The legislators also are prohibited from practicing law before the Court of Claims and from accepting payments, campaign contributions, or gifts for any service or for a particular vote.

But many questions involving ethics arise in the normal discharge of a member's duties. Legislators are aware that from time to time colleagues have been found guilty of breaching their trust, and some of them have sought a more specific code of conduct. Serving as a member of Congress is a full-time job today, but not all members restrict their activities to performing their legislative duties. Many believe the salary inadequate and feel the need to supplement it. Some, uncertain regarding their tenure, hesitate to dispose of the business interests they held prior to their election. Others want to continue to practice law. "Some people around here regard their congressional salary as a retainer," commented one lawmaker. "They spend most of their time back home making money." Inevitably, in the manner in which they carry on their noncongressional activities, a few solons arouse the ire of colleagues.

Members are in a position to assist others and to receive information that is not available to many people. There have been instances when congressmen have turned to advantage confidential information acquired as a result of their committee or legislative responsibilities. Others have been compensated for using their position to influence decisions affecting contract awards. But beyond these obvious instances of wrongdoing, many questions plague the conscientious member. Should he vote on issues in which he has a personal interest? When he accepts sizable campaign contributions from interest groups or leading businessmen is he, in fact, making it more difficult for him to act independently? To what extent should he divorce himself from business undertakings? What constitutes improper activities? There are no easy answers to these and other questions, and this fact complicates his life.

Public Relations

Douglass Cater, in "Government by Publicity," wrote in 1959:

The congressman is uniquely both a creator and creature of publicity. By the very nature of his job, with its relative insecurity of tenure, he is concerned with the process by which the public attention is attracted. . . . The American politician has always been something of a dramatist in search of an audience. . . . Recently, however, there has begun to emerge in the halls of Congress a new type . . . conditioned to the age of mass media and more keenly aware of the uses of publicity. . . . [He need not] be assiduous in preparing legislation and attending to the thousand and one chores of pushing it through to enactment. Rather he is a man versed in the subtleties of appealing beyond Congress directly to the mass audience. He knows the formula of the news release, the timing, the spoon-feeding necessities of the publicity campaign. He assesses with canny shrewdness the areas of enterprise that will best lend themselves to a sustained publicity build-up. He is a master at shadow play, creating the illusion of magnificent drama from a reality that may be quite mundane.[13]

Congressional comments tend to substantiate the validity of Cater's remarks. "Much of this job is a public relations job, and a good politician recognizes it quickly," observed one of the most serious minded freshman members. "Events and names make news," said another. "One simply has to ride the news opportunities." Frequent congressional expressions of regret and concern that it is necessary to spend so much time and energy in public relations efforts are almost inevitably followed by solemn assertions that it really *is* necessary. Competition is keen for the attention and interests of citizens, and congressmen know it. The fear is strong that unless they are unusually alert and resourceful—and persistent—there is little likelihood that their cause will be adequately stated. "The biggest problem we have is that of determining how to communicate with citizens to tell them why we have to do the things we do, why we vote the way we vote," asserts one legislator. "It is almost impossible to get across to them."

Two legislators commented on the problem in this way:

You have a responsibility not only to yourself but to your constituents to get re-elected. The functions of your office that can legitimately be used to help you get re-elected should be used. At least one third of our activities today are spent in working towards re-election. You know the saying, "You can't be a statesman unless you get elected."

*

One of the weaknesses of our political system is that congressmen are not willing to lay it on the line regarding their beliefs on issues. A lot of congressmen spend their time getting re-elected instead of studying the issues and going to their committee meetings and grinding out legislation. I find many committee members ignorant of bills their committees are presenting to the Congress be-

[13] *The Reporter*, March 19, 1959.

cause they haven't studied them. Only a few committee members are faithful in attending hearings. Now I know what the others are doing. They are going around the Capitol with constituents, answering letters, and all this other stuff. Frankly I resent it. I want them to run for election, but on the basis of what they know on the subjects that have come before the Congress and how they stood on them.

The daily newspapers are often of little assistance in publicizing the activities of members of the House, preferring to allocate their space to other matters. The activities of a congressman are not sufficiently important to be covered regularly. Weeklies, often starved for copy, are much more cooperative, and representatives fortunate enough to have many weeklies located in their district are happy to supply frequent news releases that may be printed without change. Seeking frequent mention in the press is but the first step, of course. No congressman thinks that even good press coverage is sufficient.

Unless you endeavor to supplement what might come through the news media, you can be certain your name won't be known by most of the people. It is practically a matter of necessity to figure out how you can supplement the distribution of news in your district about what Congress is doing and what your part in it is.

*

You really have to work at public relations. Even if the papers are favorably disposed to you, you must do more to make sure that you are identified with the office.

*

Take _____. He knew more about public finance than any man in Congress and handled those bills on the floor. He was hardworking, honest, and sincere and had never been identified with anything improper. He ran against a man who was inexperienced politically, and who had been a failure in business. Yet he lost. The fact is that his public relations was not good. Some of us carry on our own public relations as a matter of self-preservation, but it takes a lot of energy which we ought to be applying to what we were elected for—legislation.

There is considerable sentiment within the House that the press fails to meet its responsibilities to Congress and to the public. It is accused of focusing attention on the shortcomings of Congress while consistently ignoring its strengths. Thus the press is charged with creating a false image of the Congress. It is also accused of being superficial as well as inaccurate. "We need more think pieces on Congress," said one thoughtful House liberal. "The failure of the press to report on issues in depth is a very serious deficiency. Sometimes its reporting is absolutely scandalous." A veteran representative agreed, extending his indictment to all the mass media: "The media today are so poor in reporting what is going on that a member has a double responsibility to report to his constituents about legislation."

House members complain, too, that press coverage of congressional debate is limited to the Senate. Said one, "How much publicity do members of the House get when they speak on national issues? Damn little! If they deliver an effective and helpful speech, who is here to report it? The press fails to give the House the attention it really deserves."

One result of congressional evaluation of the importance of publicity to success is that most congressional offices are engaged in a constant search for new ideas designed to project a favorable image of the legislator into the homes of his district and to increase the number of residents who can identify him by name. Expeditious handling of incoming mail is considered an important way to accomplish these ends, but there are many others that focus on congressional initiative. At the opening session of the Brookings conference, one panelist reflected congressional preoccupation with these matters when he said:

I would be interested in knowing about the mail to their constituents that members of Congress themselves initiate. It seems to me as a freshman that it is important that I dream up all kinds of ideas for letters to ingratiate myself with the voters of my district.

One veteran Hill staff aide who had become principal assistant to a new member of the House substantiated the view that some freshmen are obsessed with developing an impressive stable of constituent-oriented projects.

I shudder whenever I hear my boss is going to have lunch with some colleagues. He always comes back to the office with new ideas for projects and wants to get some of them going right away. That's fine, but he never suggests we drop anything to make room for the new ones.

Conversations with more than fifty House members uncovered only one who seemed to place little emphasis on strategies designed to increase communications with the voter. That freshman expressed amazement at the activity that went on in neighboring offices. He issued no newsletter and had no intention of issuing one; questionnaires were more likely to cause trouble for a legislator than to help him. Some offices were "just like printing presses," and he disapproved of that. He had come to Washington, at some sacrifice, to legislate, not to take care of people's probblems. Correspondence received should be answered, and he answered it, but nothing should be done to encourage people to write in. Such actions would be regretted later.

If the congressman is right in his belief, the vast majority of congressmen from contested districts are not aware of it. They express surprise that colleagues can survive without waging an active, continuing campaign to promote constituent interest, unless a district is overwhelmingly one party in character. Even then, they warn, there is danger of primary opposition. Thus efforts to impress one's constituents take many forms; few means of contact are overlooked.

The Newsletter. One of the most effective instruments of the congressman in his continuous campaign to woo his district and, at the same time, educate it is the newsletter. *Editor and Publisher* has estimated that 90 percent of the members of Congress use this method of communicating with constituents. Discussion groups have even been organized around them.

Many regard the newsletter as an essential supplement to press coverage of the representative's activities. There is no standard pattern regarding format, content, and distribution policies, but all seek to strengthen the bonds between the legislator and his district. Issued weekly, biweekly, monthly, or perhaps even only two or three times a session, many newsletters carry the picture of the member, often with the Capitol in the background and an outline of the congressional district or state involved. Circulation may vary from more than 40,000 to a few hundred; some legislators confine distribution to newspapers in their district and a core of party workers in preference to wide coverage of individual constituents. Some newspapers refuse to publish the newsletter or print only selected excerpts; other papers regularly carry it in their columns without editing.

The newsletters vary in style and content. But whatever the form there generally is an observable effort to relate the discussion to the district represented by the congressman and often to the individual recipient himself. Full play is given to the role of the member in national and legislative events. Frequently listed at the conclusion of the report are all residents of the district who have visited the congressional office subsequent to the issuance of the previous newsletter.

Although primary responsibility for preparation of the newsletter is often delegated to an office assistant or to a person hired specifically to write it, many congressmen write their own. Indeed, some of the outstanding newsletters in the House are the products of congressmen.

Even though it is sent out franked, the newsletter can be an expensive item in a member's budget if it has a large circulation and is distributed frequently. Thus the legislators sometimes seek and obtain outside financial support, perhaps from local party organizations or a group of private individuals in the district.

Because of the importance congressmen attach to their newsletters (some identify them as their most effective single activity), there is considerable discussion about what form it should take in order to achieve the best results. An examination of these endeavors is interesting. Some letters are confined to a single topic; others attempt to discuss a dozen or more in capsule form. Some deal only with congressional action; others comment on domestic and international events not closely tied to specific legislation. The sharp content differences that are apparent in existing newsletters are conclusive proof that there is no consensus. Most legislators apparently believe it unwise as a steady policy to present detailed information regarding legislation or their stand on virtually all issues. In that connection, the following discussion between a public relations-minded congressman and a colleague whose newsletter is regarded as possibly providing the most thorough coverage of legislation before the House may be of interest. The latter may, and probably does, exaggerate the impact of a newsletter of the detailed variety. But, as his associate points out, he has been unusually successful in a district heavily weighted against him in terms of party registration.

There are two schools of thought as to whether it is a good idea to let your constituents know your attitude on all subjects and on all votes. Someone has said that every time you vote you are voting against the interests of some group, and your opponent is smart if he brings out your complete voting record because many groups will be antagonized by specific votes. Getting to _____'s newsletter, it is a good one and I read it every week. He, probably more than anyone else in Congress, lets his constituency know how he votes on every single bill that comes up. I don't do that. I don't think constituents are interested. I advised him to stop doing it but he continues. Certainly the fact that he has been re-elected in the toughest district in our large state is to his credit. Perhaps his newsletter is one reason for his success.

*

I would rather let them know where I stand than have my opponent informing them a week before the election.

*

You get into a problem when you are specific. You are voluntarily subjecting yourself to criticism as to why you acted in that way. So unless people raise an issue with you, you don't want to go over every one exhaustively in an effort to educate people as to your views. It may irritate.

*

I am not so sure about that. My newsletters are distributed all over the district. My opponents often have many house meetings and at practically every one of them there is at least one person who has received my report. If my opponent starts taking off on me, somebody is in the room to fight my battle for me.

The Questionnaire. The questionnaire has become a popular means of measuring constituent reaction to current issues and, perhaps more importantly, a device for creating a closer relationship between voter and representative. Generally, the poll results offer few surprises for congressmen, but the positive reaction that solicitation of views achieves makes it a valuable activity.

"This is the first time anyone ever asked me for my views," is a common notation written across the questionnaire by respondents. And frequently marking the appropriate response ("yes" or "no" is the normal choice) is supplemented by elaborative comments, some of which are not related to any of the items included in the poll. Some constituents write as many as ten or twelve pages about their views. There are, of course, skeptics among the recipients who doubt that the congressman is genuinely interested in the results. "I'll bet you never look at this," some respondents note. "If you do read it, send me a letter so I'll know you have examined it." "We elected you to know the answers to these questions," other constituents have written. ("My own mother wrote that to me," said one legislator.) Occasionally, too, instead of completing the form themselves, voters have returned it to the congressman and asked him to answer it and mail it back to them. "I got one like that recently," said one veteran congressman, "and I guess I'm stupid. I don't know how to answer my own questionnaire. I mean you can't answer yes or no." On balance, though, the questionnaire is well received in the district, and congressmen believe it gains adherents for them.

Radio and Television Programs. Congressmen are interested in exploiting opportunities on radio and TV. They are encouraged by the willingness of radio and television stations to carry their programs as a public service and are heartened by the prospect of reaching additional audiences in their districts. Most believe that such programs contribute importantly to their success with the voters.

> I was up looking at my TV film today—I have done one every week since I have been here—and who was behind me but Congressman _____. I'll swear he had never done a TV show before in his life but he only won by a few hundred votes last time. Now he has a weekly television show. If he had done that before he wouldn't have had any trouble.

The House provides recording facilities at cost, and House personnel will offer advice regarding format and topics. Additional assistance is available from party committees, particularly from the Republican congressional campaign committee. Some congressmen make simulcasts; for example, one southwestern member prepares nine radio tapes and four television films at the same time for weekly distribution in his district.

Programs may consist of statements of the congressman's viewpoint on current issues; frequently prominent guests are interviewed by the legislator. Cabinet officials and agency heads, colleagues, well-known businessmen and labor leaders, and even foreign dignitaries are sought for these appearances. Broadcasts of a few of the legislators have so often made "news" that they receive national press coverage.

Some members regard the impact of these activities so highly that they may delay in announcing their candidacy for re-election since such a statement brings an immediate conclusion to the "public service" time allocated by the networks. After the announcement of the party primaries, legislators must pay for network time.

Not all congressmen are convinced that radio broadcasting is particularly effective, as the following discussion among three highly respected House members demonstrates:

I have used radio for six or seven years but I am wondering how effective it is. Are we wearing out our welcome?

*

I will tell you something that may be a terrible commentary on my own ineffectiveness. I used radio for ten years, stopped it, and haven't had a complaint yet.

*

I learned more quickly than you. I did it for four.

Film and Record Libraries. Some legislators develop and make effective use of film and record libraries. Films and records are prepared on subjects of public interest and made available by the congressman's district office to schools, community organizations, and the networks. When Carl Sandburg addressed the House of Representatives on the subject of Abraham Lincoln, for example, a number of congressmen obtained recordings of the address, provided their own introductory and closing remarks (describing the scene in the House prior to Sandburg's arrival and subsequent to his address) and distributed them to schools and the networks. Reaction was so favorable that individuals sought to purchase the recordings. One congressman who prepared a recording of the Sandburg session describes his activities in connection with the development of a film library:

I have two or three films on various nonpolitical subjects. Prior to holy week I made a film with a Protestant, Catholic, and Jewish chaplain—army, navy, and air force—in which I asked them about the way in which the Defense Department made provision for the religious needs of the men in the armed forces. We made radio tapes of that as well as film. I sent it home, and most television studios and radio stations used it during holy week. I am going to write to every clergyman in my district telling them I have the film which will be on free loan. I also have a film with the author of the book, *The Ugly American*, and Senator Humphrey, in which the foreign service and our image abroad is discussed. Then I have one made by a commercial firm which details my leaving the congressional district, being shown around the House, being sworn in, and so on. I am seen talking to Harry Truman, and President Eisenhower is shown giving a State of the Union Message. It is nonpartisan and very effective.

Special Mailings on Legislative Matters. A practice that congressmen regard as productive is that of alerting various groups in the district when legislation of particular interest to them is before the Congress. Thus volunteer fire fighting organizations may be informed of a bill that would permit them to acquire equipment declared surplus by the armed forces; doctors may receive a letter telling of the status of health insurance legislation; and veterans may learn of proposed changes in the law that would affect them. The accumulation of special mailing lists—lists of union officials, Rotary Club members, bankers, policemen, teachers, automobile dealers, and almost any other classification can probably be used on some occasion—is an important activity in some offices. The expectation is that constituents will be particularly grateful to receive information about proposals bearing on their livelihood and that the congressman's thoughtfulness will not pass unnoticed.

In discussing the extensive use he made of letters directed to special groups one lawmaker said, "I think this is very effective. Voters are much more excited about what you have done in their own backyard than they are about what you do in world affairs. Congressmen have come to understand that." No group is too small to be reached if the lists are available and the congressman thinks a group will be sympathetic to his position on legislation affecting it. One man near the end of his first year in the House had sent out one series of letters to wheat growers, a second to people interested in clear streams, and a third to small businessmen, reporting on the status of legislation. Said another House freshman:

I try to specialize my mailings rather than to flood the district with all sorts of general comments. For example, when HR 10, the forced saving plan for lawyers and doctors, came up I sent letters to all lawyers and doctors telling them about the bill and its progress. Later I mailed 900 letters to school teachers explaining the status of education legislation. I also sent them a special questionnaire to ascertain their thinking with respect to federal aid. I am also starting a short newsletter which will be sent to blind people in my district. We have an organization which will translate our material to braille, and we think this will give the people a great thrill. Not too many blind people are affected, of course, but we expect the project to have a great impact throughout the district.

Use of Committee Reports and Government Publications. Some congressmen display considerable ingenuity in the use of committee reports. While most representatives make relatively little use of these documents unless a constituent writes in to request copies of them, members who write newsletters for insertion in district newspapers find them an excellent source of newsletter copy, particularly since they are less likely to duplicate other materials available to the papers. One legislator noted for his interest in constituent service explained his use of them:

I send out all the hearings and bulletins I can get my hands on. If it is an Interior Committee report I send it to a list of conservationists. If it is something from the Banking and Currency Committee I send it to the bankers or real estate owners. The Veterans Affairs Committee put out a report on pending veterans legislation which I mailed to every veterans post in my district. The report by the Government Operations Committee on civil defense in Europe and the Soviet Union has been mailed to all the civil defense people. I think that whenever you can get a specialized report of Congress from a committee and mail it out to people likely to be interested, it brings you good will for making it available.

Government publications are also distributed to groups in the community that might be expected to be interested in them. An announcement in a local newspaper that the garden club will meet the following week may lead the congressman to forward a supply of booklets about flowers (stamped with the congressman's name) to the club president; Chambers of Commerce may receive a supply of booklets about changes in regulations relating to small business. Widely circulated are the agricultural bulletins, which list hundreds of publications available from the government without charge. Constituents are invited to return the checklist indicating not more than five or six items they would like to receive. There is a heavy return of these bulletins, some respondents checking twenty-five, thirty-five, or even fifty items. Informational materials about government such as "How Our Laws Are Made" are also widely circulated.

In these and other projects the member seeks to anticipate needs of various groups and to keep them informed about matters of interest; he is not unmindful either that many people will be grateful and that he may come to be regarded as an especially thoughtful and conscientious representative.

Speaking Engagements. Most congressmen are pleased to accept invitations to speak before community groups, and many seek them. Whenever there is a lull in legislative activity or during the Easter and other recess periods, congressmen hasten back to the district and "report to the people" wherever meetings can be arranged. Between sessions in the off election year legislators may devote as much as two months to a tour of their district, spending several days in the large cities and perhaps a half day in each of as many of the small communities as possible. If no formal program has been arranged, they may just walk down the main street, stopping in the stores, introducing themselves, being seen, and learning what people are thinking. Many of them use a mobile office for this tour.

Only unusual circumstances normally can prevent the appearance of the legislators:

This is the first year I haven't gone home during the Easter recess. At that time my district was leading the nation in the rate of unemployment. There were several other local issues also. I didn't have any answers for the questions they were going to raise, so I stayed right here.

The nonpolitical engagement generally holds more appeal than the party gathering since presumably there will be an opportunity to impress favorably individuals whom the congressman might not meet ordinarily. Nonelection years offer special advantages over election years, too, because the audiences are less likely to be thinking in partisan terms. As will be clear from the following discussion, school engagements are thought by some to be particularly desirable.

I find it particularly valuable in off election years to talk before Chamber of Commerce and civic club groups. They are predominantly Republican-oriented and you can't get near them in an election year. In the nonelection year you are a congressman and welcome. Since you are talking to the people who don't normally support you, you have a chance to make friends and get good publicity.

*

The second audience that I think it especially important to reach is the school children. I find that going into the schools and talking five or ten minutes to the children, with an opportunity provided for them to ask questions, gets a bigger play than anything. Every one of those kids goes home and tells his parents. You can make more friends that way than any other way I know.

*

The best speech is a nonpolitical speech. I think a commencement speech is best of all. _____ says he has never lost a precinct in a town where he has made a commencement speech. At commencement you have an audience more prepared to like you and take you into the family than you have at any other time.

Letters of Congratulation and Condolence. Some legislators use letters of congratulation sparingly; others regard them as an effective way to link constituent and congressman. Newspapers, records of the county or city clerk, and other potential sources of information are scanned in the effort to find subjects worthy of such communication.

Advanced birthdays and wedding anniversaries are frequently rewarded with a note from the congressman; if the latter is of the same party as the President, he may forward these names to the White House so that the Chief Executive may send a letter also. Newly married couples receive the best wishes of their representative and a recipe book, *Family Fare*, a government publication. When children are born their parents are promptly congratulated (some offices carefully check death lists for a week or two following the event to be sure the baby survived) and forwarded a copy of *Infant Care*.[14]

A substantial number of congressmen send letters of congratulation to high school graduating classes, some also forwarding parchment-like copies of the Declaration of Independence. Letters are also sent out to new arrivals in the district (monthly lists of these newcomers may be purchased in many districts from Welcome Wagon), new citizens, and other special groups.

Many legislators regularly peruse all district newspapers; most of the others assign this responsibility to the staff; few offices ignore them. Perhaps the most important object of the scrutiny is to discover what local citizens have been in the news. Honors of almost any kind are noted, the article and picture often clipped, and a letter of congratulation sent from the congressman. Some members have special folders that may carry a picture of the member and the Capitol on the outside with a printed notation, "I've been reading about you." On the inside is another printed notation, "and thought you might like to have this," the clipping announcing the honor, and the signature of the congressman, sometimes with a short message written by hand. A number of offices make special efforts to congratulate everyone assuming office in community organizations as well as individuals receiving awards and important promotions.

Frequently accompanying the congratulatory message in most of the kinds of letters mentioned above is an invitation to write the representative whenever he can be of assistance.

Fewer congressmen write condolence letters than congratulatory ones, though those who do firmly believe it to be one of the most appreciated activities they undertake. Unlike most other communications from con-

---

[14] *Infant Care* is a popular item. A total of 169,615 copies were distributed to members of Congress, at their request, during the month of July 1963.

gressional offices these letters are usually stamped rather than franked. Sometimes they are written by hand rather than being typed, another departure from customary office procedure.

Acting as Host. Washington is invaded every spring by high school groups, and congressional offices are very helpful to them, suggesting some activities and arranging for others. Congressmen may sponsor luncheons in their honor, tour the Capitol with them, and have group pictures taken, with copies made available to the students to send back home. Occasionally they may even sponsor their own student groups. "_____ has been bringing down a whole busload of school children for 12 or 14 years," said a colleague of the other party. "I think it is one reason it has been impossible to defeat him. They stay here five or six days, and he pays expenses."

While most of the student intern programs on Capitol Hill are college-sponsored, in some instances congressmen have initiated their own programs. Interns are often paid a token wage enabling them to meet their living expenses and are afforded an unusual educational opportunity.

A few congressional offices function as tourist agencies. A congresswoman described one such undertaking:

We run tourist groups. They pay their own transportation costs. We put them up for three nights, and four full days and pay all of their expenses including meals, limousines and everything and charge them $55 a person. We take them to Mt. Vernon and Virginia one day, to Annapolis one afternoon, and spend the rest of the time in Washington. We try to get at least ten in the group because we lose money if we can't have ten, and we don't want more than twenty. The type of person who will come for that sort of trip isn't necessarily the student. I had two elderly ladies here last year who had never been out of their home city, and I could have cried over them before they went back. Our biggest contribution to the tour is to take one person out of the office for that period to guide them around. I don't think there has been anything greater than that program in providing a warm return for me.

The possibilities are virtually limitless. One congressman sends his allotment of the much in demand Army-Navy football game tickets to veterans' hospitals in his district, and arranges for transportation of the recipients to the game. The favorable publicity that results from such a generous action is of obvious benefit to the incumbent.

It should not be necessary to emphasize that the representatives undertake these many worthy activities not merely to win adherents. They hope that will be a by-product, of course, but in carrying on many of them, congressmen believe they are meeting their obligations to "educate" their constituents, a responsibility many take very seriously.

The Congressman as Educator

"He's a fine person and does a good job of representing his people," said a congressman of a colleague, "but he's never ahead of his district on anything. He never leads his district, merely reflects it." To many legislators the educational role is an important one, and the absence of any inclination to exert a positive influence on the thinking of constituents signifies a serious deficiency in a colleague: he is not a complete congressman. To others, the man who senses district sentiment and votes it is a practical, canny politician and one ensuring his success at the polls; he merits praise for his perception. It is likely that most congressmen regard themselves as educators to some extent, as something more than agents of their constituency. Some, however, might shy away from identifying themselves as leading their community, particularly in a direction in which the citizenry had demonstrated some reluctance to move.

There is a belief in some quarters that legislators have a responsibility as well as an opportunity to lead. Said one member:

Congressmen have an obligation to inform their constituents and to educate them as to what is going on. I try to do this in my radio broadcasts and in occasional newsletters. This is one aspect of the job which is appealing because you have a responsibility and you are in a position to carry it out.

An articulate progressive representative expressed similar views in a somewhat different way:

The obligation of a member to educate his district is a very real one and creates a problem to which I have been giving much attention. Most congressmen see their function as one requiring them to perform three main duties: (1) actively participate in committee work; (2) take care of constituents by responding to their requests; and (3) get re-elected. Too few of them go beyond that. Many don't feel they have an obligation to do very much in an educational way. I feel this obligation strongly. I am now in the process of writing four different articles in an attempt to educate the general public. Just the other day I asked a colleague for his reaction to my activity in writing the articles. He said it was okay if I was being paid for them and if I wasn't going to say anything which might be used against me in an election campaign. I'm afraid that is the attitude of too many people here! Don't say anything if it might be unpopular or misinterpreted. Don't try to educate the public because they might not appreciate it.

Yet there may be limits to one's effectiveness. It may be preferable to select certain issues on which it is regarded as particularly important to educate a district, focus on these and, over time, hope to achieve results rather than to attempt to educate constituents on a wide range of problems. Comments one congressman:

I don't think it is possible or practical to educate my constituents on everything. You have to pick and choose the things on which you can lead them; perhaps later you can cover some of the others.

The principal educational tools of the congressman are his newsletters, radio and television programs, speaking engagements, and letters in response to constituent correspondence. There is considerable concern within the Congress that the general public is not well informed regarding the way the legislative body functions, and some members consciously seek to educate their districts in this area as well as about specific public issues. The writer of one of the most informative newsletters on Capitol Hill states this as one of his goals:

I do what I can to inform the general public. One way in which I do this is to put out a newsletter which differs from most coming out of congressional offices. I try to relate things to the actual workings of Congress rather than stress the legislation which we consider. I hope it will be effective in enlightening a segment of the population in my area at least.

A colleague whose weekly report on the fate of important legislation is factual and straightforward takes very seriously his conviction that educating his district on issues and problems is "a very important phase of my activities." His newsletter is widely read in schools in his district, a fact "which pleases me more than any other aspect of it." "I specifically report what is going on week by week," he states, "but I always try to emphasize the mechanics. Every once in a while I take a bill and trace it all the way through. Sometimes I take a whole newsletter and write purely on procedure." There are other members who seek to inform the people they represent about issues but do not attempt to provide a course on Congress.

Members also seek to perform the educational function in other ways.

One Midwestern Republican concerned with the apathy of many citizens toward their government seeks to combat it by providing opportunities for residents of his district and state to become more directly acquainted with it. His program takes three forms: (a) Bringing ten university students to Washington for a week each year, two at a time. Divided equally between the two political parties, the students live with the congressman and his family and are allocated desk space in the congressman's office. To date more than eighty students have shared in this experience, the costs of their trip being shared by the political parties and a foundation. (b) Sponsoring a similar program for professors of political science in his home state, in which four of them are invited each year. The congressman regretfully noted one problem: They quickly ran through the small list of Republican professors. (c) Hiring three students at the state university as part time research assistants. Working under the supervision of a professor, they prepare research on topics of interest to the congressman. In the past the work of these students has been regarded as sufficiently valuable to warrant bringing them to Washington to testify before a Senate committee. Other legislators sponsor similar ventures though none provides as comprehensive a program. Indeed, although some congressmen consciously pursue the "educator" role more actively than others, there are few who do not in some measure seek to enlighten the people they represent. Those who regard it as their responsibility to serve as leader rather than agent of their community are likely to exercise the educative function more aggressively.

Patronage and Its Problems

Congressmen normally do not have much patronage to distribute, and what they do have tends to concern minor positions. Postmasterships and rural mail carrier jobs, appointments to the service academies, census workers at the time of the decennial census—these and other pap of similar importance are often as much a source of trouble as of gain. Indeed, patronage and the problems it involves are frequently mentioned as among the more unpleasant aspects of the job of a congressman. Explained one representative:

Patronage is one unpleasant part of this job. It is unpleasant because we have such small bones to toss to people. Party workers on all levels write and expect we can do something to reward them for their faithfulness. Most of them don't want very much. They want recognition more than anything else. It is very hard to reward people who have made a contribution and want this recognition. It is particularly unfortunate since as I have mentioned their demands are small. You feel helpless if you can't do a little something for them.

Many members have placed academy appointments on a competitive basis, the applicants with the highest scores automatically being selected for the vacancies. This has not stopped pressure in behalf of candidates, however. Much more troublesome are the post office positions. Many congressmen express amazement at the ferocity with which many campaigns for these positions are waged—phone calls, visits, telegrams, petitions, and large volumes of mail are almost standard in connection with a significant proportion of the vacancies. Most congressmen will say they wish the positions were placed under civil service, but there is little evidence of serious effort being made to bring this about. Often congressmen pass along the prerogative to name postmasters and rural carriers to county or city chairmen, and sometimes they blame these party officials for the unhappy situations in which they find themselves. "He (the local chairman) doesn't consider all the consequences of an appointment," it is said. "They can't vote against *him*." Recommendations may be submitted before full announcement of the vacancy has been made, and legislators occasionally discover some very important factors have not been considered by their designated agent. In speaking of postal appointments, congressmen frequently assert "You make one ingrate and many enemies." A rather typical comment is that of a fourth term Republican:

All the postal problems disturb me, as a great deal of rivalry exists for these positions, and it is difficult to know just who should get the job. It is pretty much dog eat dog. You know the story—after you make an appointment you have one ingrate and fifteen enemies. Nobody seems satisfied with the way you handle it. It seems to me that we should do something to get rid of this responsibility.

Another legislator reflects the position of his colleagues that making these appointments would be fine if people were pleased with the results, but the designations often create more dissatisfaction than satisfaction, affecting the congressman adversely rather than adding to his reputation. Said he, "I don't want to be running anyone's post office, nor do I want to choose who should be postmaster, especially if there is going to be a row about it. It creates ill will."

The lack of congressional patronage does not prevent constituents from writing their congressman to ask his assistance in obtaining positions of all sorts. Some legislators consider themselves harassed by requests for postmasterships and for other positions that it is not within their power to grant; others are embarrassed by the limited means at their disposal to satisfy constituent requests. Two freshmen, at the end of their first year in Congress expressed their unhappiness:

The thing I do wish could be changed is the tendency of Congress to act as an employment agency. Certainly we have far more important things to do than that. It is disturbing to find that so much of our time has to be devoted to minor things of that nature.

*

Many citizens think we are a social welfare agency. We do have a responsibility to help, but it is clear that it handicaps us in carrying out our real duty, which should be that of legislating for the nation. I'm somewhat surprised that so many people write me from my state wanting jobs right there. They seem to think I can arrange that sort of thing for them. They overemphasize my role and influence in such matters.

The last point is also one often made; citizens think that congressmen can perform miracles if only they would; they expect far more—immediately—than the congressman may ever be able to produce. Fearful of the results of disclosing inability to achieve the goals sought by the constituent, the congressman and his staff devote large amounts of time needed for other activities in seeking results. If results are achieved, they often come only after strenuous congressional effort. The constituent is less grateful than the legislator thinks he should be, partly because he overestimates his representative's power in such matters.

A congressman is administrator, educator, and errand boy, as well as legislator. In each of these roles he is mindful of his constituents. He organizes his office with them, rather than his legislative responsibilities, in mind. Though he considers his work in behalf of individuals as less fundamental to his job than work on legislation, he nonetheless gives it precedence. He both derives satisfaction from it and is dismayed by it. It often is an onerous chore, but it meets a real need, brings him valuable information, and is the activity most likely to "pay off" at the polls. He resents the time it takes, but he will not slight it.

Constant stress on how press they are for time.

III

The Congressman as Legislator

A FREQUENTLY EXPRESSED COMMENT of congressmen about their job is that they lack time to perform it, especially the legislative functions, which presumably should constitute their primary responsibility. The very volume of legislative proposals and the wide diversity of the subject matter are in themselves staggering. Mastery of the meaning and potential consequences of much proposed legislation requires not only intensive study but also technical competence that few but the specialist can hope to achieve. Ability aside, in terms of available time it is impossible for the legislator to comprehend these proposals, earnest as he may be in his desire to do so.

Though many veteran legislators have long since made their compromise with the system, for the conscientious beginner the responsibility and the task may seem nearly overwhelming. Two comments of freshman House members reflect their early impressions:

Perhaps the most impressive thing here is that the operation is so vast. If one stops to think about it, one just has to wonder how it possibly could work. We have reasonably good men working in Congress; if they weren't reasonably good they wouldn't be here. Some of them are real technicians, many are lawyers trained by long experience. But in the overall congressional picture they are merely babes in the woods, called upon to pass technical legislation in a wide, wide variety of fields. We are supposed to be experts in banking and currency activities, space activities, public opinion, world affairs, pension problems, labor matters—all of these things and many more. Obviously this is impossible. The miracle is that the member of Congress knows so much, considering how difficult his job is. People are too prone to criticize the congressman when actually he faces an impossible task and probably does as well as could possibly be expected under the circumstances.

*

I am appalled at how much congressmen are expected to do for the nation. We have to know too much. We have to make too many decisions. There is a tremendous problem in international relations and congressmen are constantly involved in this. But in addition we are supposed to know all about domestic activities—about education, water pollution, small business problems, dams, etc. No matter how hardworking and conscientious a congressman is, no matter how much homework he does, he just can't master these problems. We just don't have the time to keep informed properly.

Time-Consuming Nonlegislative Work

As though the problem of grappling with the mass and variety of legislative proposals were not a sufficient burden, the situation is complicated by the public's disposition to request personal services in such quantity as legitimately to occupy all the time of a member. Many of these requests are not significant, though they often are time-consuming, but no elected public official can afford to ignore or give cursory attention to them. The consequences of such treatment, if pursued as a standard policy, could easily be the loss of his seat, or so the congressman fears. But the result of cultivating such requests, while comforting to the ego and to his humanitarian instincts, is to decrease appreciably the already inadequate time available for the pursuit of knowledge about legislation.

At some point, nearly every House member asks himself how he can shed some of these nonlegislative tasks in order to devote more attention to legislative responsibilities. For virtually all of them the inescapable conclusion is that expressed by a fourth-termer: "The legislative role certainly suffers. We spend far too much time on the errand boy activities, probably at a cost to government. But the real question is how we can help doing that. I think the answer is that we cannot."

There are, however, dissenters who believe legislators can and should drop some of their nonlegislative activities.

One of the hardest working Republican members comments:

Many members of Congress will tell you the legislative role simply has to suffer here. I don't think that is true at all. I just don't let it suffer. Organization is part of the answer, I suppose, but a lot of my colleagues carry on many unnecessary activities. You'll never see me conducting a tour of the capitol for two or three constituents. They can do that themselves.

An important Democrat when asked whether activities associated with the legislative role were most likely to suffer in the face of the many demands on a member's time also replied in the negative. Said he:

I don't see why. A person who comes from a nearby district has a terrible problem, but one coming from a reasonably distant district has considerable choice. My own judgment is that outside of a limited [geographical] area you have a wide area of choice as to how much time you spend on legislation and how much you spend on the very legitimate services that a member should perform for his constituents. I think it is a question of organizing your office to do the one and yourself to do the other.

Most impartial observers of the congressional scene agree that congressmen unnecessarily devote excessive time to constituent requests, performing many tasks better left to staff or a department of the government. In their view, the belief of some legislators that they have no alternative but to continue to burden themselves with many menial tasks is erroneous. Sometimes, it is suspected, the decision to do this is deliberate: Some legislators do not like to legislate. Obviously, legislators differ markedly in their approach to their job and in what they find most interesting and rewarding about it. When asked to describe how his experience as a congressman had differed from what he had anticipated it would be, one House freshman responded:

I didn't realize there was so much to learn nor did I realize a congressman's position and job entailed so much public relations and service as an employment agency or a court of last resort to so many people. But I am very happy about these aspects of the position because I wouldn't be entirely satisfied if it was just a legislative job. Naturally, legislation is our primary concern but frankly it is the other things that make it interesting. I am not a lawyer whereas most members of Congress are. Drafting and enacting legislation is much more interesting to them, I am sure, than it is to me.

According to an energetic and talented House member, activities in behalf of constituents possess therapeutic value: were it not for them, congressmen, prevented by House procedure from playing an influential role in the legislative process, would be even more frustrated. In his words:

If it were not for these diversions, these administrative duties, there would be tremendous dissent on the floor of the House by many of the 435 congressmen who would thus be so frustrated under the one minute rule, the five minute rule, and the other very necessary clogs on debate, that St. Elizabeth's would be full of us. In the House this is a poultice which draws the excess energies of eager beavers. If there were no constituent pressures, it would be necessary to invent them.

There is much to be said for that view, although it was challenged by one of the most respected strategists in the House, who stated:

> I want to take issue with that because I don't believe there is any man in the House who can do a really effective legislative job on more than two bills in a year. If you do that you have a full-time job. This implies that you know reasonably well the position of each of the other members on the bill and the important amendments that may be proposed, and that is an incredibly time-consuming job. I am frustrated because I can only work on a couple of bills a year. The legislative process could absorb all our time and still cause no frustration.

Little Time for Meditation

In determining allocation of their time, congressmen constantly weigh the priority of alternatives—in terms of such factors as personal desire, urgency, political survival, and advancement. Uninterrupted periods essential to careful study of many legislative proposals and to reflection on the broader goals and trends are rare indeed in the life of a congressman. No matter how much he desires isolation, no matter how protective his staff may be, a congressman at his desk is always vulnerable to intrusion. Urgently needing time for concentrated work, it is little wonder that many legislators (and their staffs) become adept at inventing barriers to those who would invade their privacy. At the same time, motivated by the desire to strengthen the bonds of constituent support, some except "home folks" from a general directive that they are not to be disturbed.

The home is little better as a place of refuge than the office, as congressional wives readily attest. Since they particularly resent the intrusion on the relatively brief time their husbands are able to spend with their families, they have vivid memories of unnecessary and inappropriate attempts to communicate with their husbands at all times of day and night. Because the congressman is home so seldom, it is understandable that his family should resent his efforts to seclude himself while there. If he has had a busy day at the capitol, it is even more difficult for him to engage in serious study. One conscientious representative who has heavy committee responsibilities discusses the dilemma:

> The pressures are so continuous and so great that they leave little time for meditation and for study. It is very difficult to be a conscientious congressman who feels he is on top of the issues. I cannot possibly study my serious committee work except in the evenings. There are far too many interruptions during the day.

And yet when you have worked hard here all day, you don't feel much like working once you get home. Your family doesn't want you to work either and that causes problems. I take home a brief case every evening and I work every weekend, yet I can never seem to catch up.

Does Legislative Work "Pay Off"?

Many kinds of temptation lead legislators away from concentration on purely legislative pursuits, among them the desire to assist constituents with personal problems, despair at the impossible nature of the task, and greater interest in other aspects of the job. Important, too, is the recognition that such concentration usually does not provide the best means of impressing the voter. Said one member, "The footwork of Congress may be important to people in Washington, but residents of communities in my state don't appreciate the footwork at all." The following discussion illustrates congressional views about voter reaction to some of their achievements:

If there is one thing I have found my people care nothing about it is my attainments in Congress. I could say I was chairman of four standing committees. I think they relate that to being chairman of a PTA committee or a Lions committee. I defeated a good man who made much of the fact that he was chairman of a congressional committee, and people laughed about it. I had hundreds tell me, "Why you will be a committee chairman before you have been up there three months." Recently, I went home and began to talk about the _____ act. I was pleased to have sponsored that bill, but soon it dawned on me that the point wasn't getting through at all. What was getting through was that the act might be of help to people. I changed the emphasis: I didn't mention my role particularly, but stressed my support of the legislation.

*

Wouldn't you amend that to say that while the rank and file don't attach much importance to your committee assignment and your effectiveness, there are a handful of people in almost every community who will attach importance to them, and they are the ones who have considerable influence on public opinion?

*

Wouldn't everyone agree that if you can get something done that you can't justify on merit, but which goes into your district, the so-called pork barrel project, that you find it is effective? I agree there are a sophisticated few very substantial opinion molders who get the implications of this, perhaps even before you bring home the bacon. And I think the sophisticated few are pretty important.

The necessity of building a favorable image in his district and the difficulty of accomplishing this merely by achieving distinction on the Hill as an effective, conscientious legislator creates special problems. There is little in the nature of performing diligently the day-to-day legislative chores that lends itself to dramatization by, or attention from, the news media. Colleagues may recognize and admire a member's hard work and general competence, and this respect may be shared by other close observers of Congress. But this is no indication that his constituents recognize these qualities—or care about them. The temptation may become strong, therefore, to avoid the tedious but important aspects of legislative work, since all but the most unusual efforts pass unrecognized by those in whose hands the political future of the member lies.

Even the member who successfully resists this temptation may find it expedient to resort to the window dressing type of project to get publicity in his district, although it constitutes no real measure of his effectiveness or interests. It may divert him temporarily from his primary function, but it pays off in publicity and good will. He must face re-election, and if the price of continued success at the polls is emphasizing the less substantial achievements at the expense of his real contributions, it is a price he is prepared to pay. As one straightforward, hardworking congressman puts it:

I guess we all do whatever we can to stimulate interest in what we are doing here. The sad thing is that often you have to emphasize the less important things because sometimes it is easier to make a better story out of them. This whole public relations aspect of the job is a very significant one, and the effect it has on the members is also significant. You find you have to do certain things to impress the public while many of your more substantial contributions are very difficult to get across.

For many legislators this fact in no way diminishes their zeal, although they find it regrettable that their significant work is passed over so casually. For others, this realization leads to decreased interest in the hard, often boring, legislative work and concentration on the publicity-seeking accomplishments or devices. Congressmen tend to appreciate one another's problems, and while they reserve their greatest accolades for the top notch legislative experts and technicians among their colleagues, they also speak with envy and a kind of admiration of certain members who have been especially successful in keeping their names before their constituents. The inattention to legislation which characterizes certain of the showman-type congressmen, some of whom even take their committee responsibilities lightly, may irritate colleagues. At the same time, however, their mastery of the techniques of publicity (freely translated by colleagues into votes and victory) often arouses favorable comment.

Specialization

From every quarter congressmen are pressed for action and decision. Though many of the matters brought to them should more appropriately have been taken elsewhere, they usually are reluctant to decline to accept jurisdiction, particularly if voters of their district are involved. At the same time, the serious substantive legislative problems with which they must concern themselves have become more numerous and more complex, making evaluation more necessary and decision more difficult. Further, the nature of the relationship between legislator and constituent has undergone many changes over the years. A congressman today has far more constituents than his predecessors, and they are much more likely to communicate with him on a wide variety of problems.

Faced with an impossible workload, congressmen have responded in different ways, most of them seeking refuge in specialization, a tendency which is encouraged by the committee system and other aspects of congressional procedure. They become expert, or at least facile, in a particular field, earn the respect of their colleagues for their diligence and command of the subject matter, and eventually come to be recognized as one of the congressional authorities in that area, a ready source of information and advice. Such recognition is accompanied by influence and has implications both within and without the Congress, though its impact, legislators complain, too seldom extends to the congressional district.

One member discusses the process by which many legislators begin to specialize:

The nature of our set-up here in the House is such that our work on legislation suffers tremendously where matters outside the jurisdiction of our own committee are involved. We may have come here with deep interests in subjects unrelated to our committee, but we are so busy there that we never get around to thinking through or drafting legislation covering other matters. If we do draft it, and it is referred to another committee, we may not be able to get a hearing if we are in the minority and, anyway, a committee other than our own is handling it and is less interested in its success. So we begin to concentrate on the committee on which we serve, even though our interests may not lie there.

The emphasis on specialization simplifies significantly the task of the representative. Colleagues turn to him for aid in determining their own position on legislative matters which arise within his field of competence; he, in turn, settles on one or two trusted members on each committee to whom he can turn for clarification or advice regarding proposals falling within their committee's jurisdiction.

There are some legislative areas where congressmen consider themselves particularly dependent on the advice of their colleagues. Defense matters constitute an especially difficult problem since much of the information available to the appropriate committees in helping them assess defense requirements is not available to other congressmen. Though virtually no criticism is heard of the Defense Subcommittee of the Appropriations Committee, which is considered to be of unusually high calibre, there is some uneasiness in the House because there is little opportunity for most representatives to reach an independent evaluation of defense needs. This uneasiness and concern is expressed in the observations of three talented House members—a conservative Republican, a liberal Republican, and a liberal Democrat.

I'd say that not one percent of the House knows anything about the work of the Defense Subcommittee, yet it involves crucial decisions. Only the written reports provide a clue to the real issues in much legislation, and they aren't particularly helpful in connection with the work of the Defense Subcommittee. In this business you've just got to trust your colleagues, especially when it comes to the committees on Ways and Means and Appropriations. The legislation with which those committees deal is so complicated and contains so many technical amendments that it is virtually impossible for the ordinary member to have any idea about what is going on. It is an unsatisfactory way to legislate, but unfortunately there is no alternative.

*

It is pretty hard for the average member to know too much about some situations, other than those in which he is directly involved. The defense budget is beyond the comprehension and understanding of most congressmen. We have to take things pretty much on faith and on the word of those members who deal directly with the problem. Fortunately they are a pretty dedicated group, although even that just isn't enough sometimes.

*

This matter of the budget, especially the defense budget, and the whole area of executive oversight is a very difficult one. The people in Congress who are concerned with defense matters are worked awfully hard. There is a tendency for the average member to throw up his hands in handling such matters. There is also a haunting fear that if we vote to cut certain phases of the program we may be hampering national defense. It takes a lot more courage to go against recommendations in this area than it does in other areas.

Dependence on colleagues for advice does not mean, of course, that the representative abdicates his responsibility to reach his own decision regarding legislation, or to seek to ascertain the facts himself. It is but one method by which he meets this responsibility.

Becoming Informed

Although "the most important single source of information in evaluating legislation is the opinion of the trusted colleague," legislators may use many sources in the course of their deliberations. The role of each varies significantly from issue to issue and from member to member, depending on the type of legislation involved (complexity, importance, and political implications are factors, for example), the experience and philosophy of the legislator, the interest of various groups in society, etc. Among the potential sources of information are individual colleagues, informal organizations of congressmen to which a legislator belongs, committee and personal staffs, the hearings and reports of committees, pressure groups, executive departments, the mail, and floor debate. Helpful, too, may be periodicals and professional journals (some congressmen are avid readers despite busy schedules), the academic community, the Library of Congress, research units of the various political party organizations, the news media, private research organizations, and staff arms such as the Office of the Legislative Counsel and legislative liaison groups. Travel constitutes another means of acquiring significant and relevant knowledge. The contributions of several of these are touched on in the pages which follow.

The Library of Congress. Created by and for Congress in 1800, the Library of Congress with a staff in excess of 2,700, 250 miles of bookshelves, and more than 42,000,000 items, constitutes a valuable source of information for congressional committees and harassed legislators and their staffs. Of particular help is the Legislative Reference Service organized in 1914 to meet the needs of Congress for specific reference assistance. In 1962 this division answered 99,430 congressional requests for information,[1] while other units of the Library handled 42,970 more. Requests ranged from those involving readily available information, such as furnishing a single fact from reference books, to detailed reports requiring weeks of intensive research and analysis of complex problems. The majority of requests were met by forwarding prepared materials.

The importance of the Legislative Reference Service to Congress is evident from the fact that in a typical year requests are received from all members of the Senate, virtually all members of the House, and from more than eighty committees and subcommittees. During one month alone the service was used by all but fourteen members of Congress and by sixty-two committees and subcommittees.

At the beginning of each Congress, the Library sponsors a luncheon for new members to acquaint them with the services available; the congressman who is aware of the kinds of help that can be obtained is in a position to benefit tremendously. One legislator, after emphasizing the importance of becoming recognized by one's colleagues as a specialist, commented that with the resources of the Library of Congress at his disposal, this was a goal not too difficult to achieve.

In addition to preparing speeches and analyses of legislative proposals, the Library provides such varied assistance to congressmen as briefings on important judicial decisions, background reports on legislation relating to important public problems, translations of foreign language materials, drafting committee prints, the preparation of charts and graphs, and assembling of packets of materials on certain subjects. Library personnel are also lent to congressional committees for special assignments.

Library officials complain that more than one third of congressional requests represent constituent rather than member inquiries, some of which require extensive research. The impact of these demands is to limit the time available for work on matters of direct interest to members of Congress, the *raison d'être* of the Legislative Reference Service—with a direct effect on the quality and thoroughness of some of the work produced. Though performing research for the general public is in violation of the operating procedure of the Reference Service, Library officials are

---

[1] An increase of 18 percent over 1961. Congressional inquiries have increased every year in the past ten years and have about doubled since 1954.

understandably reluctant to decline to handle requests that are received from congressional offices, regardless of their point of origin.[2]

Severe time limitations and the necessity of maintaining strict impartiality between philosophical viewpoints and political parties have led to mild congressional criticism of the Reference Service. The Service is considered very good for short, factual information but less satisfactory with respect to longer, more complicated materials. An often expressed congressional comment is that "LRS is good, but sterile." Another typical observation is that expressed by one Democrat: "They have been helpful to me, but they are a bit spotty. You cannot anticipate the level of the work. You never know whether it is going to be good or bad."

Because of the heavy and continuing demands on its staff (which is in excess of 200) LRS officials admit it sometimes is "hardpressed to maintain high standards . . . frequently unable to devote as much time to inquiries as they deserved." Often deadlines are met only by replying by telephone or by forwarding materials to offices rather than by submitting completed reports or memoranda. And, when the work is prepared in more organized form, the finished product often requires substantial reworking. Even so, Congress is grateful that the Service exists. In the words of one member, "It is the best single source I have found in Washington for getting information in a hurry." Another testifies, "I have had some wonderful experiences with Legislative Reference. They have been very fine and their work very adequate. Sometimes I have had to rewrite the stuff, but from the standpoint of the specific information I want, I have had good response."

There is general recognition that much material emanating from the Library needs the personal touch of the congressman or his staff. Some members accept this as inevitable; others regard it as a weakness that should be corrected. It should be clear that, to be most effective, products of a detached research arm such as the Legislative Reference Service ought to be recast in a congressional office to reflect the personal emphasis

[2] Commented one legislator familiar with Library of Congress procedure:
"One of the problems of LRS and the Library is that they are too scared of everybody. Recently the House Committee on Administration had to pass a resolution making it unnecessary for them to translate a couple of Japanese books. I don't know why they couldn't have declined on their own initiative. One congressman got eight state newspapers, three Washington papers, and thirty-odd magazines delivered to his office as they came out and the Library asked our committee to stop that too."

and style of the legislator, and in the light of the situation and interests of the constituency concerned. If this is kept in mind, the tremendous contribution of the Service to the work of a congressional office can be recognized and properly appreciated. Without the Service, many of the more active congressional offices unquestionably would be severely handicapped.

The Executive Branch. The executive branch is potentially a leading source of information for the legislator, although some of it is more readily available to the members of the President's party than to the opposition. It is necessary, however, to distinguish between official and unofficial sources of information within the executive. Official responses to congressional requests are normally sent out over the signature of a departmental officer; if the information has political implications and will be useful to members of both parties, congressmen allied with the President may receive it first. And the executive may take the initiative in supplying them with information judged to be helpful in encounters with the opposition. Sometimes, however, the opposition party retains close affiliations with members of the bureaucracy despite a change in administration and continues to benefit from "inside" information denied it by upper echelon political appointees. As one House Democrat said during the Eisenhower administration:

In some parts of the executive, the bureaucracy can be separated from the administration. For example, there are sharp differences in Agriculture between the Benson [the Secretary of Agriculture] people and the career bureaucrats. The Corps of Army Engineers is another example. I have some pretty good contacts with them and with others in the bureaucracy and I know they often proceed independent of—and sometimes in opposition to—official policy.

Much the same point was made in a group discussion:

As a practical matter, the executive branch is not readily available to us members of the opposition party. It undoubtedly is available to our Republican opposite numbers. I think that the remnants of what used to be the Democratic executive branch of seven years ago—which still exists in sort of shadow form in Washington—is of help to some of us. There are people who may have been in the State Department and who are now practicing law or who are around town.

*

I disagree with what you say about the executive because I still have some excellent contacts in the administration.

*

They are helpful, but not on an official basis. There are friends in the Bureau of the Budget, for example, who quietly—and you have to protect them—will give you help.

Yet even by working through formal channels, it is possible for the opposition to obtain information and assistance from the executive in the preparation of materials that are in conflict with the President's program. Related one congressman, not of the President's party:

I have had much cooperation. For example, I had an agricultural bill drawn which dealt with marketing agreements and which certainly was not in accord with the Secretary of Agriculture's thinking. I contacted the Department of Agriculture and got their chief counsel in charge of marketing agreements to draw the bill for me. When he finished, of course, he said, "You understand this does not reflect the thinking of the department." But the fact is that they very willingly will lend their people to assist you in the preparation of legislation. I have had this same offer from a number of departments. They will even do research for you to back up your position.

For the administration official, however, cooperating with members of Congress not of the President's party may be dangerous. Partisans of the President in Congress complain frequently (and often loudly) that their opponents are given too much information and too soon—they find themselves "scooped" by the opposition on announcements from which they had expected to reap political benefits. When decisions have been reached to award contracts, build post offices or other federal buildings, establish new government installations, or increase ones presently in existence, it is standard procedure to inform the appropriate members of Congress of the President's party prior to passing on the information to those members of the opposition whose constituencies are also affected. One may receive the news by telephone shortly after the decision is made; the other may learn of the action by mail a day later; at the very least, the members of the opposition are informed several hours later than political allies of the President. Yet, no matter which party occupies the White House, there are occasional infractions of the general rule of giving preference to the President's party, much to the dismay of the Executive, which must bear the ire of the disappointed and angry legislator. Even when the situation relates to requests from congressional opponents for information rather than announcements of executive action, care must be taken to see that appropriate supporters of the President are provided the same information. Related one Democratic congressman who had once served in the executive branch:

> May I say from previous executive office experience that when Roosevelt and Truman were in power, there was fine liaison between Democratic members of Congress and the executive branch, both formally and informally. However, our agency once made the mistake of replying to a Republican query for more recent information than we have provided the Democratic leadership. No carbon copy was provided to the majority leadership. The Republican took the floor and used the more recent material to attack the official position being taken by the Democratic majority. The agency got thoroughly blistered for its failure to provide its own party in congress with the information they were providing the opposition. I suspect that if we succeed in getting any information in an official way from the Eisenhower administration, the Republican counterpart has a carbon copy of what we receive.

Though there were Republican complaints that Democrats sometimes got too much assistance from the executive branch when Eisenhower was President, there was general agreement that his administration was very helpful in providing both information and partisan materials to the Republicans in Congress. Said two congressmen:

> The departments are helpful. There are individuals who are very useful in discussing both the practical situation with which you may be faced—the political situation—and a comparison of different bills, the pros and cons of them. Certainly the executive branch is a potential source of great value to us, and to some extent they cooperate with the opposition too. It isn't a completely closed shop.

*

> I think that when we were in the minority and the White House was held by the opposition we got relatively little help from the executive branch. Now at least I can go and get information there, but in the previous administration you got the barest minimum of assistance.

Members of the executive branch work especially closely with those supporters of the President who are responsible for guiding his program through the Congress. Thus key committees and legislators are provided with briefings, speeches, useful documents, and strategy suggestions. Sometimes representatives of the Executive are permitted to attend executive sessions of congressional committees in order to provide first-hand information on the Executive's position on proposed legislation and to indicate where compromise between that position and the stand taken by the committee is likely to be acceptable. This may be especially important when the President's party does not have a majority in the Congress.

The presence of individuals not members of the committee—or even of the Congress—is not unusual in executive sessions of some House units. In some committees, interest group representatives also may be present, though members of the Congress not on the committee may be excluded. Participation of both executive and interest groups is pointed up in this discussion:

> The executive branch actively participated during the time our committee was in executive session on the education bill, to see if a compromise couldn't be worked out that would meet the basic principles and recommendations of President Eisenhower in this field and at the same time pay some sort of lip service to what the Democrats were agitating for.

>   *

> Many times we have representatives of organizations like the Grange, Farmers Union or the Wheat Growers Association or Farm Bureau sitting in on our executive sessions of the Agriculture Committee. They are invited, the Grange more often than anyone else. I wondered whether other committees ever invited recognized lobbyists in to consider the final details of the bill.

Intra-Congressional Groups. An important source of information for many legislators are the various groups and organizations that have sprung up in the House in recent years. One small group that made extensive use of scholars was the Liberal Project, which in 1959 included eleven liberal Democratic House members. They invited forty-six natural, political, and social scientists to develop long-term national goals in defense and foreign policy. The essays that resulted were published as a book, *The Liberal Papers*, the purpose of which, according to a member of the House group, was to "reopen the political forum" through the contributions of "intellectuals whose ideas were uncommon and provocative." The book was criticized by Republicans who sought to make it a campaign issue. A GOP group hopes to publish its counterpart, *The Conservative Papers* in 1964. A larger, less doctrinaire, somewhat less issue-oriented organization of liberal Democrats is the Democratic Study Group mentioned in Chapter I. In the 1960 and 1962 elections, leaders of this group wrote nonincumbent Democratic congressional nominees offering campaign assistance in the form of making available hearings and reports likely to be of interest to the individual nominees. The Study Group is somewhat of a misnomer in that extensive study has not been undertaken; meetings are held to determine positions and to discuss strategy and occasionally subcommittees prepare surveys of legislative proposals.

The Republicans have no comparable organization—although efforts were made in 1961 and 1962 to develop counterparts—but various social groups, which initially grew up around classes of entering freshmen but which have modified their membership with the passing of time, have meetings devoted to issues and constitute valuable focal points for information about legislation.

Breakfast group sessions of legislators with common interests often deal with issues and feature experts outside of the congress as speakers. Several freshmen cited these breakfasts as among the most valuable sources of guidance on legislative problems. There are a few bipartisan groups that seek to obtain information that will help legislators meet their responsibilities more intelligently. In one such endeavor, a first term Republican member organized a group in 1959 to receive briefings from representatives of the State Department; this successful venture has been continued into the Kennedy administration.

Academicians. The influence of the academician on individual members of Congress both in the formation of decisions and in serving as a source of ideas and advice is generally regarded as negligible, both within the academic community and on Capitol Hill. His role is thought to be greater with committees than with individual legislators and stronger in the Senate than in the House. Yet it is clear to close observers of the House that the academician does exert a positive influence on the thinking of some of the more active and thoughtful members and that he enjoys their respect and is sought out by them. The Democratic Liberal Project is but one example of the attempt to use their knowledge; the Republican Policy Committee and the Republican Conference are also enlisting the assistance of scholars and "experts" in the formulation of action programs. Individual legislators are increasingly reaching out to them. During a discussion of important sources of information, an influential House Democrat confirmed this view:

The group I find most useful in terms of information is the one I describe as the academic community, with particular emphasis on personal contacts within the group. They are either people who are academicians at present or who formerly held academic positions and are presently located in government or business or something of that nature. In that group are found the few people I really value highly and contact often. They don't have an axe to grind, or at least I am not sufficiently smart to observe it.

The comment was endorsed by another highly articulate and effective congressman. Said he, "I certainly find that group helpful too. They are, I think, much more useful than any of those mentioned."

Travel. In recent years travel, especially abroad, has become an important means by which legislators have sought to become better informed. Not until 1936 did a congressman inspect, at government expense, the United States foreign service and, according to a long-term member of the House Foreign Affairs Committee, prior to World War II, congressmen who went overseas did so as tourists or limited their travel to inspection of government-owned facilities in the territories of the United States. By 1959, however, about one-third of the House members and half of the senators were traveling abroad, nearly all in official capacities at a cost of more than $400,000 in counterpart funds alone. For 1962, more than $400,000 in foreign currency and dollar expenditures was reported by congressmen traveling overseas on committee or interparliamentary business.

The rapid increase in congressional travel abroad has been accompanied by criticism both within the congress and without, although there is much support for the practice, too. Defenders assert that the trend is a logical and necessary outgrowth of the increased role of this country in world affairs, and insist that it represents legitimate investigation by conscientious members of Congress whose legislative actions have world-wide impact. In order to legislate intelligently, it is argued, first-hand information about such matters as the effectiveness of our foreign aid program and the strength of our military bases is helpful, if not essential. Such travel has gone far to dilute the provincialism of some legislators. At the same time it has strengthened the position of the United States abroad by demonstrating to friendly nations its interest in their progress.

Critics concede that a large proportion of the authorized trips are desirable and necessary but suggest that many represent nonessential activities arranged for the convenience of members of Congress. In some instances, it is asserted, they constitute little more than a paid vacation for congressmen and their families. Trips for "lame duck" congressmen are particularly attacked. Even within the Congress there has been recognition that insufficient supervision by committee chairmen and those committees having jurisdiction for approving vouchers has resulted in abuses that serve to discredit the many worthy undertakings.

The secrecy in which authorization for committee travel was clothed until 1960 lent credence to rumors that the program was characterized by widespread misuse of funds. Revelations of certain excesses in 1960 brought about reform. An itemized public accounting of all expenditures (either appropriated dollars or foreign currencies) was required of members of Congress, congressional committees, and congressional employees, traveling either abroad or within this country. While this information was not always organized in a way designed to facilitate effective scrutiny, it represented an important step forward.

Criticism of certain trips in 1961 and 1962, however, led to further demands for control. Finally, early in 1963 the House adopted restrictions on the spending of its membership abroad. Some committees were restricted to activities within the United States. More detailed accounting procedures were also provided for. Members of congress and congressional staff authorized to travel abroad were required to use counterpart funds, if available, instead of appropriated dollars, and expenditures were limited to the maximum per diem allowed under standard government travel regulations. Only actual transportation costs could be paid, the government agency furnishing transportation had to be identified, and a report on the number of days spent in each country was required.

In May 1963 the House, with only two dissenting votes, passed and sent to the Senate a bill extending overseas travel restrictions to all House and Senate committees. Senate action was expected on the measure. To obtain more than the government's maximum per diem rate, a member would have to supply documents showing actual expenditures. Executive agencies would report any expenditures made in connection with congressional travel, and reports filed by them, members of Congress, and congressional staff would be published in the *Congressional Record* annually. Travel of "lame duck" congressmen would be curtailed.

Floor Attendance and Activity. Although the House spends less time in formal session than does the "other body"[3] and for much of it very few

---

[3] In 1959, for example, the House was in session for 527 hours and the Senate for 1,009 hours (spread over 141 and 140 days respectively); in 1960, the House sat for 512 hours, the Senate for 1,188 hours, spread over 124 and 140 days respectively.

legislators are present, the average congressman does spend considerable time on the floor. Some members, it is true, shun the floor, asserting that their time can be spent more profitably elsewhere, except when they are required to vote or when a subject of importance to them or their friends is before the House. Others, however, view attendance as a valuable learning experience, which has its ultimate reward both within the House and within the constituency. And junior members are advised that the best way to catch the feel of the House and to master its procedures is to attend House sessions as often as possible.

The presence of a member does not ensure that his attention is directed to the speaker, of course. Some members sign mail or read should the discussion be uninteresting. Others talk with colleagues about legislative or political matters of mutual interest or merely strengthen personal relationships. This practice may be even more widespread when controversial measures are under consideration than when routine matters are before the House, since the expectation of controversy increases attendance and the likelihood that the colleagues with whom one wishes to confer will be present. Related one legislator:

A two hour debate session provides a good opportunity for individual members to talk to their colleagues. Right now, for example, there are about six members I want to see, either to find out about legislation or to discuss legislation in which I'm particularly interested or which directly affects my district. While you are on the floor, you have an ideal opportunity to chat with colleagues and get business done which it proves impossible to accomplish in any other way. An opportunity is afforded to participate in a clearing house sort of operation in which valuable information can be forthcoming. It is similar to the way the London coffee houses used to be.

There is no doubt that many important decisions are reached and increased rapport developed in informal conversations held on the floor. The fact that there are no assigned seats (though some delegations or groups of members regularly sit in the same general area), promotes informality and visiting. Quite apart from the substantive work accomplished, House sessions have a socializing effect on the membership. In the words of one junior Democrat:

In 1961, the House total was 569 hours compared with 1,005 for the Senate (spread over 147 and 146 days respectively); in 1962, the House total was 656 hours and the Senate 1,159 hours (spread over 159 and 177 days respectively).

It is very important to sit in [on House sessions]. That is the way you get to know members, to assess them. It is the way you get to know the rules. Many bills which are essentially the same come up year after year; House attendance helps you acquire the background of basic legislation.

Experienced legislators emphasize the importance of being on the floor when the House is meeting as the Committee of the Whole House on the State of the Union. Here much work is accomplished with smaller quorum requirements (100) and none of the disadvantages of recorded votes. Attendance is less crucial during the period of general debate but is definitely important when a bill is being read for amendment. Under the rules of procedure, if an amendment is defeated in the Committee of the Whole, it cannot be brought up again later in the House. If, on the other hand, an amendment is successful in the committee, it remains subject to review and a roll-call vote once the House has received the committee's recommendation.

Small attendance characterizes most sessions of the Committee of the Whole. A small, unified core of members of Congress can, by defeating proposed amendments there, prevent the full membership from working its will later. Regular participants in the Committee of the Whole therefore achieve greater voting power than their less available colleagues. Respected legislators and strategists of both parties stress the importance of the work done there and emphasize the difficulty of achieving a large attendance of party adherents, even on many major issues. Since the votes taken are teller, division, or voice votes rather than recorded ones, there is less incentive for many congressmen to be present. If, as often happens, a decision is reached on a Thursday not to have any roll calls until the following Tuesday, many congressmen return to their districts for that period; at such times frantic party whip calls are of no avail. There are complaints, too, that congressmen in their offices cannot get to the floor quickly enough to participate in a teller vote once the bells have rung to alert them to the event. Many legislators, having learned from experience that the effort would be futile, no longer attempt to get there. Thus, unlike the situation that exists when roll-call votes are held, members not already on the floor seldom are able to participate in the decisions. When there is a roll-call vote, legislators who are working in their offices can get to the House in time to be recorded provided they leave when the bells ring to alert them that a roll call is under way.

In discussing the situation, one group of legislators referred to a meeting of the House of Representatives when approximatelly 100 members wrote amendments into a Rivers and Harbors bill by a two or three vote margin each time. A member of the party whip organization related that two general whip calls had been made in an effort to get colleagues to the floor. These Friday afternoon efforts were unsuccessful because the congressmen could not be found. "A whole trend," he said in despair, "was being determined by a margin of about five votes. Once members began to break through with their special projects the process could not be stopped." Commented one legislator, "it was a very discouraging experience. It seemed as though the only ones there were people interested in their pet projects, including members [of two large state delegations]." Another congressman said that the session "was rather horrifying to me." But when a colleague observed that strict adherence to the rules would bring about better attendance for sessions of the Committee of the Whole, he was told his solution was not satisfactory. He stated that according to the rules if a quorum call recorded a member as being absent, he was subject to being docked a day's salary.[4] His colleagues reminded him that his party was in the minority; a full attendance would "result in our being trounced. This way we have a chance to slip something through."

The Role of Debate

One factor contributing to attendance problems in the House is the general dissatisfaction that exists with respect to provisions for debate. The membership recognizes that the size and responsibilities of that body make some regulation inevitable. Widespread criticism of current procedures is heard, nonetheless. There is considerable disagreement with the much quoted view of the late Sam Rayburn that the rules "are pretty nearly perfect." One veteran Democrat referring to the curtailing of debate as the "greatest shortcoming of our system" went on to say. "It is most unfortunate that we cannot approximate real debate. Under the rules it is absolutely impossible to have a case argued in a manner approaching the way it should be argued, even on important issues.

---

[4] An 1872 law, never revoked, directs House and Senate officials to deduct from a member's salary a day's pay for each day's absence except in cases of illness. Periodically, individual congressmen urge the House to invoke the provision.

Major legislation may be passed following debate of only two hours; seldom does a discussion extend beyond two days. Not only are the time limitations on debate unrealistic in terms of permitting a full discussion of the issue before the House, but they serve to limit participation to a few members. Frequently, general debate is consumed entirely by members of the committee studying the proposed legislation. The representative who has been unable to obtain a seat on the committee, but who has much interest in the proposal and possesses ideas about it, is thus denied the opportunity to present his views in the House. Efforts to extend debate time are usually defeated; only rarely are motions to close debate voted down. Complained one congressman, "Despite the difficulties members have in obtaining debate time you will find nearly everyone not actually participating in a bill on the floor willing to vote to curtail the time of others who want to participate."

Legislators disagree regarding the extent to which debate affects the fate of legislative proposals. The prevailing view is that speeches rarely influence many House votes. Their main effect, it is said, is to reinforce views already held, and their purpose is to make a record for the Speaker and a case for the position he supports. There is considerable support, however, for the position that debates are significant often enough in this regard to defy being dismissed as inconsequential and to question the accuracy of the description of the House as a dividing and voting body rather than a deliberative or debating one. Its deliberative nature is far more evident when powerful personalities and leaders take opposing stands. Observed one representative:

Most House members will be more impressed by who is making a speech about a particular proposition than by what is said on the subject. I am not saying they would just judge by whether or not they like the individual. What is important is their evaluation of his knowledge and mastery of the subject and his experience in the field.

Legislators commonly believe that debate is more important in terms of public education than for member education, but there is recognition that considerable member education is involved also. And lawmakers cite specific instances when a determined and informed committee minority has upset the recommendations of the majority, once the bill has reached the House floor. Here, it is conceded, such action is more likely on bills about which the membership is unlikely to possess much knowledge or strong ideological predispositions. Even on important issues, however, debate on amendments may be determinative.

In connection with debate, there is considerable sentiment that because of the advent of television, increased restrictions on debate, and other factors, oratory has declined in the House over the years, although some congressmen deny the allegation. Not all legislators lament the passing of the art. Explained one:

> Frankly, I think it ought to be an obsolete art on the floor of the House. It is almost an insult to my intelligence to have a fellow get up and rant and rave and think he can influence my vote by tactics which should be reserved for the stump if used at all.

The advent of television is credited with having had an especially important effect on the speechmaking techniques of legislators. Members believe that "the kind of speeches which are effective on the floor of the House are not the most persuasive on television. Some of the orators don't do as well on TV."

> That is absolutely right. When _____ was speaking today I was struck by the fact that he was using a sort of "eating and meeting on the ground" style of oratory, the hell, fire, and damnation sort of thing.

*

> I make no bones about the fact that I consider myself about the least effective speaker in the House, but I will do as well as anybody on television. That calls for a conversational approach and you can be very persuasive with it. You are putting yourself in the person's home. But standing on the House floor you are trying to get attention by the sheer weight of your voice, trying to break up those conversations.

Some congressmen are concerned about their failure to participate in floor debate often, and wonder whether their colleagues think less of them because of it. Others believe the wiser course is to avoid participation unless the subject is one about which there is little division in a member's district. One congressmen reflected both these views when he told his colleagues:

> I worried about debating on the floor and the fact that I had never had any experience in such matters. After a year or so in Congress I went to my committee chairman who was a very good speaker and told him I was concerned. I wondered what he thought about the fact I hadn't made any speeches on the floor. He said, "let me tell you something, son. No congressman has ever been defeated by a

speech he didn't make on the floor of the House." I have thought about it many times because the man who told me was defeated after many years by speeches he did make on the floor. Words were thrown back to him that he had spoken twenty years before.

The Role of Parliamentary Law

In seeking to become effective legislators, apparently most congressmen do not give high priority to mastering parliamentary techniques and acquiring a thorough understanding of the rules of the House. There seems to be remarkable agreement within that body that very few members—a dozen at the outside—have thorough knowledge of these matters, only a few have a good grasp, and more than half the membership know virtually nothing about them. Freshmen cite examples of gross error and ignorance on the part of veteran members, while their seniors observe that even the acknowledged experts occasionally make mistakes.

Parliamentary expertise is commonly attributed to the leadership of the Southern bloc, although it is by no means limited to that group. "One of the greatest weapons of the South," said one liberal Democrat, "is its ability to use the rules." Long tenure, minority status with respect to issues they regard as central to the future of their section of the nation, and a special flair for, and interest in, mastering the intricacies of the complex rules of procedure are said by colleagues to explain Southern primacy in this area. Taking full advantage of the rules permits the Southerners to maximize their influence.

A firm grasp of the rules and their use is viewed as a potentially valuable asset, if it is not regarded as an indispensable tool of the average member of Congress. And for those senior legislators who have important responsibilities in connection with House action on legislation, it assumes special significance. These are the congressmen who have the most opportunity to display their knowledge, and they constitute the group of whom competence in this area is expected. Members who exhibit such skills are accorded respect and deference by their colleagues. To become recognized as an expert parliamentarian is to attain high prestige in the House.

Yet the fact remains that parliamentary skills are not considered basic to success. They are viewed as "handy but not too significant" or as "a source of help in trouble. If you have (them) in your arsenal, once in a while you can do something you couldn't do otherwise." Much of the explanation for this lies in the nature of House procedure. To expedite the work of the House, the precise rules are often ignored, and sanctions would be enforced against members who consistently sought adherence to them; the result is less reliance on certain of the formal rules. Explained one legislator:

> We do so many things by unanimous consent here that it sort of dulls the blade. If rules and correct procedure were to be followed throughout the deliberations, the whole operation could bog down in a minute. There is a sort of fraternal feeling on matters of procedure to the extent that parliamentary tactics are not resorted to frequently.

Furthermore, House practice dictates that members of the committee which has reported a legislative proposal to the House are recognized to discuss it prior to nonmembers of the committee. Since debate time usually is inadequate, members with other committee assignments, particularly the less senior of them, often have no opportunity to participate. The effect is to limit the interest of most junior members in the means by which floor action is achieved. As one able but relatively junior man put it: "There is little incentive for the average member to acquire real mastery of the rules inasmuch as he is not handling legislation as a floor manager and since usually he won't be able to be recognized anyway." A well-regarded freshman explained his indifference in this way: "To me it is like everything else. You never get down to learning it until you have to. There is no time to do so, there is no inclination since you can't use your knowledge, and there is no 'fun' involved in the process." When one particularly conscientious member of mid-seniority rank was asked by a colleague whether, as a freshman, he had not felt lost until he had gained some competence in the parliamentary ways of the House, he responded: "When I was a freshman I never had an opportunity to do anything except vote. Only when you attain enough seniority to be in charge of a bill on the floor do you really need to know what you are doing, I think." This attitude is widespread.

There is a general tendency to rely on expert advice. Juniors, it is evident, are heavily dependent on their senior allies to provide parliamentary leadership for their cause. Experienced committee clerks and other Hill professionals are queried about proper procedures. The parliamentarian and his staff are kept busy responding to member requests about simple as well as complex problems relating to the rules. The presence of the parliamentarian in the House Chamber when that body is in session, and the unobtrusiveness of his assistance to presiding officers as well as congressmen on the floor, makes it less important that even legislators entrusted with chairing sessions of the Committee of the Whole be thoroughly steeped in the parliamentary rules of the House. Experienced presiding officers do not always rule as the parliamentarian suggests, it should be noted, but deviations from his recommendations are not common.

The existence of staff specifically charged with the responsibility of interpreting the rules for legislators and for guiding them in the simplest or most complex of procedures, and the fact that relatively few congressmen are much involved in legislative maneuverings combine to strengthen the likelihood that mastery of House procedure need not become a consuming interest. After one group of legislators had agreed that the majority of House members had no competence in this area, one of the better parliamentarians among them cautioned:

> This is not to criticize. Some of them don't have to know the rules. The area in which they work is such that they don't handle legislation or they aren't making objections. They know enough about the rules to get their remarks in the Record or to get recognized on matters for which they want recogniton and that is all they care about.

There are occasions, however, where the skilled parliamentarian reaps the rewards of his knowledge. Points of order, the threat of embarrassing roll calls or quorum calls, or objections to the evasion of regular procedures may cripple the plans of the House majority. Anticipating opposition strategies, the skilled parliamentarian may force valuable concessions in exchange for silence. Even if his efforts have no prospect of success, raising certain questions and delaying or accelerating House action may prove sufficiently distressing to the majority that he may win a victory of sorts.

Although most publicity focuses on the use of the rules by a minority rather than a majority, it is clear that they may be used just as readily by the majority to frustrate the minority. Time limits may be invoked to prevent protracted discussions of proposals, closed rules may be adopted, the scheduling of legislation may be manipulated to minimize the likelihood of a serious contest. A congressman discussed a device sometimes used to forestall roll calls:

It is a very frequent tactic when the House is discussing a measure on which most members don't want a roll call to make a point of order just prior to the vote that a quorum isn't present. That gets a quorum on the floor and then you have a division or teller vote against which you can't get an automatic roll call. In other words, you head off a roll call by making a point of order that a quorum isn't present, thereby getting one. If an opponent made the point of order after a teller or division vote, an automatic roll call would be required.

A liberal Democrat describes an unusual example of the use of the rules by a minority in an attempt (unsuccessful) to prevent the passage of legislation.

The classic example of the use of the rules since I have been in Congress occurred in 1950, on February 22. February 22 fell on Calendar Wednesday, and we were bringing up the FEPC bill on that day. The Southerners wanted to avoid that. First there was a quorum call, then a roll call on dispensing with the reading of the Journal. After that came the reading of Washington's Farewell Address. When that was concluded, Gene Cox of Georgia rose and said, "out of reverence to the memory of George Washington I suggest we adjourn. I move we adjourn." Then there was a roll call on the motion to adjourn. After that came the question of taking up Calendar Wednesday, and there was a roll call on that. It was 11 in the evening before we began consideration of the bill.

We had to exert every effort to keep members on the floor. The opposition was watching all the time. Every time there was a quorum call, a group of the Republicans would leave the floor. John Bell Williams of Mississippi walked through the aisles on the Democratic side saying, "there is a cotton caucus in the cloakroom," and many Southerners would walk off the floor leaving a quorum absent. Finally, at 11 p.m. Speaker Rayburn over-ruled a point of order that no quorum was present on the grounds that it was dilatory; a similar point of order had been made just a few minutes before. Then we began consideration of the bill and passed it at 4 in the morning. In that situation one rule had been brought up after another which resulted in a form of filibuster in the House. The rules can be used in that way.

Except at crucial times in the legislative process, such as at the end of a session, the House rules may be used to delay, modify, or obstruct but seldom to defeat or destroy.

There is much evidence that a knowledge of the rules and of House procedure when combined with careful planning can be significant in promoting the attainment of a legislative goal. In the situation described below, knowledge of procedure was less important than a thorough understanding of the temper of the House and of the personalities involved, and the preparation of a systematic plan for ensuring that one's point of view would be presented effectively. Yet underlying everything was a thorough awareness of the ways in which House procedures could advance or impede the proposal.

A few years ago the Appropriations Committee cut the civil functions appropriation below the budget. We organized a little effort to override them. We designated the people to offer and prepare amendments, keeping their seniority in mind as well as the kinds of influence they would have on the floor and what they could add to the bill. _____ who was on the committee and could get recognition wanted to offer an amendment himself and wouldn't agree to work with us on this proposition. He nearly ruined everything, but we finally got it worked out. In order to get support of the liberals, we gave one of the amendments to [a prominent liberal].

To present our motion, we needed someone on the Appropriations Committee who would be entitled to recognition. We had to go pretty far down the list to find someone who was willing to buck the chairman. We also had trouble with the leader of our group who wanted to make a speech regardless of what happened. He had seniority and could have been recognized, but he wouldn't have helped the cause. When we finally had it all worked out as to who would be recognized and who would make each motion, I took the list to the presiding officer in advance, and he agreed they were the people he would recognize. That was the only time in many years in which the Appropriations Committee has been defeated on a public works appropriations bill.

The Congressional Record

The *Congressional Record* is an important element in the legislative process. The congressman uses it to build a record, and, hopefully, a favorable image and to strengthen his position with selected individuals or groups. From it he gains ideas for legislation and for political survival. Further, its "Daily Digest" section provides him with a capsule record of current activities in Congress, enabling him to become aware of matters that might otherwise escape his attention. Citizens examine the *Record* as one means by which to gain understanding of Congress.

Divided into four sections—House and Senate floor activities, an appendix, and the daily digest—approximately 45,000 copies of the *Record* are distributed every day in which at least one house is in session. Prepared at a cost of about $90.00 a page, it increased from nearly 16,000 pages in fiscal 1945 to about 30,000 pages in 1962. Educational institutions, politicians, interested organizations, scholars, and opinion leaders in every segment of national life are among the important groups receiving it. The nature of the readership is a factor in the care with which some legislators prepare their own contributions.

The process by which the *Record* is put together is remarkable in many ways. In the House, for example, seven official reporters spell one another at five-minute intervals in taking shorthand notes of the debate, moving around the House floor so as to be near the speaker of the moment. The notes are immediately dictated into recording machines from which they are transcribed on numbered sheets. These are given to the congressman for revision. Often the legislators receive these sheets within a half hour after the conclusion of their speech.

The major portion of the *Congressional Record* constitutes a record of the debates on the floor of the House and Senate, although it is by no means a true one, a fact of which many of its readers are not aware. Nor is it intended to be. Rather it is "substantially a verbatim" reproduction of proceedings. This causes concern to some congressmen who believe it *should* be a verbatim report except for allowances for minor grammatical revision. Complained one representative: "You have a record it is impossible to interpret on its face." Speeches never delivered in the Congress appear as though they had, indeed, been made there, and often there is no way to discover the truth of the matter. Other speeches have been substantially rewritten; the rule that only minor changes are to be made is occasionally flagrantly ignored. The inclusion of clever afterthoughts may sharpen the force of a member's argument, disguising his weak floor presentation and causing him to appear victor rather than vanquished in debate. Members have even been known to reverse their positions in revising copy. Deletions and additions may affect the relevance and meaning of the remarks of other members participating in a colloquy. Some congressmen have protested that their statements have been rendered meaningless by the alterations made in the presentations of those with whom they were jousting. Occasionally, according to House members, legislators hopelessly routed in debate will delay returning their revised remarks beyond the deadline for submission, so that they will appear in the appendix, rather than in the body of the *Record* adjacent to those of colleagues who have bested them.

Criticisms made in the heat of debate often are removed in the written record, but implied criticisms of colleagues never uttered on the floor may also appear in the written record within the context of remarks delivered.

Protested one irritated member:

In a controversy with the Air Force, I provoked an official of the Department of Defense to make a bitter attack on me. Later a colleague of mine made a speech on a bill under consideration. His remarks contained no reference to the controversy between me and that official. But when the *Congressional Record* appeared the next day, his speech repeated the personal attack the official had made. My colleague never made the statement on the floor.

Revise and Extend. The source of much of the difficulty is the practice of securing permission to "revise and extend" remarks. Although the occasional excesses are not condoned—they are in fact widely admitted and regretted though no concerted effort has been made to eliminate them— the right to "extend" is regarded as all but indispensable by most congressmen, and any attempt to eliminate it would be firmly resisted. Justification of the practice generally rests on two grounds: (1) it helps to conserve precious House time; and (2) it permits members to correct any grammatical errors and to modify impolitic statements made in the stress of debate. A third factor, which is sometimes advanced, is that it provides one more means by which constituents can gain insight into the thinking of their representatives.

Without the opportunity to "clean up" the *Record*, said one congressman, "it would be really sad reading the next day . . . the best comic book you ever saw." Said another: "It couldn't be used in an English composition class."

Much legislation is noncontroversial, involving no important issue that needs to be resolved. Yet because of the appeal of some such measures in their constituencies members may wish to be "on the record" with respect to them. Especially where roll-call votes are not taken, insertions become a convenient way of expressing an opinion without subjecting colleagues to the unhappy prospect of listening to testimonial after testimonial on subjects about which they are all agreed. If a roll call occurs, members may wish to provide an explanation of their vote or to demonstrate their special interest in the legislation, which, because of limited debate time they cannot accomplish by direct participation in the discussion.

On that crazy _____ bill, one of the toughest of the year, we had twenty minutes of debate on each side. Because of the brief time allotted, no one but the authors had much chance to say anything. One of the authors assured me he would get permission for every member to revise and extend his remarks so I prepared a brief statement and inserted it, so the *Record* would show what I would have said if I had been given time to say it.

Congressmen also may wish to influence readers of the *Record*, including members of the "other body," though their own view has not prevailed in the House. If the contribution has no apparent effect on the current controversy, it may help prepare the way for victory in the future.

Those congressmen who have major objections to existing extension of remarks procedures generally do not suggest the practice be discontinued, but they are inclined to press for a distinction in the *Record* between statements delivered on the floor of the House and those inserted to appear as though they had been given there. On this question, it is interesting to note, the Brookings Democratic round table divided nine-to-five in favor of the present practice: no distinction. Commented one practical legislator who prefaced his remarks by urging rules to prevent "situations where people make speeches on one side of a question and when their remarks are printed are on the other side":

Yet suggestions that we change the system with regard to extension and do like the Senate does—if you don't actually deliver the speech it appears in different type—while correct in theory are not practical. It would be hard to avoid the time-consuming situation which would occur if everybody had to deliver statements and everybody would want to make sure his name was not applied to a mere extension. The work of the House would become very cumbersome. That is why the system has never been changed in the House—to conserve time.

As a reflection of round table opinion with respect to curtailment of practices currently followed in "revise and extend" remarks consider the following discussion:

Is there a consensus that one flaw in the system has been exposed in that you have in a sense a false record, that without going so far as to be restrictive some way could be found for the record to be more accurate so a person could interpret it better? [The answer was "no."]

*

This should be said for maintaining the present system. Although it is not the accurate record we wish, it is a deliberate record. It is the way the members want the record to read. In that sense, the sober second thoughts of people—the thoughts they have had a chance to reflect upon—may be more accurate.

*

This is a record of something, there is no doubt, but of what it is a record there is some question.

*

It is the record of the way each member wished himself to be recorded. I have found the right to revise and extend in general debate to be an invaluable aid. . . . Each of us owes it to the dignity of the House to make his expressions as good as he possibly can for posterity.

Perhaps the most serious indictment of present procedures rests on the charge that they could result in the marshaling of a false legislative history, a criticism often heard. In attempting to ascertain the true intent of Congress with respect to legislation, the courts examine the floor debates as set forth in the *Congressional Record* as well as committee reports. Said one representative:

I recall writing a paper, when I was in law school, on some legal matter which involved the interpretation of an act of Congress. I researched the *Congressional Record* to see what congressmen had said in order to get an interpretation of how the law should be construed. I considered that an important element of my case. I would have reservations now as to the authority of statements reported in the *Congressional Record* as a sound interpretation of what Congress intended.

A Republican expressed his position much more sharply:

Phony legislative histories are written all the time. Extension in the body of the *Record* appears as if the words had been spoken. Therefore the court or whoever is undertaking to interpret the legislative history might reasonably assume that the words influenced the debate and hence were part of the legislative history. These words might push the meaning of the statute one way or the other, yet they had no influence whatever on debate or vote. Nobody even saw them until the morning afterwards when they appeared in the *Record*. I have observed much skullduggery and the fraudulent making of legislative history by this means. Someone ought to look into this matter closely.

Although the congressman persisted in his contention that the failure to distinguish between delivered and undelivered remarks often sabotaged the possibility of providing a proper legislative history, the majority of his colleagues were not moved. An excerpt from the discussion reflects his inability to convince his colleagues of the logic of his position:

I agree that one ought to tidy up his grammar and improve his rhetoric. And I agree that a member ought to have the right, even though he didn't speak on the floor, to insert into the record a statement disclosing his stand on an issue. What I object to is that matter appears in the record as if it had been spoken. That has the effect of constituting legislative history, but in fact it isn't proper legislative history because it is boot-strap-lifting put in the day after. I suggest that this be designated as a statement in extension.

*

Yes, but it isn't as if it is possible to record the legislative history of a bill. The facts that make the House vote as it does or the real meaning of what the House does and wants isn't going to be shown by the debate.

*

Perhaps the rules of judicial construction of legislative acts are not the best rules that could be devised, but we know what the rules are. The rules are that committee hearings and reports, conference reports, and the floor debate are considered by the court, both in federal and state courts. As long as that is so, we kid the court when we make matter appear as if it were legislative debate when it is not.

*

If the record is distorted by something put in to appear as though it were said when in fact it wasn't, those who disagree with the distortion have recourse in the days that follow. They can point out the true situation.

Developing the legislative history of a bill is a matter with which relatively few members concern themselves, but it is an important part of the legislative process, and canny representatives alert to the possibilities can do much to influence the practical effect of legislation. In connection with noncontroversial bills, it often happens that floor managers will speak only briefly to the House but extend their remarks in the *Record* to reflect more fully the position and thinking of the committee majority and to complete the legislative history. Minority representatives may do the same thing. Major legislation is more likely to involve the development of congressional intent right on the floor. Sometimes legislators will deliberately set out to make legislative history by asking questions of the floor managers to ensure that certain points are clear. There is the danger, of course, that the procedure will not always result in the accurate reflection of committee intent, as one veteran legislator observes:

> Making a legislative record by putting questions to a person handling a bill is a rather frequent occurrence. I have often thought that the chairman presumes what power he has in answering the questions addressed to him, in that he is supposed to be speaking for the entire committee. I have disagreed with my chairman when he has said "the committee feels so and so" in connection with an important point. Yet the only course is to rise and say, "I, for one, don't agree with my chairman in this interpretation," and only rarely will anyone get up and do that. That is the way legislative history is made in an interchange between the chairman and his questioner.

The Appendix. The appendix functions as a depository for materials that are not directly relevant to House or Senate proceedings but which members of Congress want placed in the *Record*.[5] These include editorials, reports, speeches, poems, essays, letters, recipes, and testimonials. Some legislators insert their own newsletters, voting records, and the results of questionnaires sent from their offices to constituents. In recent years, legislators have begun to overcome their reluctance to insert their own speeches given outside the Congress; formerly the speeches were nearly always placed in the *Record* by friendly colleagues, perhaps at the request of the member making the speech.

While most of the items in the appendix presumably have been submitted because of their purported general interest or educational value, many of them are, in fact, parochial in nature. Periodic attempts are made to exert more control over the nature of the materials incorporated in the appendix and to establish limits on the amount an individual legislator can insert in any one session. One congressman has estimated that 5 percent of the membership of the House use 80 percent of the space. And in a House speech in 1962, he estimated that the volume of material inserted by some members cost more to print than their annual salary of $22,500. There is general recognition that much of the matter is "very frivolous and of no real moment," but there is little disposition to be restrictive. One restriction provides that any insertion exceeding two pages in length must be accompanied by a statement from the public printer estimating its cost; as a deterrent this requirement is conceded to be a failure.

Most of the items appearing in the appendix have in the first instance caught the eye of a member of Congress or his staff, but some have been forwarded to the legislator by a constituent or friend with the request or suggestion that they be inserted. These communications sometimes pose problems for the member, especially if the materials are of dubious merit. Constituent initiative usually reflects genuine interest in the outcome of the request; a congressman who declines to cooperate may find he has created an enemy. That some representatives hesitate to return material is evident by this comment:

In the past ten days I have had three letters asking me to put things in the *Record* which are extraneous to the business of the House. I took them home

[5] It should be noted that much extraneous matter finds its way into the body as well as the appendix of the *Record*.

and worried about the problem for two or three days. Finally I wrote each of the persons involved a letter saying I had a rule against putting extraneous matter in the *Record* and didn't want to break it. I may have three enemies or three constituents who think I am a screwball.

Legislators reluctant to insert materials may point out to constituents that printing costs are $90.00 a page and that they do not want to add to the taxpayer's burden by submitting material not directly relevant to matters before Congress. But it is sometimes easier to ignore one's doubts and insert the material; constituents whose material has been returned may follow closely the insertion policies of their representative, seeking inconsistencies and heckling him with anything they discover. The dilemma is compounded, too, by colleagues who seem to exercise no discretion in what they place in the *Record*.

The political advantages of adroit use of the appendix are apparent to most members, just as they use extension procedures to advantage in connection with the body of the *Record*. Only rarely, as in the instance cited below, will a congressman err in anticipating favorable reaction from those whose material he places in the *Record*.

Most of the appendix materials are inserted by congressmen hoping for political gain. Some folks are sincere and believe the subject matter is worth printing and that their colleagues and public should read it. But much is political, trying to flatter newspaper editors, or something like that. A colleague from my state had an interesting experience in that connection. He inserted an editorial from the largest paper in his district prefacing it with a few remarks and sent it back to the paper. He expected gratitude, but the paper wrote a heck of a good editorial against the practice, saying they wished congressmen wouldn't reprint any of their stuff, that taxpayers' money shouldn't be spent on it.

Reprints of materials printed in the appendix are a means of subsidizing propaganda. They are obtainable at low cost, encouraging congressmen to use them for campaign or public relations purposes. In addition, legislators may strengthen their position with interest groups by inserting certain materials and making them available to the groups at cost. One private group is said to have obtained ten million pieces in this way. By distributing them to the general public under the frank of friendly congressmen, the organization saved an additional $300,000 in postage.

Far more common is the technique used by one practical congressman to consolidate support for him within various organizations in his district:

You can put something in the *Record* that you plan to reprint and send back to specific groups. During the campaign I had written a letter to all the REA people in my district—some 3,000 of them—saying that I would be for REA. It was a hot issue in my area. When the REA bill came before the House I put a statement in the *Record*, reprinted it, and sent it out to the same 3,000 people. This is standard operating procedure from what I have seen. It is a cheap way to campaign.

A substantial part of the material in the appendix is aimed directly at those who read the *Record*—colleagues, opinion leaders, students, and scholars—and is of high quality, attempting to influence them by bringing to their attention interesting and thoughtful materials which support the position of the person submitting them. Congressional colleagues are the main target of these efforts. That congressmen do read the *Record* is evident by the frequency with which they refer in conversation to provocative articles that have appeared there, and by their ability to cite examples of materials they feel should not have been inserted. One legislator who makes frequent use of the *Record* in an effort to reach his associates had this to say:

> There are several reasons for insertions in the appendix. (1) You can satisfy constituent requests that way. (2) You may have a special interest group you want to reach to indicate your support of something which is of concern to them. (3) You may be inclined to use it to lobby your colleagues, because a lot of them do read the *Record*. I have discovered that when little things I have put in happened to strike someone's fancy he mentions it to me. It is an easy way to reach members and less direct than sending them a letter. When we feel keenly about things, we write our colleagues directly, but often you don't want to make that much of the matter.

It should not be forgotten either that the *Congressional Record*, including the appendix, forms a rich resource in connection with research for speeches and campaign statements. Many a congressional staff, required to prepare effective speeches on a wide range of subjects with very short notice, have been able to do so only because the *Record* is readily available and indexed.

Introduction of Bills

The legislative effectiveness of a member of Congress is not measured by the number of bills he introduces or even by his success in getting them enacted into law, although his activities in this area constitute one means by which he carries out his legislative role. Political campaigns may even be conducted with a member's bills introduced bills enacted statistics in mind. The real contribution of many legislators may rest in strengthening the bills of their colleagues, in building majorities for proposals in which they are interested, or in effecting satisfactory compromises among opposing factions. In the House, where, unlike the Senate, cosponsorship of legislation is not permitted, few legislators succeed in getting their names on important legislation. Junior members of the House have little chance for such fame, and members of the minority party, whatever their seniority, have virtually none. They may introduce major bills primarily for the publicity value associated with them, aware that there is little prospect for passage.

Minority congressmen, realizing that committee majorities are unlikely to enhance the reputation of their opponents by voting endorsement of their proposals, often concentrate their efforts on amending the proposals of others. If a majority party member likes a proposal of a colleague in the minority, he may introduce an identical bill with his own name on it, and that is the measure which receives the attention of the committee. Credit for its passage accrues to the majority member. Said one conscientious minority member whose grasp of the detail and implications of legislation coming before his committee is recognized and used by members of both parties:

> As minority members, most of us find we concentrate a lot harder on amending bills than on introducing bills. Because we are in the minority, our bills usually are not even scheduled for hearings. This means we have to work like blazes to amend the majority ones that are scheduled in a way we feel will be more suitable. So the introduction of bills isn't the full measure of our legislative work.

The philosophy of individual legislators with respect to the introduction of bills varies widely. Some congressmen believe that a member should introduce few bills. They argue that proposals are more likely to arouse the opponents of the measure than its supporters and that at election time the legislator who has placed a large number of items into the legislative hopper is more vulnerable than his colleague who has introduced very few. They warn, too, that one can expect enactment of only a few of his proposals and that opposing candidates will attempt to make political capital out of the poor "batting average" that results. Other congressmen believe that a member should seek to introduce bills on a wide variety of subjects so that when voters ask his views on a specific subject, he can provide tangible evidence of his interest by citing the introduction of a bill on that very topic. Explained one member who follows that policy:

> I introduce about sixty bills a year, about 120 a Congress. I try to introduce bills that illustrate, by and large, my ideas—legislative, economic, and social. I do like being able to say when I get cornered, "yes, boys, I introduced a bill to try to do that in 1954." To me it is the perfect answer.

Another congressman who also sponsors many bills does so to "reflect the basic things I stood for in the campaign. I feel this is an educational process and if the bill doesn't pass this year, that is all right. It takes years for a good idea to percolate through to final conclusion. If you can merely modify, in what you think is a helpful direction, something somebody else has done previously, it is helpful."

Most legislators have not adopted the policy of the colleagues quoted above. Aside from a generous policy toward the introduction of private bills, they tend to be selective in the introduction of bills, limiting themselves largely to proposals that are in the special interest of the district or state they represent, or that reflect their preoccupation with matters within the jurisdiction of the committees on which they serve. There are sound reasons for this, buttressed by congressional emphasis on specialization. Seldom does a member (unless he is part of the majority party leadership) succeed in getting enacted into law a bill that is referred to a committee to which he has not been assigned. A study by one congressional office of bills of general application enacted into law in the Eighty-fourth Congress indicated that virtually all were sponsored by the chairman or a member of the committee majority, the latter often serving as chairmen of the subcommittees which considered the legislation. This fact underscores the importance to a congressman and his constituency of his being named to a committee that is concerned with matters of special significance to his district.

A practice that acts as a deterrent to the introduction of bills is the tendency for some chairmen of committees and subcommittees to appropriate the ideas of their junior associates. Many members with little seniority introduce bills which they regard as representing important contributions to existing law and eagerly anticipate the personal benefits to be reaped from their passage, only to discover that identical or nearly identical bills are introduced later by their chairmen. The latter bills are the ones considered by the committee. In other situations, committee consideration of a number of similar bills will result in the reporting out of a bill bearing the name of the chairman rather than that of any of the original sponsors. These are matters of concern and irritation to many of the able younger members of the House. Said one highly regarded junior congressman:

One unfortunate practice is that of allowing legislative bills to come out of committee under the authorship of the committee chairman. Even though you may have had the idea and introduced a bill on it, the fact is that if you want anything to happen to it, you often have to let the chairman sponsor it and get the credit for it. This causes members to feel they are not contributing much of substance. You sometimes get bills through, but they are very minor bills. Often you have to be satisfied with somebody else's bill. Now I agree you shouldn't merely want to get your own way on these things, that the important thing should be advancing legislation in which you believe; but the fact is that all of us like to get a little credit for what we are doing. Even though we can get vicarious satisfaction out of contributing to a committee bill, it just isn't the same thing as advancing our own.

Fortunately the practice, though common, is not universal. Some chairmen are more generous. One legislator whose party controlled both the Congress and the White House, related that at a meeting of the majority members of his committee the chairman circulated a number of bills which the administration wanted introduced and suggested that members select those they wished to bear their name and for which they desired to act as managers. A thoughtful and generous act of that kind does much, obviously, to strengthen the relationship between the chairman and his colleagues.

Even where the chairman pre-empts bills and credit, however, there are potential advantages for the junior man who introduces fresh ideas or possesses special competence in an area. His interest in and knowledge about the proposed legislation may lead to new understanding between him and his chairman, with long-range advantages difficult for him to achieve in other ways. His discussions of the proposal within the committee, and perhaps later in the House, permit his colleagues to appraise him in circumstances highly favorable to him. The introduction of bills may provide unusual opportunities for a junior congressman to become acquainted with his colleagues and to gain understanding about the legislative process. There are opportunities for discussion with committee and perhaps subcommittee chairmen regarding hearings, conversations with committee staff about the fate of similar proposals and possible approaches, and meetings with colleagues who may have introduced similar legislation. The experience may hasten the development of the member into an effective legislator.

The matter of bill referral can be an extremely important one, as many legislators quickly learn. There is much overlap in the jurisdiction of the various committees, and often there are narrow dividing lines where distinctions do exist. Where two or more committees deal with similar subject matter, it sometimes happens that one unit is so constituted as to be much more favorably disposed toward a proposal than others to which it might be referred. Discussions with the parliamentarian or his assistants, the staff of the Legislative Counsel's office, or committee staff members may reveal how the bill can be worded to ensure referral to the committee most likely to react favorably to it. The effective legislator, as a first step then, anticipates committee reaction and seeks to maximize the likelihood of survival of his idea by securing its referral to a friendly unit whenever possible.

The fact that a congressman has introduced a bill is no indication, of course, that he is genuinely interested in its advancement. In filing bills, he commonly acts as agent for constituents, the executive branch, and interest groups.[6] Many of the bills he submits at their suggestion are little more than a reflection of his desire to fulfill an obligation or request, to placate an influential person or group, or to strengthen his political position. His true feelings may be more readily discerned by his subsequent activities, if any, in behalf of the measure. His efforts to seek hearings, his willingness to testify if hearings are scheduled, and the nature of his testimony are important in this regard. Discussions with colleagues, solicitation of support perhaps from within the committee, his state delegation, or from party leaders as well as interest groups are other indicators.

Constituents should not expect their representatives to gain early recognition as sponsors of important legislative proposals; House procedure militates against this. A common experience is that related by one

[6] One congressman estimates that nearly four-fifths of the public bills enacted into law actually originate in the executive branch.

legislator who had completed three terms in the House, two of them when his party was the minority party:

> People shouldn't have any great expectations that their congressman will be the author of important legislation, especially early in his career. In my six years here I have had two bills passed, both when I was a freshman and my party was in control. One set up an Advisory Committee on Education in HEW—they never bothered to implement it after we got the bill through—and the other provided free dental care to Spanish American War Veterans, a bill which I don't suppose my constituents sent me here to push.

Only with time can a relative newcomer become generally recognized within the House as an authority. A longer period must elapse before he can expect to receive accolades as the author of major legislation. Undeniably, however, relatively junior men have made important contributions to the work of the House. The surprising thing, in fact, is that some of them can make their influence felt so quickly in that large, unwieldy body.

Voting

Voting is, of course, one of the most important responsibilities of members of Congress, and one which the vast majority of them take seriously, particularly when a controversial issue is involved. While some of the most important votes in the House are of the unrecorded type (teller or division votes in the Committee of the Whole, which affect the direction of important legislation, are often decided by very slim majorities), representatives are most diligent in attendance when roll-call votes are anticipated and demanded.

On some occasions a high sense of drama pervades the House as the voting on a closely contested issue gets underway and proceeds to its conclusion. A roll call may be preceded by division or teller votes that reveal that a surprise could be in store for the leadership or that a "cliff hanger" is in prospect. On the roll call, there may be things to watch—the vote switches that occur under the prodding of party leaders, the movement of latecomers to the well of the House to be recorded, the withholding of votes on the first call by certain legislators anxious to see the trend or to determine whether their votes are needed to bring victory to the party, the tallying of the vote by leaders on both sides of the issue to determine whether they will need to call up votes they are holding in reserve, or can release those who would prefer to vote on the other side but who have agreed to vote with them if such action will alter the outcome.

In campaigning for re-election members often point with pride to their high percentage of participation in these recorded votes; they are aware, too, that extensive absenteeism may be noted by an opponent and seized on as an election issue. During the Eighty-sixth Congress (1959–1960) the average member of the House cast "yea" or "nay" votes on 89 percent of the 180 roll calls; this percentage carried through the first session of the Eighty-seventh Congress, but dropped to 83 percent in the second session. If "pairs" were included, participation percentage would be even higher. Individual percentages varied markedly from 100 percent down to a low of 32 percent. The legislator with the poorest participation record in the 1960 session, had been present for only 17 percent of the roll calls, a figure far below that of any of his colleagues. Elected from a "safe" district where he controls the party organization, he is a chronic absentee, but his constituents do not seem to mind; he has been returned many times.

In more than half (97) of the 180 roll calls in the Eighty-sixth Congress a majority of the Democrats in the House were on one side of the issue, and the bulk of the Republicans on the other. There was no appreciable difference between the percentage of time the average Democrat and Republican voted with his party majority, in disagreement with that of the opposition party.

Considerations in Voting. Casting one's vote is not always an easy task. On some occasions the pressures on a congressman to vote a certain way are numerous and conflicting. Complicating the problem, especially where complex issues are involved, is the concern of some members that they do not possess all the facts on which to base a decision. Though there is evidence that even were additional information available, busy legislators would not have time to examine or assimilate it, there are some complaints that the Executive, to cite one source of dissatisfaction, requests the Congress to approve programs on the basis of incomplete information and is guilty of withholding data pertinent to the decision. Nor is it always easy to reconcile conflicting statements about legislative proposals. Lamented one legislator:

Another thing which disturbs me is the amazing lack of exact information which seems to be prevalent. I know it is a complex job and that we have to deal with many complicated problems. Yet it is disturbing to find people coming out with an opposite set of facts on the floor of Congress. . . . It is very difficult for a congressman to know what the truth is or where to find it when you hear such contradictory statements.

Advice regarding voting comes from many quarters. Sources and the extent of their influence on the final decision vary. Trusted colleagues, party leaders in Congress and without, the state delegation, committee chairmen, the executive, lobbyists, or interest groups, individual constituents or prevailing district sentiment, friends or family, the press— these are among the many contributors, at one time or another to voting decisions of members of Congress. Important, too, of course, is the personal predisposition of the legislator. His background, training, and fundamental social and economic philosophy play important roles in such judgments. The congressman may also be influenced heavily by the tug of party, of intra-House blocs or clubs with which he is associated, or a colleague to whom he is indebted. A representative who comes from a district in which the dominant political organization is particularly strong may enjoy special advantages over more hard-pressed colleagues whose districts are marginal politically, in that he may have greater flexibility in voting what he considers to be "the national interest" as opposed to the more parochial local interests, provided of course the organization permits him the flexibility. Said one congressman:

The stronger the party organization in your district the more independent and statesmanlike you can be, if the organization will permit it, naturally. Take _____. He can do anything he pleases and know the voters won't turn him out next time. The unfortunate thing in that situation is that the other five from that city have to do whatever he wants them to do. They have no alternative. Sometimes the type of discretion which is permitted in certain strong party areas can be very good for the country.

The fact is that the number and range of issues are so great that no one can safely rely solely on his own information and vote intelligently. Commented one lawmaker: "You have to take so much on faith on bills brought into the House; sometimes you get fooled." In that connection, deference to colleagues or to leadership opinion may be especially characteristic where the less important proposals are concerned.

One first term member, after expressing amazement at the "enormity

of the workload" stressed that it was "impossible to keep up on legislation" and mentioned his heavy reliance on committee work and committee
members with whom he had rapport. He explained:

> I turn to committee members in whom I have confidence for their integrity and
> ability and rely on them especially when the legislation is not of paramount
> importance. The best I can do is to devote my time to the major pieces of legisla-
> tion which come before the House, and rely on others for advice in connection
> with less major legislation. I admit there are many drawbacks to such a system,
> but I want to impress upon you that there is no alternative.

It seems evident that the advice of trusted colleagues is all but determinative where minor legislation is concerned and is heavily weighed, at the
very least, where the legislation is major. Where the issue has political
overtones and the congressman finds his personal views in conflict with
those of his district or the party leadership, he finds himself in a dilemma,
particularly if he is convinced his position is the correct one. On this
point one forthright veteran legislator had this to say:

> We have much leeway in voting, but we can't go against the district too often·
> I think. On *really* important issues I always vote my conviction regardless of the
> pressures which are put upon me. On less important votes politics may be
> followed on an expedient basis. I think members have to decide where they are
> going to make their stand and at what point the issue isn't too important. Some-
> times it is easier to follow what your district wants you to do.

Consider this only semi-facetious exchange:

> I think very definitely that when your own personal convictions on an issue
> are at variance with the majority opinion of your constituents you should vote
> your convictions even when you know you are displeasing your constituents.
>
> *
>
> And what district did you represent?

Little Knowledge of Minor Bills. As noted, bills that are regarded as noncontroversial usually do not gain much attention from the heavily bur-
dened legislators. This is especially true of measures on which there is not
likely to be a roll-call vote. The typical representative is virtually uninformed with respect to bills reaching the House floor via the private or
consent calendars, but in such cases his conscience is eased, for specific
responsibility for ensuring that such bills are meritorious is delegated by
party leadership to official party objectors whose job it is to screen the
bills carefully. Democrats and Republicans have objector committees

for both private and consent calendar items;[7] these representatives are on the floor when the calendars are called up. Since the majority of the bills passed are taken up by the private or consent calendar route, these committees have important responsibilities.

When a group of congressmen were asked how frequently they found themselves without strong views or even a position on matters coming before the House, they readily replied that this often happened ("all the time," "frequently," "except on very important legislation," "all the bills on the private calendar and half the others"). Because of the safeguards that existed, they were not disturbed by this.

Not ten people in Congress know the content of the bills on the consent calendar. Bills get there through request of the committee which has originally considered them, which is an indication of no opposition.

*

So that our failure to know about all bills will not be considered negligence on our part, we can point out that there are about ten thousand bills introduced each session, and about one thousand of fairly general nature reach the floor.

*

I think the problem of being adequately informed goes beyond the consent calendar items. Even with respect to bills on which there is a roll call I often have a hard time finding out what the issue is.

*

Lest we leave the impression legislation is too haphazard, we should remember that every piece of legislation which gets on the consent calendar has cleared the committee and has been cleared with the leadership. In addition, it must get past official objectors designated by each party. All of these hurdles have to be passed before you get it on the floor. There are other basic rules for the consent calendar, too. For example, an expenditure of less than $1 million must be involved, and the measure cannot have had an adverse report from the executive department concerned.

Occasionally, of course, errors occur. In 1960, for example, while

[7] According to a statement submitted in the opening days of the 88th Congress by the majority and minority objectors for the consent calendar, the following requirements should be met before a bill is passed by unanimous consent in the House: (1) It must involve aggregate expenditures of less than $1 million. (2) It should not change national or international policy. (3) It should not affect a majority of the congressional districts. If it does, and meets other requirements, it will be "passed over without prejudice" one or more times to permit congressmen to become informed as to its content. (4) It must not run counter to the President's program and should be the subject of reports from the Bureau of the Budget and the executive departments affected by such legislation.

trying to aid certain rural businessmen, the House voted to take minimum wage protection away from 14 million covered workers. The faulty proposal was offered as an amendment to a measure raising the minimum wage to $1.15. With only about twenty minutes debate remaining on the bill when the amendment came up, it slipped by on a voice vote, without opposition and with little discussion. It was intended to bar some farm processing workers from the coverage of the law, but as worded it actually removed all workers except those in cities of 250,000 or more. Remedial action followed quickly.

Primary Dependence on Self and Colleagues. Members of Congress indicate a heavy reliance on two main sources in arriving at a final decision regarding a vote: (1) their own personal judgment and (2) the views of trusted colleagues, usually those sitting on the committee having jurisdiction over the proposal under discussion. Most emphasize that the ultimate decision is their own, but the trusted colleague is mentioned nearly as frequently, particularly by representatives who have served more than one term. Since the colleagues consulted are nearly always of the same party as the member seeking advice, one could cite the practice as an indirect reinforcement of the influence of party in voting. Freshmen seem more anxious than their more senior associates to mention their independence of their districts when their own views conflict with those of their districts, though some are not anxious to publicize this independence. Said one freshman: "I came with the intention of voting my own convictions and not necessarily the will of the district. I consider that to be the proper view, although I don't think I would have wanted my constituents to know that while I was running for office."

Sources of Advice for Freshmen. When a group of freshmen members of Congress, interviewed separately, were asked to whom they turned in forming their judgments, they indicated in their responses that they placed great value on their own judgment. Beyond that, there was much divergence—colleagues, family, and friends, business associates, constituents, personal and committee staffs, party leadership, and state delegation deans being among the groups cited.

I cannot say I lean on any particular individual. I am likely to trust my own judgment first. I study the issues as best I can, then I contact key people in our district in whom I have confidence.

*

I listen to my fellow freshmen and I tend to turn more to junior congressmen in whom I have confidence, than to senior men. A Wednesday morning breakfast group which contains many new members and junior members has been very helpful.

*

Frankly the give-and-take between junior and senior congressmen is quite limited. I'm the sort of person who likes to make up his own mind. I do consult with my administrative assistant and talk with my law partner at home whenever I have a serious problem. Another source of assistance are my former associates in the state legislature. I talk occasionally to the dean of our state delegation. If the matter relates to my committee work, I often consult the committee counsel.

*

I am trying to become an expert in my committee assignment, and I rely on people of other committees to help me on other legislative matters, if I feel I don't have the information. Inversely, there are people on other committees I watch just because I expect to be on the opposite side from them.

*

When I was first elected I asked a friend, whose judgment I value very much, which member of the state delegation could be most helpful to me, was most likely to be informed on legislation, and could give me some idea of what a good congressman should do. I followed his advice, got acquainted with the member he suggested, and have never regretted it. I don't always agree with him, but I know I can go to him for honest advice.

*

I believe in party responsibility and I follow the President's lead wherever possible. Certainly there should be no criticism within the party for that action.

*

Primarily I depend on myself for decisions. I also turn often to my administrative assistant, and to my wife—she occasionally feels strongly I am doing the wrong thing. I also try to take advice from businessmen in my state. I turn also to senior members from my region regarding procedure and discuss issues with many of the new members, particularly those on my committee.

Relatively Little Leadership Pressure. Many new members of the House express surprise that so little pressure is exerted by the party leadership regarding voting. Clearly they had anticipated more frequent guidance or instruction. Their more senior colleagues also indicate that leadership intervention is minimal. Activities of the party whips prior to a vote generally consist of little more than perfunctory requests to be on the floor or occasional checks regarding the intended vote of the member. Seldom is advice given or a party position urged.

As long as the veteran Democratic and Republican leaders, Sam Rayburn and Joseph W. Martin, retained power, it was likely that leadership would be moved by pleas that, on certain issues, prevailing constituency opinion required individual congressmen to deviate from the official party position. It was also likely that relatively few demands would be made on members of the House, although adherents of both parties indicated their belief that "pressure" was more understandable when exerted by the party in control of the White House. Member consensus is that one should support one's party whenever it is possible to do so, and one or two veteran members caution that where a party position is known and one intends, for whatever reason, to vote contrary to it, it is wise to inform the leadership of that intention as early as possible.

As might be expected, constant deviation from the party position is likely to affect adversely the career and influence of a member of Congress. One of the most promising members to appear in the House in many years discovered early in his congressional career that his frequent votes in opposition to the stand taken by a majority of his party colleagues was the subject of much discussion and seemed destined to limit severely his influence within party councils. After a careful assessment of the situation, he set about to remedy it, with extraordinary results. On very important issues about which he has strong convictions, he stands firm despite his divergence from his fellows; on less crucial issues, he goes along wherever possible with the majority of his party. Conversations with some of his early critics reveal an almost complete reversal in their assessment of him. Though he is still regarded as somewhat atypical within his party (and has been denied the committee assignment he wants), respect for him has increased sharply, and there is no doubt that he is more effective than he would have been had he pursued his initial voting pattern.

In discussing the problem of casting intelligent votes in the House, one congressman declared that occasionally when members are called to the floor and arrive in the midst of a roll call, they may have difficulty in discovering what issues are involved in the vote or even the subject of the vote. In such instances, he complained, an inquiry at the party leader's table may result in advice on how to vote without an explanation of why that position should be supported. In illustration of his point he said:

Usually we have the bills and reports before us prior to voting, and ordinarily I take a look at those and make up my mind before going over to vote. Once in a

while you get there and are not prepared to cast a good vote or have not anticipated the vote. Usually, you ask some of the party leaders what the bill is all
about. Sometimes it is difficult to get any information. For example, today we
were voting on a not too important item because one of our people had demanded
a roll call. I went over to the leader's table and said, "What is this all about?
What are we voting on?" Do you know what I was told? "The vote is no." I
said, "Okay, the vote is no. Why should it be no? What is the issue?" The answer
was, "Someone is trying to give away a couple of hundred thousand dollars,
and we are against it." They don't seem to like it when you ask why you should
vote a certain way. I had to wander around to find someone who could explain
the issue to me. Then I voted.

Representatives, like most politicians, speak often of their independence, especially when voting is discussed. They resent actions which
might be construed as efforts to tell them how to vote. Yet, while emphasizing their determination to arrive at their own decisions, the legislators
may express irritation with the party leadership because of its failure to
state vigorously, and campaign aggressively for, its position on certain
proposals. Irritation of this kind is not infrequent and is almost always
expressed when the party position coincides with that of the outraged
member. Failure of the party to achieve success with respect to measures
in which congressional interviewees were especially interested, for
example, was commonly attributed, in part at least, to weak, half-
hearted leadership. "We could have defeated that bill," grumbled one
Democrat, "if Sam Rayburn had just applied the pressure instead of letting the word get out that while he hoped people would vote against it, he
realized we had to bear in mind the views of our districts." Liberal junior
Democrats, in the last days of the Eighty-sixth Congress, were especially
distressed by what they regarded as lack of effective leadership.[8] Many
of them were equally dissatisfied in the Eighty-seventh Congress, though
the leadership had changed.

Executive Leadership or Executive Pressure? Congressional members of a
political party that controls the presidency but has minority status within
the Congress find themselves under special psychological pressure to
support the administration's program, especially if the issue involved is
one on which the opposition can be expected to take the contrary position.
Passage of the President's program will normally be difficult enough

[8] A major cause of this dissatisfaction was the passage of the Landrum-Griffin labor
bill, which most liberals in the House opposed.

when his party is in the minority, and defections are regarded as somewhat more serious than would be true if he possessed a working majority.

During most of the Eisenhower administration, Congress was controlled by the Democrats, but the President's problem was further complicated by the tendency for the congressional Republicans to be more conservative—some of them inflexibly so—than the President. Unity was essential, but in the face of widespread hostility or unenthusiastic support for certain aspects of the program, how far could the President go in marshaling congressional Republicans behind his proposals? In view of the situation, it was not surprising to find within the ranks of the Republicans expressions of dissatisfaction with the efforts made to unite the party on legislation. Criticism of this sort, understandably, came largely from people who, favoring the administration's position, believed that its position was not clearly stated or that insufficient efforts were being made to ensure party support for it. The frustration of one member of this group is evident in the following discussion:

There have been some instances when I have felt the Executive should have taken a more positive position. Take a bill like Jenkins-Keogh, which the administration was against,[9] yet completely ignored for a while. I felt if they wanted us to vote against the bill they should start calling us up and sending arguments and making statements out of the White House. Yet nothing happened. The day we were to vote on the bill the Secretary of the Treasury came out with a statement against it.

*

One reason they didn't make a fight is that they figured the bill was going to be killed in the Senate. You must remember, too, that they can lose face if they make an all-out fight for a lost cause.

*

One problem I had was that accountants and lawyers from my district were badgering me to vote for the thing. I would say that the administration was against it, and they didn't know that. I called Treasury and said, "If you expect us to vote with you on this you'd better start publicizing your position." If the administration feels it is important to vote against or for something they have to build towards that end. They may not get their congressmen to go with them but they sure ought to try.

*

I have never seen the unconscionable pressure that was applied to me on the Reciprocal Trade Act which I opposed. Carrots were offered to one of my in-

[9] But which was supported by a majority of House Republicans.

dustries and then the whip was offered to me. I had some of the very high people in our government calling me personally and trying to persuade me.

There were attempts in the course of the same discussion to distinguish between executive leadership and executive pressure with respect to legislation.

There is a fine line between pressure and leadership. I would say that in the last four years I have heard more gripes among Republicans because they didn't know what the administration's position was than gripes about having too much pressure put on them. We occasionally have been embarrassed in our committee work because we haven't known the administration's position.

*

I think we all expect that on an important issue we should hear, directly or indirectly, from the administration as to its position. I wouldn't consider it pressure to be informed by them, directly or indirectly, of their position. I consider that to be leadership and if I choose not to vote with them that is my own decision.

Republicans generally agreed that the replacement as minority leader of Joe Martin by Charlie Halleck resulted in stronger party cohesion in the House and more effective leadership, in the Eighty-sixth Congress. However, there was some criticism that failure of the Republican administration to pursue its position energetically on legislation had provided an opportunity for the more conservative party leadership in the House to drag its feet occasionally. An excerpt from one discussion of Republican members illustrates this point. The group was talking about an action of the House in approving an appropriation for construction of a prison. Most of the members present had opposed the appropriation, but two who had supported it commented:

What irritated me was the fact that the story being spread was not factually true. It was said the administration was half-hearted in support of the legislation, which isn't true. The Attorney General testified for it. Those members of our party from the state concerned who opposed the legislation did so for political reasons. They felt passage might help the sponsor in his district, and he had defeated a Republican who was popular here.

*

The Attorney General was very clear that the prison was needed, that he wanted it, and that it was part of the President's program. Then on the floor I heard one influential Democrat argue the amendment was ridiculous because $10 million was needed for the prison and only $2 million was requested. I called the head of the Bureau of Prisons. He said that was absurd, $2 million was enough to get the thing started, the prison was needed and he was for it. I ran into the minority leader right before the vote and asked, "What is your position on this prison?" He said, "I hope to God we kill it." I asked, "What is the administration's position?" He said, "I don't think they really want it."

The experience of members of Congress with respect to receiving pressure from the party leadership—either that within the Congress or the administration—differs significantly. A partial explanation for the divergent testimony on this matter, it may be assumed, rests with differing interpretations of what constitutes pressure and what should be regarded as an expression of leadership. None of the Republicans attending the Brookings sessions had ever received a personal phone call from the President requesting their support for or against a measure, and the majority stated that no direct pressure had ever been applied to them. Although in many instances this might be attributable to the fact that on the important votes their preferences were known to be consistent with the party position anyway, in other cases their stand was in opposition to that of the leadership. While no one had been subjected to pressure often, several legislators identified specific measures on which they and colleagues had received strong overtures from the executive branch. Some participants often not sympathetic to the administration reacted to their testimony with genuine expressions of surprise.

The experiences and reactions of some members of Congress with respect to executive pressure are revealed in the exchange presented below, which also identifies several ways in which the executive attempts to influence votes.

I haven't been requested by anybody in the House or in the executive departments to vote a particular way on any measure. I have had representatives of the leadership say, "If you feel you can, we would like to have you go along on this bill." But as far as saying or intimating it might influence my future, that has never happened.

*

I have never had pressure but once and I am shocked to hear anyone say pressure is put on Republicans to vote a certain way.

*

Pressure *is* put on and I know about some of it. For example, one of the first problems I ran into was when the administration decided they wanted to extend the excess profits tax. I received calls from people in my district that were the result of calls to them from the administration. I made it very clear I thought the tactics were pretty lousy.

*

The use of the carrot is much more effective than the use of the stick. Placement of installations, judgeships, postmasterships, selection of appraisers by the Veterans Administration, jobs in the executive—these are made with votes in mind.

*

Last year the President listed three measures as criteria for determining support of the administration and even suggested he might go out and fight you if you voted against them—foreign aid, reciprocal trade, and defense reorganization. Several of you were, like myself, in the position of having to oppose him on at least two of the three. Were you subjected to any pressures? I wasn't even asked to support them.

*

An Assistant Secretary of Commerce, knowing my antagonism to the Reciprocal Trade Act, approached me with a booklet showing the amount of business being brought into my district by the measure and the number of jobs involved: he did that for every congressional district in the country. I don't think that is pressure. The executive did a better job selling members of Congress on this legislation than any other legislation I know of. It was a demonstration of leadership.

*

I don't mean to contribute to your disillusionment, but as far as I can see it was a case of executive pressure. Until just before the vote I felt the proposed amendments [weakening the act, in the opinion of its supporters] would carry. Then things happened. Cabinet officials were calling congressmen with whom they had the most influence, the bait was held out of direct subsidies on lead and zinc, and things just went "a-scooting." Also it was an election year and many Republicans wanted to be with the administration.

*

Don't you think it might have been a combination of pressure plus presentation?

*

I'd say that westerners were pretty much inclined to vote against the bill until the Mineral Stabilization program was announced with the blessing of the administration. I am not going to say they didn't buy a lot of votes with that program. I have always been for reciprocal trade and probably would vote for it again, but I know a few boys who voted for it for that reason.

*

There is another, indirect pressure on us Republicans, too. I know I feel it frequently because of the fact that I often find myself in disagreement with the administration position. When it comes right down to party responsibility and you know your vote may make the difference between passage or defeat of a measure, it is much more difficult to vote against it than it is when you can say, "Oh well, it is going to pass anyway and I can vote as I see it."

*

This is all sort of amazing to me. I guess I have the poorest record of any Republican in support of the administration, except for one or two members. But no one has tried to put pressure on me. When I was going to vote against the administration position on reciprocal trade, a cabinet member spoke to me about it and asked whether I couldn't go along on it. I said no. On a couple of other bills, people have called me, but they didn't try pressure. They didn't offer to do anything for my district, or promise to campaign for me, or offer me any bribes. It was the sort of action I would call leadership, executive effort to get their position across.

One device used by the executive to strengthen the base of its support in Congress is to encourage important community leaders and organization officials to write their congressmen urging them to back or oppose certain proposals. Although there is widespread agreement that the Chief Executive has a right—and perhaps a responsibility—to seek passage of measures in which he believes, some legislators are not enthusiastic about his resorting to that particular technique, especially when more direct approaches are not fully used. Congressmen clearly believe that Congress should be consulted in advance by the Executive. While risks are involved in such consultations, many a worthwhile proposal has foundered because of a failure to adhere to this policy. The following discussion took place in the Republican group:

The President made no bones about the fact he had written to about fifty top executives saying, "Do what you can for my military organization plan."

*

He didn't write and ask them to get in touch with you and try to persuade you, did he?

*

Yes. Don't you think he did? It was reported he had done so. The men who wrote me were all loyal Republicans and large contributors to the party. They were of such a calibre that they wouldn't have accepted a suggestion from anybody who wasn't pretty important. I don't see why the President shouldn't do that. I think a Chief Executive has the right to write anybody he wants to.

*

I am not condemning him for his action. I think I would have done the same thing under the circumstances if I felt strongly about that bill. You use any tool that comes to your hand. You want to change minds.

*

As you will recall, he had a love feast with the Republican House members this spring and said that his support would go to members who supported three bills—foreign aid, reciprocal trade, and defense reorganization. And a good batting average was 33⅓ percent—we all tried to get at least that.

*

I heard that speech and I didn't think there was anything wrong with it. That is my idea of leadership. I think a Chief Executive is entitled to do that. I have a feeling that over his shoulder might come the thought that all Republicans are valuable to him at this particular time because when they are getting scarcer and scarcer people might be allowed latitude to express their own feelings.

*

Well, *I* object to it until the reasons and facts are presented to the people involved. I don't object to the Executive taking a strong position if he is doing so with knowledge of the issues and after consultation with members of his own party in the Congress who have some knowledge of the subject.

Influence of the District. Those legislators who decide that the best way to ensure continued success at the polls is to adhere closely to district sentiment on issues often discover that ascertaining the preferences of the constituency is not always an easy task. And, some solons declare, the public is fickle: legislators may be held accountable for judgments which, though consistent with prevailing district views at the time they were made, eventually prove to have been unsound. As one conference participant stated, "You must be as smart in prospect as they [the voters] are in retrospect."

To gauge the thinking of district residents with respect to important issues, members of Congress rely heavily on their own conversations with friends and acquaintances, party leaders, and newsmen back home to provide them with information as to local reaction. Congressional mail may be an important factor, although it should be clear that the form letter and the mass mailing ordinarily have little impact. District newspapers are generally read by the congressman and/or his staff, but they tend to be considered a somewhat less accurate index of district opinion. Another rough guide is the questionnaire "poll" which a majority of the House members distribute annually within their constituencies. In recent years, an increasing number of legislators are turning to scientific samplings of district sentiment undertaken by professional polling organizations.

Some representatives believe efforts to stay attuned to district sentiment are doomed to disappointment since the citizens themselves are subjected to so many cross-pressures by the mass media that they cannot reach very firm judgments on public issues; nearly every legislator agrees that constituents do not give or withhold electoral support solely, or even primarily, on the basis of recorded votes. Said one congressman:

The huge bombardment of our citizens means they have little time to concentrate on what congressmen are doing. Things are so complex now and there are so many media providing information to individuals that I don't think they know which way to turn. There are millions of stimuli and it is difficult to know how they arrive at a decision.

Uncertainty regarding the preferences of constituents distresses many congressmen. True, discretion in voting becomes more permissible or acceptable if it is concluded that no strong mandate is evident, but the danger exists that a serious misinterpretation of local views or ignorance of firmly held opinions may prove fatal to the elected official. Thus, as one able congressman put it, how far you go beyond your interpretation of district preference depends primarily on whether you think the proposed deviation is "viable." The following discussion of Democratic congressmen includes many points commonly raised with respect to the issue.

The key is that we members of Congress behave as one would normally expect us to. We represent our districts.

*

We go beyond the district. You left the party's farm program, for example, and I have stayed with it, for reasons that relate to our districts. TVA is still viable as an idea in your district, but the farm program no longer is. It is in my city which has 67 percent of its income based on agriculture and the remainder based on manufacturing.

*

Who knows what is viable? That is the big question I have. I think it is almost, if not completely, impossible—at least in city districts—for a representative to know what a majority of the people think. I don't think there is any way of finding out.

*

All I am saying is that we decide we are able to stick with our ideologies, our views, our judgments, with relation to the effective opposition in our district.

*

I think in terms of pressures being imposed and I don't think the majority of the people put pressures on you. Your pressures come from organizations and you respond to the organizations. For example, take the bill which came to the floor yesterday. The doctors and lawyers were for it, and many congressmen voted for the bill because of them. Yet I think if it were explained fully, a majority of the people wouldn't be for it.

Votes May Not Be What They Seem. It is true, too, that recorded votes do not always mean what they seem to mean. Measures may be passed by one body by large margins after assurances that the other body will scuttle them; the purpose may be to permit congressmen to be recorded so as to enhance their stature back home. Sometimes understanding colleagues rally behind an associate who needs support in his district, secure in the knowledge that a House-Senate conference will eliminate the not-too-meritorious measure he is sponsoring. The following discussion concerns a bill passed by the House:

His friends certainly rallied around and showed up today. Yesterday afternoon when [the bill] was first discussed no one was on the floor, but today everyone was out backing him. The Appropriations Committee had stricken a $10 million budget item and he moved to put back $2 million believing his district would get the construction.

*

Rumor has it that _____ [an important committee chairman] wants the project in his own district. I heard that he got the subcommittee to keep the item out of the bill until he got an agreement from the administration to have it built in his district.

*

It was amazing. Of all congressmen except _____, the sponsor could be expected to have the smallest following in the House. Yet he got out the vote.

*

There were other things involved, I assume. The money was included in the President's budget and that made it easier than pushing for something not in the budget. He made an excellent presentation, and he did an excellent job of contacting people in advance to get them on the floor to help him.

*

I talked to a Democrat from my state who wasn't around today when we voted, but who was working hard in opposition to the amendment yesterday. When I asked him why he was missing he said the leadership had agreed to give a favorable vote because they had gotten agreement from the Senate that they would knock it out of the appropriations bill and then in conference nobody would push for it. The House sponsor wouldn't be put on the conference committee. What harm had been done? He had made his pitch and was successful, would be regarded as a big hero back home, and yet the bill could be killed.

Logic Not the Sole Determinant. Congressional voting is a complex process which involves many considerations not always readily observed or understood by the outsider. Perhaps the best explanation of why its mysteries sometimes escape many observers is that offered by one freshman member of Congress. Said he:

> You've got to realize that not only are we sitting there trying to analyze legislation, trying to do the best job we can, but that factors other than absolute reason are always entering the situation. We are not participating in this process in an academic environment, secluded from pressures and other factors which may not be competely relevant to the situation at hand. We are operating in a political environment, surrounded by lobbyists, constituents, the leadership, and jangling telephones and we virtually have no time alone to think and reflect upon the problems before us. The big miracle is that somehow all of this works. On paper, looking at the situation, you'd say it couldn't possibly work and yet the fact is that it does.

The legislative process is, as it should be, the central interest of most representatives. The congressman is both attracted and humbled by the difficulty of making wise decisions. He is frustrated by his inability to master all subjects of legislation, but he finds ways of informing himself, or of getting cues from trusted prompters in voting, and so evolves his own scheme of decision making. Yet he sometimes worries lest some inadvertent slip or unpredictable circumstance turn his constituents against him. His knowledge of the House grows with experience, but he never ceases to be amazed by the nuances of the legislative process itself.

IV

Pressure Groups and Legislation

THE impact of lobbyists and the organizations they represent on the course of legislation in the United States has been a popular subject for scrutiny in recent years. Because of the publicity given to early, blatantly improper attempts to influence legislators, the general public views with suspicion anyone classified as a lobbyist. The constructive services that are provided by today's professionals are often little known. Congressmen frequently comment on this fact, generally expressing regret that the functions, activities, and motives of lobbyists are so commonly misunderstood: "It is unfortunate that the term lobbyist is associated in the public mind with somebody smoking a cigar, lurking in the corridors, trying to lure congressmen to parties, and that sort of thing."

Although most legislators seem to regard the executive branch as the principal source of legislation, it is recognized that in certain subject matter fields the influence of interest groups is strong. As the following discussion illustrates, there even are congressmen who believe that these organizations are the primary source of legislative proposals. Certainly they seek to maintain cordial relationships with as many members of Congress as possible, particularly those whose committee assignments are most relevant to the activities of the pressure groups.

Both the executive branch and the party leadership rank higher in the review or veto category in terms of what comes out of committee, but from the standpoint of inspiring legislation I think the special interests are the principal source. Their role is even greater than that of the executive.

*

The interest groups have two swings at legislation. They intervene at the executive level and then again at the legislative level through members of committees. I don't think there is anything heinous about that practice. They are entitled to a voice in what is done in Congress and to have their proposals reviewed and considered.

*

A lot of people seem to think that lobbying is a bad thing. I think that is one misconception which still needs to be corrected as far as the general public is concerned. Lobbying is an essential part of representative government, and it needs to be encouraged and appreciated. [Lobbyists] are frequently a source of information. If they come to your offices and explain a program or factors contributing to the need for legislation, you get a better understanding of the problems and the answers to them. If you have your independence, and I think we all do, they can teach you what an issue is all about, and you can make your own decision. There can be bad lobbying techniques, of course, but basically lobbying is a good thing.

There is no doubt that the representations of interest organizations are considered by members of Congress, even though they may have little discernible effect on the ultimate determination of the position of the member. As one highly respected liberal congressman puts it:

These pressure groups do complicate matters or influence congressmen more than just in the sense of how many battalions they have at election time. Maybe this is a confession of my own weakness, but if I receive a corporate or institutional position, it means a little more to me than an individual representation. This includes the whole spectrum of interest groups, from the Chamber of Commerce and N.A.M. to the more radical unions, although of course the effect of the plea depends somewhat on the nature of the group making it.

Congressional testimony regarding the percentage of legislative measures on which they are aware of organized pressure varies from one third to one half on up to 100 percent. The number of measures on which they feel "pushed" is considerably smaller, however, and, to the surprise of some members, on many very important pieces of legislation there is virtually no pressure or expression of organized opinion at all.

Lobbying to influence legislation has become a major activity. In 1962, more than three hundred lobby organizations reported spending in excess of $4,200,000 to influence legislation, seven of them listing expenditures of over $100,000,[1] on the ground that influencing legislation is not their principal purpose. This figure is not a true measure of the extent of lobbying activity since the provisions of the act under which the organizations file reports are so vague that some groups which lobby Congress do not file at all. Others vary significantly in the percentage of their operating costs they report.

[1] The seven were: National Committee for Insurance Taxation; AFL-CIO (National Headquarters); United Federation of Postal Clerks (AFL-CIO); American Farm Bureau Federation; United States Savings and Loan League; the American Legion; and the National Housing Conference.

Techniques of Lobbying

The techniques of interest groups actively engaged in attempting to influence legislation vary, depending in part on the size, power, interest, and scope of operation of the organization involved.

While most members of Congress can identify individual lobbyists and organizations they find distasteful and irritating and whose methods they regard as unfair, there is virtually unanimous accord that the bribery and direct approach, which characterized an earlier era, is practically nonexistent today. Only one participant in the Brookings round tables indicated he had been subjected to anything of that nature, and after he had related the circumstances, there was emphatic agreement that such a proposal was most unusual. Said the congressman:

Several years ago one of my colleagues came to me and told me he was a director of a corporation that had some plants in my area, or was establishing some. He said the people in his group had no particular bill of goods to sell, but that they were trying to establish a good atmosphere for themselves in this new operation and needed some public relations help in that field. He asked me if I was active in public relations work. He knew I had been associated with a newspaper and knew a lot of the editors and newspaper people in the area. When I told him I was not in public relations work, he said that what his group had in mind was nothing more than somebody to get out a release about once a month about something of general interest to the plant. He pointed out, however, that it was important to find someone with contacts, who knew all the editors. He added that he did not expect the work would take much time and that they could not pay too much for it, not more than $400 or $500 a month. I asked whether it was something that would be used in relation with my being in Congress, and he replied in the negative, adding that contacts I had before I came to Congress was all that was needed. I didn't see how I could do that but saw that it might provide an opportunity for me to set up some sort of business I might move on to when I got moved out of this job. I knew two or three newspapermen at home who could set it up, with whom I could be a silent partner. Thus I said that I would be interested in talking about it. The president of the company was interested in legislation before our committee at that time but, of course, he didn't mention it to me. The legislation came to a head within a few days, and my viewpoint did not coincide with his. I have never seen him since. I feel sure that was an effort to do some pretty direct lobbying.

Although there are occasional exceptions, it is clear that the most satisfactory means of obtaining individual congressional endorsement for a group's legislative goals is to provide support in the form of research, campaign workers, and money rather than to bring pressure to bear. In many ways this is the age of the "soft sell" in lobbying work. Fear of reprisal at the polls for failure to support a powerful group's position on legislation is, of course, a factor of varying importance to the legislators. But gone are the crude attempts to buy support; today's efforts to bring about enactment of specific proposals—or to prevent tampering with favorable legislation already on the books—are far more subtle. The professional lobbyist seems to have discovered that fact, logic, assistance, and goodwill achieve the best results over the long term. Belligerent, shady, or bombastic advocacy may be effective in an isolated situation but tends to jeopardize or destroy future relationships and thus seldom is worth the gamble.

Votes versus Money. When the question of the effectiveness of lobbying groups was raised at one discussion, a member of the House commented "you would have to put the question in terms of how effective certain pressure groups are in elections, and if you got back to that first point you could talk a little about how effective they were after elections." Another congressman explained: "We are more interested in votes than we are in any particular economic group." After a colleague had remonstrated that "that is a rather callous way of putting it," the speaker persisted "we are representatives in Congress, and we are thinking in terms of the votes in our districts."

In the same vein another congressman said:

When you measure pressure, you measure it in terms of what the groups do in an election period. In my area, railway labor's Political League is one of the most aggressive and active campaign organizations I know. It really does a job of informing its members of who has been friendly to railroad labor. Their activity, of which they give you tangible evidence during a campaign, is certainly a factor to think about when you look at the group's position on a bill affecting it.

A further comment on the activities of railway labor's Political League emphasized an important point: "While contributions are always gratefully received at campaign time, even more appreciated is organizational assistance in lining up votes, furnishing campaign workers or perhaps even providing advice as to strategy at crucial points." Observed one of the most astute members of Congress:

Their influence should be defined as ability to influence the electorate rather than in terms of the campaign kitty. When railway labor and management work together, they can get a bill through Congress without trouble. When labor was on one side and management on the other, labor had enough votes to override a veto. This shows congressmen are thinking in terms of influence with the voters and ability to convert this influence into votes rather than in terms of money.

This is not to argue that financial assistance does not result in substantial advantage to the contributor. As one representative stressed in making the point that bribery and similar methods are all but passé, campaign contributions often constitute a wise investment for the group seeking to influence elected officials and public policy.

Obviously the smart operator now is not going to offer a bribe or even put someone on his payroll. That is a rather crude way of doing things. But campaigns cost more and more, and if you are going to have any influence on a candidate, you are going to do it the legal way and help him in his campaign contributions. Now I don't think that a congressman looks back and votes according to campaign contributions received, but he can't help being indirectly influenced by what his friends think. He knows that his friends are the ones who back him financially in a campaign so indirectly they are going to influence his decisions.

Providing Information. Congressmen recognize that lobbying as ordinarily practiced represents a relatively efficient and effective means for an interest organization and its membership to present its case, and they appreciate the informing and watchdog functions such groups perform. In many instances lobbying organizations constitute a valuable source of information, sometimes providing worthwhile ideas for legislation as well as protecting the legislator from embarrassing errors.

The interest group that is in a position to furnish relevant research material to congressmen tends to profit from such activities. If drafts of speeches and public statements can be supplied, so much the better. And interest group rapport with some committees is occasionally so close that their representatives may be invited to sit in on executive committee sessions when legislation is being drawn or discussed.

The evidence is strong that many congressmen are not aware of the variety and volume of assistance that is available to them from lobbying groups. Those members who have discovered and tapped this source are usually well satisfied and come to regard it as an important adjunct of their regular resources. Anyone utilizing the research facilities of the larger organizations realizes that many of them will go to extraordinary lengths, in terms of both time and expense, to fulfill congressional requests for information, briefs, and speeches. Once congressmen learn to trust them, they turn to them often. Explained one Republican:

You get to know certain groups who have to be regarded as lobbying and you know their position. On numerous occasions I have called on the Farm Bureau and said "I feel this way about legislation. Would you give me some material on it?" They perform a very valuable function. I have contacted them several times but to the best of my knowledge they have never contacted me. The Library of Congress can be used under certain circumstances, but quite often I don't have confidence in their research or its quality. I prefer to call on someone who I know agrees with my position.

All the activities mentioned, if undertaken on a wide scale, expand and complicate staffing and workload problems of the organizations involved. At the same time, the expansion of these services indicates that such endeavors have proved effective in establishing good working relationships between lobbying groups and congressmen.

Not only individual legislators and committees but various blocs within the Congress have learned that interest groups can be of substantial aid in promoting a cause in which a bloc is interested. In addition to providing debate materials, the groups assist in planning strategy and contact congressmen outside the bloc. For their part the interest organizations have discovered the value of teamwork. A joint effort by groups interested in the same legislative result permits a pooling of resources and a more efficient distribution of workload as well as increasing the number of congressmen who can be drawn into the effort.

Staffing Congressional Offices. Interestingly enough, some Republicans feel that organizations such as COPE and ADA do far more than furnish their opponents with speeches and other materials: they are sure these groups actually staff the offices of many Democrats. Said one Republican, "I understand there are a hundred on the other side who have legislative assistants put in by COPE." The opinion, though unsubstantiated, is not an isolated one. It should be noted, too, that office assistance has sometimes been provided on a temporary basis by interest groups to members of Congress of both parties.

Letter Writing Campaigns. Mass letter writing campaigns usually fall short of their goal because they are so obviously inspired. Most such undertakings consist of mimeographed appeals to which a constituent has signed his name, or of form letters that have been carefully—sometimes not too carefully—copied by voters and mailed to their congressman. This method risks antagonizing the recipient and is ineffective unless the number received reaches staggering proportions. As a rule the congressman is only mildly irritated by this approach, largely because he dismisses the letters as an inaccurate reflection of constituent opinion and the work of an interest group. Says one member:

> Pressure groups often go off the track in that they fail to take into consideration the mentality of the members of their organizations. I have received letters starting off: "Dear Congressman: Please write your congressman and senators and tell them so and so." You can tell from the letters whether the people are really thinking, whether the issue really is important to them, or whether they are writing just because they have been told to do so. I pay little attention to the form letter that comes in. It obviously comes from some headquarters.

Though recognizing volume mail of the variety described as practically meaningless as an index of district sentiment, congressmen can occasionally turn it to advantage as did the freshman who said "I liked them (mass letter campaigns) when I first came down. They gave me a mailing list." And frequently an organization member will resist the request of his leadership to write a letter on one side of an issue and instead send off a letter describing what he has been asked to do and why he does not agree with the group's position. Such a communication can be very damaging to the group's chances of influencing the congressman. This is especially true if the letter is but one of a number, and the congressman is undecided or leaning away from them already. A common congressional reaction is that "one original letter has more weight than one hundred form letters."

There is no doubt, however, that genuine expressions of opinion from home are carefully considered by congressmen, and that the organizational appeal that can produce a moderate supply of thoughtful, self-composed letters on an issue has advanced the cause considerably. Congressmen do not weigh the pro and con mail to determine their position, as is sometimes charged, but they are highly sensitive to informed district opinion.

Testifying before Committees. Some interest groups welcome—and eagerly seek—opportunities to testify before congressional committees, while others are less prone to engage in such activities. Occasionally, interest group testimony will influence legislation.

One hears congressmen state they have changed position on pending bills as a result of testimony presented before their committee or after reading committee hearings and reports, and sometimes legislation is suggested by such testimony. Often, however, the results are less encouraging to the pressure groups. Some representatives complain that year after year the same interest groups, represented by the same witnesses, appear before committees and present essentially the same testimony, offering no new evidence or fresh ideas. Said one congressman at the conclusion of lengthy hearings before his committee: "Any objective person who will review any of our major hearings on any subject over a period of years will agree that a preponderant part of the testimony is to a large extent repetitious or covers obvious and minor points." Further, the severe time limitations under which most congressmen function make it unlikely that testimony contained in hearings will be read by more than a small minority of the House. These same limitations cause committee members to suggest that the number of witnesses and the time provided for testimony should be reduced sharply. Prospective witnesses are often urged to submit prepared statements for insertion in the record and to forego a personal appearance.

If the purpose of testifying extends beyond the desire to impress the organization's membership with the vigor and activity of its leadership, there are skeptics who believe the results disappointing. Most organizations can find congressional sponsors for their proposals, it is argued, and need not rely on exciting a member's interest at a hearing. While it is important to demonstrate that a bill possesses support or faces opposition, congressmen are not particularly moved to learn that groups whose position can logically be surmised are indeed maintaining that position. At the very least, however, testifying before a committee affords a forum from which a group can obtain national publicity—a subject of irritation to some legislators—while at best the results can be more far-reaching. Though hearings may be poorly attended and reports little read, the most interested and ambitious of congressmen are more likely to be reached, and the organization can always hope its position will awaken the interest and support of some of them.

Sponsoring Meetings. The breakfasts and dinners sponsored by pressure groups are less favorably regarded than most of their activities. When asked to name some of the least appealing aspects of their job a substantial proportion of the congressmen queried mentioned attendance at such functions. Some flatly decline to attend, pleading other commitments; some put in an appearance, seldom remaining for the length of the affair; others gamely attend, regarding it as a necessary though aggravating part of their duties; only a few seem not to mind them. Many congressmen follow a policy of accepting no such invitations unless some of their constituents are going to be present. Interest groups, realizing this, now often mention in their communication that residents of the member's district will be coming to Washington to be present, occasionally even listing them; sometimes the constituents themselves extend the invitation or supplement that of the organization with a note that they will be present and hope to see the congressman there also.

Occasionally, members fear that their absence from organizational gatherings will provoke unfavorable comparisons with members of the other political party. Lamented one congressman:

> I resent all the dinners and receptions to which we are invited because they are such a waste of time. But you really have to go because the host organizations see to it that delegations from your district are present. You go there and eat a much too rich dinner and listen to a not too interesting program. All these dinners knock the tar out of your work. One problem for me is that it becomes a competitive thing in a mixed delegation. I am the only member of my party from my state. The other members of the state delegation here would like to make me look bad so they go, which means I have to go too.

Organizationally sponsored meetings do not always achieve the results desired, of course. During the 1959 debate over labor legislation the Teamsters sponsored a series of breakfasts for congressmen which were well attended, but much criticized by opponents of the Teamsters position. In commenting on one of these meetings, one of the most liberal Republicans, a man often favorable to the labor position on legislation, said:

> I think pressure groups sometimes influence congressmen in the opposite way from what they hope. They become so concerned with their own particular views

they are likely to not even recognize the fact that there could be another. In their eagerness to blast home their position to the members of Congress who may attend their gatherings, they may alienate some congressmen who are, to say the least, pretty free thinking individuals. I think the Teamsters group has had that impact.

Another of his colleagues, also of liberal bent, agreed:

I was at another Teamsters breakfast with the same result. I went with an open mind. When they were through talking and giving their pitch, so much of what they said was inaccurate and not factual and there was so much demagogic nonsense that I was repelled by the whole thing.

A representative of more conservative persuasion had a similar reaction:

It was to be a sweetness and light breakfast, and every effort was made to conciliate. Yet it became ugly before it was over. It was a little like the Vice President of the Teamsters Union in my district who called on me one Sunday morning saying he merely wanted me to see what a teamster looked like, that perhaps I had the wrong impression.

Visiting Congressional Offices. There is little doubt that the increasing complexity of government and the rapid extension of federal authority into virtually all aspects of life have complicated the task of the Washington lobbyists. Their ranks have increased markedly, creating a serious problem. With congressmen pressed on all sides for allocations of their time, it is increasingly difficult for all but the closest of friends, or representatives of the most powerful of groups, to gain the access necessary to provide the legislator with complete information about the organizational position. Frequent visits to congressional offices are usually not appreciated, either by the congressman or his staff. Virtually any Hill employee can cite instances where lobbyists, apparently oblivious to their true status with a legislator, have worn out their welcome by dropping by too regularly, intent on talking with the congressman rather than with his aide. Though circumstances may cause the member to be reluctant to refuse to see the lobbyist, there is little doubt that he would prefer to spend his time in other ways, especially when the visit seems largely social.

At the same time, despite the large number of lobbyists in Washington, many legislators report that few call on them, a situation they do not find displeasing.

Decentralization of Activities

The trend toward centralization of government has somewhat para-
doxically led to decentralization of many lobbying activities. In recent
years, increasing attention has been focused on the development of activities in the locale of individual representatives rather than solely on
those of the national office. Grass roots lobbying, which the 1950
Buchanan Committee investigations found had come to represent the core
of effective lobbying, has both supplanted and supplemented Washington
activities. There is little question that the impact is greater when a group
can make its case to a congressman by using its officials and rank and file
membership in his area, preferably people known to the legislator. This
is true whether a committee ("committees on the whole are more impressed by the guys from the field") or a single congressman is involved.
("Lobbyists are effective only as grass roots media. The state organizations are pretty effective. Naturally the best ones are those which can
use men from your area to convince you, rather than someone at the
national level whom you don't know.")

Even when the congressman is unsympathetic with the general philosophy of the organization, he sometimes is reluctant to dismiss lightly
the views of its local representatives. As one Democrat explained it:

> The National Farm Bureau has absolutely no effect on me. I just toss this
> material away when I get it because I know they don't represent the views of the
> farmers in my district . . . on the other hand, the president of one of the county
> farm bureaus in my district would have much more weight.

Two other Democrats discussed the successful shift in focus on the
part of one interest group:

> One special interest lobby, which has perhaps done the best job by withdrawing
> from the Hill, is the private utility lobby. About ten years ago they were here in
> force with a big office and were working like mad. Soon they realized that the
> way to get to the congressman was back home with the voters. Today their real
> effort is made at the grass roots. And they can control more votes among in-
> dividual congressmen than any other special interest lobby.

*

> The private utilities have spent millions of dollars on slick newspaper ad-
> vertising against public power. Almost any magazine you pick up has had a full
> page ad about taking the taxpayer's dollars out of his pockets and putting them

in the pockets of someone under a public power project. They have done a tremendous job at the local level: they get back to the original source of votes and stir up the people.

*

They pinpointed. They did a real legislative job. They started a long time ago and analyzed where they were and what they had to do, and they got the right person to carry the ball for them. They were among the big spenders and they were ineffective. Eventually they pulled back, began to spend more money on analysis and local operations and today they are four times as effective as they were then.

Withdrawal to the local level for one phase of lobbying activity has not resulted in eliminating the necessity of maintaining a strong central organization. Indeed in many ways it has served to demonstrate the importance of such an operation. The effectiveness of the local appeal depends in large measure on the alertness, the persuasiveness, and the ingenuity of the central office. It can help promote favorable contacts with an individual congressman by providing him with special services of a research nature. In addition to furnishing the legislator with factual information, many such groups are able to pinpoint the power and influence of the organization in terms of his district. Thus organizations representing postal employees and railway labor have prepared materials indicating their numerical strength in individual congressional districts. They can assist their cause by maintaining elaborate fact sheets on individual congressmen which include information as to their close friends (both within Congress and back in the district), voting record, hobbies, and organizational affiliations, as well as lists of opinion leaders among their constituents. The central office is thus often in a position to advise the locals on the most effective approaches to legislators. Its familiarity with the practical operation of the Congress enables it to provide the field forces with excellent guidance should they come to Washington. By following congressional activity closely it can often anticipate a legislative crisis likely to confront the organization and develop an over-all plan with which to meet it. One congressman described the way in which some central offices alert their membership:

They are very good at sitting in offices here and figuring out ways to get their people back home scared. I got back to the district, and my wife told me that in five minutes the association against raising the minimum wage would be there. About fifteen of them arrived. One fellow served as spokesman and said,

"Now, Bob you tell the congressman what this minimum wage will do to you."
They went around the room, and it took an hour for them to finish. I told them
there was not going to be any minimum wage legislation this year and that there
was no need to commit ourselves completely now. They said they knew better,
that their organization had informed them it was imminent—the corner druggist,
the retail stores, etc. would all be covered by the minimum wage.

In addition, by creating an atmosphere in which a candid, objective
exchange can take place between representative and lobbyist, the staff can
sometimes develop a situation in which legislators like to deal with them
and are predisposed to be sympathetic to the group's activities. As the
congressman said:

> The people who come from the districts are not very well trained in lobbying.
> The regular Washington representatives are really the capable ones. Not only
> are they the most capable but they are the most help to us because we get to
> know them and learn to respect them. They give you the truth and we learn to
> depend on them for information.

Lobbyist Types

There are many types of interest groups, and their aims and influence
differ markedly. Many of them appeal to only a small minority of the
members of Congress; a few have nearly universal impact. In describing
railway labor, one congressman said:

> It is one of the few groups that has an almost across-the-board effect. It has
> influence on people from the far right of the conservative spectrum all the way to
> as far left as we get in American politics. It is nearly unique in this respect—most
> groups have very limited effectiveness in terms of influence, not geographically so
> much as ideologically.

Certain groups and categories of groups earn special congressional
comment. Thus, noting the unusual success with which conservationist
organizations seemed able to arouse their membership to communicate
with their legislators on even minor legislative proposals, one legislator
observed that while such groups "may not always be the most effective,
they certainly are the fiercest." There is general accord that they do
possess crusade-like fervor and that they are remarkably successful in
persuading their membership to make their wishes known to their representatives.

Another member stated that the lobbying of the "noble minded" was unusual and the more effective because few of the programs they advocated provided direct benefit to their members. Whether they are more effective is questionable. Though many congressmen are sympathetic to these groups and the programs they support, they seldom regard their admonitions as being as significant politically as the "bread and butter" lobbies, which restrict their advocacy to matters of direct concern to their membership. Many legislators regard the latter as the most consistently effective type. They not only have a genuine interest in the causes they espouse but an economic stake in success. Thus they are more likely to deal firmly with recalcitrant legislators whenever it is within their power to do so. A weakness of certain of the church and idealistic groups is that their Washington representatives are often neither realistic nor practical either in their approach to the Congress, their analysis of the issues, or the strategy they choose. The result is that though they are given a pleasant hearing, they are not influential in changing votes.

Calibre of Lobbyists

There is little doubt that the effectiveness of a lobbying group is affected appreciably by the calibre, personality, and approach of its representatives. The best lobbyist is the reasonable man. Observed one legislator:

An important point is whether the pressure group is represented by reasonable people or people who give the impression of being reasonable. Recently our committee held hearings and heard testimony from many groups. The representative of the Anti-Defamation League of the B'Nai Brith came in and had the entire committee, including the Southerners, eating out of his hand. Testifying on the same side of the issue the next day was the representative of the American Jewish Congress who antagonized everyone. It was just the approach which made the difference.

Another House member made a similar point:

I have found you can't depend on all the lobbies. I think the most dangerous person I have ever seen is _____ who has no scruples of any kind, who would resort to almost anything to get his point across. He is completely dishonest. I think he is going to lose and in the process his group will lose too.

The individual referred to has succeeded in arousing the antagonism of many members of Congress. One member observed that state officials

of the organization the lobbyist represents "think he is the most dangerous man representing any group." Another was reminded of testimony
the man had given before his committee in which the lobbyist had
implied that anyone not supporting his position was a communist and
subverter. Few lobbyists, it should be emphasized, trigger such unfavorable reactions from congressmen. Where they do, it should not necessarily be inferred that the lobbyist is ineffective, though often that is the
situation; sometimes he is both aggressive and effective, arousing violent
reactions from legislators who disagree with his position.

Although congressmen are quick to note that the calibre of lobbyists
varies tremendously, most seem to believe that, on balance, it is relatively
high. As one member stated:

> Lobbyists can be over criticized. Actually they are a pretty reasonable bunch,
> not normally stupid, and seldom offensive. On balance they are a plus. They tend
> to be articulate and to use the right approach. The important thing is to be able
> to respect the man you talk to and to approach his problem with an open mind.
> I think that in general lobbyists respect congressmen, and their approach tends
> to be that of a man who wants to present his case but not in such a manner as to
> make it offensive.

Another is less equivocal:

> The calibre of lobbyists is good, and they perform a valuable service. I have
> never been asked to do anything against my conscience or anything I have con-
> sidered less than above board. In my opinion lobbyists are well informed and
> effective and well worth what they are paid.

While not all congressmen are convinced that lobbyists are of high
quality, few assert that they are incompetent as a group. Yet this view
is expressed occasionally. One junior congressman—a northern liberal
who has fought hard for the labor position on legislation—had this to say:

> I am not impressed with lobbyists. As a matter of fact, I have been quite sur-
> prised at the mediocrity of the individual lobbyist. During the struggle over the
> labor bill last session, I was shocked at the labor lobbying. Not all labor lobbyists
> fall into that category but a great many of them do. They were unsure of what
> they wanted, and they changed their positions from day to day. The ones who
> were intelligent were so different from the others that they stood out. Probably
> we do not see the top representatives of lobbying groups, but the ones we do see
> are not persuasive and tend to know little.

Impressing the Membership

A Democrat who has had executive branch experience did not doubt the ability of lobbyists but had a more serious criticism:

I feel very strongly that the lobbies need to be exposed. Lobbyists mislead their own members much more than they inform Congress. They seem determined to keep their membership inflamed in order to justify their existence. Ninety nine percent of the information they disseminate is misleading and many false statements are made. The reaction of the public shows that the people just don't know what is going on. The lobbyists as they presently perform their responsibilities are not rendering service to the nation or to the people they represent. For the most part, they are pretty intelligent men, and I can't understand why they do what they do, but nearly all of them seem determined to distort the true picture in order to justify their own existence.

The charge noted above, that interest groups and their spokesmen frequently agitate more to impress their own membership with their diligence and devotion and to increase their retainers than to achieve legislative results, is one often made by legislators. Said a highly respected Republican:

The worst kind of lobbyist is the fellow seeking to achieve legislation because it means his job. There are many here who are attempting to justify legislation only because they are adding something to what they have done before. As long as they add something they can go back and get their contract renewed or their support bolstered.

Closely linked to this criticism is the belief that much lobbyist activity is wasted effort. Two Democrats discuss this point:

I think the really significant thing about pressure groups is the incredible amount of money they must waste on correspondence. You go into the office on a Monday, and your desk is piled about a foot and half high literally—expensive, beautifully printed stuff, most of it. And all of it almost entirely meaningless. The real impression I get from pressure groups is that they waste their time and their money to an incredible degree.

*

Once an organization establishes a public relations office in Washington, it feels it has to do something to justify its existence. Many times the members themselves don't really feel strongly about particular measures. Yet the central

office will generate something to try to get their members to note the activity
and say "well, look what our office is doing out there."

Another criticism that is heard is that some lobbying groups are too
unyielding in their demands with the result that not only are legislators
antagonized but no beneficial legislation is obtained. In some instances
the group is powerful enough to be able to get the bill out of committee
but lacks sufficient strength to bring about its ultimate passage. Two
comments which bear on this point are given below:

The reason we are considering such an ill-conceived bill is because the _____
[a pressure group] has such far-reaching influence and got formal commitments
from committee members to support a particular bill without any real regard to
what it contained. I have talked with members who put the bill in who really
don't know what is in it. I am not saying that generally speaking the _____
influence is not benign. In this instance, though, they are very unwise to press a
poorly written bill, which is far more comprehensive than most of us want to go.

*

At times, because of the nature of their leadership, the pressure groups push
for legislation which is so unrealistic that the people they represent don't get
any help at all. They could have gained something if they had been reasonable.
The best example of that are the _____ groups. On numerous occasions I have
had the feeling we could have passed something benefiting them, but because
their leaders were so insistent on getting so much, they lost the whole thing.

Advice to Lobbyists

Most of the time individual legislators are not particularly concerned
with lobbying groups, though on specific issues and at a given point in
time, they may regard them as undesirable irritants or as powerful allies.
Most congressmen are politically sophisticated and alert to the needs
and desires of significant bodies of opinion and power within their district. It usually is not necessary to bring pressure to ensure action to
protect and advance these interests. In a very real sense the congressman
is an instigator as well as a subject of pressure. He needs and appreciates
information on the impact of proposed legislation on the nation and
especially his district. Such information is not always forthcoming.

One congressman observed in the *Harvard Business School Bulletin*,[2]

[2] Frank M. Coffin, "How to Get Action from Politicians: Congressman Tells
Businessmen," *Harvard Business School Bulletin*, Vol. 33 (Fall 1957), pp. 13–17.

that often important segments of the economy fail to participate fully in the process of enlightening legislators, with the result that their fortunes suffer. Addressing himself to small businessmen, he observed that they were facing a critical period, beset by many problems but "what we know about these problems, with a few notable exceptions, comes from practically every source but the businessman himself. . . . The absurdity exists that Congress will act in a field directly affecting small business with relatively few businessmen making their views known. This is despite the fact that their views are both sought and welcomed."

In presenting the case for increased communication between the businessmen and the legislator the congressman argued:

> One precious commodity which the businessman has, and the congressman knows he has, is knowledge of the facts of life as they exist in his very small corner of the world. These facts the political representative needs if he is to draft sensible legislation. Respect for these facts will build the bridge of understanding so badly needed between the small-business community and those whose law-making efforts will help or hurt that community.

One lawmaker offered the following advice to lobbyists:

> If I were giving advice to lobbyists as to how they could maximize their influence here, I would say there are four basic rules which should guide them: (1) They should know the facts of the situation with which they're dealing; (2) They should be courteous in all their discussions with congressmen, whether these members happen to agree with them or not; (3) They should know the opposition and the kinds of arguments which are being advanced by the opposition; (4) They should stick to the facts.

Congressmen as Lobbyists

The belief is widely held in the Congress that the most effective and persuasive lobby is the built-in lobby of the congressmen themselves. Even members who declare themselves to be largely immune to the lobbying efforts of their colleagues refer to the prevalence and success of the practice. For most, it is difficult to deny a colleague, particularly when one's own district is not adversely affected. Some members, however, insist it should not be awkward to resist a colleague. One representative explained:

> It is not very difficult for me to say no to a congressman. He shouldn't put

things on a personal basis anyway. There is too much of that around here. We should be able to convince a person on the merits. Some people think that just because you play ball and golf together you should vote together on anything of special interest to them. That is not logical. I can see doing it for the party if it is a party issue because I believe in team work. But with that exception I'd say the approach is not very effective as far as I'm concerned.

During a Democratic discussion of effective lobbying practices the following exchange took place which illustrates the member's dilemma:

Lobbying by other congressmen is the most difficult for me to resist. The spectacle of _____ standing by the door saying "help us out" recalls to me that he helped me out on an Indian bill.

*

You are right, that is the biggest pressure. Outside of the few major things of importance in my district the strongest pressure I feel is from other members of Congress.

*

It is purely sentimental. You know you have got to see this guy every day and you know he will know if you try to double time him, so this is very effective. He knows all about teller votes and divisions and record votes and everything else. There is no way to evade him.

*

But you know he will understand if you can't go along.

*

You can tell a member, and I have done so, "I am sorry, I would like to help, but I can't."

*

Either I am extraordinarily weak or I am the only honest man here.

There is considerable evidence that the last speaker, a northern liberal Democrat, is not unusual in his reaction to the entreaties of his associates. At the same time, as is indicated in the colloquy above, members understand each other's problems, and few expect associates to support them at the risk of forfeiting support at home. As one person put it:

Certain members function as lobbyists, and as pretty effective ones. When one of them votes with you on something in which you're interested, it is pretty tough to turn him down when he comes to you later and wants some assistance on a matter of importance to him. There is a great deal of logrolling in Congress, and it's not going to be changed. It is particularly apparent on a close vote. Now I vote against any farm bill despite the fact that members who would like my support on those bills often support me on other things. People know my stand on the farm situation, and they just don't bother trying to get me to go along. This doesn't affect our relationship on other things, however. I think most of us recognize a cardinal rule in the House and that is that you don't ask a member to support you if such support is going to be going against his district or against a particular project in which he happens to be interested. We all respect one another's views on those matters.

It is apparent that many congressmen honor personal requests from colleagues for support of legislation of local importance partly to avoid the embarrassment involved in declining to do so, particularly where no overwhelming reason exists to act adversely to the request, and partly because they are mindful of the potential advantages of cooperation. Support for a colleague's project now may normally be expected to result in his support when you need him later. Beyond these factors, however, and short of a genuine belief, after careful study, that the proposed legislation is both necessary and appropriate, the sympathetic understanding and spirit of camaraderie with which members view one another often cause them to want to cooperate if it is possible. This is illustrated by the following congressional comment:

> Congressmen tend to have a high regard for one another, and if someone has a pet bill, you tend to make efforts to accommodate him if it is at all possible. When Congressman _____ had his cranberry bill, everybody said, "let's do something for good old Nick," and so they passed the bill. It wasn't a very good bill and probably shouldn't have passed; but the "good old Nick" slogan was enough to do it. No lobby could have pushed that bill through. It was just a personal hand for a member.

Some congressmen express the opinion that colleagues, wishing to retain the good will of their peers, tend to be judicious in selecting issues on which to solicit support. Said one, "most requests from congressmen are quite reasonable. They rest on a sound basis and can easily be supported."

Although the legislators are sympathetic to the pleas of colleagues that they support projects that may be expected to benefit the latter in home districts, they react in a much more detached and objective way to the arguments of associates who have come to be recognized as spokesmen for important interest groups. The importance of the local project to electoral success is a matter of which they are quite aware, and a member pleading his own cause receives attention, understanding, and usually cooperation, particularly if he does not request the support of his colleagues often. Congressmen who represent large interests are less successful. Explained one legislator, "Some congressmen can become mouthpieces for various groups, but in general they are not too effective because everybody comes to recognize them as such."

It is not surprising that congressmen seek to impress their constituents with tangible evidence of their influence by seeking new installations and special contracts for their districts. Veteran legislators may feel under special pressure to produce these benefits both as a matter of personal gratification and as a deterrent to potential opponents. Once a project is reported as under consideration, failure to obtain it for the district may be humiliating. Pleading that failure would be regarded as a sign that he had no influence with his own associates, a member may suggest that his prestige, perhaps even his political future is at stake. Congressmen understand that language.

A legislator whose committee responsibilities result in his being lobbied extensively by his colleagues discussed the dilemma which he and others within the House face:

Certainly congressmen are very effective in lobbying for their own point of view and their own projects. The most difficult situation to face here is a personal request of a colleague. All members feel this at one time or another, but men on the appropriations committee may feel it more often and directly than most. They're subjected to a great deal of pressure. The phones of people sitting on conference committees dealing with public works, military construction, etc. ring constantly in the days prior to the conference. Some congressmen are so effective as lobbyists that they get all sorts of unnecessary construction projects in their districts. I don't think you could drop a bomb anywhere in Texas, for example, without hitting a military installation. You'd be surprised at the people who try to influence you, when items important to their districts are involved.

The congressman recognizes that Congress is an arena for the struggle of competing interests in society. He seeks to analyze their influence at national, state, and especially district levels, and the potential impact of their programs. He is neither surprised by lobbying nor normally resentful of lobbyists. Indeed, he has become adept in using their information and assistance to best advantage and discriminating in reacting to their methods. On the whole, congressmen are sanguine. They do not feel that the public interest is endangered by the existence and activities of the special interests, and they are confident of their own ability to use the lobbyist's help properly without being improperly used themselves.

V

Committee Assignments

"Congress in its committee rooms is Congress at work," wrote Woodrow Wilson in 1885 in his perceptive and enduring study of the Congress. Today, though many congressmen would also insist that much of their time and energy is devoted to nonlegislative activities related to the interests of their constituents, they would not dissent from Wilson's observation. The committee system is still the crux of the legislative process, far more important to congressional decisions than activity on the floor. The assignment to a committee, therefore, becomes the first order of business for most new congressmen.

Not only is the fate of most legislative proposals determined in committee: to an important degree the fate of individual congressmen may be decided there too. A person's congressional career may rest largely on the kind of committee post he is given. A "good" assignment may greatly enhance his value to his constituents and provide unusual opportunities to publicize his activities in Congress; here he can develop the expertise and the reputation as a "specialist" that will enable him to influence his colleagues and important national policies. This is not to say that a "bad" assignment is an irretrievable setback, since effective work on an unimportant committee can identify a new man as a "comer" and lead to a better assignment. Indeed, it usually does. But being named to a committee in which he has little interest defers the day when a congressman can begin to acquire seniority on a committee of his choice. Precious time is lost. By the time an opening to which he is entitled develops, he may be so far up the ladder on another committee that he will hesitate to surrender his seniority and status there for the lowest spot on a committee to which by training, inclination, and the interests of the district he represents he may be more congenial.

The importance of the initial assignment is not always apparent to newcomers, however. Some approach the matter casually. Said one member:

I came to Congress without any ideas about what committee I should be on. I had had enough trouble getting elected! Although I flattered myself that I was reasonably well informed and that I kept up on current problems by doing a normal amount of reading, I recognized I had no depth of knowledge in a specific area. There was no special niche I wanted to fill. I just put myself in the hands of my representative on the Committee on Committees, feeling he would obtain a decent assignment for me.

Similarly, some new congressmen become preoccupied with selecting staff, making arrangements to leave their business enterprises, and preparing to move their families to Washington, and do not concern themselves seriously with the matter of committee assignments. Sometimes inaction results neither from lack of interest nor a faulty assessment of priorities, but rather from uncertainty about what to do. One close observer of the committee selection process asserts that far too many newcomers are unsure how to proceed, and need guidance:

I think it would be helpful to write new members following their election to tell them at least the minimum steps they should take to get their committee assignments. Some just wander in here and operate on a hit or miss basis. They don't even tell anyone they are here. They just wait to be assigned. Since the Committee on Committees often knows virtually nothing about new members, this can be very harmful—even disastrous—to their interests.

Whatever their preparation and expectations, however, freshmen congressmen are likely to find the assignment procedure far more complex than they had expected—far more unpredictable, and dependent on many subtle considerations that they did not anticipate.

Party Mechanisms for Making Committee Appointments

Until 1911 the Speaker customarily appointed the chairmen and members of House committees, although on rare occasions committees were permitted to select their own chairmen. In that earlier period the road to assignment was clearer than it is today: requests were directed to the Speaker or his close associates. However, since the 1910–11 revolution which curtailed the power of the Speaker, the House has, in the opening days of each Congress, elected the chairmen and members of the various committees, following the designations made in party caucuses. On rare occasions a contest develops in the caucus. Usually, the recommendations of the party Committee on Committees are accepted without challenge and the slate is ratified by the House. The Committee on Committees for each party has a dual function. Most of its work is concerned with assigning first term members of Congress to committees. Another important responsibility is that of acting on requests for change of assignment from congressmen who have been re-elected. Once on a committee, a member usually can stay there as long as he wishes; it is not always easy to transfer to another committee, however, even if a vacancy exists.

The Democratic Committee on Committees. Democratic members of the Committee on Ways and Means serve as the Committee on Committees for their party, having one vote each in balloting on committee assignments. Each member is assigned to a "zone" and has the responsibility of representing the Democrats within it. Zone boundaries are determined by the committee members and are changed with fluctuations in Democratic party fortunes in the House or to facilitate the attainment of a current objective of the leadership. In setting boundaries, an effort is made to unite a varying number of states (from one to six in 1963), usually contiguous and hopefully congenial, into approximately equal groups of Democrats. In 1963 the smallest group had ten members, the largest had twenty-three.

There has been considerable criticism from Democrats that the coveted seats on the Ways and Means Committee are not distributed properly, that certain states seem to be regarded as "entitled" to seats, regardless of the qualifications of their candidates. Although departures of members from North Carolina, Minnesota, Rhode Island, and Montana have not led to replacements from those states, it is asserted that there is a tendency to replace a departing member with someone from the same state. For example, deaths of committee members from Tennessee and Pennsylvania, retirements of members from Texas, Michigan, and Virginia, and the defeat of members from Kentucky and Tennessee, resulted in the designation of other congressmen from those states to fill the vacancies, irrespective of other considerations. Where this procedure is not adhered to, it is often because potential candidates from the state or states concerned are not acceptable to the party leadership. Critics of the practice assert it is difficult to justify a policy providing for automatic inclusion of Kentucky and Tennessee members on a committee with the subject matter jurisdiction of Ways and Means.

Complained one congressman, "Why should there be a Tennessee seat, a Kentucky seat, a Pennsylvania seat? To say Pennsylvania should have a seat is to say that New Jersey can never have one, even though it may have a well qualified man, because the two states are in the same region. That doesn't make sense."

In explanation, one of the most perceptive members of the House states:

> Actually, what we mean when we talk about a Pennsylvania seat or a Tennessee seat on Ways and Means [or the Committee on Committees, since they are one and the same] is that we are resorting to a "don't-rock-the-boat" technique. So many problems are involved in selecting people that it just proves easier to stick to tradition and fill the vacancy with a man from the same state.

A similar explanation is made by another keen student of the House:

> The zone areas are shifted from time to time for strategic purposes, just as the decision to fill a vacancy with a man from the same state as a man going off the committee is often determined by circumstances. The tariff question is a key to Ways and Means appointments. The leadership checks carefully with potential candidates before putting them on the committee. This year the candidates for the vacancy from one area were people who would not vote "right" on the tariff issue. And many tended to be close to special groups with strong positions on matters coming before the committee. That is why the leadership prevailed on _____ to go on, even though he had not applied and didn't want the spot.
>
> Doughton of North Carolina had been chairman of Ways and Means for twenty or thirty years when he retired, and he wanted someone from his state to replace him. But some of the North Carolina representatives had too much seniority on other committees to want to shift to Ways and Means, and those who were proposed were not right on the trade issue. So no one from North Carolina got the seat. The reason a Tennessean got Jere Cooper's place was partly because he was from Tennessee but also because his stand on tariff was satisfactory. By naming him, on the basis of precedent, the party leaders could avoid a situation where the vacancy would go to someone who wouldn't be on the train.

Designating the Ways and Means Committee as the Committee on Committees is not without its disadvantages to the Democratic party in the House and to some members of the committee itself. The jurisdiction of Ways and Means involves some of the most complicated, technical legislation to come before the Congress. Yet some congressmen who have little interest in the subject matter seek the assignment because of its important role in the selection of the Democratic membership of all committees. They may not carry their share of the work load in connection with the committee's legislative jurisdiction.

The Republican Committee on Committees. Unlike the Democrats, the Republicans do not assign a dual role to their members of the Ways and Means Committee. Their Committee on Committees consists of one member from each state having Republican representation in the House, each member casting a vote equal to the number of Republicans in his state's delegation. The Republican system was developed in 1919 in the aftermath of a factional contest for the party leadership, and represented an attempt by the defeated group to prevent the victors from controlling the committee assignment process. Because such a large group is un-wieldy—in 1963 the Republican Committee on Committees had thirty-eight members, including the minority leader,—a special subcommittee is designated to prepare the party list, subject to the approval of the full committee and the party policy committee.[1] Although the subcommittee includes representatives of the small states, they possess little real power since there, as in the full committee, they can cast only the votes of the Republicans from their states. In 1959, the nine member Executive Sub-committee included two members with one vote each, the other seven members coming from the seven states sending the largest Republican contingents to Congress. They represented about two-thirds of the House Republicans. Beginning in 1961, the size of the subcommittee was increased slightly to include a representative of the large number of freshmen Republicans in the Eighty-seventh Congress. In 1963, another sizable group of new Republican members was elected and they, too, won a seat on the committee.

Evaluation of the Committees. One liberal Democrat who has been critical of the method by which his party arrives at its committee lists compares it with that of the Republicans:

For some time I felt the Republicans had a better device for naming people to committees. After talking to colleagues who are close to the process, however, and after watching the system operate for several years I have come to the conclu-sion that ours is by far superior. Each Democratic member of the Ways and

---

[1] In the 88th Congress the subcommittee was composed of Rhodes of Arizona (1 vote), Utt of California (14 votes), Arends of Illinois (12 votes), Adair of Indiana (7 votes), Morton of Maryland (2 votes), Bennett of Michigan (11 votes), Battin of Montana (1 vote), Osmers of New Jersey (8 votes), St. George of New York (21 votes), Brown of Ohio (17 votes), Dague of Pennsylvania (14 votes). Battin repre-sented the Republicans first elected in 1960; Morton represented those first elected in 1962.

Means Committee has one vote in determining committee appointments under our system. For the most part the system seems to operate in a reasonably democratic fashion with an honest vying for position. On the Republican side, most members of the Committee on Committees have no role at all. Three or four members get together and control the appointments.

A liberal Republican protests that the individuals who make his party's assignments are "all of similar viewpoint." He concedes that a party conference would, in most instances, uphold their choices, but he is unhappy. In his view:

> On the Republican side of the aisle the business of filling vacancies simply boils down to a decision to be made by about four people. If you don't sit well with any one of them, you can't get on. They come from big states and they have the votes to select whomever they want. They parcel out assignments and exercise veto power according to what they think is best for the Republican Party. They think alike and they are very senior, and they are not representative of what most people would like the Republican Party to be. To them, the sine qua non is to "be regular" according to their views of regularity, and regularity is rewarded.

But another colleague of more conservative bent is more sanguine about the system:

> The subcommittee is a very practical device because it is picked by, and consists of, members who together control the majority of the votes in the party conference. It wouldn't make any sense to have people on the subcommittee who don't have the power to back up their own decisions. It is true that sometimes it results in stacking committees. I don't approve of that, but I don't know any way around it either as long as we have a system of majority rule.

A third member said, "In a nutshell, our system is a combination of the power of the combined votes of a few men and the veto power of our top member of each committee. In fact this group can fill any vacancy."

The Assignment Process

Members of the Committee on Committees of both parties do not take their responsibilities lightly. Nor do they lack guidance. They are approached by incoming members who make known their preferences and qualifications and solicit support; colleagues interested in the fate of individual candidates seek them out; committee chairmen or the top minority members may wish to indicate reactions to applicants seeking service on their committees. In addition, both party groups are provided with materials (somewhat more detailed and elaborate for the Democrats) designed to facilitate their work. These materials include biographical information about first term members; party ratios, vacancies, and names of applicants for each committee; and in the Democratic Committee, an indication of who has endorsed the various candidates. What is prepared is impressive, but no matter how great the effort, it is impossible to provide full information.

Assignments by the Democrats. Although the source of supporting letters that are directed to the chairman of the Democratic Committee on Committees in behalf of individual candidates is included in the printed material furnished to members of that committee, no notice is taken of letters written to anyone else. Nor is there any record of telephone calls— which may be far more effective than letters—or other communications.[2] It is not unusual for returning members who desire to transfer from a committee, or to add another, to speak directly to members of the Committee on Committees rather than to submit written requests. This practice is more common among Democrats than Republicans.

By the time the committee meets, the majority party has come to an agreement with the minority on the size of each committee and the party ratios to be maintained thereon. These ratios tend to reflect the relative strength of the two parties in the House. However, a two to one margin is given the majority party on the Rules Committee and a three to two edge is provided on the Appropriations and Ways and Means Committees. Sometimes, in order to inconvenience as few congressmen as possible, committees will be permitted to deviate from the appropriate division.

The Democrats divide the twenty House standing committees into

[2] Although many Democratic newcomers to the House state in their requests for assignment that they have letters of support from party leaders such as Adlai Stevenson, Harry Truman, state governors, and other party men, few of these appear to be directed to the Ways and Means Committee chairman since reference to endorsements by these party luminaries is rare in the official notebook prepared for Ways and Means Committee members. One member of this group suggests that letters of endorsement from prominent Democrats and also from respected House colleagues could, with advantage, be directed to the chairman and entire membership of the committee.

three categories. For the Eighty-eighth Congress, party members serving on committees in the first group (exclusive committees—Appropriations, Ways and Means, and Rules) were not permitted[3] to serve on another standing committee. Congressmen assigned to committees in the second group[4] (nonexclusive) could serve on any two of them or any one plus any one of those listed in the third group.[5] Members of committees in the third group could serve on any one of them plus one included in group two.

In the executive sessions of the Committee on Committees, the standing committees are generally called up alphabetically—Agriculture, Appropriations, Banking and Currency, and so on—although on occasion a committee may be called up out of turn in order to dispose of an especially difficult problem early in the deliberations. As nominations are opened for each committee, members of the Committee on Committees proceed in order of their seniority to nominate candidates from their zone. Discussion of individual candidates takes place as they are nominated, and their names are written on a blackboard. Once the junior member of the Committee on Committees has completed his nominations for the committee under consideration, secret balloting takes place without further delay.

It is important to note that a candidate can only be nominated by the representative of his own zone. If his zone man fails to nominate him, he has no chance to get on the committee he desires. Though normally the zone head will be willing to nominate a person about whom he is not enthusiastic, he may decline to urge his selection vigorously, or he may merely place the name in nomination leaving it to a colleague to explain why the choice may not be appropriate. Sometimes, however, a zone representative finds himself in a dilemma. He may have four congressmen in his area desiring service on the Agriculture Committee with no more than four vacancies existing on the committee. Knowing his region cannot win all of the vacancies, he is likely to select one or two and concentrate

---

[3] With a single exception—Howard Smith of Virginia, Chairman of the Rules Committee, who also serves on the District of Columbia Committee.

[4] District of Columbia, Government Operations, House Administration, Interior and Insular Affairs, Merchant Marine and Fisheries, Post Office and Civil Service, Un-American Activities, and Veterans Affairs.

[5] Agriculture, Armed Services, Banking and Currency, Education and Labor, Foreign Affairs, Interstate and Foreign Commerce, Judiciary, Public Works, Science and Astronautics.

on gaining spots for them. This may antagonize those who fail to be nominated, but it probably will increase the chances of success for those whose names *are* put forward.

A zone man may also block nomination because of a disagreement over an issue of public policy. One congressman who was confronted by this situation when he sought his initial assignment described his predicament in this way:

> I was anxious to serve on Public Works because the St. Lawrence Seaway proposal was before the committee. I armed myself with supporting letters from Adlai Stevenson and many other national leaders. However, my regional man on Ways and Means was the author of the water diversion bill, a source of conflict between my state and his. He was not going to permit an opponent of his bill to gain a seat on the committee considering it, so I had no chance. He would not even consider anyone from my state. Without his support, I could not even be nominated.

Thus a Democratic congressman interested in obtaining a committee assignment is at the mercy of his representative on the Ways and Means Committee. There is general agreement, however, that this power is seldom exercised arbitrarily.

Assignments by the Republicans. The procedures followed by the subcommittee of the Republican Committee on Committees are similar to those of its Democratic counterpart, although, as has been noted, the weighted voting gives the decision-making power to a hard core of the subcommittee. Although they have a smaller working group and are more informal, the Republicans also follow regular parliamentary procedure. As the name of each standing committee is called, nominations are declared in order, and if a contest develops, voting is by secret ballot.

Unlike the Democrats, Republicans do not divide the twenty standing committees into three formal categories, although only rarely do members of the Appropriations, Rules, and Ways and Means committees serve on another standing committee. Nor are subcommittee members made responsible for protecting the interests of Republicans from specific zones. Because most states designate senior members as their representatives on the Committee on Committees, that group is likely to be somewhat more conservative in outlook than the conference of all Republican representatives.

The Influence of the Party Leadership. Deliberations of the Committee on Committees in both parties follow many informal discussions, both among members of the committee and among committee members and other colleagues. Although participants in the Democratic Committee on Committees sessions state that in the course of their formal sessions no one says, "this is the man the leadership wants," there is ample opportunity for word to reach key members on the preferences of the leadership, and applicants to fill vacancies offer extensive evidence that their views on issues likely to come before committees for which they are applying are often solicited in advance of the decisions.

The extent to which the formal party leadership injects itself into the selection process is the subject of disagreement. It should be noted that the Republican leader acts as chairman, without vote, of his party's Committee on Committees, whereas the elected Democratic leadership is not represented on the Democratic committee and exerts its influence indirectly. There is general accord that the leadership of both parties exerts much influence on committee assignments and that it should do so, but it seems clear that most House members feel that this power should be—and usually is—exercised with discretion and with a light rather than a heavy hand. It is apparent that differences in the manner in which the Democratic and Republican Committee on Committees are formed make it far more likely that the Republican group will include the actual if not the formal leaders of the party than the Democratic committee.

The feeling is strong that with respect to the selection of Ways and Means Committee members the hand of the leadership of both parties is evident and generally decisive. This interest is justified on the grounds that tariff and tax policies are more likely to be "party" matters than most other issues, with the added factor on the Democratic side that it is this group that functions as the Committee on Committees.

Of all the committees, a freshman is least likely to be able to obtain a seat on the Ways and Means or Rules Committee, not only because of the competition of seniors but also because, in the words of one leading House member, "It would be too risky to put on a person whose views and nature the leadership has no opportunity to assess." One freshman Democrat who withdrew his request for the Ways and Means Committee has this explanation for his initial action:

As a student of public finance, I felt I had a special interest in the Ways and Means Committee. I had just completed a tax study and had worked on others so I asked two colleagues whether I could request an assignment to Ways and Means. One said, "By all means, do." The other said, "You haven't got a chance." Torn between the rival advice from senior members I went ahead. Of course I got the discouragement from the leadership that a freshman should expect when he asks for a committee to which freshmen just don't get named. But since there was going to be a vacancy and since I knew of no rival for the spot, it seemed proper for me to make inquiries. At that point I was concerned purely with the tax functions of the committee, not its Committee on Committees functions.

With respect to the filling of four Democratic vacancies on Ways and Means at the beginning of the Eighty-sixth Congress, one Democrat states, "Everybody understood that the leadership would select the nominees for Ways and Means and that these nominees would be elected. I assume this is one way by which the leadership insures it will have some influence on future committee assignments made by this group." In the Eighty-eighth Congress, on the other hand, the leadership permitted a three-way contest for two vacancies to be decided by the Democratic caucus. The caucus rejected one of the candidates supported by the leadership. But the victorious aspirant was considered more likely to support the leadership's position on important issues than the man he defeated.

Veteran members of the House note that leadership candidates for positions on the Ways and Means Committee have been defeated in the Democratic party caucus twice in recent years, but add that the issues on those occasions were not clear-cut.

The Role of Committee Chairmen. It is not unusual for the leadership to escort an applicant for a particular committee to the office of its chairman or ranking member, thereby lending support to the application. This practice leads one to ponder the influence of these committee leaders in assigning party members to their committees. It seems evident that they have an important role. Sometimes, depending on the personalities involved, they are less reluctant to express a preference than the leadership. But their influence obviously varies: to be influential they must be respected by the leadership or the Committee on Committees, preferably both. According to one Democrat, "Generally the chairman or the ranking member of a committee has a veto power in the assignment of members of his party to his committee, but sometimes the senior party man is not in good standing and his views are a matter of indifference to the leadership."

Although the chairmen are not present in the Committee on Committees when assignments to their committees are discussed and, in the procedure followed by the Democrats, no formal communication is directed to them by the selection group, they ordinarily know the identity of the applicants for their committees since most of them will have paid a courtesy call or written a letter indicating interest. If the chairman reacts strongly—favorably or unfavorably—to any applicant, he thus has an opportunity to make his wishes known to various members of the Committee on Committees. Ordinarily the chairman of that group will consult with him informally as a matter of course. On occasion in the Democratic party, a chairman requests zone representatives to nominate specific congressmen for service on the chairman's committee but "in some cases the regional man doesn't even nominate them. The views of committee chairmen are considered in some instances and ignored in others."

According to a member of the Republican Committee on Committees, that committee is careful to check with ranking Republican committee members, and "if a ranking member objects to service of a man on his committee, that is two strikes against the applicant." As another member expressed it:

> I don't see how the Committee on Committees could have the nerve to ram somebody down the throat of a committee chairman or ranking member who doesn't want that candidate. It would be natural to consult with your top man on the committee, and unless some unusual issue is at stake, his wishes would be adhered to.

One congressman related that prior to the decisions of the Committee on Committees he and some colleagues were consulted by the ranking member of the committee on which they served about the vacancies on that committee. The ranking member had a short list of individuals who were acceptable to him, and "when the committee lists were published no one who was not on that list joined our group." One result of heavy reliance on the advice of senior committee members when filling vacancies is that the basic unity of the party's membership on the committee tends to be maintained; and men and women are selected who may be expected to work well with their new colleagues and to function quickly as members of the team.

The veto power possessed by many top committee members is sharply attacked by those whose applications are affected by it, and, indeed by many of their colleagues. Occasionally, the veto may even be used to deny a place to an applicant whose main crime is that he supports the position of the acknowledged leader of his party on an important issue within the committee's jurisdiction. Complained one critic, "Why should the ranking member of Ways and Means on the Republican side have the power to prevent anyone supporting the Republican President's position on reciprocal trade from getting on his committee just because he does not happen to agree with that position? In my opinion he doesn't represent what I consider to be the Republican view on reciprocal trade." And one congressman against whom the veto was invoked had this to say:

A man from my state was leaving Congress and his seat on an important committee, one which he had held for years. Nobody else within our delegation wanted the post, and everyone said he would be glad to push me. In this instance there were an unusually large number of vacancies on the committee. Our state is reasonably entitled to a seat there, and yet I was bypassed by someone who hadn't even requested it and who was junior to me. The reason is that I didn't know the right people, that somewhere along the line I had made the wrong impression, by votes or otherwise, on the people who had the power to blackball me on committee assignments. The basic negative attitudes towards me came from within the committee to which I wanted to be assigned.

The "arbitrary" power of senior committee members led one Republican to declare that "the committee selection system is pure and simple government by crony."

A number of congressmen concede that the system does not always function in the most equitable fashion but point out that a member who feels he has been unjustly deprived of an assignment has the right to appeal to the full party conference or caucus, which has the final responsibility of settling such contests. They emphasize that a party selection committee that did not reflect the general outlook of the conference could not prevail in the face of such challenges to its decisions. On those grounds one conservative Republican dismisses criticism of the appointments to fill his party's vacancies on Ways and Means. Says he, "I think it was perfectly proper to select only people who opposed President Eisenhower on reciprocal trade for assignment on Ways and Means because I think they represented the majority Republican sentiment in the House."

Competing for an Assignment

One strategically placed observer believes that "as a minimum, when his party is in the majority, a freshman Democrat should make his committee preferences known to the Speaker, the Majority Leader, the chairman of the Ways and Means Committee, his zone man on Ways and Means, and the chairman of any committees in which he is interested."[6] To this list one could add all others of his party on Ways and Means, the party Whip, and the dean of the member's delegation.

In addition, conversations with state colleagues may be helpful in providing information about the outlook, interests, and idiosyncrasies of key participants in the committee selection process, which can be useful in determining the approach most likely to achieve favorable results. One seasoned congressman emphasizes the value of the face-to-face encounter.

It may also be helpful to enlist the support of any national or state party leaders who enjoy the respect and confidence of key members of the leadership or the Ways and Means Committee.

The pattern for a freshman Republican is similar. He would be well advised to communicate with the leader of his party in the House, the top Republicans on the committees in which he is interested, his representative on the Committee on Committees, and all members of the special subcommittee of that group, particularly those representing states with large Republican contingents. He also may wish to confer with the party Whip and to seek the assistance of prominent Republicans outside of Congress who possess influence with those whose views are likely to be decisive.

Normally an elaborate campaign is not essential to success. Sometimes delegation and regional leaders will, in order to obtain more effective representation for their area, undertake to intercede for the candidate and cover the important ground, making it unnecessary for him to do much. In other instances not even that is necessary; some freshmen do virtually nothing to press their claims for a particular assignment and yet,

---

[6] If the Democrats are in the minority, the minority leader and senior minority member of Ways and Means would be substituted for the first three men mentioned.

because of the post being sought, existing vacancies, and the background of the applicant, succeed in obtaining it. When the entering class of party freshmen is large, the task of the Committee on Committees becomes especially difficult and having an influential friend to espouse one's cause may become crucial to the newcomer. Unfortunately, too, it is often difficult to isolate early the problems and factors involved in any particular vacancy. Thus members have found it wise to explore many avenues to the desired goal.

Not all of one's endeavors may be effective, as one member relates:

I first got letters of support from people of national prominence who had helped me get elected. I concentrated them largely on Joe Martin [then minority leader] and the dean of our state delegation. At first I divided my shots between two committees. Rather quickly I discovered that other people from your state won't tell you what they are doing, so you have no idea where the focus is being put. I asked another freshman what his preference was, and he refused to tell me, saying that the delegation dean had told him never to indicate what he was going for. At that point I said to hell with checking with colleagues.

Many of my initial efforts were wasted because Martin was not re-elected leader. Then our dean got sick. I spoke to Halleck [Martin's successor] about my choices, but he gave me no commitments or encouragement. I also talked with the man next in line to the delegation dean, but later he relinquished his responsibilities on the Committee on Committees to still another member to whom I then turned. About halfway through the negotiations I discovered that another man in the delegation had the support of our two senators for one of the committees in which I was interested. I quickly dropped that one and concentrated on my other choice. By some miracle I got it, chiefly, I think, because there were relatively few applications. Helpful, too, was the fact that another member of our delegation who had been on the committee decided not to continue there.

A member who has a strong interest in a particular committee assignment may work hard to maximize the likelihood he will get it, as the statements of several congressmen will indicate. As one described his efforts:

The day after election I called the dean of my delegation and told him my committee preference. He said he would speak to our man on Ways and Means. On the way back from my vacation, I stopped by Bonham, Texas, and spent about five hours there [with Rayburn] and let him lead the conversation. When he asked me what committee I was interested in, I told him. Then I had Adlai Stevenson, the national chairman, and some other people write the Speaker, the Majority Leader, the Whip, and the chairman of Ways and Means in my behalf, and

I wrote all of those people myself. Some frineds who are close to John McCor‑
mack wrote to him and went to see him on my behalf. Another important party
leader wrote McCormack and my Ways and Means man about my background,
which happened to be appropriate for the committee I wanted.

In addition I phoned some people once I learned they were leaving the commit‑
tee. I also talked with several other members of Congress whose judgment I
valued. Then I called on the committee chairman. I didn't know whether there
would be competition for the committee, but I wanted the assignment very
much. The process was a great education to me.

A congressman from one of the larger states related the route by which
he managed to obtain his objective:

Getting the committee you want is a combination of planning and luck. I came
here with one of the largest groups of newcomers in recent years and was the only
freshman to be assigned to Armed Services. I campaigned very hard for the
assignment. Even before I was elected, I wrote to the head of our Committee on
Committees and to my representative. I got the mayor, the board of supervisors,
everyone of importance in my area, to say I had to be on Armed Services. Things
got to the point where my man on the Committee on Committees wired me "Call
off the barrage. I get the point." One factor of great significance is that my dis‑
trict has many military installations in it and thus is a logical one to be repre‑
sented on the committee.

My problem was complicated because three members of our delegation wanted
the spot. By pointing out that our state already had three members on the com‑
mittee, only one of whom was from my part of the state—he was of the opposite
party—I eliminated one aspirant. At that point, the fact that I came from a mili‑
tary district swung the delegation's decision in my favor.

Only because we changed from the minority to the majority, thus opening up
more seats on the committee, did I have a chance. Then my active campaign, plus
the nature of my district, turned the tide. I bumped a man with several terms
seniority who made a floor fight of it. Normally, a freshman hasn't a chance in
such a contest, but my representative on the Committee on Committees stood firm
and lined up other support so that I just barely made it.

Although effort is not conclusive in determining whether a member
gets on the committee he desires, it often is a factor. Contrast, for ex‑
ample, the experiences of the two men whose comments follow:

I wanted a seat on the Agriculture Committee. My experience in the state
legislature made me realize you just don't get things automatically. You have to
go after them. I had the support of our member on the Committee on Committees
and I also sought out other influential members of that committee. I talked with
Charlie Halleck and the ranking Republican on the Agriculture Committee. I

pointed out that there were no people from my area on the committee. I represent a family farm-type constituency. In numbers, the family farm outnumbers other farm types, and yet there was no one to represent this important group. I emphasized that point and made my case successfully. Our farm problems are different than those of states further west. We grow a different kind of wheat, for example. People keep talking about the wheat surplus, but there is no surplus of the kind of wheat grown in my area. The distinction is important, and it is very helpful to have someone from my region on the committee to emphasize the difference. I got my subcommittee assignment in pretty much the same way I got my committee assignment—by pointing out how important such a spot would be to my state and my district.

*

I feel that it was unfortunate for me that I came in as a member of the majority and also from a safe district. My predecessor had been here for many years and was the top man from our party on his committee. The work was of special interest to me, and I took it for granted that I would be considered for the vacancy created by his retirement. No one else in our delegation wanted the assignment. I made no organized effort to get it but rather naively thought it would fall into my lap like a ripe plum. I think it was partly because I came from a safe district that I lost out. They told me there was no chance of my getting the slot I wanted and offered me two other committees. I ended up on both. I was able to get off one after two years, but I am still stuck with a committee I never asked for. I have tried desperately and unsuccessfully to get off of it.

A congressman who makes little personal effort to ensure his designation for an important committee post he seeks faces the possibility that he will be unsuccessful. One man emphasizes that it often is necessary to do "a little political bargaining" in order to attain one's ends. Says he:

We had a classic case of a raw deal on committee assignments this year. It was a combination of circumstances—bad luck and poor politicking on the part of the candidate. He was just too gentlemanly and thought all the logic was on his side—which it was—without really getting down and doing a little political bargaining. It seemed that everything that was attempted worked out badly.

The Influence of Seniority. Traditionally, seniority has been regarded as the most significant factor in the committee process, including the designation of new members where differences in seniority exist between applicants. A modification of that assumption seems in order: An applicant's outlook on controversial issues currently before a committee, or on issues likely to come before that committee, is often far more significant in determining the outcome of his quest than is seniority. As one close observer of the process said:

> Seniority may control if all others things are equal. But other things usually are not equal. Sometimes you begin to think seniority is little more than a device to fall back on when it is convenient to do so.

Indeed, one victim of the failure to enforce seniority complained:

> I should think seniority would be more of a factor in committee assignments than it seems to be. Certainly juniors get seats their seniors would like, which is not what the rule book says at all.

Such statements are not unusual among representatives, particularly among those who have watched the committee appointment process over a period of several sessions. Such comments as the following are heard: "Once you get on a committee, seniority counts but not much before that." "Seniority can play a part in getting on a committee, but as many congressmen can testify, if they want to mess with that rule, they can trim it a bit and keep a person off." "Seniority is tied in with committee assignments, but it isn't always binding." "Seniority is more an excuse than a governing factor."

This is not to deny that seniority remains a powerful factor in congressional life. The senior majority member of a committee nearly always serves as its chairman. Once on a committee, a member can remain there as long as he wishes unless a reversal in his party's strength in the House results in the loss of sufficient seats that, under the seniority rule, he is not entitled to one of those remaining to the party. Traditionally, on some committees the subcommittees are determined by seniority. But given a contest for an important committee assignment, in which returning members of Congress may wish to transfer from another committee and find themselves competing with each other and with freshmen congressmen, seniority is not infrequently brushed aside, if it will not bring about the outcome desired by those making the decision.[7]

As will be shown, there are many general principles that have become

---

[7] The importance of seniority in making committee assignments varies from party to party and from one house to the other. It is followed most closely by Senate Republicans and least closely by Senate Democrats, with the House groups falling somewhere between them.

associated with the assignment process, and it is the seniority system which gives way to one or more of the others whenever it is believed something crucial is at stake. The evolution of a set of principles has given a large measure of flexibility to the system, thereby increasing the power of the Committee on Committees by enabling it to justify virtually every appointment on some grounds that will seem sufficiently plausible to achieve acceptance.

In each recent Congress, for example, cases can be cited from both parties to demonstrate that seniority operates where there is no plausible reason to upset it, but ceases to be the crucial criterion for appointment whenever the senior candidate lacks the support of those responsible for preparing the party lists.[8] Thus, in the Eighty-sixth Congress, on the Democratic side, to mention several examples, a respected returning member who aspired to service on the Committee on Education and Labor saw the party's five vacancies there go to entering freshmen, largely because the leadership was aware that his views on important issues before the committee were not in accord with the ends they were seeking to achieve; a candidate for the Appropriations Committee found himself nudged out of the spot by a slightly junior colleague who was supported by the leadership; and another veteran Member who sought service on the Foreign Affairs Committee was not able to obtain one of the seven vacancies, several of which were awarded to first termers. One of the men assigned to that committee, incidentally, was later told by a party leader that he never would have been given the spot had the leader known his views on certain issues.

On the Republican side, in the same Congress, a candidate for the Appropriations Committee, regarded as a "spender" by its ranking member, saw a freshman get the seat. The successful candidate had powerful forces working for him beyond the ranking member's evaluation of his competitor. The recently defeated minority leader whose friends controlled the Committee on Committees was anxious that he be named since they were from the same state. Then, too, the state had been represented on the Appropriations Committee for many years by a man who had retired the

---

[8] It should not be necessary to observe that those who act to deny an individual a committee post to which by virtue of seniority he is entitled, may well reflect the view of the party majority, or the leadership, or both.

previous session. A liberal candidate for the Ways and Means Committee was not able to get one of four vacancies even though—or because—the liberal alone of the five men involved had supported the Republican President's position on reciprocal trade. He was particularly distressed because one of the seats went to a junior who had not originally applied for the assignment. A man who had once served on the Rules Committee and who had expected to return found himself shunted aside in favor of a junior who had never seen service on the committee; the explanation, in the words of one party leader, was that "our leadership didn't trust him because, in the past, he had made deals on legislation which were detrimental to our over-all program. The man who got the spot was safe from that point of view. There is nothing to hide about that situation. It is just a cold political fact."

A member considered "difficult" by some of his colleagues and much respected by others endeavored in vain on several occasions to shift committees. Success was made contingent on agreement to become less difficult; it was too great a price to pay.

The Influence of Issues. A member's stand on critical issues is important in determining his chances for a seat on the prestigious Ways and Means Committee. One widely recognized test of eligibility is the position of an aspirant on tariff questions. For many years a condition of appointment on the Democratic side has been support of reciprocal trade; and on the Republican side, opposition to it has often been the determining factor. According to one informed Democrat, "There is no question that the tariff issue is an acid test of who goes on Ways and Means." Another colleague said, "The Ways and Means Committee is an example of a committee where a stand on legislation determined who got on the committee. All of our people had to favor reciprocal trade." One rising Democrat who sought service on the committee was unsuccessful because the interests of his state, if adhered to by the member, would require him to desert the party position on certain tariff questions. When the party leadership asked for assurances that he would support the party's position on such matters, he issued a statement that in conflicts between party position and district interest, he intended to follow the interests of his people even if doing so would bar him from service on an important committee such as Ways and Means.

On the Republican side, the line was held in the late 1950's despite the fact that a Republican administration was aligned on the other side of the issue. Protested one GOP member "I have been blackballed because I supported a basic part of the administration's program." Another congressman said, "I was right in the middle of some maneuvering, and I know for a fact that anyone who was pro-reciprocal trade would have had a mighty hard time getting on Ways and Means." This evoked the comment from still another member, "Hard time? It was impossible!"

One need not aspire to membership on Ways and Means to be quizzed on controversial matters. It is common practice in connection with assignments to certain committees. In 1959 no one unwilling to take a certain position on labor legislation was permitted by the Democratic leadership to gain a seat on the Committee on Education and Labor, though five vacancies existed. And some years ago when St. Lawrence Seaway legislation was before the House, potential members of the Public Works Committee were carefully screened on the basis of their position on that proposal.

As one congressman relates his own experience:

My predecessor in Congress had been chairman of the Public Works Committee and I requested service on it too. Every time I talked to members of the Committee on Committees about the matter they asked me how I stood on the St. Lawrence Seaway. That was the decisive question. I didn't have any stand and that made me acceptable to the leadership because I was able to go along with them; I was the only new man to join the committee that year. About that time President Truman began to work very hard to get the St. Lawrence Seaway legislation passed, and there were five changes on the committee within a year in order to get members more sympathetic to the legislation.

His story led another legislator to comment:

I know a similar case on the other side of the aisle. A colleague who now has eight or ten years seniority is a contractor by profession and requested service on Public Works, when he first came to Congress. One day he was asked how he felt about the St. Lawrence Seaway. His honest answer was, "Well, I say to myself, isn't it inevitable?" He didn't succeed in being named to Public Works until this year when the seaway was a reality.

Considerable support exists for the view that where there is a recognized party position on an important issue, sympathy for that position should be a minimum requirement for being named to the committee having jurisdiction in that area. Members would like to be certain, however, that the position is a party stand. After one congressman protested that he was barred from a committee because of his stand on certain issues, a colleague said: "I think a person's outlook on issues should be an important factor in determining certain assignments, because a policy can be built up or stopped at that stage. The problem is that occasionally a position is established arbitrarily by one individual and does not reflect majority opinion."

The Influence of the District. A large percentage of the House membership request assignment to committees that deal with matters of considerable importance to their districts even though, other things being equal, they might prefer another post. Often a congressman's predecessor has served on the committee and the newcomer considers it detrimental to his prestige and interest not to be able to serve there also. Sometimes, too, a committee assignment becomes a campaign issue. A member described his situation:

Shipbuilding and sea food are the important industries in my area. Traditionally our district has been represented on the Merchant Marine and Fisheries Committee, one of my predecessors having served as chairman. When I challenged the incumbent in our primary, his supporters pointed out that membership on the committee was important to our district and that therefore he should be re-elected. When I won the primary, I came to Washington and told our delegation it was very important that I be assigned to Merchant Marine and Fisheries. They talked with the chairman of the committee, and he not only assured them he would do everything possible to get me on but he appointed me as special counsel to the committee before I became a member of Congress. From September to December I traveled, working on a special project which provided me with technical information which has been of value since and also gave me a better understanding of the problems before us.

Another representative substantiated the view that if committee assignments become an issue during an election campaign, the claim of the victor to membership on the committee in question may be advanced:

No one from my state had ever served on the committee I wanted and got. Its work is of much importance to my district. It even became a campaign issue at which time I stated I would try to be named to the committee if elected. Right after the election I wrote a letter to our party leader and also to our top man on the committee. Later in November I came to Washington and began seeing everyone I could. I knew the Committee on Committees made the decisions and that it was similar to a political campaign: line up the big states and you have a chance. So I sought the support of New York, California, and states like that. Our delegation's representative on the Committee on Committees worked hard for me too. The fact that I had campaigned on the issue and that our state had never been represented helped me a great deal.

Role of Interest Groups. Interest groups have influence in the disposition of committee seats, although their impact varies from committee to committee and from period to period. There is general agreement that various farm organizations play a role in the selection of members of the Agriculture Committee, for example. Other groups are interested in the composition of committees, too, and even offer to press the claims of members for particular assignments, as these comments from two veteran members illustrate. One said:

When I first came to Congress I requested and got a good committee. When the assignments were made they ended up with one vacancy on Education and Labor. The first I knew of it was when some labor lobbyists came to me and asked whether I would go on if they could get me on. I'm sure they had checked me out and knew what my general point of view was. They went ahead and got me on. I neither asked for it nor lifted a finger for it.

The other member stated:

Some business people came to me and pointed out there would be a vacancy on Ways and Means. They told me they hoped I would consider serving on the committee and asked whether I would mind if they wrote letters suggesting me for service there. They also offered to assist in any other way I thought they could be helpful.

Other Considerations. If a member has a strong claim to a particular assignment and possesses influential support in asserting that claim, it is possible that the leadership will find a way to enable him to serve despite the absence of a vacancy. This may take the form of persuading a member of the committee to resign in favor of another assignment, or it may result in arranging with the opposition leadership to increase the committee's membership to allow an additional seat for each party. In other instances congressmen sometimes voluntarily give up committee posts with the stipulation that specific colleagues be named. One legislator tells of the complications involved in giving him the assignment of his choice:

When I arrived, there were no openings on the committee I wanted and there were many candidates. One member from my state was on the committee and also had another good assignment. She decided to resign in my favor, making her resignation contingent on my appointment. Thus it became more or less automatic for me to get my choice. But a congressman from another state obviously had spoken to the leadership and had definite commitments for the first opening. To solve the problem the leadership enlarged the size of the committee, enabling them to seat the person to whom they were committed.

Another member described a situation where the leadership intervened to resolve a difficult impasse which had arisen:

This year there was considerable interest in a number of vacancies on an important committee. Eventually, a tie vote developed within the Committee on Committees for the final opening. After two ballots it appeared a stalemate had been reached and the assistance of the leadership was sought. Since senior members of the standing committee were opposed to increasing its size, the leadership persuaded one member of the committee to resign in order to permit both deadlocked candidates to be named. The resigning member was given two other assignments.

A member of the leadership indicates that it sometimes is necessary to wage an active fight if a congressman is to get the assignment he wants:

Several years ago I wanted a particular committee and had my representative on Ways and Means committed to me. I also talked to other Ways and Means members and some of the leadership. When the selections were announced, the successor to a man who had just died had been chosen on the grounds that his state had always had someone on the committee. He was a freshman and I was in my third term. For the other spot they selected a man also junior to me and gave the same reason. I was mad, and went to everyone I could think of. They enlarged the committee by adding one member from each party and I was put on.

Sometimes failure to obtain one's first choice, even when it is a major committee not normally open to freshmen, will lead to special effort by the leadership to provide an acceptable substitute, provided the candidate has impressed the leadership favorably and has strong backing.

When I came to Congress the man I succeeded had been on the Appropriations Committee and I decided to try for it too. My delegation agreed to support me. So I talked with John McCormack who also agreed to help. Eventually, though, he told me that the leadership had given a great deal of consideration to my request but had finally decided on someone with more seniority. When I said that I realized the leadership has particular problems, that I didn't want to be difficult and that I'd go along with whatever they wanted he seemed very pleased. Actually, what alternative did I have? He told me the leadership would support me for any committee other than the one I had requested and asked my preference. Soon afterwards, the Democratic whip took me up to meet the committee chairman. I guess I satisfied him because I got the assignment.

Where competition for vacancies exists, choice assignments are often given to members representing "marginal" congressional districts as opposed to those from districts firmly held by the party. A congressman who has scored an impressive upset in gaining his seat may argue successfully that he needs a good initial assignment if he is to keep it. In criticism of this practice one legislator from a "safe" district observes:

Those making committee decisions at times at least have a complete blind spot as to the political value of placing "x" on a committee rather than "y." Men in their late sixties or early seventies are given good spots rather than men in their early forties. Also they are too often inclined to give a good seat to a man from a swing district who, despite his good points, may be defeated. A person from a safe district can afford to take controversial positions more easily. He also provides more continuity and is more likely to work up to a senior position.

Another representative expressed a similar view when he said, "When I first came to Congress, our party went from the majority to the minority. Though I waged a strong campaign for a good committee assignment, I couldn't get one. What few decent openings were available were given to those elected from marginal districts." On the other hand, Speaker Rayburn often stated that he preferred men from safe districts for service on committees like the Rules and Ways and Means. There the party's political stakes are high. It is important that committee members be able, where necessary, to resist the natural interests of their districts and support the party position without endangering their congressional seats. An important requirement for membership is that the individual be a "good party man."

The experience of one freshman who had been elected against heavy odds illuminates many phases of the process by which seats are allocated:

I came to Congress with unusual publicity for a first termer. In early December I came to Washington and saw the chairmen of the two committees in which I was interested, told them of my interest and qualifications, and pledged myself to work hard if selected. Both told me they were not in a position to choose me, that the decision would be made by other people, but both stated they had no objections to my serving on their committees. Later the congressmen from our section met together to talk about committee preferences and to estimate the possibility of success in achieving them. Our representative on the Committee on Committees said he would help me, as did the majority leader. Finally, I got the bright idea of talking to all members of the Ways and Means Committee. I assured each of them they would have no cause to regret voting to give me either of my committee choices, that I knew the fields and would work hard to justify their confidence. Few asked me for my views on legislation although several asked me general questions about agriculture. I think I could have gotten that committee if I had pushed my interest sufficiently, partly because of my experience, but I was given my other choice, also a good committee. Because so many people regarded my victory as an upset they may have felt they had to give me one of my choices.

Occasionally, a newcomer may even benefit from a factional struggle within his delegation. He may be given a first-class assignment because delegation leaders want their state represented on a certain committee, yet do not wish to give the spot to a more senior colleague whom they do not like. One member describes such a situation:

I came to Congress with no deep convictions about committee assignments. I introduced myself to the dean of our delegation. He asked about my organizational affiliations and interests such as my interest in veterans organizations. I told him I had been active in state bar association work, and he said I sounded like a good man for the Judiciary Committee. When I replied that the majority of congressmen are lawyers and that I thought it would be presumptuous of me to come here as a freshman and think I could get on Judiciary, he said that though it might be presumptuous of me to push it, there was nothing wrong with it being his idea, and he thought it a good one.

A week or two later I was back in my state and met our party leader. He said, "What are you up to in Washington?" I asked him what he meant. He replied, "You have been in Congress two weeks and you have the delegation split right up the middle." I had no idea what he was talking about and told him so. He said, "I have been getting phone calls from members of the delegation wanting to know who the hell you are. They say that though you have only been there a week or two people are saying you must go on Judiciary. Other members from our state have been trying for years to get on that committee and can't make it." When the committee lists were published I was on Judiciary.

Although it often is helpful to obtain the endorsement of influential partisans in pressing committee claims, not all communications from party leaders outside Congress are meant to be helpful to a candidate, as this story demonstrates:

I lined up enough votes to go on the committee I wanted and then, to my surprise, didn't get named. Some months later I discovered that a former member of Congress, then a federal judge in my district, had written to every member of the committee on our side whom he knew, saying how horrible I was. That one action turned the trick against me.

In the absence of firm operational criteria, irrelevancies can become important. Apparently even a hobby can tip the balance when competition exists for assignments. According to one Republican:

I first came here when the Republicans had just lost control of the House. Our party lost many committee seats and old timers were stumbling around for decent spots. I looked over the situation and decided to go after the only good committee which appeared to be left. I didn't think I had much chance because members bumped from other committees were eyeing that one too. One day the man handling assignments for my state phoned and said, "Say, aren't you interested in Abraham Lincoln?" I said that it was a hobby with me. He told me that the top Republican on the committee in which I was interested was also a student of Lincoln and that this mutual interest might be helpful to my candidacy.

He took me around to meet the fellow and we talked for half an hour about Lincoln but nobody said anything about the committee. I became worried and kept looking at my colleague, but he didn't say a word. Eventually we excused ourselves. When we got outside I told him I had thought he was going to help me, and he hadn't done anything. He said it wasn't necessary, that he felt sure I'd get the assignment. He was right. The next day I had a call from the ranking member asking if I would serve on the committee. That was one time a man's hobby really paid off because there was much competition from members senior to me.

Decisive Factors in Committee Assignments

In the preparation of party committee lists in the House a number of general propositions appear to be influential. Depending on the circumstances, candidates will seek to capitalize on one or more of them to advance their cause. In the interactions of these guide rules, it is not always possible to predict accurately the outcome of assignment contests. The propositions include:

The role of the leadership, where it wishes to exercise a role, is likely to be determinative. When an important issue of great interest to the leadership is before a committee, an aspirant for a vacancy on the committee whose views conflict with those of the leadership will not get the appointment regardless of his seniority.

A member is likely to get the committee of his choice if there is a vacancy and if little or no competition exists, unless he has aroused the antagonism of the leadership and/or the senior man of his party on the committee. It is possible to cite instances in which, in order to block the applicant, other congressmen who have not requested the assignment have been persuaded to file for the same spot, but this is infrequent. The "reasonable" and "responsible" legislator is given preference.

The role of chairman and ranking minority members of committees is significant, provided they are in "good standing" within their party.

A member who has more seniority than his rivals for an assignment is likely to be given the appointment unless, in the view of those responsible for the decision, there are other overriding considerations. Such considerations often exist.

An attempt is made to match committee assignment with the experience and background of the congressman. Usually, this works to the advantage of a candidate. Sometimes, of course, this may prevent a person desiring to vary his experience from doing so, as the testimony of one man indicates:

> Because of my background you may think I wanted the committee to which I was assigned. I didn't, but I had no real choice. I was told that I was a "natural" for the committee and that, because of my experience, I would have a better chance than other people from my area of getting it. Though I should have preferred to expand my experience, it was clear the interests of my section would be best served if I went on that committee.

A member who is removed from a committee because of a cut in the number of seats allotted to his party usually has priority when vacancies subsequently occur on that committee. Thus two Republicans "automatically" rejoined the Ways and Means Committee at the beginning of the Eighty-sixth Congress and another returned to the Rules Committee. But, as noted elsewhere, a second Republican seeking to regain his old seat on the Rules Committee was unable to do so because he was not regarded as "reliable" on some issues.

In the preparation of party lists for most committees, geography is a factor and, given the proper circumstances, a member may be able to capitalize on underrepresentation of his region or state in asserting his qualifications for appointment. That certain committees such as Agriculture, Interior, and Merchant Marine and Fisheries should have strong regional overtones in composition and thus deviate sharply from the general pattern is inevitable, given the inclination of members to seek posts related to the welfare of their district. Less easily explained is the fact that until recently four states accounted for the ten Republican places on the Committee on Education and Labor.

States sending a large party delegation to the House are usually regarded as "entitled" to one or more seats on the important committees, and designation by the delegation generally suffices to ensure election to fill "our" vacancy regardless of seniority claims of other candidates. Once it has a place on a committee, a state is reluctant to relinquish it. Because senior people in the delegation may already have good assignments, an aggressive campaign by a state to retain a seat on an important committee may lead to its designation of a relatively junior member to important responsibilities early in his career.

An attempt is made to assign a member to a committee which will help him in his district. Party leaders want their party colleagues to be re-elected and will keep this goal in mind when allocating committee seats. A member's claim that a particular assignment will significantly improve his chances of re-election will receive serious attention from the Committee on Committees.

Some Consolations

In retrospect some congressmen are convinced that their failure to be placed on the committee of their choice was in their best interest politically.

I had a lot of federal employees in my district, so I told our Committee on Committees man that I thought Post Office and Civil Serivce would be a good committee. He said right away, "Don't go on that committee. It has too much to do with your people. If you go on you will be hurt." I took his advice and backed off, and I have come to believe that his advice was sound.

*

In my first year the leadership saved me from my own folly. I desperately wanted to be a member of the Interstate and Foreign Commerce Committee, but I did not fully appreciate the work of the committee and didn't realize that probably the worst thing that could happen to me would be to be given that seat. Had I been a member of that committee I would have been continuously embarrassed, given the nature of my district, about the votes I would be required to cast.

Many members who were denied posts on the committees of their preference have found unanticipated advantages to their eventual assignment. One Democrat explains why he is content:

> I asked for the Judiciary Committee because of my background but, despite impressive support, I was not successful. Then I was asked whether I'd be willing to serve on the Space Committee, and I said yes. It is a new, noncontroversial committee, and I enjoy it although I regret that more floor work is not involved. Since being named to the committee I have found that it provides many opportunities for effective public relations and for increasing my contact with my district. I'm certain that eventually our committee will be one of the most important in the House. Certainly its work is extremely interesting and significant.

The process by which members seek and are assigned to committees is thus seen to be a complex one, influenced by factors that are far from constant. Numerous precedents, many of them contradictory, afford flexibility to those possessing the power to determine assignments and to the candidates as well. At the same time they complicate the task of candidates.

No single strategy can assure the newcomer of the assignment he wants. No single precept can guide those who make the decisions. Perhaps the only certainty is that a good assignment is worth striving for.

VI

The Committee System

"NO ONE WILL BE ABLE to understand Congress unless he understands the committee system and how it functions," said one congressman at the opening session of the Brookings round table conference. The House and Senate must, of course, work their will on legislative proposals that are cleared by committees, but it is in the committee rooms that the real work is done. There, choices are made between alternative proposals and decisions are reached to pigeonhole or kill outright other bills. The latter actions virtually eliminate the possibility of further consideration by the House or Senate; the former involve determinations that generally govern the reception of the measure in the parent body. By weighting a measure with unpalatable items though reporting it, a committee can hasten its demise. By amending a bill so as to weaken the opposition it can almost guarantee success. By endorsing a measure strongly, a committee increases significantly the likelihood that it will be accepted. Close House and Senate adherence to committee recommendations is the practice, although recommended legislation in controversial fields, such as agricultural policy, may face defeat on the floor. Normally, few substantive changes are made during floor debate. The volume and complexity of legislative proposals, the strong tradition of deferring to the "specialist," the search for ways to reconcile often conflicting pressures on congressmen, the very size of Congress—all conspire to enhance the authority of committee action. According to a congressional committee study, 90 percent of all the work of the Congress on legislative matters is carried out in committee.

The influence of committees in the legislative process is bolstered by the practice, particularly prevalent in the Appropriations Committee, of confining efforts to defeat or modify a proposal to activities within the committee itself. Once the battle has been fought and resolved there, those in the committee minority often do not press their case on the

House floor. If they do intend to press it, they are careful, at the time of the committee vote, to "reserve" the right to do so. But the emphasis is on closing ranks and presenting a united front.

Committee pre-eminence and the difficulties involved in setting aside measures receiving committee endorsement have led party leaders on occasion to ignore seniority in making assignments to committees handling crucial or controversial legislation, as has been illustrated in Chapter 5. They also have led the Executive and the interest groups to concern themselves with the assignment process.

The central role of committees in the legislative process has also underscored the importance of strategic referral of bills to committee: by careful attention to the wording, a congressman may have his bill sent to a committee more favorably disposed to it than the one to which it might otherwise have been referred.

Powers and Procedures

Committees are virtually autonomous bodies, hiring their own staffs, establishing their own rules of procedure, proceeding at their own pace for the most part, and resisting on occasion the urgings of the party. Chairmen may openly and successfully flaunt the party leadership, or they may have such stature that they are seldom requested to follow specific courses of action. And the reports of committees or their subcommittees may become as binding on executive departments as if they were law.

Committees differ tremendously in composition and method of operation, and may change significantly from one year to the next. As one congressman said, "Each committee tends to be unique in its unwritten rules—an organism in itself. The character changes with different chairmen and with different congresses." Some rely heavily on staff, interest groups, or the executive; others are relatively free from all such influences. Some are characterized by a lack of partisanship and generally report measures to the House floor by unanimous or nearly unanimous vote; strong partisanship is typical of others. In view of the central role of committees in the legislative process, an understanding of the working relationships that exist within the various committees is very helpful—often indispensable—to those who desire to influence legislation.

Just as different personalities alter procedures, the impact of a committee on the outlook of its members may be perceptible also. For example, service on the Appropriations Committee seems to make members more conservative. This is true in part because the membership is recruited carefully from the ranks of representatives likely to be susceptible to the socialization process. Although their attitudes toward issues vary, they are considered "reasonable" and "responsible," capable of adjusting easily to committee procedures and committee thinking. The fact that there is little turnover in committee membership tends to promote a group identity that is unusual and that aids in the assimilation of new members. Explained one liberal who sits on the committee:

The Appropriations Committee develops a strange sort of breed. As soon as you get on the committee somehow you become more responsible as a member of Congress. You find you have to justify expenditures and you cannot pass over any situation very lightly. As a result you become more conservative. I think it is fair to say that on the whole the members of the Appropriations Committee are more conservative than most members of Congress. Committee members pause long before they support various programs. They are always thinking of what additional taxes are necessary to carry these programs out. Most congressmen, on the other hand, are just thinking how worthwhile the program would be, neglecting the point of how much additional taxes would be required.

The important work of committees takes place in closed rather than open sessions. It has been estimated that in recent years from 30 percent to 40 percent of committee meetings have been held in executive session. While House committees dealing with money matters and unusually technical or sensitive legislation, such as the Appropriations, Ways and Means, and Foreign Affairs committees are concerned with, are more disposed to meet in private than most other groups, nearly every committee makes fairly extensive use of this procedure. Closed sessions facilitate compromise, promote candor and serious discussion, and eliminate the temptation to "play to the spectators," which occasionally overcomes members of Congress. Party representatives may have met together prior to a "mark-up" session in order to determine strategy and the party stand on a bill. But partisan stances are often sublimated and an atmosphere conducive to thoughtful consideration of legislation is more likely to prevail. Here representatives whose names the general public would not recognize may develop reputations among their colleagues based on their insights and their capacity for hard work. Despite the obvious advantages of holding executive sessions on many kinds of problems, there are persistent complaints, particularly from the press, that too many committee sessions are conducted behind closed doors. Far from promoting better legislation, these critics assert, closed sessions are often detrimental since, there, decisions are reached that would not be tolerated were the proceedings conducted in public.

Majority-Minority Relationships. The degree of cooperation existing between majority and minority members of a committee may be more dependent on the personal relationships between the chairman and ranking minority member than on the subject matter area involved. These two individuals usually have served together on the committee for an extended period and may have learned to work together comfortably. Retirement of one of them may alter intracommittee relationships. As one congressman illustrated:

> We had excellent relationships in our committee between the chairman and
> _____ [long-time ranking minority member]. But since the latter's retirement
> last year things have changed. I have sensed a strained relationship between the
> chairman and _____ [the new ranking minority member]. I don't look for close
> liaison to continue. I think a sharp clash is going to develop very shortly.

Intracommittee relationships may be changed in other ways, too. The leadership may seek to alter the kind of legislation reported by a committee by deliberately "packing" it with people of different philosophy than those who have long held control. A single issue may so solidify party lines that years of cooperation and harmony will be swept aside. Or interference by the Executive in the normal committee operation may have drastic effects. One Democratic congressman described such an incident:

> _____, who heads one of our subcommittees, doesn't always support our
> Democratic party's position. When the _____ bill came along, he supported
> President Eisenhower's proposal, and we had to maneuver for months and months
> to get him straightened out. That was the start, really, of unity among the committee Democrats. The Republicans had to be for Ike's plan because pressure was
> put on them. They finally stood with the administration on all parts of the bill
> instead of going along with the old procedure whereby we took care of committee members and other individuals. There were so many weaknesses in
> administration policy that we were able to unify all of the Democrats to vote
> against everything in the bill. In the course of considering it, interparty relationships got so bad that they have carried over into other programs. Recently, every

vote on an important measure in the committee has been almost a straight party vote. That is fine with us because it is much easier when you can write the legislation among the Democrats. The Republicans started having caucuses and we started having them too.

That statement led to the following discussion regarding the cooperation between majority and minority on committees:

On our committee we have a close relationship with the ranking minority member. In House tradition the minority member is consulted in scheduling legislation, but I wonder how many committees do this. I have been critical of consultation because I think we fail to get legislation passed if we try to iron it out with the minority ahead of time. In your committee, the minority isn't consulted at all about legislation, I suppose.

*

It is consulted to a degree. But last year we didn't tell them in advance that we were going to vote on the TVA bill. They had hundreds of amendments to offer to it, and we suggested that they offer them all en bloc. So we had ten minutes to consider the bill. That's democracy in action! It is all contrary to the textbooks, but it is the only way we ever could have gotten a bill out of the committee.

As the first speaker noted, consultation between leading majority and minority members of a committee is not uncommon. Members of some committees and subcommittees work in such close harmony that even the questions the chairman and staff intend to put to witnesses are furnished to the minority prior to hearings.

A Republican was sharply critical of one House committee, attributing what is generally regarded as an undistinguished record on legislation to excessive partisanship and domination by the chairman.

Everything that could be wrong with a committee is wrong with that one. The chairman has all the power to schedule legislation; he won't schedule anything. He makes trades on things in which he is interested. When hearings are scheduled, he is abusive to departmental witnesses. He and the ranking member on his side take up the time; anyone below the ranking one or two members on our side has no opportunity to say anything. The committee is nothing but a propaganda agency. That is demonstrated by the fact that no substantive legislation in the areas of its jurisdiction has been passed in the time I have been in Congress. More of that committee's bills are defeated on the floor than those of any other committee. There is no discussion between Democrats and Republicans on the committee, and the Republicans never know what is going to happen.

Another Republican told of one way in which committee staffs may be used for partisan purposes.

I am on two committees which practice a good deal of partisanship. The chief clerk of one of them kept a record of how many subcommittee meetings I attended. It included not only the subcommittee on which I served but those to which I did not belong. It included the amount of time I spent in each, and what I said. The information was forwarded to my opponent. I couldn't figure how my opponent knew so much about my activities last session, or why the chairman of the committee made snide remarks about me during meetings. Finally I found out. I was in the district talking about southern domination of our committee, and it got back to the chairman.

Problems of Jurisdiction and Intercommittee Coordination. Many thoughtful members of the House are concerned about problems of overlapping jurisdiction, intercommittee coordination, lack of proper liaison and exchange of information, and situations in which committees hearing testimony and presumed to possess special competence do not actually make the decisions. Matters relating to defense and national security, foreign policy, and science are among those for which it is often difficult to determine jurisdiction. Rivalry may develop between committees with common interests as they seek to establish their primacy in a certain field or to undertake hearings or investigations which promise to arouse widespread interest and publicity. Committees are jealous of their prerogatives and resent intrusion. Information gained may not be shared with competitors. When there is duplication of effort, prospective witnesses suffer too.

The following discussion illuminates some of the jurisdictional questions that plague the House:

Conflicting committee jurisdiction is a real problem. Take the missile field, for example. The Armed Services Committee, the Appropriations Committee, the Military Affairs Subcommittee of the Government Operations Committee all have had jurisdiction. Then the Space Committee was organized this year and began questioning all the military leaders about the missile program. As a consequence, people from the Pentagon are testifying before four different House committees and then going over to the Senate and doing the same thing. That is time consuming and unnecessary.

*

Another kind of problem arises when two committees share interests, and there is no liaison between them. For example, railroad retirement and unemployment insurance for railroad workers was brought to the floor by the Interstate and Foreign Commerce Committee although Ways and Means has the bulk of unemployment insurance programing and social security. There was no liaison between the committees' staffs. It is important to have the committees in agreement on some fundamental propositions so whatever is passed on railroad retirement will be somewhat in conformity with other unemployment insurance programs and social security.

*

Another example is foreign trade. The Foreign Affairs Committee has an interest, as has Interstate and Foreign Commerce by its very definition. Yet I dare say Ways and Means does the bulk of the legislating in that field because it gets reciprocal trade within its jurisdiction. There is no liaison between committees. In addition to overlapping jurisdiction you have piracy. Foreign Affairs developed the idea of distributing surplus foods abroad as a means of furthering good foreign relations. The Agriculture Committee took it over.

As a result of the confusion and overlap, there is much feeling among representatives that there should be more coordination of committee activity within the House itself, even though they express little enthusiasm for joint House-Senate committees. A coordinating body is sometimes suggested, though the point is made that much of the coordination could be accomplished by the committees concerned if attention could be directed to the problem. "It wasn't by accident," said one congressman, "that when the highway bill was before the Public Works Committee, Ways and Means people sat in. Liaison was necessary, and we made sure it occurred."

Another lawmaker observed that there was very little exchange of information between the Appropriations Committee and the Government Operations Committee, "yet Government Operations' job is to follow federal expenditures to see whether they are in accordance with the law and spent efficiently. The testimony and information they get is very valuable to Appropriations." In corroboration of this observation one member of the Appropriations Committee said: "There still isn't enough of that. We seldom get members of a Government Operations subcommittee appearing before us to give us the benefit of their work. Nor do we get any staff liaison. I think it is unfortunate."

The Appropriations Committee is often resented by legislators assigned to other committees, in part because of its power over the congressional purse. Some congressmen who do not themselves take the initiative to ensure that the results of the deliberations of their committees are,

where relevant, made available to the Appropriations Committee believe
the latter group is negligent in failing to seek out such information. And
some believe that members of other standing committees should be invited to sit in on appropriations subcommittee meetings where appropriate, as is the practice in the Senate. Commented one legislator:

> Theoretically the weapons system is authorized by the Committee on Armed
> Services, but that is only in theory. On the missile programs that have been
> permitted to go ahead, decision is made by the Appropriations Committee
> through the language of reports and through riders. The committee which heard
> all the testimony and is presumed to have special competence is not the one
> which makes the decision. If we are going to take the trouble to develop men
> with specialized knowledge in a given field, then we should give them the right to
> sit in and second guess on Appropriations. There is no point in having hearings
> before Armed Services and then have the final decision made by Appropriations.

That statement led to the following comment:

> Isn't it a little more complicated than that? Isn't it a fact that the Armed Serv-
> ices Committee doesn't really make decisions on major problems, that it involves
> itself more with housekeeping and peripheral matters? I suspect that if we had an
> Armed Services committee that made substantial policy decisions rather than
> accommodations between the weapons systems, then the Appropriations Com-
> mittee would not be in a position to do what it now does.

While many House members resent the Appropriations Committee and
believe it to be somewhat arrogant in its attitude, there is wide recognition that its members work diligently. Membership on the committee is
eagerly sought, but it is realized that the committee has a heavy workload
which successful applicants must help to shoulder. There is, therefore,
sympathy within the House for the heavy responsibilities of the committee and even for the committee itself when it is bypassed.

> Wouldn't it be better to require that bills for which there is overlapping
> jurisdiction be re-referred to another committee before they come to the floor?
> Agriculture passed a bill increasing the authorization for special school milk
> programs by $3,000,000, and it went directly to the floor, bypassing Appropria-
> tions. How can Appropriations have control over total government expenditures
> without having every bill involving expenditures re-referred to them before com-
> ing to the floor? Another ridiculous thing is that although the Foreign Affairs
> committee sits for weeks deciding what to put in the Mutual Security bill, the
> proceeds used for local currency under Public Law 480 is under Agriculture.
> Appropriations is bypassed.

Committee Chairmen

Committee chairmen rank high among the most influential members of
Congress. Sometimes respected, sometimes feared, often criticized by
their colleagues, the majority have learned well the traditional privileges
of their station. As men of authority and power, they are fair game for
detractors who charge they often fail to discharge their duties in responsible fashion. Some appear unmoved by such criticism, regarding it as the
inevitable result of power; most, at times at least, regard their actions as
"misunderstood." Even House members who have words of praise for
their own chairman are quick to document the "arbitrary actions" of
others. As one congressman said: "All committee chairmen are despots.
Some of them are benevolent despots, as is the case of my chairman, but
in any event they are despotic. They can run their committees as they see
fit, and they usually do." In the face of such comments, it is not surprising
that chairmen have a reputation in the House for moving to each other's
defense if their power is threatened.

Characteristics of Success. An effective chairman is much respected in the
House, earning even the grudging admiration of those who oppose him on
legislative issues. In analyzing the success of one Democratic chairman, a
Republican commented:

> The prime requirement for any chairman who wants to be an effective leader
> is to demonstrate that he is informed about the subject matter of his committee,
> and clearly this committee chairman is informed. And in demonstrating that
> he is, he commands the respect of the committee and of the House.

But knowledge of his subject is only one of the essential attributes of a
successful chairman. Realism in perceiving his support and skill in exploiting it can make a chairman strong. An awareness of the realities of a given
situation—of what is possible and what is not possible—is basic. Observes
one representative:

> The really skillful chairman understands where he stands on the floor. Judge
> Smith seems, perhaps more than anyone else among the chairmen, skillful in
> manipulating this relationship. He works in relation to the House as a whole. He
> is aware, or thinks he is aware, that he can get away with stalling a bill quietly
> when the House is not for it. He is aware he cannot stall a bill indefinitely if the
> majority is for it.

Some chairmen have virtually no influence in the House and very little influence in committtees. Others have influence out of all importance to their committees because of their personal prestige. So you have an incredible variety in the role, the position, and the power of the chairman.

The chairmen who are best liked by their committee colleagues are usually those who consult their associates on important matters, follow regularly established procedures, are amenable to reason, are not disposed to retain all committee perquisites for themselves, and do not discriminate against junior members by denying them adequate opportunity to participate fully—almost equally—in committee activities.

Sources and Uses of Power. The power of a committee chairman is impressive, varying somewhat according to committee tradition and the personal impact of the incumbent. He calls committee meetings and presides at them, exercising discretion in the recognition of his colleagues when they desire to speak. He decides the order in which bills are to be considered in the committee and when hearings should be held. Committee staffing is largely his prerogative. It is he who creates subcommittees, selects their membership, designates the chairman, and determines which legislative proposals shall be heard by each. He passes on requests for committee travel, initiates or approves special projects, acts as floor manager of legislative proposals voted out of his committee (a responsibility which carries with it the often crucial decision as to which members share in the limited debate), or designates the manager and, should such proposals go to conference, generally functions as head of the managers representing the House.

If he does not choose to have his committee governed by formal rules, his resistance may be sufficient to overcome efforts to provide for them. Should he determine to ignore established rules, it is only rarely and with great difficulty that his opponents can succeed in forcing him to acknowledge them.

In the last analysis he is, of course, responsible to his committee colleagues and can be called to account by them. Yet he often successfully avoids and sometimes flouts established procedures. Discontent may smoulder, but it seldom erupts in victorious rebellion. A freshman member of Congress says:

I knew committee chairmen were powerful, but I didn't realize the extent of the power or its arbitrary nature. Recently, when my chairman announced he planned to proceed in a particular way, I challenged him to indicate under what rules he was operating. "My rules," he said. That was it, even though there were no regularly authorized rules permitting him to function in that manner. There is great reluctance to challenge committee chairmen even though you don't agree with them. Everyone seems fearful; all members have pet projects and legislation they want passed. No one wants to tangle too much because they realize what the results would be.

Primarily, a chairman's strength rests on personal relationships under-girded by tradition. As chairman, time and again he is in a position to grant special consideration to the request of a committee member—a request which, were normal procedures to be followed, might not be acted on promptly if at all. His power is cumulative: association with his colleagues over a period of years enables him to build a strong residue of personal good will and IOU's in the face of which open revolt is most difficult.

Colleagues are grateful when he assigns them a subcommittee of their own and the right to staff it, and they want to retain this power. They know, too, that the chairman, by virtue of his position, possesses influence and leverage with other committee chairmen that on occasion, may prove helpful. In short, they recognize it is within his power to bestow certain privileges, and they hesitate to antagonize him. One Democrat describes the problem faced by would-be reformers:

The toughest kind of a majority to put together is one to reform a committee in the face of opposition from the chairman. As you get closer to the top of the hierarchy, the pressures on people who normally would be counted on to aid reformers are enormous and even people who would be classified as among the "good guys" rather than the "bad guys" tend to chicken out. It is the second and third termers who really have to lead the rebellion. The new fellows are still in a dream world and after you get beyond two or three terms you are part of the team and begin to see some merit in the system.

Another representative describes a recent attempt to bring about reform:

Our chairman is a lovable fellow but we have had no rules and no subcommittees. Inspired by the examples of some other committees last session, a number of us drew up some rules, setting up subcommittees and so on, and moved their adoption. The matter was brought to a vote after much anguish and finagling, and we were voted down. How? A couple of freshmen who had been interested in reform were "detained" in their district on this particular occasion. Some of the older people near the chairman in seniority, who nevertheless were spiritually on our side, voted against us because they had received pap from the chairman and there was more coming.

I should add a happy sequel. With this Congress came some changes in membership, and the chairman saw the handwriting. So now for the first time in history, we have a few subcommittees and a much better situation.

Majorities are Pickwickian things. You really have to have about a two-thirds majority like we now have in order to get results. Last session we had a simple majority spiritually in our favor, but they would not stand up and be counted.

A third member confirmed that many chairmen are resourceful in maintaining their power:

One chairman calls freshmen into his office and points out "if you vote for this set of rules, the chairmanships will all go to the senior members, but if you play along with me, you, as a first termer, will be selected as chairman of an important subcommittee." That gimmick has worked now for I don't know how many years. And he does appoint first termers as subcommittee chairmen.

Yet there is evidence that when contrasted with the authority of predecessors of several decades ago, the outside limits of power of today's chairmen are declining. The process has been gradual—so gradual as to be imperceptible to some congressmen. One leader in the movement to curtail the unrestricted freedom of chairmen by providing regularized procedures for committee operation explained the difference in this way:

When talking about a chairman's powers, one can differentiate between negative and positive power. Prior to the Reorganization Act when there were thirty or forty committees, you had the classical picture of what I call the negative chairman. A chairman, functioning within a system of smaller committees with narrower jurisdiction, was able to pigeonhole any bill referred to his committee to which he was opposed, provided there was not overwhelming sentiment in the House that action had to be taken. He could simply say, "There will be no hearings. We are not going to take up this bill."

This negative power of chairmen still exists today in the sense that chairmen can employ delaying tactics, by failing to call hearings, for example. But it is much more limited than it used to be, although the political scientists haven't completely caught up with that fact.

When we talk about the positive power of a chairman, we are talking about the chairman who not only is influential in his committee, but who has tremendous power and prestige on the floor. He will seldom be overruled. But the great power of pigeonholing legislation that chairmen once exercised simply by saying autocratically, "I am against this bill and there will be no hearings," has all but disappeared. Minor bills have been stalled in this fashion, but I challenge anyone to name a major bill that any chairman has killed in that way, except at the very end of a session when the time factor becomes important.

While there is considerable agreement with the views expressed above, there also is vigorous dissent. One congressman said he thought the speaker "a little too charitable and too satisfied with things as they are." He continued:

Look at all the committees that prevent consideration of legislation. Ways and Means will not consider any fiddling with oil depletion allowance. You can go on with example after example where there are taboos because of the chairman, very largely. The fact is that most of the committees, despite the valiant efforts of some members, are not reformed and the chairman is, if not omnipotent, at least the wielder of a tremendous negative influence.

In support of the position that chairmen still exert autocratic influence one lawmaker said:

The _____ committee offers a good example of complete and total dictatorship in action. The chairman runs the committee with an iron hand. He puts people on subcommittees, takes them off, and announces transfers at will. About a year ago a subcommittee was considering something to which he was strongly opposed, but which seemed likely to pass. Just as the meeting opened, in walked four additional members of the full committee two Democrats and two Republicans. Without forewarning the subcommittee chairman, the chairman of the full committee had added four men to the group. In less than an hour there was to be a vote on a very important issue about which the four could not possibly have been fully informed. The chairman assumed that all four additions would vote with him against the legislation. It looked as though he had won until much to his distress one of the four broke ranks. But the action in increasing the subcommittee size was taken solely and arbitrarily by the chairman. Subcommittee chairmen do a lot of grumbling, but when the chips are down they vote with the chairman.

Consensus appears to be that while it probably is true that a chairman could not so flagrantly defy the will of the House today as formerly, efforts to proceed in the face of his objection depend primarily on the intensity of the pressure which can be brought to bear to get him to act, the nature of the majority aligned against him, and his own personality and conviction. Even today, opposition from a committee chairman to a proposal coming before his committee can be extremely detrimental, and sometimes fatal, to the measure. To overcome the obstinacy of a recalcitrant chairman requires a firm and determined majority strongly and skillfully led. Yet it is also true that legislators feel that fewer chairmen execute their responsibilities in the fashion of the stereotype of the autocratic committee head of old who kept his own counsel and regarded "his" committee as completely subject to his will. A definite trend in the other direction is discernible, though it would be erroneous to conclude that all chairmen are "reformed."

Today's delaying tactics are likely to be more subtle ("The judge is a much shrewder man than_____. He uses a bowie knife where_____uses a meat axe.") and less irritating than those of the past, but the results may be the same. Observed one member, "I don't think there is a chairman in the House who will say, 'I won't give you a hearing.' They don't need to say that. A skillful chairman will schedule hearings and action on a bill in such a way that by the time it gets out of committee, it won't have time to get by the House." One chairman is drawn in this fashion:

> _____ is one of the most charming and delightful chairmen in the House, and highly skillful. He doesn't sidetrack us by ever refusing anything. He just schedules a workload in other areas which makes it impossible for us to get our legislation heard. He always keeps us busy, never refusing anyone a hearing on legislation, always holding out hope. I have eternal hope. But he has one of the fullest schedules you will ever encounter.

A chairman is sometimes also criticized on the grounds that, in the words of one congressman: "Often he is trying to squirrel away information. He doesn't even want some of the committee members to be well informed, much less the average member of Congress." It is charged, too, that many of them have a lien on committee staff members, requiring them to perform assignments which should be undertaken by the chairman's personal office staff, thereby diverting hardpressed committee aides from their primary responsibilities. Although the House itself is reluctant to interfere in the activites of its committees or in committee expenditures, on occasion it has done so, generally as a rebuke to individual chairmen. For example, it reduced sharply requests of two committees for funds in the Eighty-eighth Congress, and, in one case, even specified the allocation of the funds authorized and required that the appropriate subcommittee chairman co-sign all authorizations for spending.

Preference for a Strong Chairman. As critical as some congressmen are of chairmen who seek to dominate committee proceedings and decisions, most of them seem to prefer a "strong" chairman to a "weak" one. For example, one representative stated, "I sometimes think I would prefer a despot to a man who is a pile of jelly." Another lawmaker agreed, and although a member of the minority party, had high praise for his chairman:

The chairman of my committee is often considered a despot. I think he is a strong leader. He runs what is called in the Navy a taut ship. You know where you are headed. Sometimes you have to fight to get your point across, but if it is a good point you can get it across. I would prefer to have a committee run like that to one functioning without real leadership. Our chairman is responsible to the committee and we are very loyal to him because of the quality of his leadership. He has a record that is unparalleled for getting legislation through. Seniority, experience, and responsible leadership are the basis of his power.

Seniority and the Choice of Chairmen. There is no evidence of significant support in the House for modifying the present system for selecting committee chairmen by seniority. Though some freshmen express dissatisfaction with seniority as a test for capacity to lead a committee, nearly all of their more experienced colleagues assert there is no more satisfactory alternative. Even many freshmen support the present system. Indeed, there is some feeling that opposition to selecting chairmen by seniority is concentrated among those who write about the Congress, many of whom, it is said, possess little understanding of it. Acceptance by the Congress of seniority does not signify that members are enthusiastic about it. They are not. Rather they fear that the alternatives involve even more disadvantages. As one liberal House Democrat has written, "It is not that Congress loves seniority more but the alternatives less."

It is admitted that the present impersonal and automatic system for designating committee chairmen fails to distinguish between outstanding and mediocre House members, occasionally elevating a man incapable of leading or who possesses a record of inattention to committee responsibilities. It is also agreed that the system is not conducive to the maintenance of party discipline and that committee chairmen as a group are neither ideologically nor geographically representative of the House as a whole.

The characteristic congressional response to these criticisms is that seniority avoids the "politicking," logrolling, and factionalism that would accompany any system likely to replace it. It promotes stability by pro-

viding for an orderly transfer of authority to an heir apparent whose selection is assured. It is also suggested that to substitute another method
might result in the loss of valuable talent. Said one congressman:

> Suppose you picked the number four man on a committee as a chairman.
> Wouldn't you immediately do away with the usefulness of the first three? They
> would be unhappy that they hadn't been picked and the chairman would always
> be regarding them as possible rivals and probably wouldn't want to give them
> stature. You are dealing with people, and human nature must be considered in
> deciding the method to be used.

Selection of a chairman by vote of committee members—more precisely, by the majority members—is thus regarded as unsatisfactory: the
present impersonal system avoids the rivalries likely to develop among
the more experienced committee members. In rewarding experience, the
seniority system, it is asserted, generally places in positions of power men
and women who through long exposure to the subject matter and to the
process by which committee work is carried forward have become alert
to the technicalities of legislation and its possible ramifications, and to the
kinds and sources of pressures affecting the key issues before the committee. They are adept at handling relationships with the executive branch
and with their own colleagues. From the minority's point of view, the
present practice may result in the designation of an individual less motivated by partisanship and therefore more amenable to "reason," than
election procedures would bring forward. It seems clear that many congressmen are not anxious to replace seniority with a system in which adherence to party would become a major determinant. They enjoy the
flexibility of voting and degree of independence which seniority promotes. When it was suggested by one representative that where the
Congress and Presidency are controlled by the same party, it is important to have committee chairmanships in the hands of legislators sympathetic to the President's program, another congressman said firmly:

> I think you make a basic mistake when you assume that it is desirable for the
> committee chairman to be in harmony with the administration on every issue.
> Don't forget this is a tripartite form of government. I think it is a healthy thing
> sometimes to have competition if not conflict between the legislative branch and
> the executive branch.

An influential liberal Democrat has said that when he first was elected
to Congress he shared the public image of "aging tyrannical chairmen

ruling their committees with iron hands, pigeonholing bills willy-nilly and generally running Congress the way Henry VIII ran England." Eventually, however, he came to realize there was "a wide discrepancy between political folklore about the seniority system and fact about [it]."[1] He and other members believe seniority has become a popular whipping boy, unfairly charged with responsibility for many weaknesses of the committee system. Seniority, it is observed, does no more than designate the chairman; his powers and duties depend on rules of procedure adopted by the committee on which he serves. Committee inertia may produce too strong a chairman, but the remedy is clear: reform rests with the committee itself.

The tendency for committees to establish formal rules of procedure ("one man rule is on the way out") is but one of many influences that may mitigate the sometimes undesirable results of seniority. As has been demonstrated elsewhere in this volume, the seniority principle is not firmly applied in making committee assignments when there are strong reasons pointing to another choice. And the proliferation of subcommittees and select committees provides an unusual opportunity to grant early recognition to able and restive junior members of Congress who might otherwise be required to wait years to assume positions of leadership.

Though the general principle of seniority is well established as one of the basic tenets of the congressional system, there is nothing in the existing rules of the Congress to cloak it with legitimacy. It is a custom of convenience. It is clear that the elements of stability it lends to a system otherwise noted for its uncertainties and maneuverings have increased the reluctance to cast it aside.

Committee Rules

Closely linked to the question of the power of committee chairmen is the matter of committee rules. In the absence of committee action, the relevant rules of the House and those set forth in the Legislative Reorganization Act of 1946 are the only official guideposts. Each committee has the privilege of adopting supplementary rules of procedure, and about half have done so. Concern with the dictatorial tactics of some com-

---

[1] Emanuel Celler, "The Seniority Rule in Congress," *Western Political Quarterly*, Vol. 14 (March 1961), pp. 160–67.

mittee chairmen led Congress in the 1946 act to provide for regular meetings of committees, more complete records, open hearings, and prompt reporting of legislative proposals once a majority of the committee voted to support them. As has been indicated, however, these provisions are often ignored. Referring to that legislation, one congressman has written: "Much of the impetus for committee reform derives from that [the 1946 act], for implicit in it is the concept that the committee and not the chairman is sovereign. If we still have a dual system—reformed committees and unreformed—it is because a few committees have never understood the spirit nor taken advantage of the letter of the Reorganization Act."

There is much sentiment within the House of Representatives that strict adherence to the appropriate rules would obviate the need for "major" action in the individual committees. Although congressmen tend to favor additional rules that would restrict opportunities for chairmen to act arbitrarily and without consultation, many emphasize that the main problem is enforcement of existing rules rather than creation of new ones, desirable as the latter may be. The sections of the rules of the House that pertain to committee organization and operation are among those with which newcomers to Congress are particularly urged to acquaint themselves in order to be aware of their rights and in a position to protect them.

It is evident that members of Congress are less concerned about committee rules than are political scientists. Most congressmen seem to regard rules as convenient and desirable, while at the same time recognizing that on occasion it may be equally convenient to ignore them by tacit consent. Their very adoption and existence offer a measure of protection to those committee members who are unhappy about the way the unit is proceeding. Most chairmen—even tyrannical ones—it is asserted, will be guided, in part at least, by the knowledge that such rules can be resorted to if a sizable and vocal group within the committee desires to embarrass or harass. One congressman of independent bent argues that where such rules exist the chairman is vulnerable. "Get a special order," he urges, "and take the floor and expose him. Prepare releases for the press and document his arbitrariness. Challenge him in committee. If people are persistent they can force a chairman to toe the mark." In most situations, however, committee members, while disapproving, and sometimes resenting, failure to adhere to the rules do not feel that enough is at stake to warrant a struggle. While the tools may be available to bring about changes in committee procedure, most legislators seldom regard an issue as of sufficient importance to justify their taking time from other necessary duties to do battle. Generally, the action has to be extremely arbitrary and of a recurring nature to arouse enough ire to lead to reform.

In nearly every instance where a chairman is criticized as arbitrary, it is possible to uncover defense of his actions and sympathy for the difficult nature of his responsibility. In the absence of a strong and clear history of similar performances by a chairman, and providing the action is not particularly flagrant, considerable sentiment often exists that in the face of the tremendous volume of work with which a committee is concerned, priority and even pace must primarily rest with the chairman who, it is noted, will find it impossible to satisfy everyone. For this and other reasons, there is a predisposition to accept his judgment, and this makes the likelihood of successful revolt rather slim. Thus one of the most respected members of the House, when asked to explain how his chairman had been able to take and enforce a certain arbitrary action that the member disapproved, replied, "He acted under the rules he uses. I don't know where they come from, but those are the rules he uses, and that is the way he proceeds." It was clear he regarded the chairman as firmly entrenched and in a position to exercise near sovereign authority.

Says one congressional reformer, "Where you really need the rules is where you have hostility." Another comments, "Rules of committees are designed to take the sting out of seniority and clip the wings of an arbitrary negativist chairman. The obstinacy of the chairman has to be weighed in determining the need for and nature of rules. The equation: If you have a nonexistent or compliant chairman, rules are unnecessary; a medium type chairman, medium rules." Yet the first speaker warns, "We really ought to shoot for rules everywhere because then you will have a tradition and established practice. You will have reasonably democratic procedures no matter who takes over."

Among legislators who have been most sympathetic to the movement to establish regularized methods of operation, there is agreement that reform is best advanced under bipartisan auspices arising from an issue cutting across party lines. If the reform attempt has the appearance of being a partisan effort by minority members of the committee, it becomes awkward for sympathetic members of the majority to "break ranks" without incurring the wrath of party leaders outside the committee. If the attempt is primarily that of "young Turks" within the majority party, with no prior attempt to gain the support of minority party members, the latter may refuse to inject themselves into the dispute, being content to watch the majority engage in intraparty conflict. Or they may provide sympathy or outright support to the senior members of the majority, an action attributable in part to the concern felt by senior members of the minority for the plight of their peers in the majority.

A small, vocal group among the freshmen and junior men is likely to be particularly restive under dictatorial rule, since they are least likely to be consulted or informed about committee activities, although newcomers have been somewhat conditioned to expect little by the much cited, but not quite accurate, admonition that freshmen "should be seen but not heard." Most legislators want the respect of their colleagues very much, and, lacking support from fellow legislators of stature and longer service, newcomers are likely to be reluctant to unleash or join a full-scale attack on existing procedures they may find irritating. In fact, as has been noted, the most junior members often are not the most reliable and constant of allies for the reformers; the general view is that the middle group must carry the burden of the battle.

The ease with which legislation is reported out of committee bears no direct correlation to the nature of the rules by which the committee is governed. Thus it is possible to demonstrate that committees with no formal rules, or fragmentary ones, may be far more successful in reporting bills than those which operate under relatively complete and "enlightened" rules. This, of course, may depend far more on the nature of the legislation and the pressure, as well as on the chairman, than on rules or the absence of them. The point is that many congressmen think the reformers among their colleagues are excessively optimistic in their claims for the advantage of detailed rules.

A committee can lack formal rules and still function in an orderly way because of respect for informal norms of procedure. One of the leading advocates of formalized committee rules recognizes this. As he describes the situation:

It seems to me there are two forces at work. One is written rules, if any, and the other is simply an unwritten tradition of the committee which can be very powerful. For example, in the committee which has a beautiful set of rules, there is also an unwritten code of having things done in a certain way because they have been done that way and everybody recognizes it is a good way to do business. If you had a change of leadership, and the new chairman tried to violate the unwritten tradition and practice, he would run up against tremendous opposition.

In many of the committees which operate without any rules, an unwritten tradition of doing things has developed, that is recognized as an acceptable modus operandi for everyone. If the chairman changed and the new man completely overturned many of the existing practices, tremendous resistance would develop. It might even lead to the setting up of written rules.

One of the main arguments heard in advocating committee reform is that formal rules prevent a chairman from delaying or ignoring committee business in which he is not interested. Yet in some situations the lack of rules is regarded as a means of expediting action rather than delaying it. Said one legislator, "In our committee during the past session we got things done by resisting all this reform business. If we had had a reform, we wouldn't have gotten any legislation out." Later he charged that attempts to reorganize committee procedures were purely partisan in nature and were specifically motivated by a desire to impede committee action: "The Republicans on our committee are all in favor of reform, such as outlawing proxy voting and having regular meetings and things like that. They advocate it for the purpose of obstructing good legislation." The congressman dismissed the suggestion that rules provided protection should a change in party control or leadership occur. When a colleague observed that, though he might be satisfied without rules at the moment, situations change and in different circumstances the absence of rules might be detrimental to his cause, he said: "We'll worry about that when the time comes."

Few individuals who wield important power voluntarily relinquish their prerogatives; congressional committee chairmen are of this mold. Yet, having fought unsuccessfully to retain the full measure of their authority, some surprise their colleagues and themselves by rapid adjustment to new rules. One chairman who resisted reform for years, yielding only when a rebellious majority within his committee forced rules upon him, apparently found the results more palatable than he had anticipated. Relates one participant in the rebellion:

We had a fantastic experience with our chairman who admittedly is one of the hardest people to deal with. His method of running a committee was to do nothing.

Two or three months would go by without a meeting even though the jurisdiction of the committee includes a couple of the most vital and controversial subjects before the Congress. Finally we pushed through some rules. After two years of operating under rules, which provide not only for subcommittees but fixed jurisdiction with bills automatically being referred, I went to talk to the chairman. I was amazed to find he was ready to give up further power. "This new system we have works very well," he said. We relieved him of his responsibilities and he likes it!

Another member of the same committee added that the transformation had been so great that when the time came to assign new members to subcommittees, the chairman called them all to his office and told them to select the ones they wanted. A few years ago, it was agreed, such an event wouldn't have occurred.

Participation in Committee Work

Committee work is often unexciting and routine, involving time consuming chores of no apparent value to a member or his constituents, and sometimes it is concerned with technical subject matter beyond the comprehension as well as the interest of a congressman. Nor is it likely to be as relevant to the question whether he will retain his congressional seat as some of the other tasks that continually vie for his time. The temptation is strong, therefore, to select carefully the points at which he will permit himself to become deeply involved in the work of the committee or committees of which he is a member.

Veteran legislators urge their juniors to resist this temptation. They regard such a decision as short-sighted in terms of its effect on their relationships with their colleagues, and in terms of the educational value of committee work in enabling a congressman to become familiar with all aspects of the legislative process before he becomes engulfed by the more pressing responsibilities that accompany increased seniority. They also warn that lack of participation limits severely the potential scope of a member's influence within the committee and the House. The man who attends to his committee work, they emphasize, is the man who is listened to. He is the man who gets ahead.

One congressman explains his presence on a major committee:

When I first came to Congress I was placed on two committees. I enjoyed those activities and I worked hard at them. What I really wanted was a spot on the _____ committee, however. It wasn't too long before I was given that job, and I'm sure that I got it largely because of the work I did on the committees to which I was originally assigned. Around here, one of the things which is most wanted is a worker. When they find out that you are a worker you tend to get what you want.

It is difficult to generalize about the degree of member participation in committee work since it varies not only from committee to committee but also from subject matter to subject matter within a single committee. House personnel like to cite instances when a representative, unhappy with a committee assignment, may even decline to attend committee sessions, but such examples are rare. Congressional estimates are that from one-third to one-half of a committee's membership constitute the hard core that can be depended on in nearly every activity, other members injecting themselves when they are interested in the subject under discussion. The core of "workers" find that their diligence leads to an increased workload in other ways: they are the ones who carry the responsibility with respect to floor activities of the committee, and it is they who are consulted and deferred to when decisions are being made on whether to support or oppose legislative proposals.

One congressman describes his committee in this way:

About half the members of our committee participate actively in the committee work. The other half are not present at the majority of the meetings and hearings, although they are present at the time of a vote and simply vote their party position. I have noted a very close correlation between participation in committee and active participation on the House floor when issues of concern to our committee come up. The same group which is not active in committee don't know enough about the hearings on the bill or the technicalities involved to be able to speak intelligently on the legislation when it is brought up. Usually they keep quiet.

Committee procedures, as well as subject matter, can play a major role in determining how faithful and attentive members are in meeting committee responsibilities. In this respect, the chairman is in a position to be an important factor. Explains one member:

Participation is also reflected somewhat by the method which the chairman establishes for questioning witnesses. When we hold important hearings, our chairman regularly follows the procedure of querying the witness himself, and then moving down the membership of the committee in terms of seniority, alternating between parties. There is no time limitation on any member. The low men on the totem pole soon learn that whenever important witnesses are before the committee, they will never be reached to ask questions. The effect has been that they become discouraged from attending as regularly as they otherwise would. It is my understanding that many other committees establish time limitations for questioning by individual members, but that has never been true in our case.

Such an experience is in sharp contrast to that of junior members of the Ways and Means Committee where, according to one Republican, "The chairman frequently begins at the lower end of the seniority scale and works backwards. In the entire time I have been on the committee I have never seen anybody who wanted to ask questions fail to have adequate opportunity to do so." And a freshman member of the Foreign Affairs Committee has words of praise for its presiding officer. Says he, "He is a good chairman who believes all members are entitled to participate fully in the deliberations of the committee. Senior members have no particular advantage."

Some committees are so organized that the really important deliberations and determinations customarily take place in the subcommittees rather than in sessions of the full committee. In such situations the full committee generally meets to approve in routine fashion the work of its subordinate units. This too can affect attendance, as one congressman observes: "While we don't have as good attendance, as we might like in the full executive committee meetings, there is an obvious explanation. The burden of our workload occurs in subcommittees, and there we have had very good attention to the legislation."

Members of Congress agree that much of their congressional life is spent in committee activities. For conscientious members of active committees, the responsibilities can be onerous and staggering. Attending committee sessions and preparing for them can easily consume a major proportion of a member's time, for months at a stretch. For such congressmen, a strong personal staff able to assume the burden of more than routine matters relating to constituents is particularly essential. They have no alternative but to delegate many activities they would prefer to perform themselves if they are to carry out their committee duties diligently and effectively.

The House was in session 141 days during the first session of the

Eighty-sixth Congress. In that period the Defense Subcommittee of the Appropriations Committee, to cite one of the more important and active groups, met sixty-five days, nearly always in both morning and afternoon sessions. For nearly three and one-half months the subcommittee met almost daily on the dual meeting basis. In 1963, the Defense Subcommittee met seventy-two and one-half working days, excluding the period required for marking up the Defense Appropriations bill.

Since members of the Appropriations Committee serve on two, and sometimes three, subcommittees, it is not unreasonable to assume that a member of the defense unit may find himself in committee two days out of every three the House meets. In addition, of course, this is often accompanied by a heavy schedule of study and preparation so that the congressman can fulfill his committee chores properly. The Defense Subcommittee of the Appropriations Committee passes on more than half of the federal budget—a responsibility one does not accept lightly. It is not surprising, therefore, that conscientious members are sometimes irritated by colleagues who fail to respond to their duties with equal dedication. Nor is it surprising that a capacity for hard work should become a condition for membership on the more important and busier standing committees.

It is precisely because of the magnitude and the importance of committee work that the representatives who come to be known as "a congressman's congressman" are those who attend to their committee duties, master their subject, develop expertise, and command respect. Because this situation exists, also, a junior member of ability can often successfully bypass many of the normal seniority routes to prominence and rather quickly become recognized in the House.

Burdensome as committee activities can be, some members point out that committee work is too often cited inaccurately as an explanation for absence from the floor of the House. Commented one lawmaker:

Committee work is sometimes used as an excuse by members for not participating fully in other activities associated with the job of a congressman. I'm sure that many times you've read or heard it stated that congressmen are in committee when they're not on the floor. That's a lot of baloney. Many members fail to meet their committee responsibilities. I'd say on my own committee less than one third of the members are really hard working and conscientious in terms of attending the meetings and assuming their share of the workload.

The Subcommittees

The workload of most congressional committees has made it increasingly difficult for them to meet their obligations to the Congress without formal subdivision of work among committee members. In 1963 only three standing committees of the House—Rules, Un-American Activities, and Ways and Means—functioned without subcommittees. In recent congresses the Ways and Means Committee has sometimes established subordinate units to meet specific needs, but once their purpose has been met, they have been dissolved.

There is wide disparity in the use committees make of subcommittees. While Ways and Means "almost invariably operates as a full committee," the most important work of the Appropriations Committee is carried on at the subcommittee level. About half the legislation coming out of the Armed Services Committee passes through the full committee route, including nearly all items of major importance. Although the Foreign Affairs Committee has ten subcommittees, it, too, considers the bulk of its major legislation such as foreign aid, peace corps, and armament control in the full committee. Indeed, though many standing committees consign important legislation to subcommittees, there is a tendency to reserve the major proposals for consideration by the entire committee.

If some committees exist without subcommittees and others often bypass them when important legislation is involved, it must also be said that no pattern of subcommittee organization is evident among those committees where they are important. Subcommittees may be established by number rather than by subject matter, or their titles may be so general that they do not identify jurisdiction. Both types permit wide flexibility to committee chairmen in bill referral, thereby enhancing their influence. Education and Labor, for example, presently has six subcommittees, three dealing with education and three with labor. Those in each category are titled "general," "special," and "select," which reveal nothing about subject matter. Even committees that establish subordinate units by subject matter do not follow a consistent formula. The Agriculture Committee, for example, has some subcommittees that are commodity-oriented (Tobacco, Cotton, Wheat), and others that are problem-oriented (Conservation and Credit, Domestic Marketing, Family Farms).

In part the greater dependence on subcommittees is but a natural outgrowth of the Reorganization Act, which reduced the eighty-one existing standing committees to thirty-four—nineteen in the House of Representatives and fifteen in the Senate.[2] The sharp decrease in the number of committees was accompanied by a corresponding increase in jurisdiction, making inevitable ultimate dependence on a division of labor within them. The number of subcommittees has risen steadily. In 1963 there were over 250 in Congress, the majority in the House.[3]

House Committees now have as many as fifteen subcommittees, many of them rather specialized.[4] In some instances, it is charged, they have been established because of a desire to create additional chairmanships for members of the majority party, but frequently a more impelling need has been demonstrated. And the trend to more subcommittees provides an early opportunity for recognition of less senior committee members and decreases criticism of congressional organization.

Occasionally, a subcommittee will become so powerful that its influence will exceed that of the full committee. In describing the impact of certain of these groups, one legislator points out that: "The reports of the Appropriations subcommittees are more important than statute law because these are the bibles of the operating agencies for the coming year." These reports are important in part because it is difficult to challenge them, or to test their accuracy as a reflection of House opinion. A rider or amendment can be defeated on the floor, but a committee report is not subject to that kind of verification. Subcommittees have become important instruments of policy because of the tendency of the House to follow the recommendations of its standing committees and the practice in many committees of approving in routine fashion the findings of their subordinate units. Subcommittee chairmanships are eagerly sought not only because of the prestige, publicity, and perquisites that go with

[2] Now twenty in the House and sixteen in the Senate.

[3] A comprehensive breakdown of congressional committee structure prepared by the Senate Government Operations Committee showed that, as of July 18, 1961, Congress maintained a total of 303 committee units, including 36 standing committees, 3 special and select committees, 11 joint committees, and 253 subcommittees. Of the total number, 127 units were in the Senate and 152 were in the House. Added to this were 11 joint committees which had 13 subcommittees of their own.

[4] Thus the House Agriculture Committee has the following subcommittees: Cotton; Dairy; Poultry; Forests; Livestock and Feed Grains; Oilseeds and Rice; Tobacco; Wheat; Conservation and Credit; Departmental Oversight and Consumer Relations; Domestic Marketing; Equipment, Supplies, and Manpower; Family Farms; Foreign Agricultural Operations; and Research and Extension.

them but also because of the opportunities they provide to affect the direction of legislation. Congressmen agree that only in rare instances are the actions of subcommittees subjected to anything approaching a searching examination by the full committee, or on the House floor. This fact underscores the importance of the composition of certain subcommittees —particularly the distribution of chairmanships—not only to individual congressmen and state delegations but also to various interest groups. "Friends" strategically placed at the subcommittee level can reduce appreciably the effort that otherwise might be required to gain favorable action on proposals of concern to organizations, and it is not surprising that many groups should seek to maximize their influence at the subcommittee as well as the committee level. The truth is that congressmen are generally more concerned with the work of the subcommittees to which they belong than in the activities of the committees themselves.

The right of standing committee chairmen to designate subcommittee heads is put to various uses and has been all but unchallenged, although in 1957 a sizable minority within the Committee on Education and Labor unsuccessfully sought to force the chairman to allocate these posts on the basis of seniority.[5] This attempt was made because of his refusal to provide such an assignment to the next ranking member of his party on the committee. Ordinarily, as an examination of the House committee lists shows, senior members receive subcommittee chairmanships. Sometimes nearly everyone on a committee benefits from the subcommittee system: the House Select Small Business Committee formerly provided subcommittee chairmanships for each of the majority members. Not only can a committee chairman strengthen his control by means of the power to allocate these much coveted positions, but he often serves as a voting member of all subcommittees.

While the chairman's discretion in appointing subcommittees is widely regarded as unlimited, in fact his stature and traditional committee practice may serve to create practical limits to the exercise of that discretion. Once the seniority principle has been developed as an important criterion for selection, for example, it may be difficult for a chairman to ignore it. Even then much latitude remains. Some subcommittees are more important than others, and although it may be necessary to make a chair-

---

[5] Ironically the action was taken by the junior members of the majority party, most of whom ordinarily are not strong advocates of the seniority system.

manship available to all senior committee members, it does not always follow that the most seniors are assigned to the most important committees. And though subcommittee chairmanships are eagerly sought, sometimes they are not distributed as widely as it is possible to distribute them since certain congressmen may head more than one.[6]

Some committees make no provison for ratification of subcommittee assignments by the full committee. Even when committee approval is required, the action is likely to be a perfunctory one. When asked whether assignments were referred to the full committee for action, one congressman replied, "Oh, sure, it is done with the approval of the committee. It is one of those 'without objection it is so ordered' actions."

The latitude of "strong" chairmen in changing subcommittee chairmanship assignments at will is illustrated in part by the following statement, although it is important to note that in the instance cited the man affected was given another, albeit lesser, chairmanship.

The chairman of the _____ committee has taken a strong dislike to a certain issue which regularly comes before one of his subcommittees. At the beginning of a recent Congress he just demoted the subcommittee chairman of some years who had been sympathetic to the program and put on as chairman a man dead set against it.

Yet it is also true that in different circumstances another "strong" chairman in disagreement with a subcommittee chairman may take no such action, partly because of the practice prevalent within his committee of permitting members to select subcommittees on the basis of their seniority and partly because his control of the full committee is less complete than that of his colleague mentioned above. The following description of the operation of one subcommittee makes this point. It also makes the more important one that in some instances subcommittees may be the private preserve of their leaders, operating outside full committee control.

The chairman [of the subcommittee] has the power of life and death over claim bills coming before the subcommittee because he exercises the right to assign a particular bill to a particular member with a known philosophical persuasion. The chairman of the full committee does not agree with the present procedure.

[6] While ten of the twenty-two Democrats on the House Agriculture Committee head subcommittees, one of them is chairman of three and three others are at the helm of two. If each were limited to one chairmanship, five additional committee members would benefit.

He thinks the work should be done by a staff system, with the staff processing the claims cases and reporting recommendations to the subcommittee. The subcommittee chairman refuses, however, and retains the traditional practice of signing out the raw file to individual congressmen on the subcommittee. Because of the extensive workload it is impossible for members to go into the detail of all the bills so they pretty much rely on the recommendations of the man studying the bill.

The degree of participation of members in the selection of subcommittees on which they are to serve varies. Just as committee chairmen occupy a dominant position in the determination of subcommittee chairmen, they often decide which members of their party shall serve on which subcommittee. Sometimes, by their leave, members are able to select their own spots; sometimes subcommittee heads shape the direction of their work by requesting certain colleagues; sometimes congressmen are assigned arbitrarily and without consultation. In a committee such as Agriculture, they are likely to be named to units the work of which is important to their district. But on House Appropriations (in contrast to the practice followed by its Senate counterpart), a congressman generally is not assigned to a subcommittee of special concern to his district, on the grounds that his judgment would be less objective than that of a member whose constituency is less directly involved. In large part this decision is a deliberate one made by the conservative committee leadership in the hope of holding down appropriations.

Sometimes the subcommittee chairman not only names his own party's representatives but will even possess the power to veto potential minority members. In one such case, a subcommittee head, hesitant to accept the minority list, declined to approve one nominee until he had met with him, lectured him on the work and aims of the subcommittee, and quizzed him regarding his general philosophy with respect to matters within its jurisdiction. Only after he had extracted from the candidate a promise to work diligently, loyally, and without histrionics did he agree to the selection.

Committee chairmen may have personal reasons for making certain assignments not readily apparent to other members of Congress. In one situation, a full committee chairman also heading a subcommittee refused to accede to the pleas of the two top members of his party in Congress to make a certain appointment to his subcommittee. As one of the congressmen involved tells it:

One day I got a call from my committee chairman, who told me there was a vacancy on his subcommittee and that he was going to name me to the spot unless I had some reason for not wanting to serve. I was pleased because it was one of the best subcommittees. A few days later I met _____ [a congressman from Texas] in the hall. He told me he had wanted very much to be on the subcommittee and that although he didn't regard seniority as sacred, he was senior to me and thus entitled to the assignment. He said he had gone to Lyndon Johnson and Speaker Rayburn in his efforts to get the spot. They called the chairman in his behalf but reported back that the latter insisted on my being named. My colleague wanted to know why the chairman was so anxious to have me on the committee and I told him that I just didn't know. Now I think I know the answer: the chairman had hopes of going into a problem on which the Texan would be likely to disagree with his position and I would be likely to agree. He didn't want to risk the possibility that the Texan would vote with the Republicans, thus forcing the chairman of the full committee into the embarrassing position of having to write a minority report for his own subcommittee.

Many congressmen are skeptical about the success of the 1946 reorganization of committees. The skepticism is expressed in many ways. It may be little more than a "feeling" that things have not improved:

We have given so much jurisdiction to standing committees now that many items never get consideration that would receive attention if there were a larger number of committees. A byproduct of change is, if you had more standing committees, you would develop people who know more about committee business and parliamentary procedure than would otherwise be true. Of course, as a practical matter we accomplish a lot by dividing ourselves into subcommittees, but I have never been convinced that jumbling a lot of jurisdiction into nineteen committees instead of fifty has accomplished what it was thought would be accomplished.

There is some comment that the purposes of the act were circumvented. The reform legislation had envisioned House members serving on one standing committee. But as one member observed:

Another change has been in the direction of making more and more committees nonexclusive. A criticism used to be that in putting a member on three or four committees he didn't have an opportunity to give attention to his committee work. But now over 150 members have two major committee assignments, and the committees have more than twice the amount of jurisdiction the former committees had.

Other congressmen complain that legislative proposals are subjected to less careful scrutiny under the present system:

The full committee fails to perform an integrating function. I think there is less attention on the part of the membership of the full committee than we would have if we had individual committees in these jurisdictions. Rarely do the committees on which I serve bother to probe into the findings of a subcommittee.

Customarily, members of the full committee have little or no oppority to review the findings of its subcommittees prior to determining whether to accept those findings. In many instances, no formal written reports are issued; when a matter comes before the full committee, the subcommittee chairman presents an oral report, which is usually followed by comments from the ranking minority member. Then the committee votes. In other committees, such as Appropriations, extensive reports are prepared. But usually:

> Reports are not available to the full committee until the morning the committee is going to pass on them. You can't go through 400-500 pages of testimony and try to appreciate what the subcommittee has done. Unless you have previously served on the subcommittee and thus know what it has been doing you are in the dark. You pretty much have to rely on the oral reports.

A sore point with some members is that consolidation of committees has, in the words of one congressman, "concentrated the plums more than pre-1946." As important as many subcommittees are, heading them seems less impressive than chairing a full committee. "Responsibility and opportunity are both concentrated more today," complained one member. "I am on three subcommittees of the _____ committee and the chairman of the full committee is chairman of all three." Stated another, "I think we have as much committee work assigned to members as we have ever had, but we have fewer opportunities for them to develop a little leadership." A common criticism of the present situation is that the former system was a better training ground for members.

The Conference Committee

Although political scientists have long written about the impact of conference committees on legislation, members of Congress believe that even many students of government do not really understand their significance. And congressmen who have not had much conference committee experience often display a lively curiosity about what really goes on in these meetings, in which differing House and Senate versions of legislation are reconciled.

One legislator who often serves as a representative of the House on conference committees said:

> When I came to Congress I had no comprehension of the importance of the conference committees which actually write legislation. We all know that important laws are drafted there, but I don't think one person in a million has any appreciation of their importance and the process by which they work. Part of the explanation, of course, is that there never is a printed record of what goes on in a conference.

This led another congressman to comment, "I wonder if other committees have the same experience we have on appropriations. I know you can never recognize the report on appropriations measures when they come back from conference; they are completely changed."

Conference committees vary markedly in size and in the nature of the membership, though traditionally the senior senator on the committee serves as chairman. Often three or five members of the standing committee that has considered the legislation in dispute will represent the body in which they serve. Sometimes all members of the appropriate subcommittee will act as conferees, as is normally the custom when the House Appropriations Committee is involved; this may increase the House group contingent to nine or more. The House and Senate need not appoint the same number of conferees since votes are taken within the House and Senate units on the committee rather than in the committee as a whole. To report a bill out of conference a majority vote of each delegation is required.

There are many other variables, some of which are the subject of much comment. While both political parties are represented in the delegation of each house, the proportions vary. Representation may be in terms of party strength on the standing committee concerned, or the majority may merely be allotted one more conferee than the minority. There is a tendency to overrepresent the minority party. Seniority within the committee or one of its subcommittees usually is the criterion by which the committee chairman or the bill's floor manager recommends conferees to the presiding officer, but this is not always true. On rare occasions a conferee may be chosen who does not even serve on the committee. Where seniority is followed, the outcome of a conference may be influenced by whether the basis for selection is seniority on the full committee or seniority within the appropriate subcommittee. Different conferees may have different outlooks and varying interests to protect.

Criticisms. One of the most serious criticisms of the conference committee is that the delegations that compose it often are so constituted as to defeat the will of the body that they are supposed to represent. It is quite possible under selection by seniority that a majority of the conferees of the House, for example, have been recorded against the items for which they are supposed to fight. Conferees are instructed, of course, to seek to preserve the measure as it passed the house in which they sit. The question immediately arises how hard they will struggle for a position which they oppose, particularly if the representatives of the other body have taken a stand against the position. Commented one lawmaker: "There is a little line in the instructions which says that the chairman of the conferees will attempt to carry out the will of the House regardless of his own personal feelings about it. Now, I have never seen that rule observed."

When one group of legislators was asked whether there was a feeling that conference committees often were not faithful to the intent of the House, several members responded that was indeed their view. One congressman took the extreme position that: "The average conference sets out deliberately to circumvent the rules of the House." But another participant was more cautious:

> I think it depends on the chairman of our conferees. Take _____ committee matters. The House generally goes beyond the views of the committee chairman in passing bills relating to the committeee's work. Yet he acts as chairman of our conferees when these matters go to conference. Since he is not favorable to the action of the House, he doesn't defend it very long, and you usually get a different result in conference.

A brief discussion in another congressional group, which included several members who have served on a number of conference committees, indicated that rigid adherence to House views when in conflict with those of the individual conferee was not always to be expected. One member remarked: "I think you go over there with the idea that you are representing the House view and not necessarily your own." A second added: "That may be, but you don't have to stand there and die fighting for a position you really don't believe in."

Another major criticism of conference committees is that they regularly exceed their authority. Said one congressman, "The new legislation that comes out of conference is sometimes almost as important as the basic legislation." Officially their power is restricted to the specific subjects in controversy; they are not authorized to delete sections which have been approved by both House and Senate or to add others which have not been included in either version of the bill. In fact, however, conference committees often are guilty of both of these actions, particularly the latter. Though points of order may be raised against changes of this type, they seldom are made. The subjects are complex, debate time is limited, and most legislators are willing to believe their representatives on the conference committee have done as well as could be expected.

More legislating can be done in a well organized conference committee that really knows what it is doing than at any other place around the capitol. The conference committee on a controversial and involved bill is very, very influential. It is particularly powerful because when the bill returns to the House and Senate, members feel they have already expressed themselves on it and ordinarily don't take too much interest.

*

You are right. We can argue for two days on the floor about $10,000,000 and yet the conference committee can bring back a report of $20,000,000 and it will pass in five minutes.

*

In part, I think that is due to the difficulty of following the reports of conference committees. You have one hour of debate on a very complicated bill. And the control of debate time is entirely in the hands of the chairman of the conference committee. Action usually is perfunctory.

*

There is more opportunity for an individual to dominate a conference committee than a standing committee. It is important to note that fewer people are involved in giving consent there than in any other step in the legislative process. A powerful person who knows the bill and what he is trying to accomplish can dominate in that situation.

Relation to Legislative Strategy. Members of Congress agree that it is almost impossible to defeat a conference committee recommendation. As one representative stated, "In the final analysis the committee is almost determinative of the House position. For all practical purposes they decide what we are going to do, and we usually do it." About the only way in which a conference report can be defeated is if the leaders of the delegation are unsympathetic and have agreed to bring in a report they refuse to accept, hoping their colleagues will vote it down, thereby strengthening their hand in conference.

Because of the wide latitude of action enjoyed by conference committees, some congressmen believe that, where the outlook is uncertain, it is unwise to risk House or Senate defeat of a proposed amendment to legislation likely to go to conference. Even if the other body incorporates it in the bill, it is said, once one house has defeated it, its chances for inclusion in conference have been adversely affected. According to that view, one hopes the provision can be added in the other body and retained in conference, or one may even seek its inclusion by the conference committee as entirely new material. To a question whether it is wise to avoid a test in the House if the result is in doubt one member replied:

> It depends partly on the composition of the House conferees. If they are going to be conservatives and it is a conservative position you want to sustain, the conference committee is a good place to do it. But if the conferees are going to be liberals—and you can pretty much tell who they will be by looking at the standing committee concerned—and you want to carry a conservative position, I would rather risk the House than the House conferees.

Quite apart from the substantive issues involved, House-Senate conference committee negotiations are often regarded as contests, as tests of the skills of the principal negotiator of each body. The prestige of each house is also regarded as being at issue and conferees dislike to be forced to return to their colleagues with the information that they have capitulated in conference. It sometimes seems that it is fully as important to many members to demonstrate the power of the House or Senate as to retain or delete features of a bill on which the body has expressed itself.

To gain an objective, many devices are used. Bolstered by specific House action or House instructions, for example, House conferees may become adamant in their position. They may threaten stalemate with the prospect of obtaining no action whatsoever. They may return to the House "for instructions," an action frequently dreaded by their conference committee opponents. It is likely that the House will follow recommendations of its conferees and "instruct" them to stand firm; such action is likely to destroy whatever opportunity exists for any compromise on that particular issue. Firmness of position is particularly effective at the end of a session, or when a program must be reviewed or face expiration. It is not unusual in some conference committees for House or Senate conferees to walk out of the conference several times.

I recall an appropriations bill last year where they brought a conference report back with many items in disagreement and the House had to vote on each. I think we had four or five roll calls.

*

I was a conferee on that bill. We adjourned three or four times because we reached an impasse. But the conference on _____ was worse. _____ [top House conferee] did what _____ [who annually heads House conferees on another bill] has done on occasion. He said, "Gentlemen, we just won't budge. The House has spoken." We picked up our papers and walked out several times.

The importance of "saving face" and the leverage provided by timing, given uncompromising leadership of the conferees, are evident in the following story:

Last year there was a difference of about $400 million between the House and Senate versions of the foreign aid appropriation. The chairman of the House delegation in the conference took a very firm position that we had to end up with slightly less than 50 percent of the difference as a matter of prestige. It was the day we were to adjourn. We were in conference until about 10:30 p.m., and the Senate wouldn't give in. I think the difference between conferees was only five or ten million dollars. The Senate was fighting for its prestige, and our chairman for his. At 10:30 he started to close his book and got up saying he would get instructions from the House. All the rest of our conferees did the same. That prospect was too much for the senators. They capitulated.

The heads of the House and Senate delegations are usually the key figures. Some of these men relish the jousts with their opposites in the other body. Sometimes, too, they know their adversary wants a bill so badly that he will capitulate if he believes his opponents will not yield:

My only experience on a conference committee related to agriculture and resolved itself into maneuvering between two consummate artists, Senator _____ and Representative _____. The chairman of each group knows how much he wants to give and where he wants to stand firm, and he maneuvers his group into position. Gradually the edges start to smooth out and you finally come to a compromise. We approach the conference committee with the idea that there has to be a compromise, but we recognize there are certain places where you cannot compromise.

*

It all depends on how badly one chairman wants the bill as against the other. I sat in on the conference on _____ where we had changed the Senate bill completely. Senator _____ was the only member sitting on from the Senate most of the time, holding all their proxies. He had sponsored the legislation, and he wanted it very badly. Our conferees didn't want a bill so they just said to the Senator, "You either take this or there won't be anything." And he had to acquiesce all the way.

The Senate is nearly always more generous than the House in appropriating funds. In discussions about appropriations, many members cannot resist mentioning the quip that, "The Senate is called the upper body because it always ups the appropriations of the House." The various government departments regard the Senate as a court of appeals from the cuts that the House committees almost invariably make in their budget requests. And representatives whose projects have been excluded from House-passed bills transfer their efforts to the Senate, occasionally with the assurances of House leaders that if the Senate acts favorably on their request House conferees will accept it in conference. The departments, the House, and the Senate, all have come to anticipate House trimming and Senate restoration (at least partially) of these requests. Everyone then looks to a House-Senate conference to compromise the differences.

Knowing that certain measures will go to conference, it is not uncommon for astute House and Senate managers to seek to insert on the floor provisions that they cannot and would not hope to retain but which can be used in conference bargaining. Other provisions may be included to placate an important House member whom a chairman may not want to offend, or to make a member facing a difficult fight for re-election look good in his district even though the project involved is not particularly meritorious; such items may be yielded quickly in conference. Thus, occasionally when congressional colleagues not privy to the strategy complain that their conferees have not held the line, they may be quite wrong: the line may not be what it appears to be.

Sometimes, it should also be said, the likelihood of a conference affects congressional voting. Members may consider a measure less carefully knowing that there will be an opportunity in conference to alter it. On occasion, failure to examine a proposal closely may lead to unanticipated results. Stated one congressman:

Often one body will pass legislation hastily with the expectation that the other will pass a version, and there will be an opportunity to compromise. After we had passed the _____ bill, for example, I spoke to one of the senators. I said, "Boy, you sure threw the hooks to us. You sent a bill over here after only forty minutes debate and by voice vote. It arrived right in the middle of our debate and just clobbered our side." He said that wasn't the way it was supposed to have worked. "We thought we would send it over to you and you would pass a good bill. Then it would go to conference and we would accept your version."

One thoughtful legislator suggested that more serious attention would be accorded legislation if the power of conference committees to write new legislation in committee were to be curbed:

The lack of responsiveness of conference committees to House and Senate action has another bad effect. On many issues people tend to vote irresponsibly on the floor because it is generally believed that the action will be fixed up in the conference committee. There is an annual ritual that is gone through on foreign aid appropriations in the House. Traditionally, they are slashed heavily. People are willing to go along with the cuts because they know that ultimately the conference committee will restore many of them. Some change in the rules or traditions of conference committees in the direction of making them more responsible might result in a little more thoughtful voting on some of the substantive issues.

The fact that no records are kept of conference committee deliberations has important effects on the results. As one frequent conferee pointed out, "You certainly get some different attitudes in a conference than you would anticipate by listening to speeches on the floor. There is one senator, for example, who is known primarily for a particular position on foreign aid. Yet in conference I never saw anyone fight more ardently for a different position." Participants, secure in the knowledge that there is no indisputable means of revealing their performance, may be more candid in expressing their true position and quicker to desert that which they are charged to uphold. They may threaten, cajole, and bargain more directly than would be possible were a written record maintained.

Few people are present other than committee members and this also promotes candor. Representatives of the Legislative Counsel's office are usually there to assist in the preparation of the sections to be revised and to interpret their effects. Other experts and personal staff of members sometimes attend, but only if no objection is raised. The House has been known to pass a resolution requesting that the Senate conferees withdraw their advisers.

The information leading to a compromise on a particular bill may be so narrowly held that only a small minority of the members of the House and Senate are aware of any of the details. Floor discussion of the details of conference negotiations is rare. Certainly the reporting requirements are not designed to encourage disclosure. Often a committee's report will consist of little more than recommendations that the House or Senate recede from its insistence on certain parts of the bill. Unlike the Senate, House rules also require a statement by its conferees setting forth the effect of the proposed changes to the measure passed by the House. But since the report is required to be inserted in the *Congressional Record* only one day prior to the vote, there is little opportunity for opponents to prepare their case. The prospect of reviving the conference committee and seeking new compromises is not regarded as attractive, either, under most conditions.

While conference committees are basically committees of compromise, it is clear that, "You get all kinds of compromises that don't make much sense except that they are a way to solve a problem." This is particularly true when the point at issue is one of dollars: How much is to be spent for a particular program? There the simplest solution is to halve House-Senate differences, though, as has been suggested, managers for each body sometimes try assiduously to tip the balance at least slightly in the direction of their original figure as proof of their skillfulness. Some conference problems are far more knotty than that, however. On public works appropriations bills, for example, the areas in which the compromise is to take place must be determined. Which projects are to be eliminated? Whose district is to be affected? On such matters congressional interest is high, and conferees are often under tremendous pressure to "save" various projects. As one veteran congressman told a House conferee with respect to a project that had been included in a Senate bill but not in the House version and was likely to be lost in conference: "You've just got to save that project for me. I've been here _____ years. What will my people say if I can't retain that item after being in the House that long? I didn't mind that the House failed to include it in our bill. But now that the Senate has put it in, I've got to see that it stays in."

It seems taken for granted that conferees will protect the interests of their own constituencies. One congressman pointed out that the gum and turpentine workers of Georgia were not covered under social security until Senator George of that state left the Finance Committee. He also asserted that one reason peanuts were included in the list of basic crops was that for many years the chairman of the House Agriculture Committee, who served as chief House conferee on such matters, was from a peanut growing area. Where projects relating to areas not directly represented on a conference committee are concerned, House members are somewhat suspicious that Senate conferees are more protective of their colleagues' interests than are House conferees:

I once sat on a conference committee dealing with a public works bill. The Senate conferees always took a strong position on projects in their states. If a project was outside the states of the conferees, compromise was in order, but they didn't compromise very much on those affecting their own constituencies. I should say some of the House members had the same attitude.

*

I would take a little different view. I have been in conferences where a senator not on the conference committee had persuaded Senate conferees his projects were to remain in the bill. The Senate conferees would not change their views till they had gone out and contacted the Senator concerned. If he sent word he was firm, that the project was essential to his welfare, the Senate conferees held firm unless they were forced to give in in order to work out a solution. There is a close liaison between senators whether or not they are conferees and regardless of party affiliation. It is generally understood that all senators have to do to get a project included is turn in a list.

Because of the stability of conference committees, where appropriations bills go to conference annually, understandings are sometimes reached that affect future bills as well as the one currently under consideration. According to one representative:

You will recall the situation with respect to the two _____ [installations], one in the state of _____ and the other in _____. For the past three years they have been knocked out of the House bill on a point of order and then, in the Senate, Senator _____ has gotten the one in his state back in the bill. Then it goes to conference. This year the House conferees said they would not go along with that provision; the Senate conferees said they had to go along. We argued back and forth for some time. We had lost the first two years, and finally we lost again. The Senator concerned was engaged in a primary the day after the conference was supposed to break up, and it was argued he should be protected. We went along but with the solemn pledge of every House conferee speaking directly to all Senate conferees: "This is the last year for this item and we want you to know it." That was the only basis on which that rider was approved last year. It never will be approved again and they know it.

Thus, the wide discretionary powers of conference committees are evident. While it is true that only 11 or 12 percent of the public laws enacted in recent congresses have gone to conference, the number is not a proper index of the central role of the conference committee in the legislative process. Submitted to these House-Senate negotiators are many of the most important measures before the Congress, including most appropriations bills. Conference committee deliberations may be brief—one congressman appointed to his first conference arrived ten minutes late and found the meeting adjourned—or they may continue over extended periods. Some have lasted several months. But even the time spent in conference provides only a rough index of the importance of the issue or the degree of difference between the two houses. Deliberations may be under way prior to the selection of conferees and, in order to maximize the tactical advantages, designation of conferees may be delayed for considerable time. Since the congressional system places heavy reliance on specialization and deference to colleagues in their particular area of work, it is not surprising that conference committees, composed as they generally are of the men and women most informed about the matters in disagreement, possess tremendous authority. This would tend to be so even if their preeminence were not reinforced by the one hour limit on debate of conference committee recommendations in the House (increased somewhat for appropriations measures), the tight control of debate time exercised by the managers of the bill, and the feeling that prolonging the conference would not produce more favorable results.

Committee Staffs

Congress was slow to develop professional staffs for its committees. In 1856 the Committee on Ways and Means became the first House committee to hire a full-time clerk. Only three years earlier, four clerks had been authorized to serve all House committees.

Not until about seventy-five years later, however, in the 1920's and 1930's, did committee clerks begin to assume semiprofessional duties. At that time it was customary for these staffs to sit in the office of the committee chairman rather than in separate quarters specifically set aside for committee use. Indeed, a 1929 Legislative Pay Act automatically made the three senior assistants on the personal staff of Senate committee chairmen the clerk and assistant clerks for the committee concerned. At the outbreak of World War II, only the House and Senate Appropriations committees and the Joint Committee on Internal Revenue Taxation employed "well trained technically qualified staffs with continuity of tenure." The 1946 Legislative Reorganization Act marked the real beginning of a professional staff for committees.[7] As of April 30, 1963 nearly 500 people were working for House committees, the majority of them for special and select investigating committees rather than for standing committees.[8]

Members of Congress generally agree that today committee staffs tend to be of high calibre, and that competence has become a basic criterion for appointment to the professional staff. This has not always been so. Traditionally, a committee chairman brought a friend from his home district to serve as committee clerk. The clerk's main qualification was loyalty to his patron, and his duties were not onerous. What few files were kept were regarded as the personal possession of the chairman, and when he left the committee, the records and the clerk usually left with

[7] It provided that "each standing committee of the Senate and House of Representatives (other than the appropriations committees) is authorized to appoint, by a majority vote of the committee, not more than four professional staff members in addition to the clerical staffs; on a permanent basis without regard to political affiliations and solely on the basis of fitness to perform the duties of the office; and said members shall be assigned to the chairman and ranking minority member of such committee as the committee may deem advisable."

	EMPLOYEES
[8] Standing Committees (other than Appropriations)	191
Standing Committee on Appropriations	44
Investigative Staff, Standing Committee on Appropriations	4
Special and Select Investigating Committees	251
Total	490

Each of the standing committees, other than Appropriations, was entitled to 10 employees (including four professionals), except for Armed Services (12), Interstate and Foreign Commerce (14), Judiciary (13), and Ways and Means (26). Salaries of the regular employees of all standing committees totaled more than $3 million annually and special and select committees were expending a like amount. Most standing committees were using their full staff allotment but the House Administration and Rules Committees each had only 3 employees and the Ways and Means Committee had 5 unfilled staff positions.

him, with obvious effects on the activities and effectiveness of the committee. Not until 1946 were committee records required to be maintained separately from those of the chairmen and declared the property of the Congress and available to all members of the committee.

Staff Appointments. The notion of making purely political appointments to committee staffs has not died easily—indeed, some prominent examples remain—but the sharply increased volume and complexity of committee work, as well as the desire to be in a position to watch the Executive closely, have served to bring about a change in the criteria of appointment for most positions, however reluctant a chairman might be to accept it. Though some committees lag behind others, the unmistakable trend is to the qualified, trained staff; about half of professional committee staff personnel are lawyers.

One much respected head of a House committee staff comments about the experience in his committee:

> Staffs vary tremendously according to the chairman. When _____ was chairman of our committee, he preferred to work with the people in the executive branch. His view was that they were Democrats and we were Democrats, so why duplicate effort with a lot of congressional staff work. His staff was not selected for competence but rather on the basis of personal friendship, and for political reward. His successor's outlook was much different, and he really built up the staff during his short term as chairman. Later chairmen have followed the same philosophy and now a tradition of professional competence has been developed that it would be difficult to change. When congressmen see the kind of assistance it is possible for them to get, they become less and less satisfied with incompetent or uninformed staff members and begin to insist on professionalization.

The attitude of the chairman is crucial in determining the nature and quality of a committee's staff, for generally he has the appointive power. This control leads to some grumbling, not only that he fails to recognize the need for well-qualified people or an expanded program, or that staff selection should be a joint rather than individual endeavor, but that occasionally staff appointed by the chairman will work primarily, or even exclusively, for him, neglecting their responsibilities to other committee members. Commented one congressman: "I have the feeling that on occasion the staff is an adjunct of the chairman's office or of the ranking minority member. It sometimes appears to be private property."

Criticism of this sort usually emanates from junior members of Congress, who sometimes assert that their requests for assistance receive low priority from well-entrenched committee personnel. There is no question that it is not always possible for the staff to be of as much help to members as the latter would like. Nor is there any question that staffs work more closely with the chairmen than with other members and that they assume many duties which in other situations would be undertaken by members of the congressman's personal office staff, including answering the chairman's legislative mail. In some cases, they even sit in the representative's office rather than in that of the committee.

The general view, however, is that most chairmen exercise discretion in making staff appointments and that many of them consult with other senior members of the committee before reaching a decision. The practice of permitting subcommittee chairmen to name the staffs for the units they head has gone far to mollify the senior members of the full committee since it is they who are most likely to receive such assignments. A few committees establish bipartisan subcommittees to handle personnel matters and require bipartisan agreement on new staff appointments. In some committees the staffs themselves play a major role in the selection of personnel.

Most congressmen, while willing to grant broad appointive powers to a committee chairman, want him to recognize that he possesses them subject to the review of his colleagues on the committee. One House member states:

I am a firm believer in letting the chairman select the staff and holding him responsible for its quality and performance. If the staff isn't good you can raise hell with him. Having a committee try to supervise a staff is impossible. The committee should, however, have a clearly understood power to veto staff nominations of the chairman and to direct discharge of an unsatisfactory employee.

Some committees adhere to the principle of a professional, permanent staff, even though a substantial element within the committee including the chairman, prefer a staff to be selected on a partisanship basis. Once the tradition of a professional staff is established, it is not likely to be easy to revert to a system of appointment with political overtones. Paralleling the recent emphasis on qualified personnel is the tendency to retain staff members despite a shift in the control of the House from one party to another. Although the latter is not without disadvantages, it appears that in the judgment of most congressman the continuity of records, experience, and personnel which it ensures far outweighs the drawbacks.

Said one member of the staff of the Joint Economic Committee:

> Tradition has a great deal to do with the naming of a staff. You can have a staff that is fairly well stabilized, such as that of the Joint Economic Committee where the chairman has pretty full control but the committee maintains a veto. From the date of the creation of the committee in the Republican Eightieth Congress, we have had a tradition of a high level of professionalism, and we have maintained much the same staff. The Democratic staff director was first named by a Republican chairman and retained by the Democrats. When the Republicans came back in the Eighty-third Congress, many of them wanted to make it a partisan staff, but we picked up one of their members and held the line. We came back in the Eighty-fourth Congress and our Democratic chairman thought it might be nice to change it around, but some of us refused.

There is, of course, no standard formula for selecting staffs or for determining the way in which they are to function. Some staffs, such as that of the Joint Economic Committee, are "integrated" in the sense that they serve both parties equally. Others designate one or more staff members to represent the minority with little attention to their party affiliation or ideological inclinations. In still another category are the committees that permit the minority party to fill a specified number of staff positions. In a few instances separate offices are provided for the minority.

Majority and Minority Staffs. Though nearly all congressmen support the concept of a professional staff ("You can't criticize the idea of a professional staff which does so much to make your job easier"), division of opinion is apparent on the question of providing special minority staff and on how partisan or nonpartisan staff work should be. Said one Republican:

> I am inclined to favor the career system for staffs of committees, but I do think that it ought to be grounded in some political protection to both parties. I mean by that, if there are going to be career Democrats, there ought to be career Republicans as well. There are certain proceedings, certain tactics which a Republican member wouldn't want to discuss with a Democratic counsel and vice versa.

Understandably members of the minority party are far more convinced than those in the majority of the desirability of having designated minority staff members, preferably with sole power of selection in the hands of the minority. "When the chips are really down," said one member, "the staff is tipped towards the majority and the minority doesn't get much help. We need our own people to do essential research." On some committees, it should be noted, majority and minority reports are prepared by the same person. The point has been made that a staff man's primary allegiance in such a situation is likely to be to the majority position. Beginning in 1962 and continuing in 1963, a group of House Republicans demanded that the minority party be given the right to appoint up to 40 percent of committee staffs if a majority of the committee minority request it.[9] The House Republican Conference adopted the position in 1963. The Democratic majority refused to accede to the request, but some increase in minority staff was provided in certain committees. As late as 1962, however, there were instances where ranking minority members of committees had failed to fill positions assigned to the minority.

Congressmen who support increased staff for the minority tend to emphasize the need for more professional staff. At current levels, they assert, time pressures on staff workers mean that the minority gets little assistance. If the minority is to perform adequately its function as the responsible opposition and develop constructive alternatives to the proposals of the majority, it must have staff with which to do it. This is particularly necessary when the opposition has control of both houses of Congress and the executive. Minimal staff assistance for the minority may mean that it is not possible to file minority reports; it clearly restricts the possibility that separate research can be undertaken.

Leaders of the fight for increased minority staff have pointed out that there are committees which are bipartisan or nonpartisan and where the minority seems well satisfied. But they point out that some committees are strongly partisan and have much controversial legislation referred to them. In 1962, two of these partisan-charged committees had budgets of nearly $650,000 each, yet one had only two of its forty staff members

[9] In the Eighty-eighth Congress, 1962–64, the minority held about 40 percent of the seats in the House.

specifically assigned to the minority, and the other had only three of seventy-seven. To advocates of increased minority staffing, the basic issue is who controls the staff, not how many Democratic or Republican staff members there are. They assert that the powers of appointment, control, and dismissal should rest with the minority rather than the committee chairman. Anything short of that is meaningless. Some chairmen may bar minority members access to staff arbitrarily without prior clearance; in other instances minority staff are not allowed to sit in on subcommittee hearings.

Those who deny the need for increased minority staff assert that increased partisanship would tend to sabotage congressional operations rather than improve them. This is not to say that nonpartisanship cannot be carried too far. In the view of one congressman:

> Our committee has one of the finest staffs anywhere. But a year or two ago when we were engaging a new staff member, I innocently asked a question of one of my seniors as to the man's political affiliation. I was quickly told that such an improper question had never before been asked in our committee. Although I have no objection to any members of our staff, I think you sacrifice a great deal when you go to such lengths to get a nonpartisan point of view. Something can be gained from the healthy exchange of differing viewpoints, and this is more likely to occur where the two parties have some staff of their own.

Party affiliation, of course, is no certain test of sympathy for your point of view. Said one representative: "A committee staff can be bipartisan and still be biased. You must remember that the splits within the two parties are sometimes more strained than between the two parties. You can end up with a bipartisan staff that is loaded one way or another, conservative or liberal." At the same time he went on to say, "I think it is important that we draw lines of difference, and in order to do that a minority counsel is necessary."

But the idea of an essentially "neutral" career staff is clearly endorsed by the Congress, especially if provision is made for one or more "party" staff assistants for each committee. Congressional operations are considered to be essentially nonpartisan in nature and most legislative activity is noncontroversial. And most legislators would insist that the number of committee employees specifically labeled as minority is not a true measure of the total actually providing assistance to minority members of the committee.

The weight of testimony of members who have worked closely with committee staff is that staff tends to be competent and objective. In one such endorsement, a minority member paid tribute to the staff of the Ways and Means Committee:

> We have a majority and a minority counsel who shift positions when control of the House shifts from one party to the other, but the rest of the staff is used jointly by the two parties. Policy questions are presented to the full committee in an honest fashion without slanting the information. The staff will be discussing a topic and will say: "If you decide it this way and use this language, you will be involved in a policy question which is. . . ." Then it is our problem to reach the policy decision and to proceed from there. I have never found the staff to withhold information or to present it falsely. Any error that might be made is just human error.

Criticisms and Limitations of Staffs. Criticism of committee staffs is concentrated on two situations: those in which the chairman fails to appoint qualified personnel, and those in which the staff is admittedly partisan. Partisan staffs become controversial. Majority party members tend to defend them as thoroughly competent, though partisan; minority members sharply attack their bias.

Although there is little concern in the House that committee staffs exert excessive influence on the members they serve, there is some feeling that staffs occasionally attempt to assume the role of the congressman in determining the direction of an inquiry. The reaction of two imaginative and able partisan Democrats indicates that definite limits exist for the exercise of staff initiative. In discussing the merits of nonpartisan staffs, one of these men said: "I would much prefer to have a quite dispassionate professional than a partisan professional. I think I can provide the partisanship myself. I get annoyed with the staff man who tries to tell me how to be a partisan." Support for that position was voiced by the other congressman:

> The real secret of a good staff is to have one which functions in a way such as to let us make an objective judgment. You want professional competence in review and analysis and in achieving your purposes, and what you object to is a staff member trying to tell you either what the wise thing to do politically or what your objectives ought to be.

Are House committees sometimes the captives of their staffs? If they are, the congressmen are not aware of it. Continued close association between a chairman and his top staff assistants may develop confidence and the delegation of important responsibilities and may facilitate a frank exchange of ideas, but few House members believe committee staff personnel achieve sufficient power to be able to exert excessive influence on the direction of committee work and program. Staff influence is likely to be greater in the Senate than in the House because senators are likely to serve on more committees and to be involved in so many activities as to have no alternative but to delegate broader authority to personal and committee staffs. Former Senate employees now serving as congressmen speak of significant differences existing between the two bodies in that respect.

Staff influence tends to be greater on subcommittees than on full committees, according to congressmen and staff observers. One of the outstanding staff men on Capitol Hill who adheres to this view points out that subcommittees are often "one man shows" facilitating staff initiative, and adds that the subject matter is less controversial and involves much less policy than matters heard by the full committee. But where staff influence is strong, he insists, "it is not true in the bad sense. It may be true to some extent in the _____ committee, but there you have a couple of men who have been around for a long time and who are acknowledged as experts. If staff people pull a couple of booboos they are not around very long, and staff assistants know it. If they are given a free hand, it is because they have proved themselves. Congressmen have too much at stake to put up with staff mistakes."

An all but universal lament is that while the quality of committee staffs is high, numerically they are inadequate to perform the tasks that confront them. Members point to increased committee workload, emphasize the importance of having specialists for each of the major jurisdictions of a technical committee, and complain that, in the face of the more generous staffing of executive agencies, the Congress is frustrated in its efforts to perform properly its surveillance function.

One Democrat explains the need this way:

We need both in our own staffs and in committee staffs the competent probers who can uncover the necessary data so that we can make intelligent judgments. For years Congress functioned on the premise that the administration was engaged in a cooperative activity with the Congress. Suddenly we found ourselves having to live with a situation of noncooperation or hostility. We simply haven't reorganized the Congress to overcome this limitation.

Because the volume and nature of staff work varies so much from committee to committee, the provisions of the 1946 act authorizing up to four professional staff members for each standing committee failed to correct certain inequities.[10] Subsequent legislative action has provided additional staff for various committees, although it is recognized that many of them could use to advantage still further increases. At the same time, one or two committees are sometimes cited as being overstaffed. One valuable source of temporary professional staff assistance is the Legislative Reference Service of the Library of Congress, which, on request, sometimes lends personnel to congressional committees for special projects, the committee assuming the expenses involved. Temporary personnel may also be borrowed from the General Accounting Office on a reimbursable basis.

There is much sentiment that committee staffs fail to undertake research independent of hearings, and that they give insufficient attention to digesting, comparing, and distributing materials that could be of much use to committee members. They are accused of lacking creativity and of failing to possess imagination, although their critics add that, in most instances, given the present committee workload, they would be hard put to accomplish much more than they do. Staff limitations necessarily impose restrictions on committee activity, some of which can impede programs significantly. Speaking of the adverse consequences of insufficient staff, one member of the Department of the Interior Committee said:

I can see area after area of improper public management of the resources of this country, and yet we are doing nothing about it. The only thing we will consider in the hearings of the Interior Committee are bills which have been introduced and upon which we have had a report from the administration. There are many, many fields of management where legislation is not possible until you have had a thorough investigation but, because of staff limitations, we lack the flexibility in committee to go out and make that kind of investigation.

While it is apparent that demands on staff time vary considerably between committees and that professional, technical assistance is far more essential to some than to others, the consensus is that rapid strides

[10] No maximum was set for the appropriations committees.

have been taken in the past ten years to improve the quality of staff and to broaden their assistance to the committees and to the Congress. Realists acknowlege that progress has been uneven, but assert there are few examples of flagrant disregard for professionalization; defects are more often attributed to limitations on staff size and to reluctance to strike out into new lines of inquiry.

Hearings and Reports

Committee recommendations so often determine House action that it is important to consider the role of committee hearings in the decision process and the manner in which the findings are communicated to colleagues. Committee hearings are of two general types—legislative and investigative—with tremendous overlap between them. An indication of the importance of hearings is the fact that congressional committees spent more than $10 million on them during the Eighty-fifth Congress (1957–58). Authorizations in the Eighty-seventh Congress rose to in excess of $15.5 million. In the House, the Government Operations committee generally receives the largest allocation, a sum in excess of 1 million in recent Congresses.

The Role of the Chairman. There is general agreement that the quality of hearings and the reports that follow depend in large part on the chairman of the committee or subcommittee that conducts them. Staff calibre is an important element, too. Unquestionably the attitude of the chairman greatly influences the direction of the hearings. As one congressman said:

Hearings depend on the subcommittee chairman and his attitude and interest. Within our committee we have several subcommittee chairmen, and they differ completely. There is no particular standard. One is fair and tries to give both sides an even time break and every consideration. Others don't act in that impartial manner. I am thinking of one subcommittee chairman who is author of a bill before it. He is not sympathetic towards witnesses opposed to the legislation and tends to cut their time short. He tells them to put their statement in the record and summarize it for the committee. He is greatly concerned, however, that anyone favoring the measure have sufficient time to develop his testimony.

One important power of the chairman is that of recognizing colleagues to permit them to interrogate committee witnesses. Junior members often complain that their senior colleagues—particularly the chairman and ranking minority member—monopolize the time with the result that the newer members may have little or no opportunity to ask questions. The hearing may even be adjourned before their turn comes. Committee rules may provide time limitations, but they are seldom adhered to. One House veteran has so antagonized his colleagues on both sides of the aisle by his tendency to talk interminably in hearings that, although he is considered an able congressman, he has virtually no influence with his associates. This is by no means an isolated case, but it is one often cited by members of Congress. It is so unusual for junior members to seek to limit the question time of their seniors that such actions may not readily be forgiven. Said one legislator:

> During my first term when Mr. Meany came before our committee the ranking minority member, now the chairman, went into his second half hour of questioning. One of my freshman colleagues brashly made a point of order that he had held the floor for over ten minutes, and House rules didn't provide for that. The congressman who was shut off hasn't forgiven him yet.

Value of Hearings. Hearings can serve many meritorious purposes. By providing an opportunity to interested parties to present their views on an issue, they increase the likelihood that proper consideration will be given to the potential effects of congressional action. They also represent one means by which members can obtain detailed knowledge and understanding of a proposal.

Hearings also inform the public and interested groups that a particular measure is under consideration, thus providing the voters with an opportunity to make their wishes known in advance of congressional action. In making this point one congressman said:

> The hearings serve a very useful purpose because, as a whole, they are open hearings, covered by members of the press and given considerable publicity. They constitute one of the few places where any publicity goes out over the country that a bill is moving along. By informing people the bill has reached the point of hearings, correspondence is stimulated before you reach a vote on it.

Another representative disagreed:

> All a hearing does is give an opportunity to the vested interests to beat the drum and get letters out on their side of the issue. It doesn't necessarily go to the

merits. I don't think those publicity campaigns result in the kind of mail that is of any value to me in deciding whether the bill is good or bad, and I think they can do a lot of damage. If you sprang legislation on a public that hadn't adjusted itself to it there might be a reaction, but I don't think good legislation has necessarily been enacted because of the publicity attendant on hearings. The Mc-Clellan committee hearings, contrary to most, have aroused public opinion to the fact that there is something wrong that needs attention, but even they haven't gone into the question of which approach to the problem is appropriate.

Another valuable function of hearings in the view of some congressmen is that, by prolonging the decision, they provide time for the political climate to change, thus facilitating acceptance of the program under discussion. Legislators were quick to point out another advantage. If hearings are to be scheduled, congressmen can more easily answer the demands of lobbyists that they take a position on the legislation. "You can tell them that it is very important to have the benefit of the hearings, that you intend to determine your position after listening to all the evidence."

Hearings may prove beneficial in pointing out implications of the language of a bill which had not been foreseen. Explained one member:

The English language is fraught with the danger of misinterpretation. Everyone might be agreed on purpose and still disagree as to language to accomplish that purpose. A phrase might mean one thing to one man and something quite different to another. In one such case recently a bill suggested by an executive agency was completely redrafted after a short committee hearing.

Committee hearings may also serve as a source of ideas regarding legislative proposals not directly associated with the subject under discussion. Testified one lawmaker:

I sometimes get ideas about legislation just by sitting in on hearings. For example, I got a bill on a gas tax into the Ways and Means Committee tax bill because the smaller companies were being discriminated against. I never would have gotten the idea if I hadn't been a full participant in hearings before my own committee.

Criticisms of Hearings. Despite the many salutary effects of hearings, the general impression among thoughtful legislators is that considerable improvement in hearings procedures is in order. Prior to 1955, there was considerable criticism within the Congress that too little protection of the rights of witnesses was provided in certain types of investigative hearings.

But reforms of that year led to established rules of procedure that have eased the situation considerably. Criticism on these grounds is now seldom heard or strongly pressed. Among the most frequent criticisms are these: hearings are preceded by insufficient planning; the scope of subjects covered by them is much too limited; too little effort is made to evaluate the information presented; the same witnesses representing the same groups tend to appear at hearing after hearing; the junior members of Congress are often not accepted by their seniors as full participants in the hearing process; chairmen are sometimes too arbitrary in their exercise of authority; and too often little effort is made to obtain a full discussion of a controversial measure.

Certain major investigative hearings are not investigations as much as dramatic presentations. As one careful observer has noted, "The most notable committee investigations are seldom in point of fact 'investigations' once the public hearings begin. They are planned deliberately to move from a preconceived idea to a predetermined conclusion."

The following remarks bring out some of the criticisms noted above:

We need research to develop facts. For two weeks our committee has been listening to witnesses in the fair trade legislation hearings. In almost every instance we could write their testimony in advance on the basis of the group they represent. Yet the committee has undertaken no independent studies of the effects of fair trade legislation as it has worked out in the various states. We have made no effort to evaluate some of the claims of these groups appearing before us.

*

One of the chief areas where House prestige has declined and that of the Senate has grown immeasurably results from our failure to conduct depth hearings with the type of expertise you are talking about—with good staffs doing creative work.

An important basic criticism about hearings is that inadequate preparations precede them, and that no one concerns himself with what they could accomplish. Often hearings represent crash programs where the problem is to get enough material and witnesses together to bring off what will be regarded as a "successful" undertaking. The staff involved in the preparation and conduct of the hearings, it is asserted, are too often technicians lacking broad understanding of the issues before the committee. Insufficient use is made of well-qualified extra-congressional personnel to prepare background materials and to help guide the sessions to successful conclusions. A corollary point is that, customarily, little effort is exerted to have the staff assemble materials independent of those to be presented in the hearings and to digest and circulate them to committee members. Legislators mention favorably occasional staff efforts to compare bills covering the same general subject or to place legislative proposals in historical perspective. At the same time, they express regret that more of this is not done.

Hard pressed public officials are required to spend far too much time on the Hill testifying before committees with overlapping jurisdiction, say critics both in and out of Congress. While the testimony itself is time consuming, it does not reflect all the time involved. Preparing for the hearings may involve an even greater period. As one congressman pointed out:

> I don't think there is any question that in presenting a program on the part of the [executive] every word which a witness is going to utter is carefully rehearsed and reviewed. The stage management that goes on in preparation for a hearing is far more complete than that which goes on in advance of a Broadway opening.

Dean Acheson has estimated that approximately one-sixth of his working days in Washington while Secretary of State were spent appearing before congressional committees or preparing for them. For one seven-week period during his tenure, he states that fully half of his time and energy was so spent. In 1962, Secretary of State Rusk appeared before congressional committees 54 times, and Secretary of Defense McNamara spent 203 hours in such activities.

Following a six-week period in which men closely associated with our military effort had made frequent appearances before Hill committees—a summary for the first month showed eight men including the Secretary of Defense, the service secretaries, and the Joint Chiefs of Staff had made thirty such appearances before four committees—one congressman wrote in his newsletter:

> Congress, of course, must be kept informed. . . . Nonetheless, I am concerned at the excessive amount of time which the Secretary of Defense and other military leaders must spend in testifying on Capitol Hill. Since Congress convened in January, Secretary Gates has spent nine days before five committees of the House and the Senate. General Twining, Chairman of the Joint Chiefs of Staff, has made ten appearances to date. Such key figures in our defense effort cannot

attend to their other duties while testifying. Furthermore, briefings and preparation are essential, and must require at least an additional day before each appearance as a witness.

Last year, according to reliable estimates, 465 Defense Department witnesses testified before various congressional committees. Of this group, about 120 witnesses were civilian, the balance military personnel. These witnesses made approximately 700 appearances. Assuming these 465 witnesses spent one day preparing—as they must for their appearances—almost 1,200 days would be consumed. With a six day work week this represents four man years of effort lost in one year by our top military and civilian leaders during a single session of Congress.

Noting the reluctance of Congress to rely on joint committees, the congressman went on to suggest that Senate and House committees with comparable responsibilities and a common interest in testimony from the Defense Department could meet together for such briefings.

Congressmen are not optimistic about the power of hearings to change the views of legislators with respect to important legislative proposals. Said one representative, "With respect to hearings I think you come out about where you go in. Not many minds are changed which I should think would be their purpose. Nor do I believe that hearings have resulted in many changes in the legislation that comes out on the floor." Yet there was some feeling that with respect to less important features of a bill a shift in viewpoint was possible:

I doubt that hearings change the minds of many members when controversial or emotional issues are involved; on most issues, members are looking for things to bolster the decisions they already have reached. Where the issues are less consequential, however, I think hearings can make an impact. There, the member is looking for information to help him make a rational decision. I have had my own mind changed many times on bills before our committee—bills on which I had a pre-formed opinion—where the weight and logic of the evidence presented demonstrated to me that I was wrong.

*

You aren't going to change your viewpoints with respect to the general principle. There remains, though, a smaller area with respect to individual provisions in the bill where you are still flexible and where the hearings can sway you. That is where hearings do have an impact.

The Reports. Committee reports that summarize the hearings and subsequent committee action are regarded as containing much useful information, although they sometimes are criticized as possessing too little analytical material. Congressmen prefer to have recommendations before them, accompanied by a criticial analysis of the pro and con arguments. They are willing to make the judgment, but they want more specific guidelines leading to the point of decision than are often found in committee reports.

Congressmen are aware that reports are read carefully by executive agency personnel, who are often reluctant to act counter to any expressed wish of the Congress or those of its committees possessing jurisdiction over the department or agency. Thus, some legislators seek to make their influence felt at the report level.

Reports are also regarded as excellent sources of materials for campaign speeches, whether they are drawn in partisan fashion or not. For some congressmen, regardless of their politics, the minority reports are valuable in illuminating the main points of controversy:

> I read the minority report before I read the majority report. Then I have some indication of the arguments against the legislation and in reading the majority statement can see how well those things stand up. Members in failing to read the minority report, miss a great deal of information about the legislation.

Not all reports are favorably received, of course. Occasionally, certain committees are singled out as disposed to issue reports that are excessively partisan or which are of little assistance in explaining the legislation. Observed one congressman: "Often committees don't really explain the legislation and what is involved in it. Reports, instead of serving to illuminate the truth, seem to be designed to hide the facts to advance the position in which the committee is interested."

By far the most common congressional criticism of reports, however, is that too often they are not available in time to assist the legislator in reaching a decision. Frequently, they are issued just prior to a vote so that the congressman has little or no opportunity to study them. This serves to strengthen the dependence of the House on those legislators who have participated actively in committee discussions about the bill.

Influence of House Leadership

There is agreement that the intervention of House leadership in the committee process tends to be minimal. It seldom is evident with respect to minor legislation and occurs less frequently than might be expected when major bills are being considered. Leaders expect to be informed of the progress of legislation within committees and of the problems involved, and may make routine checks of this nature. But seldom is their role one of harnessing committee members to the party will; where the chairman is strong and reliable, that function is ordinarily left to him.

Leadership activity varies with the particular committee and personalities involved as well as with the importance of the legislation. Party leaders are always available for consultation and advice, and senior committee members are often encouraged to take advantage of this availability. But the leadership intervenes directly sparingly, and then often with reluctance, sometimes on request. Aware of the sensitivity and traditional independence of committee chairmen and mindful of the consequences of attempts to give direction to "strong" ones, the leadership "is careful not to over-use its potential."

In virtually any situation, leadership intervention can bring about faster committee action, and it may be exerted to expedite the reporting of legislation. Attempting to dictate or influence heavily the detail of legislation is a more delicate matter, however, and one which has traditionally been avoided. "But," said one congressman, "if the Speaker wants to talk to a key man about a key bill he can help shape the proposal in a way he thinks will expedite its passage through the Rules Committee and the House. He may not shape the whole bill, but he can knock some rough edges off the thing while it is still in committee just by a word to the wise." Occasionally, when conflicts develop between committees about the jurisdiction of legislation, the leadership may exert an active role in bringing the two groups together. By assisting in the wording of measures so as to send them to "friendly" committees or, whenever possible, by assigning bills they do not want passed to "unfriendly" committees, the Speaker and his immediate subordinates may exercise a major role in determining the fate of legislation.

The Joint Committee

Discussion with members of Congress of the advantages and disadvantages of joint committees revealed no real enthusiasm for them although one congressman who has served on two—the Joint Committee on

Atomic Energy and the Joint Economic Committee—defended both as effective and hardworking. It was his opinion that the Senate did not dominate committee proceedings, and he argued that on "the big questions" there were substantial advantages to the joint committee procedure.

It was evident, however, that many House members fear Senate predominance in joint committees, while House members carry the workload, and believe that any significant increase in the number of such groups would result in the reduction of House prestige in relation to that of the Senate. Concern was expressed also about the tendency for some senators to have members of their personal staff attend joint committee sessions in their stead:

There is a fundamental difference in the way the two bodies legislate. This is not a criticism; it is a question of work load. Anyone sitting on joint committees knows that while it is inconceivable that a member of the House will be represented by his staff, it is not at all unusual for senators to be represented by their top man, who will even participate in the discussions. It is the difference between direct individual participation by the principal and pseudo-participation by the man who presumes he speaks for his principal.

One congressman noted the opposition of the late Speaker Rayburn to extension of the joint committee system and indicated that opposition was determinative. When plans were underway to create a standing committee on Space and Astronautics, he related, a House group recommended that a joint committee be established, but the proposal was removed on the House floor. After the Senate had amended the bill by inserting the joint committee feature, the matter was sent to conference. There Senate conferees found the provision had been deleted from the compromise bill. When one senator asked why this action had been taken, he was told "that decision was reached at the Texas level," a reference to the fact that both the Speaker of the House and the majority leader of the Senate were Texans.

The Role of the Executive

The role of the executive in the committee process is necessarily a major one, for it not only requests funds from the Congress to carry out its work but it provides the legislature with most of the information on which decisions about executive programs are based. As Dean Acheson has written: "When one speaks of the executive working with Congress, one is using shorthand. The center and focus of legislative-executive relations lie in the congressional committees and in the method of their operation."[11] Acheson's statement explains direct intervention by the executive in the committee assignment process. Sometimes executive influence on committees is so strong that in many instances an agency almost makes a committee its tool by its constant year-to-year relationships with that particular committee.

While it is true that the continuing interaction between executive agencies and the committees often leads to close cooperation, the results sometimes work to the advantage of the legislative branch. Some committee veterans are so knowledgeable about the intricacies of operation of certain agencies that representatives of the executive may be no match for them during hearings. And when the executive branch is held by one political party, and the legislative branch by the other, it sometimes happens that congressional committees make effective use of certain executive personnel to lend support to their own position and to undermine the official opinion of the administration. The influence of some congressional committees with the departments and agencies with which they are concerned is also well known. Some even possess the power to effect policy changes, as the following comment notes:

> The best example I know of, of a committee that has had a substantial effect on policy decisions is the Joint Atomic Energy Committee. Over a period of time they have substantially modified executive policy, as I understand it. They have demonstrated conclusively that this can be done by a congressional committee and in retrospect their decisions appear to have been correct.

Clearly, whatever turn the relationship between congressional committees and the executive branch takes, the effect usually is close liaison.

Congressmen are aware of, and sensitive to, the influence of the executive with respect to legislation. In speaking of the reluctance of congressional committees to schedule hearings on legislative proposals in the absence of a statement summarizing the reactions of the executive, one congressman said, "we abdicate many of our responsibilities to the executive." Progress of virtually all legislation awaits initial executive evaluation, although an adverse recommendation does not necessarily prove

[11] *A Citizen Looks at Congress* (Harper & Brothers, 1956), p. 61.

fatal to measures: agency disapproval is generally determinative in connection with minor legislation, but other factors may outweigh it where major proposals are concerned.

The committees on which I sit make executive branch recommendations almost imperative before they will go ahead with any bill. They may not agree with the recommendations or follow them, but until the executive comes in with a report or recommendation of some kind, these two committees will not consider a proposition—at least it is most exceptional for them to do so.

*

That is the general practice. It should be pointed out, however, that a lot of executive branch recommendations are forthcoming only because the committee tells the department or Bureau of the Budget, "we are going to consider this bill and you'd better get your report in." If the executive branch thought it could stop some measures by failing to submit a report, it would do so. The committee sometimes has to put pressure on the executive to get them to report. There is some justification for the time it takes the executive to submit reports, especially when several departments are involved, and the Bureau of the Budget has the final word.

The trend toward the primacy of the executive branch in the drafting of legislation is another matter of concern to some members of Congress who fear the influence of the legislative branch vis-à-vis the executive is declining. Congress may lose whatever initiative it has possessed and become little more than a judge of the proposals of others: "A large percentage of the bills that come through our committee originate in the executive department and are introduced by the committee chairman or the members. In a broad sense the Congress has been reduced to a sort of veto power."

Even when the Congress does not accept the adverse views of the executive with respect to undertaking a new proposal or establishing the guiding principles for it, the latter, noting congressional insistence on the program, may submit suggestions regarding execution of the details, and these may be followed:

Executive position is strongest where the controlling congressional leadership is least at variance with it. Where we are inclined to go that way anyway, we will accept the executive's advice on how to do it. But even where our position is contrary to that of the executive, we may take their advice on detail. They say, "If you are going to do it, do it this way."

As another congressman observed, it is very difficult to get anything past the Appropriations Committees involving an expenditure of money that has not been requested by the executive. Congress is in a poor position to initiate major new programs independently of those recommended by the administration.

Still another indication of close coordination between the two branches of government is the fact that executive department officials will meet regularly in closed session with congressional committee members to work out the details of some major pieces of legislation even though there may be disagreement between the two groups about the kind of bill that is desirable.

A sore point for many congressmen is the dependence of committees in reaching decisions on information provided by the executive. By selecting which information to provide and which to withhold, they assert, the executive may well determine the fate of legislation instead of leaving the decision to congressional judgment. Said one legislator particularly sensitive to the problem, "I think the situation exists today where the Congress is faced with a responsibility for legislating very basic policy and fiscal policy, but is without the ability to compel the production of information which gives us the facts as a basis for legislating." To that statement, a colleague with service in the bureaucracy commented, "I absolutely agree with that position." The first speaker continued:

You can't get facts now. The executive says you can't have them. Today the executive asserts a new type of privilege which holds him above the law. He executes faithfully now only those laws he likes. And he can withhold from us and our agent, the comptroller general, all the facts of government under the claim of executive privilege.

His colleague then replied:

We got caught in this situation because for a long time [when the Democrats controlled both Congress and the Presidency] we presumably had liaison cooperation which has been severed [with a Republican in the White House]. And we have not built into the congressional structure the necessary research personnel, the necessary lines of informal communication to elicit the information. What we are dependent on, I assume, is informers.

A later discussion re-emphasized the dependence of congressional committees on the executive and indicated congressional concern that the executive might not, itself, always arrive at the proper conclusion. Some congressmen were not willing to concede that constant involvement with the subject matter gave executive officials wisdom greater than that possessed by legislators with more diverse interests and responsibilities. The discussion also brought out that, occasionally at least, executive determinations of the most desirable course of action were tempered by the necessity for placating the narrower interests of key congressional leaders.

Don't you think the point that should be made is that unless the administration volunteers the information, Congress generally is pretty helpless? We lack the expert staff to do the effective cross-examination needed to get the facts.

*

The terrifying thing is that what we are talking about is the ability of Congress to make decisions on the basis of information furnished by the executive, and the indications are, on relatively superficial study, that in the field of defense we don't have an effective decision making apparatus in the executive. [Disagreement within the Joint Chiefs of Staff group had recently been disclosed in the press.] The basic decision is never made by Congress. We may choose between "A" or "B" missile systems, but we never get all the facts to determine whether the choice should even be made between "A" and "B." Perhaps the choice should be "C" or "D."

*

Even if we had better functioning committees, there is a question of whether we are in a position to make such a decision.

*

I think we have to assume that we have as much intelligence as the men over there at the Pentagon. We have the constitutional responsibility.

*

I don't mean that our intelligence is inadequate. I agree we should do more, but I have considerable question as to the type of committee organization we need, and how much decision we can make in this field.

*

As a member of the executive branch before I came to Congress, I heard the sharp criticism that House decisions were made basically on what was thought to be good policy as modified by the necessity to trim to personal circumstances and to whims of strong individual members of Congress. There is a great temptation on the part of some members to home-town decisions, particularly in this area. In the process of home-towning, the executive agency makes a decision not in terms of what is, even in their judgment, necessarily the wisest combination for the good of the country, but what is the one which will ruffle the fewest significant feathers in the House.

The important role of the Bureau of the Budget in the administrative process is a source of much congressional dissatisfaction. During the period the Presidency was held by a Republican and both houses of Congress possessed Democratic majorities, the Democrats particularly resented the tendency for the Budget Bureau to reduce—sometimes sharply—departmental requests for funds. Many thought the efforts of congressional committees to act judiciously and in the national interest were severely hampered by the restrictions placed on departmental administrators who appeared before them. The departments knew far better than the Budget Bureau what their needs were, the legislators argued, and their representatives should be completely free to press those needs on the Congress. The Bureau of the Budget was, in effect, making policy for all of the executive branch and this was dangerous.

The question of what is official policy is a question of what the President and the Director of the Bureau of the Budget finally lay down as official policy. If you are going to have one voice speaking for the executive, you have to have some coordination. It is proper that the executive office have a coordinator.

*

That is where you and I disagree. The Secretary of the Interior and top Interior officials are confirmed by the Senate after the President submits their names. The Secretary is the President's spokesman on problems relating to his Department. I don't think the Bureau of the Budget is the authority on problems of the Department of Interior. I don't think the Budget Director is supposed to be Secretary of Defense. Don't we have a right to look to the Secretary of Defense rather than to the Director of the Bureau of the Budget to speak for the administration position on defense matters?

*

Let me put this in focus. Right now we have aid to education legislation before our subcommittee. The Secretary of Health, Education and Welfare and his subordinates are strongly pro-education. They would like to have a school construction bill with some money in it and get going. The President and Bureau of the Budget are on an economy jag right now and don't want any money spent. I suppose ideally this question should be resolved with the President as the arbiter. The Budget Bureau should present one point of view and the Secretary the other and the President should decide. The reason for your complaint is that Budget has taken over and is dominating all policy, overriding the people who normally serve as spokesmen and who normally prevail at least half the time.

*

You say the President should act as arbiter between Budget and HEW. Budget has no position. Only the President has a right to have a position. The

Bureau is to carry out the programs and policy of the President as is the Secretary. There cannot be conflict in presidential policy; it must be the administration position.

*

That is a lot clearer in textbooks than in operation.

The impact of executive leadership on the decisions of congressional committees and of the Congress itself receives attention from congressmen. Both Democrats and Republicans believe that executive leadership was lacking under President Eisenhower, but they emphasize that the personality of departmental emissaries frequently affected significantly committee reception of particular programs. Excerpts from a discussion of Democratic members of the House illustrate some reactions:

I think the 81st Congress had more executive leadership than any in which I have served. Truman was not always popular, and he didn't always have his way about things. The votes were very close, but he stood for something. It wasn't just a matter of taking an objective viewpoint about everything and if it went through, fine, and if it didn't, saying, "Well, I have done my best or stated my position."

*

Whether Congress works "best" when Executive leadership is strong and positive depends on what you mean by "best." Certainly a program is more likely to be achieved with a strong Executive whether it is good or bad.

*

It isn't just "the executive" that is involved; it is the plan and its spokesman. If he inspires confidence even though he is of the opposition party, if you trust him and feel he is not slippping a knife between your ribs or destroying something you believe in, if you think he knows what he is talking about, you will cooperate with him. If you don't trust him or believe he doesn't know what he is doing, you treat him with the contempt he has earned. I saw this happen to Roosevelt's executives when the Democrats had substantial majorities. He had weak executives and they couldn't carry a paper bag down the Hill.

President Kennedy has exerted more effort than his predecessors to establish rapport with committees, and particularly with committee chairmen. Although previous presidents conferred frequently with chairmen of major committees, Kennedy is the first systematically to schedule personal talks with every committee chairman. First undertaken in the Eighty-seventh Congress, the practice has been continued in the Eighty-eighth. In these meetings, the President discusses legislation within a committee's jurisdiction, seeks to ascertain the priority for its consideration as well as the chairman's general attitude toward it, and indicates his own views with respect to certain issues. These preliminary sessions are followed up from time to time by presidential phone calls. And on occasion entire committees or their leading members have been invited to the White House for briefings or to participate in special presidential conferences dealing with matters within their ken.

Writing three quarters of a century ago, Woodrow Wilson spoke of "government by the . . . standing committees of congress" and referred to congressional committees as "little legislatures." "Legislation as we nowadays conduct it," he said, "is not conducted in the open. It is not thrashed out in open debate upon the floors of our assemblies. It is, on the contrary, framed, digested, and concluded in committee rooms."[12]

Today committees remain the kiln in which the stuff of legislation is baked, the important point of entry to the congressional power elite, a major route to attainment of the respect and deference of colleagues that members eagerly seek. Congressional size, workload, and rules promote, if not compel, their primacy. It is not surprising, therefore, that, in their efforts to influence the course of legislation, the Executive, the interest groups, and party leaders should be much concerned with control and persuasion of the committees. Nor is it surprising that critics of congress and dissidents within that body often should seek to launch their assaults on that venerable institution by concentrating on reform of important elements of the committee structure such as seniority and rules.

For the student of congress there is drama and even aspects of mystery in the significant differences in procedure between committees, the often fascinating interplay of personalities within a single unit, the rivalries between committees and the attitudes of resentment that membership on one may give rise to with respect to another. If "congress is organized to buck responsibility," as one bright congressman insists, then, as he says, "the committee system is a major instrument in that. There, it is often difficult, if not impossible, to place responsibility." The strengths and weaknesses of congress are illumined there as nowhere else, for the committees, in truth, are at the core of the legislative process.

[12] *Congressional Government* (Houghton-Mifflin Company; 1885).

VII

The Leadership

LEADERSHIP IN THE HOUSE is diffused—divided between elected leaders, members who have risen to power by means of seniority, and a few individuals who are influential because of their personality and expertise although they do not enjoy official standing in the House or party hierarchy. In recent years, the formal instruments of leadership, such as the party caucus and the policy committee, have not been central elements in its exercise. The absence of official party apparatus that could give direction to the elected leaders has strengthened the hand of the Speaker and the majority leader, increasing their authority and freedom of action. They have not appeared dissatisfied with this arrangement.

The Speaker

Originally not a particularly powerful force in the House—early Presidents designated their own legislative leaders from whom the party majority took its cue—the speakership has developed into one of the most important positions in the governmental system. Once merely a presiding officer, the Speaker now is a recognized party leader. In discussions of the office, the words of former Speaker Thomas B. Reed that "the Speaker has but one superior and no peer," are often quoted approvingly

Although two nineteenth century Speakers, Henry Clay and William Pennington, assumed the position when they were first elected to the House, the trend has been toward selecting a man with long experience in that body.[1] In this century, all Speakers have been elevated to the position from the post of floor leader and have averaged more than twenty years House service at the time of their designation. Their long tenure has provided an opportunity to develop friendships and influence within the House and has meant that Speakers bring to the office important sup-

[1] The Speaker need not even be a member, though only members have been elected.

280

plements to the power realized from the authority of the office itself. They already possess an extensive network of allies, have had an opportunity to study closely the strengths and weaknesses of their colleagues, and have influence based on service and achievement.

Prior to 1910, the Speaker had come to exercise near absolute powers. He appointed all members of committees, including the chairmen. He could arbitrarily refuse floor recognition to those whose purpose ran counter to his. He served as chairman of the Rules Committee and designated its other members, thus being able to ensure a majority for any action he wished that strategically placed group to take.

His control over the Rules Committee was especially important. The committee became a major instrument of leadership by means of which the power of the majority could be maximized. Through the committee, the Speaker could prescribe limitation of debate, avoid consideration of most unpalatable measures, and rebuff attempts to modify the rules themselves. Control of this group and the power to alter committees at will made the House all but subservient to the Speaker's will. He could determine the legislative program almost without restraint.

The authoritarian manner in which some prerogatives were exercised and the insensitiveness of the Speaker to various elements in the House, especially to some within the majority party itself, eventually led to the revolution of 1910, which stripped him of much of his power. He was removed from the Rules Committee, lost the right to name committees, and forfeited his absolute power of recognition. Though his authority was diminished, his overall influence remained great. Building on their experience in the House and the positions of pre-eminence they have already achieved there, it has not been difficult for recent Speakers to exert extraordinary influence, firmly based on personal leadership. Each Speaker makes his own impact on the position, and with each occupant the post assumes a different form. There is, however, a characteristic deference in the House to the Speaker's suggestions and requests.

In addition to the power achieved by the force of his personality and the esteem in which he is held, the Speaker has important functions that strengthen his authority. Along with the majority leader and the party whip he regularly represents the House in the weekly conferences of congressional leaders with the President (when they are of the same political party). With them also he determines party strategy in the

House; he is supreme commander of his party's forces there. He makes certain appointments directly and, when he desires to do so, influences strongly regular committee appointments. He presides at House sessions where he rules on points of order, retains discretion in the matter of recognition, and refers legislative proposals to committees. As a member of the House, he may vote and participate in debate.

The Floor Leaders

Leader of his party's forces on the floor and bearing responsibility for the scheduling of the work of the House, the Majority Leader, like the Speaker, owes much of his power to his personal influence with his colleagues. Designated by the Speaker prior to 1910, subsequent to that date he has been elected by the caucus of the majority party and has succeeded to the speakership whenever a vacancy has occurred in that office. Scheduling legislation to obtain maximum results is a tricky matter, and the effective majority leader possesses a canny sense of timing. Working closely with the Speaker he assumes major responsibility for the passage of his party's legislative program, seeking accommodation between conflicting forces within the party and the House as well as attempting to reconcile jurisdictional disputes between committees. He endeavors to keep recalcitrant members in line with party policy, and he watches closely legislative developments within the committees. The Republican floor leader serves as chairman of his party's Committee on Committees. The Democratic floor leader, though not a member of the group making his party's committee designations, can heavily influence selection by expressing an opinion or preference.

The minority leader performs many of the leadership and consultative functions carried on by his counterpart, the Majority Leader, but there are obvious differences. He generally has little to say about the scheduling of legislation, for example, and since the speakership is held by the opposition, he is leader of his party in the House rather than chief assistant leader.

The Whips

The Democratic whip is appointed by the Majority Leader (after consultation with the Speaker when they are of the same party) and is then approved by the party caucus; the Republican whip is elected by his party's Committee on Committees. Each, aided by regional assistants, works closely with his floor leader to coordinate information and to ensure maximum attendance of colleagues when crucial votes are to be taken. The whip has responsibility for notifying party members of the legislative schedule and for furnishing them with materials relevant to the current program. The measure of his influence depends in large part on his relationship with the floor leader.

The Seniority Leaders

The chairmen and ranking members of House committees have positions of power by virtue of their seniority on committees and are well situated to affect the course and form of legislation. They clearly constitute an important element of House leadership. It is equally apparent that their influence varies markedly. House reliance on the committee system serves to increase the role of these men. If they are respected members, in good standing with colleagues and the leadership, they are given wide discretion in the determination of party policy with respect to matters falling within the jurisdiction of the committees they head. The formal leadership generally restricts its intervention in committee activities to difficult situations where there is an apparent conflict between the party position and the committee (or chairman's) position.

But not all seniority leaders perform significant roles in party affairs or in the determination of party positions, even with respect to matters falling within their ken. They may be consulted by the formal leadership more as a matter of courtesy than as a means of formulating party policy. And when a senior committee member is powerful, it is as an individual, not as a member of a group of committee chairmen or ranking minority members, as this discussion among House Democrats indicates.

The committee chairmen operate as a kind of policy committee with the leadership with regard to matters under their jurisdiction. Wouldn't you say that was more or less an understanding?

*

I would underscore "kind of" and "more or less."

*

I think the chairmen do consult the leadership and vice versa.

*

But they don't do it collectively. The majority leader and the Speaker consult with individual chairmen not with an assemblage of chairmen.

The discussion[2] which follows reflects the fact that statements by certain committee chairmen who enjoy the confidence of party colleagues tend to be accepted as establishing party policy, while actions by other chairmen whose positions in the party hierarchy are less secure are less regarded. All the discussants are Democrats.

Wilbur Mills [chairman of the House Ways and Means Committee] today announced that, in his opinion, there would be no tax increase or cut in the current session. This is setting Democratic party policy in the House. He didn't check with me before making the statement, but I have a notion he checked with at least a few people. Party policy has been set on taxes without a party caucus.

*

Mills' statement is more or less a consensus of the views of the Democratic members of the Ways and Means Committee. From his vantage point as chairman of the committee, it appeared to him unlikely that we could or would do either of these things.

*

I am not quarreling with the system. I am just saying this is the way our party policy on taxes is made. Over the years enough tradition has developed so that people in places of power, like Mills, don't have to go to any informal organization before speaking. I doubt very much whether he conferred with more than a half dozen people. He is in a position where he has the authority through his prestige and his office so he makes a statement based on his experience.

*

Is there a distinction between Mills' personal viewpoint and party policy in terms of what the tax program will be? He happens to occupy the position which determines what will happen. His statement becomes quasi-official if not official.

*

But consider the matter of what kind of labor legislation is going to be passed. There are three main alternatives, including that proposed by the Democratic chairman of the House Committee on Education and Labor, Mr. Barden. Few Democrats will support Barden's bill.

*

That is a good point. Barden put in his bill the same day Mills made his statement. Both are committee chairmen. Mills' statement is policy; Barden's probably will not reflect party policy. The difference is that Mills is in good standing, Barden is not.

[2] This took place in 1959.

The Identification of Leadership

An important effect of the diffusion of leadership has been uncertainty within the House regarding what constitutes "the leadership" and the real sources of power. There is general agreement that the term "the leadership" includes more than the principal formally elected leaders— the Speaker, floor leader, and party whip—but beyond that there is less accord. The officers of the party caucus or conference are rarely mentioned, for example, although the chairman of the Republican Policy Committee and at least certain key members of the committee itself seem to be regarded as within the elite group of their party. Of late, the chairmanship of the Republican Conference has assumed more importance. Many of the seniority leaders occupy positions of power, but few of them are regarded as part of "the leadership."

Some Democratic congressmen discuss the matter:

Can you precisely, or even approximately, define the leadership of the House? Is it the Speaker, the majority leader and the whip, plus the whip organization, or is it the Speaker and the Senate majority leader and, on fiscal matters, the Secretary of the Treasury, and, on international matters, the Secretary of State?

*

I'd say the formal leadership consists of people who are elected to lead. There certainly can be no controversy about the Speaker and majority leader. Would you say there is anybody in the Democratic party with more power than those two?

*

At the end of the session when Uncle Howard [Chairman Howard W. Smith of the House Rules Committee] goes home to look at his dairy farm [thereby delaying legislation], I'd say "yes." When you consider the entire session, the Speaker and majority leader constitute the main source of power. But in that final period before adjournment when tensions are high and the desire for action is the greatest, the Rules Commmittee chairman is one of the most important members of the House.

*

The fact that the Rules Committee chairman can block legislation doesn't mean he is a leader. I think one should distinguish between positive leadership and negative leadership. The chief power in a committee chairman is a negative one. By and large the legislative product depends less on the chairman than on the composition of the committees.

Power accrues to a member by virtue of the office he holds, although

the measure of this power and the individual's position in the leadership
cannot be determined by the office alone; the personality involved bears
significantly on this point. As one congressman put it:

The opportunities for power compare roughly with the positions occupied,
but these opportunities are translated into exercise of power by individuals and
their personalities. Any member of this body, on any issue, can become a leader,
and because of his leadership of the moment have power in guiding legislation.

Certain influential House members are occasionally identified with the
leadership even though they hold no elective position in the House or in
the party and do not occupy the senior party posts on the committees on
which they serve. And it is agreed that within the House and within each
party there is an informal inner circle of leaders (many of them appear to
be top subcommittee members) who enjoy special deference from their
colleagues, whose pronouncements noticeably affect House voting, and
whose support is eagerly sought because of their unchallenged position of
influence. Explained one representative:

When a man has demonstrated ability, regardless of his formal position of
power, by the force of his personality, knowledge, and effective talent he becomes
an informal locus of power. He is the true leader who automatically wins followers, regardless of position. In every social structure you are going to find people to
whom, for certain purposes, people will automatically turn regardless of their
formal status in that group.

All of this tends to reflect the view that the leadership core (Speaker,
majority leader, whip) expands with respect to specific issues to incor-
porate party specialists in good standing. Speaker Rayburn's "Board of
Education" was an extremely powerful though informal group whose
membership was not constant. In calling these men together, Rayburn
was continuing a practice of earlier speakers, who, in fact, had given the
group its name. Charles Halleck organized "The Clinic" as a Republican
counterpart. Leadership—even "the leadership"—then, is an inconstant
thing as many congressmen see it, varying somewhat from one issue to
the next. Often it is difficult, particularly for junior members, to identify
with precision the real wielders of power.

Successful Leadership

Whether the setting for the exercise of leadership is the House itself,
the political party, or a committee, persuasion rather than coercion or

threat constitutes the main instrument by which it is attempted to attain most desired goals. There may be tacit recognition by all principals that it is within the power of the leadership to inflict sanctions (or distribute largesse) if that is necessary, but seldom, according to the testimony of numerous House members, is that fact verbalized, and rarely is it invoked should a member find himself unable or unwilling to comply with a request.

The most effective leaders know how much flexibility individual colleagues possess in a given situation and the direction in which their inclinations would take them. They know, too, how best to achieve a favorable result. One measure of true leadership is the ability to exercise strategic deployment of arguments and allies so as to elicit the support of diverse elements within the House. The success with which the conditions can be established that will make it possible for members with different problems and different outlooks to stand together on a proposal is another indicator. Careful selection and use of lieutenants is important. Sometimes it is necessary to try to dissuade an individual entitled to serve as a floor manager for a bill from exercising this prerogative if it is concluded that his participation might endanger prospects for success. At the same time, designation of a revered House luminary, or a respected representative of a faction from which more support is sorely needed, may turn potential defeat into victory. Strategy is important indeed.

The leaders must be sensitive to the "mood" of the House, always prepared to defer a showdown on an issue when the House appears to be in a negative or rebellious frame of mind. The leaders function, too, as catalysts for party groups and are generally remarkably responsive to situations existing within their party. Whatever their natural inclinations, they cannot ignore the attidudes of any significant element if they are to retain the confidence of their party colleagues. When they attempt to run counter to these views they may suffer defeat. Repeated defeats would jeopardize their influence in the House.

They may lose, too, if the extra-congressional groups on which the leadership can normally rely to lend support to its position are arrayed against them. Thus legislators attribute the defeat of a gas bill, in which Speaker Rayburn himself was vitally interested and for which he and his cohorts thought they had the votes, to the active intervention of organized labor in an effective last minute effort to switch committed members. According to some supporters of the bill, what had been a comfortable majority the day prior to the vote dissolved by the time the House met to decide the bill's fate, largely because of the widespread defection of forces susceptible to labor influence.

The Light Touch of Leadership. In recent years both parties have been led in the House by men (Rayburn and Martin particularly) who firmly believed that the first obligation of a congressman is to himself and his district rather than to his party. ("Vote your district first.") This has resulted in marked reluctance to enforce discipline against recalcitrant members, particularly if the latter can plead plausibly that their district's interests run counter to the party stand. The party encompasses many diverse elements, this reasoning holds, the future of some of which might be jeopardized if they were forced to conform to certain official positions. It is recognized that individual congressmen have more flexibility on some issues than on others and that the substantive areas of flexibility vary from one district to another. Said one party leader, "One of the things many members tend to assume is that since they tend to have a certain flexibility on a given set of issues, everyone has the flexibility. In my judgment that is a great mistake."

The prevalence of this doctrine of permissiveness at the upper echelons of the party hierarchy affects the nature of the legislative party itself as well as the impact of the party caucus and the utility of arms of the leadership such as the whip organization. It has also resulted in only rare direct solicitation of votes by the formal leadership; where a request is made, it often comes from a party lieutenant. This practice has one salutary effect: Because a member is so seldom personally requested by the leader to vote in a certain way, he may be inclined to accede to such requests if it is at all possible to do so. "The Democratic leadership makes very little effort to weld their people in line," observed one party member. "They do so little asking, in fact, that if they did ask me I'd do my darndest to go along with them." But, the same man stated, failure to solicit support very often "may actually hurt the party in the long run by keeping it from becoming more effective."

The following excerpt from a discussion of House Democrats reflects their experience with respect to appeals by Speaker Rayburn; he rarely requested their votes. It also sets forth the views of certain members that much greater maneuverability is possible in the absence of party caucuses.

As a substitute for the caucus the leadership attempts to exert a personal persuasive influence. I have only experienced this on two issues, one of which was the farm bill just prior to the 1956 election. My district opposes the party position on farm policy. The Speaker called me and said. "This is very vital to the party, particularly with the national election approaching. Can you possibly go along with us?" It was a personal appeal from the Speaker on the day of the vote. I told him that I had a strongly Democratic district, and if my vote would make the difference I would vote with him, but, if possible, I wanted to wait until the second round on the roll call and, if my vote was not needed, vote my district. He said, "That is fine. That is all I want." Friends told me he talked to them also. In effect he buttoned the thing up by that type of personal appeal. He could have gotten us all in a caucus and made a speech that wouldn't have been half as effective as ten or twelve phone calls.

*

I think most of us have had a somewhat similar experience. He has never asked me to vote any way on a single issue. He senses the operation; he knows what you can do and what you cannot do.

*

He is able to do a lot more planning, negotiating, packaging, and timing than he could do if he had any need to bring major issues before a caucus.

Despite testimonials that top leadership is slow to invoke discipline against recalcitrant legislators, some members insist that today "the House is run by a close clique of too often willful men." This belief affects behavior. Junior members especially seek the approval of those who have command positions. They want to "go along" whenever possible on important votes. They know the leadership can single them out as men with a future by designating them for special assignments and trips, volunteering to speak in their districts, tapping them for the annual honor of reading President Washington's Farewell Address, or to make the motions to adjourn the House. Being invited to preside is another important honor, and the ambitious member looks forward to the day when he may be asked to chair sessions of the Committee of the Whole House.

On the other hand, if they lose the confidence of the top leaders, they risk isolation and loss of prestige. Party leaders have many indirect ways in which to retaliate. Said one disillusioned congressman, "They can give you the silent treatment. And the real whip is the delayed action. You may think you are not going to be punished for your failure to stay in line because there is no immediate penalty. Months later, however, something happens which makes you realize they were just waiting for the proper moment to strike. There is no doubt about it. If you are going to be independent around here you are going to pay a steep price for it."

Working With the Opposition. An important element in the effectiveness of the leadership relates to its ability to work harmoniously with leaders of the opposition party. As one influential congressman put it: "The only way the House can operate is through accommodation between party leaders. You must have confidence in the work of the other fellow if things are to move along well." For many years the friendship and confidence which the two House leaders—Sam Rayburn and Joseph W. Martin—had for one another was an important factor in determining the fate of legislative proposals and promoting more efficient operation of the House. One effect of close cooperation between leaders of opposing parties is evident in the following exchange between House Democrats:

When top leaders of both parties take the same position on a given piece of legislation, the real minority on the issue may actually be deprived of its rights because the leaders protect the recommital. The motion to recommit with or without instructions is an important part of the process, but party leaders can often negate that when they are allied. By setting impossible alternatives they can deprive the House of a real choice. To make the recommital motion, it is customary for the Speaker to recognize the senior minority member opposed to the bill who sits on the committee which has considered it. When the leadership groups are agreed, he sometimes can get the opposition to make the kind of motion he wants made. This helps get maximum support for their position.

*

That happens. You may regard it as a good protective device or as a frustrating one, depriving the House of a real choice, depending on whether you are for or against the position.

Cooperation and accommodation between parties may be highly desirable, even essential, in some circumstances. But the search for agreement is not without its congressional critics. Cooperation can be carried too far, it is said, and the result may have serious consequences for the national interest. Consider the comments of a conservative House Republican:

Many times I think we practice this effort of bipartisanship too strongly. Sometimes we ought to draw the lines and fight back. For a long time, I have had the feeling that we sometimes choose a minimum course of action because it is the maximum area of agreement that we could easily reach. The country itself sometimes loses because we are so eager to have bipartisanship that we take the lowest common denominator.

Sharper criticism of the close personal relationship that existed between the veteran Democratic and Republican party leaders in the House came from a man considered to be among the most practical politicians in the Democratic liberal ranks:

The Republicans did a cruel thing to Joe Martin, kicking him out after he had served them for so long and after he had grown old. But events indicate that though it was cruel, it was wise. One liberal Democrat said to me, "Halleck is the best thing that has happened to Congress in years." And I guess he is—he plays to win as one should in this political game. Cronyism had become bipartisan, with not only fellow Democrats sticking together because of friendship or vulnerability, hesitating to disagree openly with one another, but with Rayburn and Martin, the Democratic and Republican leaders, participating in cronyism themselves. One would say to the other, "Am I really going to hurt you if I do such and such?" And if the other said, "yes," the first person altered his plans. They tended to forget that the two leaders should not be waltzing with one another here but instead should be pushing their party's program. Rayburn isn't going to do much waltzing with Charlie Halleck; Halleck doesn't operate under the Marquis of Queensbury rules. He elbows and bucks and kicks. He fights with whatever he has, and he makes maximum use of his troops. He plays it smart too. When he knows he has no chance, he doesn't put up a real fight.

Criticisms of the Leadership

The leadership is blamed for what many legislators characterize as lack of communication and consultation and poor scheduling and coordination. Criticism on these scores is widespread.

Poor Communication and Scheduling. Grumbling is especially apparent in the ranks of junior members since without general party caucus sessions— which have been rare indeed in the House[3]—there is little opportunity for them to make their wishes known or to learn what has been decided by party leaders. The leadership (and this is particularly true of the Democrats since they lack the active policy committee mechanism of their Republican counterparts) functions in an informal way, taking soundings by soliciting opinions and suggestions from the more senior colleagues; the junior members feel ignored. "We function without party caucuses,"

[3] The revitalization of the Republican conference in 1963 following the election of Gerald R. Ford of Michigan to the chairmanship has provided an important outlet for the energies of Republicans of middle and junior seniority.

said one third term member. "We have little opportunity to express views to the leadership about party programs except through the filing of a bill or a speech on the floor." And a ten-year veteran Democrat regards the failure of the leadership to keep the rank and file members fully informed as but one example of the general lack of communication which prevails in the legislative body:

> One disturbing thing is the lack of communication which seems to characterize the whole congressional operation. In both parties there is a lack of communication between the leadership and the other members. A lack of communication is also apparent in connection with committee activities. There are so many non-major issues coming before us that it is impossible to keep up. The way we get the word about them is through the operations of the committees—actually through the subcommittees. Under our system, members who are not on a committee or subcommittee are apprised of action only when the bill comes out. There is little opportunity to get the information in other ways, so the reporting of a bill is the important event in bringing it to the members' attention.

A policy of infrequent caucuses and weak policy committees may provide desirable maneuverability to the leadership, and some party members may believe this to be the most effective way to proceed. But the lack of formal communication between leader and follower also gives rise to criticism that the leadership is not properly responsive to the views of colleagues, that, in fact, it may not even be adequately aware of these opinions. Complained one representative: "Those who are in control run the legislative program without much consultation. Certainly they haven't always been responsive. The rules are made for the leaders and that isn't the way it should be." A companion complaint is that the decisions of the leadership are often not fully shared with their fellow party members. One Democrat on the fringes of the leadership commented privately: "One of the real problems here is that we don't know the party position except on something like the override of a veto." Following an observation that the leadership is negligent in crystallizing policy and in disseminating it, a member pointed out that there was a two-way deficiency of communication:

> I think we feel we should have more to say about what the party line is. I think he is saying there isn't enough party line. At first we were talking about the filter up and now we are talking about the trickle down. There is no party policy as such that is built at the grass roots and goes on up from there and directs the leadership. And we don't get the word from them either.

Understandably, most criticisms about the need for more strict accountability are heard from junior members or congressmen who are impatient for more positive legislative action. Said one well regarded freshman Democrat:

I have been rather disturbed at various times as to how and why leadership decisions have been arrived at. I am not always in disagreement with the decisions, but I often disagree with the methods which have been employed in arriving at those decisions. Often, I fear, the facts of the 1930's have more bearing on what is done than the facts of the 1950's and 1960's. The House is so big and unwieldy that some sort of central policy making body is necessary. The leadership is going to be defeated on many questions unless it takes into account the views of the average member of the House. It is very difficult to ascertain those views until the leaders approach the matter on a more systematic basis than they have thus far.

In similar vein another freshman said "I expected more caucuses and more leadership, and I thought there would be more small groups getting together to attempt to give some direction to the leadership."

If the lack of means for formal expression of party opinion aids the leadership in making its own determinations of policy, another factor of importance in this regard is the fact that some newcomers find congressional machinery bewildering at first.

Commented one freshman:

The machinery in Congress is so complex and in the hands of so few, that the average congressman is lost and his influence is limited. After eight months in Congress I'm just beginning to learn about things. But I must confess that there is a great deal which still eludes me. I was worried about this until I talked to colleagues who have been here several terms. I find that they, too, are in the dark regarding many of the situations which have developed in this Congress. That's a little comforting, but it isn't the answer. It is only after you've been here a number of terms and participated in some of the final work itself that you become aware of what is going on.

Criticism of programing and scheduling procedures is particularly evident toward the end of a session when pressures and tensions mount in the attempt to act on as much legislation as possible. Some legislators deny that Congress moves slowly in the early months of a session: that may appear to be true, they declare, because little legislation reaches the House floor, but actually the committees are busily at work, sifting and perfecting thousands of proposals.

Yet, in recent years, there has been widespread comment that insufficient and inefficient planning characterizes the congressional operation. "One of the least appealing aspects of life in Congress is the way the legislative order is handled," asserted one representative. "It is inexcusable for us to have to sit around doing very little while there is substantial work ahead. We waste too much time." The members think more attention should be given to establishing and adhering to work schedules and to the matter of developing longer range, coordinated programs. One congressman expressed it this way:

> Recently I have been giving a lot of thought to the way we representatives operate. We don't sit down and plan ahead. We have no real political strategy on a long-term basis. That is necessary if we are going to get across what we believe in. For example, we should be planning a farm program for the next election right now. What will happen is that the executive branch will throw farm policy into the President's State of the Union speech without consulting Congress and we [members of his party] will be stuck with it. That isn't right and it isn't smart politics.

The "Tuesday to Thursday Club." Another common criticism is that the leadership often fails to exert sufficient precautions to ensure the presence of members of the party on crucial votes. In speaking about one party defeat, a Democrat said: "The leadership should have been more careful about seeing to it that congressmen were present for the vote. There were a number of unnecessary absences. We could have had and should have had those votes." Another Democrat commented about a failure to override an Eisenhower veto: "We should be able to override vetoes. There are too many people away from Washington—or the floor—when these issues come up. In most instances there is no excuse for such action. The absentees should be brought back."

Closely linked with problems of absenteeism and scheduling practices as a subject for sharp criticism are the members of the informal "Tuesday to Thursday Club." These are representatives who generally represent districts sufficiently close to Washington that they can go home weekends to visit constituents, deliver speeches, perhaps practice law or supervise a business. Only rarely are votes scheduled on Mondays or Fridays in the House, and often the subjects taken up on those days are of

less than average significance. Knowing this, and convinced of the importance to electoral success of frequent appearances in the district, some
incumbents become accustomed to limiting their attendance at Congress
to the period from Tuesday noon through the close of the session Thursday. Other scheduling practices beneficial to members who wish to spend
maximum time in the district include the informal understanding that no
votes will be taken on days when any state is having a primary election
or during the annual Easter recess and the periods set aside around
Lincoln's and Jackson's birthdays to permit legislators to accept speaking
engagements throughout the country.

Some critics of Tuesday to Thursday members deplore the practice but
place primary responsibility for the situation on the leadership and the
scheduling procedures they establish: if things were arranged differently,
they state, the Tuesday to Thursday club would dissolve. Said one
Easterner not a member of the club, "Something should be done about
those Tuesday to Thursday people. We could have been out long
ago if the leadership had seen to it that they were here to carry their
share of the load and vote." Two other Eastern legislators treat their
colleagues (and themselves) more gently:

In my opinion, the attacks on the Tuesday to Thursday congressmen are not
justified, at least not so far as many easterners are concerned. The system under
which we operate lends itself to a Tuesday to Thursday operation. If we didn't
waste so much time, there would be little incentive or opportunity for members
who live nearby to spend a great deal of time at home. It is also true that many
members just don't have interest in the types of legislation which come before
Congress the first or last of the week. When, for example, items of interest to
the District of Columbia are brought before the House there is little necessity
or incentive for most members to listen to, or participate in, the discussions. I
think that if the scheduling were changed you might find a change in attendance
and procedure.

*

Ninety-nine per cent of the Tuesday to Thursday congressmen would willingly stay here throughout the legislative session if it meant the session would be
shorter. The Mississippi primary is to be held next Tuesday, and so it has been
arranged that any roll calls coming up on Monday or Tuesday will carry over
until Wednesday. In addition, we are not going to do anything this Friday. That
gives people a five day breathing spell when they know there will be no recorded
votes. It is bad enough to make that provision for Monday and Tuesday. But,

given those circumstances, the least we could do is to work hard and carry a full legislative program on Friday.

At the same time, other critics of House procedures look at the situation differently, tend to absolve the leadership, and direct their main indictments at the Tuesday to Thursday group. Although defenders of the latter point out that "many members do a very conscientious job and yet go back to their districts frequently," their detractors believe that such members fail to assume their proper share of the legislative burden, adding to the work of already over-worked colleagues, and specify committee and floor activities as particularly relevant in that connection.

The Tuesday to Thursday people are not here on Mondays or Fridays, which tends to slow down legislation; often they are not as conscientious about their committee work as the rest of us either. It may be that all the blame is not with them, though I think they bear a large share of the responsibility. The main problem is that the habit has been established. The majority leader just announces every week that there will be no votes on Monday, that any roll calls which develop will go over until Tuesday. That is utter nonsense.

*

There must be some way to get better legislative action than we do. There are hundreds of bills which really don't get a fair hearing and are pushed through at the end without adequate examination, or which get no attention at all. Even major bills are often slighted. This Tuesday to Thursday crowd needs to be broken up.

This group is often blamed, too, for the inability of members to spend more time with their families; by prolonging the sessions they make it impossible for congressional families to vacation together or spend much time together. As one man said: "The fact that you are so often separated from your family is the least satisfactory part of this job. But it is unnecessary. Congress could get its work done if it really wanted to and if it didn't permit the Tuesday to Thursday group and other groups to run the Congress."

Still another charge is that these legislators contribute toward the somewhat unfavorable public image of congressmen, although some members wonder whether the voters know what the term "Tuesday to Thursday Club" means.

That group hurts the whole Congress. It creates a very bad impression.

*

Out in my state I don't think the public knows what you are talking about when you talk about the Tuesday to Thursday club. I would say West Coast members unanimously feel the Tuesday-Thursday club causes us to be in Washington an extra month—a month which could be spent in our districts. They pressure the leadership, and the leadership concedes to accommodate them.

*

I would go home more often, but I find that when I do go home during a session, people ask: "What are you doing here? What is Congress doing? I thought you were in Washington." I think the policy depends in part on your district. I couldn't get by with going home every week.

Whether justly or not, the Tuesday to Thursday people are implicated in many of the shortcomings of Congress!

Instruments of Leadership

In view of House attitudes toward the responsibility of leadership, it may be worthwhile to examine the views of members regarding four potential instruments of leadership and of the party—the party conference or caucus, the whip organization, the policy committee, and the Rules Committee. The first has seldom been used by the Republicans (as noted, it was revitalized in 1963) and even less frequently by the Democrats; no one was found in either party who thought the second a strong arm of party control, though some congressmen would like to make it so; the Democrats have no policy committee, a fact that caused no concern to round table participants, at least.[4] Republicans have activated their policy committee and seem pleased with the result; once a major instrument of party policy, in recent years the Rules Committee has often served as an obstacle to the enactment of party programs.

The Party Caucus. Called a caucus by the Democrats and a conference by the Republicans, the meeting of all party members in the House was at one time important in promoting party responsibility. In the period around World War I, party members were often bound by caucus decisions, and the stands adopted by the majority caucus were usually endorsed by the House. Today the situation is much different.

---

[4] In 1962 the Democratic caucus voted to establish a steering committee, but it was not anticipated it would be very powerful. Its subsequent performance strengthened that view.

The rules of the House Republican Conference do not provide for the binding of its members. Rules of the Democratic caucus permit such action but only in certain circumstances; the provision has not been used for years.

The primary function of the caucus has become that of selecting party candidates for the speakership and of electing party officials and members to committees at the beginning of each Congress. For some years prior to 1963 an occasional conference was held by Republicans to discuss legislative issues and an informal vote might even be taken. In the first nine months of 1963, however, eight meetings of the conference had been held, indicating that a return to a somewhat more active role might be underway. Democrats have virtually eliminated the caucus except for the organizational meeting. Two main reasons are advanced for this: caucuses are not needed, particularly when the Democrats control the House, and there are stronger ideological differences in the Democratic party than in the Republican party and caucuses may accentuate them.

Although virtually no attempts are made to bind members as a result of caucus action, it is clear that caucus decisions constitute something of a subtle discipline in themselves. As one Democrat stated: "If you have participated and have had an opportunity to make your wishes known, you are somewhat reluctant to break with the caucus decision even though you don't agree with it." The following discussion of Republicans makes essentially the same point:

It [the party conference] doesn't bind the members, but it is useful in arriving at a consensus.

*

Do you mean to say that if you get up in one of the conferences and vote for something that you are not bound to follow through? We have had two votes so far this year. After I stood up and was counted on those two issues, I felt morally bound by my action unless conditions changed appreciably.

*

I don't think anyone feels he is bound, morally or otherwise. However, I do think a decision openly arrived at in a conference does have a great psychological effect on the individual member when he is reaching his own personal decision. I believe that, consciously or unconsciously, his decision is influenced by the knowledge that the vast majority of his party colleagues have a fixed position and conviction about a particular issue.

Members do believe that the psychological impact of a caucus action is great, and they believe, too, that it usually is useful to "talk out" issues on which there is division of opinion. The undecided members are influenced by the discussion, and coordination or modification of the party program is facilitated. Another important caucus function is the opportunity it affords to learn the plans of the party leadership and to discuss and even challenge them. In a system where it is difficult to hold the leadership accountable and to remain informed, the more junior members are particularly desirous of such a forum. Systematic and frequent briefings are seen by caucus proponents as sufficient reason for reinstituting the practice on a regular basis. Explained one junior Democrat:

> The big defect here is lack of information. In order to get the scoop on anything you really have to go out of your way on your own initiative. The leadership is opposed to the caucus idea, but a discussion group caucus rather than a policy making caucus would be very helpful to me and others. It would provide an opportunity for people to sound off and also would enable us to receive information.

Another member also advocated the caucus, though he recognized there were potential dangers involved.

> Our party should caucus frequently. True there might be dog fights, and we might come out worse in some respects, but on the whole it would be worth it. It is very important to have an expression from all House members.

Stated a third Democrat:

> Even if the caucus were not a policy making body, it could serve a useful function. It should be used for briefings on foreign affairs, for example. It would be very valuable to have party experts in particular areas fill us in on latest developments—but all this talk about caucus is just a dream anyway. The Democrats are so deeply split in philosophy that they cannot encourage anything which might divide them even more. Unlike the Democrats, the Republicans are a disciplined group and therefore they can use the caucus.

It is apparent that some House Democrats who are not really convinced of the validity of the argument that Democratic caucuses are likely to be divisive rather than cohesive and therefore should not be used are sufficiently troubled by the possibility that the argument *may* be accurate that they do not press too firmly for caucus revival. Said one liberal Democrat who in the past has fought hard for other reforms:

> I don't think the caucus will be used more often. A senator who had long experience over here said that it had been his experience that we Democrats

were so obstreperous that we came out of caucus more divided than when we went into it. It probably relates to the stormy history of the Democratic party on the civil rights issue for the past twenty years or more. There was never a caucus but what somebody got up and waved the red flag, and there was a reply. Some of us have the feeling that maybe in specific instances, with very limited uses, it might be used with some effect now.

But when the point was made that the basic reason the Republicans caucused more frequently than Democrats was that "they do not have the deep ideological division we have—the difference between the traditional Southern conservative and the liberal Democrat is almost polar," there was disagreement. The Democrats believed that the caucus could be expected to work better for the Republicans primarily because the latter were more susceptible to direction from their leaders. Indeed, the lack of independence of the Republicans formed a recurring theme in Democratic discussions. The caucus, in their view, was one means used by the Republican leadership to reinforce its position. Stated one Democrat:

> We look at the caucus and see that it operates for the Republicans but not for us. We abandon it because of sectional differences. I think there is a far more important reason why it operates better for them. It isn't because they have more areas of agreement or fewer areas of disagreement than we do, but because they have more effective control over the campaign pocketbook of their members. That is the whip they use with great skill to produce a high degree of unity. The Democrats, lacking an effective party organization for the financing of campaigns on a national basis and for the underwriting of the day-to-day propaganda activities of individual members, have not the whip necessary to make the caucus work.

Republicans, on the other hand, said that they were not discriminated against in allocation of funds and services from the party committees even though they had often failed to support the party position on legislation. And they tended to deride the failure of the Democrats to hold party sessions. It was because Democrats were so subservient to the leadership that they supported the leadership position meekly and sought no opportunity to express their true opinions, asserted the Republicans. There was Republican testimony, for example, that Democrats (who at the Brookings meetings expressed no concern that reforms were needed within the party structure) privately congratulated them for installing new, more aggressive leadership and for strengthening the arms of leadership. The sentiments had been accompanied by expressions that they would like to make changes within their own party. With respect to the caucus, then, as with other matters, members of each party protested their own independence and that of their colleagues and depicted their opponents as sheep blindly following a leader.

The reasoning of those House Democrats who see little need for increased use of the party caucus is apparent in the following discussion:

I think you should ask the question, "Why do you want it to function?" Why change your wing combination when you have a winning team?

*

If you have good leadership which gives you results, there is no need for a caucus. Republicans have needed a caucus because they had to get positive decisions on some things.

*

When you are in the majority, if you have any cohesiveness between the committee chairmen and the leadership, what is coming out of the mill is a program to which you are usually committed. There isn't the need to define positions that exists when you are in opposition and must figure out with respect to any given issue whether you are going to oppose it completely or seek to modify it.

*

I think the Democratic party in the House has operated pretty much the same way whether we were in the majority or minority.

*

The speaker [Rayburn] is a traditionalist in determining legislative programs· With rare exceptions, he stands by the committee which considered whatever bill is up. If we want a representative sampling of the majority viewpoint that is fairly satisfactory. Assuming that the committees are representative of the Congress, what they push out to us and what we are able to get through the Rules Committee comes to the floor.

*

In the Democratic party, a caucus can't really bind. We could meet and get a heavy majority on one side of an issue. The person who felt he had to oppose it would get up and say so, or he would go out on the floor and oppose it; he would not be bound so what is the point of a caucus? The Republicans will be bound so they have their caucuses.

The Whip Organization. As noted earlier, each party elects a chief whip who in turn appoints regional assistants. Democratic area whips are initially designated by the Democratic members of the states for which they are responsible. The chief tasks of these organizations are to ensure that there is maximum turnout of party members for votes taken on the floor and to inform the leadership how much support they can count on to sustain its position. Criticism of the whip organizations is common in the House, with the main source of discontent centering around the failure to perform the informing function. Occasional situations in which the party clearly has the votes to carry its position but fails to get them to the floor lead to temporary flurries of activity, which quickly subside, demanding a re-examination of the efficiency of the whip organization. More serious and sustained criticisms are that it is not used as a means of informing members of the party position and urging them to support it, that it is merely "a reporting agency," "a group of poll takers," and often not even that. "All they do is call up and say we should be on the floor," said one representative. "They should give us some sense of direction as to what is going on and what we should do about it." Explained one Republican whip: "If you ask somebody how he is going to vote on a certain bill, often he will ask what the party position is and you will tell him. But as a regional whip I never tell anyone unless he asks me."

Assistant whips in both parties stated that only infrequently did they do more than seek to get all the members of their party in their area on the floor: there were relatively few requests to poll the members. When a vote is approaching, routine calls may be made to congressional offices to ask secretaries to inform the legislator that the Speaker, party leader, or whip wants the legislator on the floor. One representative relates his first experience of that nature:

> My first year in Congress I stayed on the floor during most of the debates. One day after I had been here about three months I left the floor and returned to my office. As I entered the office, having left the floor five minutes before, my secretary said, "Mr. McCormack wants you on the floor." I said, "How did that man know I had left!" I thought he was an amazing person and turned around and went back.

The discussion which follows took place among House Democrats several months following the opening of a recent session of Congress. The chief participants, both liberal Democrats, sought a more active role for the whips. One Congressman was serving as a zone whip (one of four principal aides to the chief whip); the other was an assistant whip.

> I think the whip organization is beginning to take a little more form as a policy sounding and measuring body than it has been heretofore. For the first

time in four years we have had discussions in our whip meetings of several bills and their possibilities.

*

Our whip organization has been somewhat passive in the past. It has had two main functions: (1) to ascertain in advance how many votes are available for a particular piece of legislation. This helps the leadership decide whether or not to schedule a bill. For instance, the Upper Colorado Project was very important to the West. A whip check last July showed we didn't have the votes. Thus it was carried over until January when the votes were available; (2) the other function of the organization comes when the leadership wants members on the floor because of the partisan alignment on a particular issue. Attendance is particularly important in the Committee of the Whole. Each office is called and members are notified that the Speaker wants the member on the floor in five or ten minutes. The chief whip is very consciously trying to broaden the role of the whips. An attempt will be made this year to give them an active floor function. They will know precisely what the position of the leadership is and may do actual recruiting on an issue in a limited way.

*

On some whip checks where we have asked people how they will vote, we ask what their objection is if they indicate opposition to a bill the leadership wants. If you can determine that there are enough members objecting to one feature of the bill and that elimination of that feature might move the bill, it can be a very valuable piece of intelligence. In our last meeting there was quite a debate between assistant whips as to what constituted policy and how it was derived. The nearest thing you could say was this: there is a presumption that when a committee dominated by a Democratic majority brings out a bill that is Democratic policy.

*

The zone whips meet with the chief whip each morning to get the picture. One goal is to obtain a better communications system in terms of letting members know why a particular piece of legislation is part of the party program and what the essentials of that legislation are.

At the conclusion of the legislative session, the assistant whip was asked whether his expectations of a more active organization had been fulfilled. Somewhat sadly he replied, "No. We haven't done much whipping this year, though I thought we would." Congressmen who prefer a loosely knit party organization in the House and who desire to continue the policy of gaining support for party programs by means of persuasion rather than pressure are reluctant to strengthen the role of the whip organization. They resist attempts to give it a more positive role.

The Policy Committee. One of the major recommendations of the Joint Committee on the Organization of Congress, incorporated in the Legislative Reorganization bill in 1946, was that party policy committees be established in each House. Because of the hostility of House leaders to this feature of the bill, it was eliminated before final passage of the measure. The Senate then proceeded to establish its own policy committees and made provision for professional staff to serve them. The House took no action, however, each party being content to continue the steering committee arrangement, which the Republicans had inaugurated during World War I and the Democrats had instituted in 1933 at the time of Franklin D. Roosevelt's election to the Presidency. Neither group met frequently nor possessed much power.

Although the Republicans changed the name of their steering committee to the Policy Committee in 1949, it remained relatively impotent until 1959 when, following the election of Charles Halleck to succeed Joseph W. Martin as Republican leader, it was activated, assumed new responsibilities, and became an important force in House Republican affairs. A new, enlarged role for the policy committee is said to have been a condition for support of Halleck by some Republicans in the leadership contest.

In 1963 the Republican committee consisted of thirty-six members: a chairman elected by the Republican Conference, fourteen regionally elected members, three at large members, ten ex officio members, and eight members representing the five most recent Republican clubs.[5] Prior to 1963 the Republican club representatives were denied a vote. In 1963, they were elevated to voting status.

Although some Republicans have thought the Policy Committee too conservatively oriented or have believed it might be preferable to select members so as to provide committee rather than geographic representa-

---

[5] The ten ex officio voting members included the minority leader, whip, chairman and secretary of the Republican conference, chairman of the congressional campaign committee, and the five Republican members of the Rules Committee. Geographic representation is provided by dividing the fifty states into nine regions, each region being entitled to one member for every twenty (or fraction thereof) Republicans in the regional delegation. Each of the five most recent informal freshmen groups from the current and the four preceding congresses is provided one or more members on the same basis.

tion, there has been considerable agreement that its establishment represented an important step forward in party organization and coordination. And in both the Eighty-seventh and Eighty-eighth Congresses, as it happened, all but one of the standing committees were represented. "Republicans tend to know more about where they are going and what the issues are now and that was long overdue," said one House Republican a year after the group had been reorganized.

While Congress is in session, the committee meets every Tuesday afternoon. Leading Republicans from committees that have studied the legislative proposals to be discussed at the meeting are invited to be present and explain the issues involved. Following the discussion, the Policy Committee may vote to recommend a party position on a measure, may defer decision, or may decide to make no recommendation. During the Eighty-seventh Congress, the committee took an announced stand on fifty-three items of major legislation. The chairmen informs House Republicans of all decisions made by the committee and presents the basis for those decisions. Many individual regional representatives supplement these statements by reporting more fully to those they represent either by letter (California and the Northwest Central group) or in open meeting. The New York and the New England delegations, for example, meet subsequent to each policy committee session for a firsthand report.

The committee employs a small professional staff, which is augmented from time to time by volunteers. Occasional reports on various controversial issues have been prepared under its direction. In the preparation of these reports, academic and professional experts in selected fields have been solicited to furnish technical papers. And teams of Republican House members have been organized to set forth the Republican position in floor debate.

When the Republicans occupied the White House, the first part of each Policy Committee meeting centered on a report from the party leadership summarizing the regular Tuesday morning conference of legislative leaders with the President. The committee also served as a means by which the leadership and the President could obtain a broader sounding of House Republican reaction to an issue prior to the determination of a final administration position. Said one Republican:

Pennsylvania Avenue became a two way street. The White House knew a little bit more about what congressional Republicans were thinking before policies and ideas were formulated and crystallized. One of the big weaknesses in our leadership had been the fact that the White House didn't know how we felt on legislation. The Policy Committee became a chart that at least pointed out the shoals and reefs for the administration. They knew what they were up against if they brought up certain legislation. They never had known that before. They were often amazed to bring up legislation and find the majority of House Republicans opposed to it.

Said another influential Republican:

Prior to 1959 a rather general criticism of the Policy Committee was that no action occurred until after the White House had formulated an opinion and expressed it publicly by a message to Congress or by some other means. Then we had a choice of supporting the administration or taking no action. Establishing an active policy committee corrected that. Our new arrangement permitted us to inform the President or administration of what we considered to be the position of the majority of our party in Congress on specific proposals before a decision was made. Our views could be weighed along with other factors.

The same congressman suggested that when there is a Republican President, House Policy Committee members should be recalled to Washington in December prior to the convening of Congress to permit more effective, and earlier, liaison between Congress and the Executive and to expedite the promulgation of the administration's legislative program.

That Policy Committee recommendations and dissemination of information have had a positive effect on the attitudes of rank and file party members is attested to by one independent-minded Republican:

We get reports right after each Policy Committee meeting so we know what the general consensus of the committee is on any given subject. The reports have been helpful to me in establishing a position for the purpose of answering the mail and in deciding how I am going to vote on legislation. The Policy Committee reports that came out on the Airport Act and the Housing Act, for example, gave both points of view and pointed up the weaknesses in the position of the Democrats and the strength of our position. It prevented us from answering mail without knowing what the points were. The Policy Committee has made me more of a team player. It has caused me to recognize the validity of the [Republican] administration's position better than I ever had before.

The Democrats, unlike the Republicans, have not established a policy committee. Speaker Rayburn opposed the idea, and that was sufficient to make certain that no action would be taken during his tenure. Indeed, following Mr. Rayburn's election as Speaker in 1940, even the steering committee was all but ignored. Eventually, vacancies in the group's membership were not filled. The Speaker much preferred the less formal "Board of Education" as a means of keeping abreast of House sentiment. The "Board" fulfilled the functions of a policy committee although it had no fixed membership and could not be found on an organization chart.

Rayburn's death and the ensuing struggle for control of the leadership brought new efforts by junior, more liberal elements with the Democratic caucus to establish a policy committee. This was not seriously considered. Speaker McCormack did, however, lend his support to a move to revive the old steering committee, and this was done. The twenty-four member committee consists of the six elected party leaders[6] and eighteen regional representatives elected by individual regions. Though it has been given no policy-making responsibilities—its expressions are not binding on the leadership—the new group is to "cooperate and consult" with the leadership on bills reported by the legislative committees. It provides a means by which the rank and file can communicate their views to the party leaders, but it is not likely to become an important force in party councils.

The Democratic participants in the round table expressed no sentiment for the creation of a policy committee in the House and revealed little sympathy for the attempt by some Senate Democrats to liberalize the Senate Democratic Policy Committee. Privately one or two participants volunteered the opinion that it might be helpful to have such a body, provided it was representative, but they did not press hard for it. Some Democrats who favored organizational reform in the form of increased use of the party caucus believed that the caucus, the leadership triumvirate of the Speaker, Majority Leader, and Whip, and the tendency to rely on Democrats on committees to set policy in the subject matter areas under their jurisdiction would provide sufficient leadership. Reconstitution of the Rules Committee to make of it a group that could be granted policy committee functions was also suggested. On the whole, though, there was less Democratic agitation for a formal policy group than one might have anticipated in the face of expressions of dissatisfaction surrounding the formulation and dissemination of the party position. The fact that the

[6] The Speaker, majority leader, whip, chairman and secretary of the party caucus, and the chairman of the campaign committee.

Democratic party was the majority party of the House was sometimes mentioned as a major reason a policy committee was not essential to the Democrats: Democrats on the committees could determine the party position following consultation of individual chairmen with the leadership.

Democrats knew Republicans had a policy committee, but they appeared somewhat unclear as to its function. Said one member, "the Republicans have a policy committee which meets weekly. I don't know what it does but it meets. You read about it." In discussing the "discipline" they thought evident in Republican ranks, the Democrats centered their attack on the Republican party conference rather than on the policy group, which at the time was by far the more active and effective of the two.

The Rules Committee. The Rules Committee possesses important powers, and its actions can go far to determine the nature of the legislation passed by the House. Thus control of the committee is eagerly sought by legislative leaders, and its resistance to suggestions of the Speaker and his allies inevitably leads to demands for reform of the group.

A center of controversy in recent years because of its occasional defiance of the wishes of the majority leadership, the Rules Committee was once a central element in the centralization of party responsibility in the House. It represented an important source of the Speaker's power; it was, in effect, *his* committee. He chaired it, determined its membership, and it bent to his will. Curtailment in 1910 of the Speaker's power of appointment has made the committee more independent of the leadership, despite the fact that in recent years the majority party has maintained a two to one edge in its membership. Since 1937 occasional coalitions of its Republican and conservative Southern Democratic members have functioned to thwart certain programs of the Democratic leadership when that party has controlled the House.

Most bills of any importance that are reported out of the legislative committees reach the House floor by means of a "rule" presented to the House by the Rules Committee. This resolution establishes the condition of debate on the bill: it specifies the time allocated for discussion and may stipulate the number and kind of amendments that can be offered. A rule from the committee does not guarantee House consideration of a measure—the leadership occasionally fails to schedule measures so reported—but it makes consideration likely. Committee refusal to grant a rule, on the other hand, usually means the bill will not be considered at all. The power of the committee to determine when to report out a bill is not an inconsiderable one either: timing is an important element of legislative strategy and delaying or expediting a bill can do much to affect its fate.

Measures are reported from the Rules Committee under an "open" rule, which places no limitation on the number or kind of amendments permitted during floor debate, or a "closed" rule. The latter is used less frequently and either permits no amendment or specifies those that are permissible. Closed rules are confined largely to complicated, technical measures, generally fiscal in nature, which come from the Appropriations or the Ways and Means Committee. Proponents of a bill may seek a closed rule to prevent the possibility that crippling amendments will be added; when they can get one, they gain an important initial advantage. Additionally, the committee may provide for waivers against points of order which could normally be raised against inclusion of non-privileged matters in privileged bills, such as legislation in an appropriations bill.

Generally, the Rules Committee cooperates with the legislative committees and the House leadership both in scheduling hearings on bills and in reporting them to the floor for House action. Seldom will a rule be granted for a measure opposed by the leadership, for example. But a bill it supports may occasionally either not be reported out or will be given a rule not favorable to the position of the majority party. In other instances, bills may be delayed in the Rules Committee until agreement is reached with the legislative committee regarding the nature of its activity on the floor: the Rules unit may elicit a promise to seek to amend the bill to conform more closely to Rules Committee preferences, or it may demand assurances that the committee will oppose amendments designed to disturb certain features of the bill. If the legislative committee declines to make the desired commitment, the bill may languish in the Rules Committee.

Few rules reported to the House are defeated. When they are rejected, the reason is more often opposition to the bill itself than a belief that the rule is unsatisfactory or unfair. The special orders under which measures proceed from the Rules Committee to the floor require only a majority vote; in effect they constitute suspension of the House rules, an action that ordinarily requires a two-thirds vote. Thus Rules Committee support eases the way of a measure.

Defenders of the Rules Committee maintain that while the committee has not always been responsive to the entreaties of the leadership, it has almost always been an accurate reflector of House opinion. Where it has clashed with the leadership, it has often expressed the judgment of the House. To charges that the committee flouts the will of the House, it is said that no committee that flagrantly ignored House opinion could maintain its power for long. And, it is asserted, the committee renders a valuable service to congressmen by refusing to act on bills on which the House does not wish to be recorded or in drafting rules so as to protect colleagues from difficult votes. The committee, it is said, often serves as a convenient whipping boy for the leadership or even the rank and file when in fact the latter groups privately applaud the actions taken. Stated one representative:

> There are many House members who spend time excoriating institutions like the Rules Committee, yet in their heart they thank Providence that the Rules Committee exists. They can't wait to get back home to make the Rules Committee a scapegoat. We could have done this or that, they say, if the reactionary Rules Committee hadn't bottled things up and prevented us from working our will. These people are secretly pleased that organizations like the committee exist to slow down the process and prevent bad legislation from developing. In a sense the Rules Committee takes them off the hook.

Explained another congressman, "Members are always going around to the Rules Committee and asking them to let a bill die there. Then they turn around and berate the committee for not reporting the bill out."

Although the values of the committee are appreciated, there is recognition that with respect to certain legislative proposals deemed important, if not crucial, to the program of the House leadership the Rules Committee has proved uncooperative and obstinate. It is often charged that the committee exceeds its "traffic manager" functions to perform a policy-making role rather than leaving determination of policy to the House itself. Undeniably the committee leaves its imprint on major legislation. As its chairman, Howard Smith, says: "My people did not elect me to Congress to be a traffic cop." One Democrat is particularly outraged that in certain circumstances a rule must be obtained to send a bill to conference. Said he: "After a bill has passed both houses, to let a half dozen men prevent the will of the majority of each house from being carried out is just outrageous."

While critics assert that the committee has denied the House the opportunity to vote on good legislation, friends of the Rules Committee unit retort that if a majority of the House desire action on a measure, there are sufficient means available to get it before the House despite lack of cooperation by the committee. Stated one House leader, "The Rules Committee which is nothing more than a committee on agenda has been unfairly used as a whipping boy. It never has had the power to bottle up legislation the majority really wanted." The main ways in which the Rules Committee can be circumvented are by (1) unanimous consent; (2) suspension of the rules; (3) Calendar Wednesday; and (4) discharge. All of them are difficult ways by which to attain enactment of major legislation.[7]

The occasional reluctance of the Rules Committee to respond to leadership requests and its assumption of policy-making roles, combined with the difficulties inherent in seeking to bypass the committee by resorting to any of the procedures mentioned above, have led proponents of party responsibility to seek to return the committee to its earlier status as an instrument of the majority party. Failing that, they have sought to provide a more satisfactory means of circumventing the committee.

In recent years, critics of the committee have been successful on two

---

[7] A single objection can prevent consideration of a bill by unanimous consent, making it unlikely that controversial measures can be disposed of in that manner. Under suspension procedures the Speaker may, on the first and third Mondays of each month, recognize a member to move suspension of the rules and immediate consideration of a bill. But the Speaker has absolute power of recognition and may entertain or refuse to entertain such a motion. And, even if the Speaker is cooperative, suspension requires a two-thirds vote, which may be difficult to obtain. Calendar Wednesday provides that on Wednesdays the Speaker may call on committee chairmen (in alphabetical order by committee) who may call up for a vote any bill that has previously been reported out of their committee. But the measure must be disposed of in the same legislative day, and dilatory tactics may make this difficult. Further, hostile chairmen heading committees further up the list may prevent consideration of the bill in question by bringing up a bill from their own committee. The discharge petition is a difficult procedure since a majority of the membership must sign the petition to bring about action, and many legislators refuse to sign any discharge petition as a matter of policy.

occasions in imposing restrictions on the independence of the group. In 1949 they secured adoption of the "21 day rule." This provided that the chairman of a legislative committee could bring directly to the House floor any bill reported out of his committee for which the Rules Committee had failed to grant a rule within twenty-one calendar days of a request for action. The twenty-one day rule lasted only two years, falling victim to reduced majority party strength in the succeeding Congress. In 1961, the Democratic House majority sought to make the committee more responsive to its leadership by enlarging the membership of the committee from twelve to fifteen, maintaining the two to one party division. Explained one Democrat closely allied with the leadership: "The Rules Committee is a bit too powerful. If what we really want is to have a representative body and to have the majority will prevail, then it is clear something should be done to modify the Rules Committee."

And some Democrats who felt the need for an effective party policy committee believed the Rules Committee might be reconstituted to meet that need: "We need some kind of effective party instrument such as the policy committee. The Rules Committee might perform this function provided it is increased to make it more representative of the party point of view. As it stands now, it is not an effective instrument of Democratic party policy."

Although the 1961 changes did not make the committee a potential policy committee, they clearly made it more responsive to majority party leadership, for the time being at least. Even so, despite the increased majority, the leadership was not able to dislodge from the committee some measures in which it was interested. In 1963, the House voted to make permanent the larger committee size. The importance of the committee in the legislative process soon was emphasized by the intra-party struggle which developed when it was announced that a member of the committee from Texas would leave Congress to accept a judge-ship. A tentative agreement between the Speaker and the Texas delega-tion as to a successor was quickly challenged by liberal Democrats, who feared the views of the designee would lead him to be less cooperative with the leadership than the congressman leaving the committee. Wheth-er the move by the liberals was designed to substitute another congress-man as the successor to the seat or merely to wrest concessions from the member designated was not immediately apparent.

Discipline and Pressure

That congressional leadership relies on persuasion and personal appeal to effectuate programs rather than on discipline, sanctions, and pressure has already been noted. Congressional party groups, for example, have displayed extraordinary reluctance to discipline nominal party members who may even have failed to support the party's presidential nominee or who have openly endorsed the candidate of the opposition. Though threats have occasionally been made to strip the dissidents of their choicer committee assignments, such threats have usually originated with legislators far removed from the real sources of power and have received almost no serious support. It is much more difficult to deprive a representative of status already achieved than to prevent those who stray from the party position on national or congressional issues from advancing to better committees, being designated for prestigious trips, or from obtaining eagerly sought projects for one's district.

The congressional parties not only fall far short of being well disciplined, powerful organizations, possessing the means for effective permanent enforcement of sanctions against recalcitrant members, but the leaders are reluctant to move against the rebels, generally preferring whenever possible to attribute the deviation to district problems faced by the legislator rather than to reluctance to cooperate on an issue. Congressmen indicate that the use of pressure and discipline in the House is much exaggerated. They express surprise that such is the situation: they entered Congress expecting to find much more. The explanation for the relative lack of pressure is not difficult to find: congressmen in terms of philosophical outlook and commitment are usually disposed to support the party position, and there is no need to bring pressure on the faithful. Where they do part company, the cause may indeed be attributable to desire to adhere to what they believe to be district sentiment. In discussing the difficulties of enforcing strict discipline, one leading liberal Democrat said: "I think one of the greatest mistakes many of us make is to fail to recognize the role that the district plays in our attitudes and in the attitude of the leadership towards achieving conformity. We are an extraordinarily diverse party."

The comments of two freshmen Democrats tend to substantiate the observation:

I am dismayed by the lack of leadership on the Democratic side of the aisle, especially in view of the tight Republican discipline. I have never been pressured to vote in any particular way. We have all, I think, been left to our own decisions. I like that but I am disturbed because I keep hearing rumors that I am too independent, that people are saying, "he didn't go along with us, why should we help him later?" I come from a conservative Republican district and that fact must be kept in mind when I consider my votes. I am no flaming liberal Democrat, and people should understand my situation.

*

I expected stricter discipline on the part of the leadership and thought they probably would invoke penalties if their suggestions were not followed. I haven't found it that way. On the Democratic side, we are asked if we can support legislation, but the same friendliness exists whether we do or not.

It is relatively easy to cite instances where all or some members have been requested to support the party's position, and it is even possible to point to instances where sanctions have been imposed. But, on balance, there are relatively few reprisals. The emphasis is on tremendous flexibility in voting, excessive flexibility according to some legislators.

Member Responsibility to Party. The question what constitutes one's responsibility to his party in voting matters is one which not all congressmen have resolved. Should independence be punished? When, if ever, are party considerations more important than personal conviction or district sentiment in determining one's vote? Do those who occupy positions of prominence in the House have a greater obligation to conform than the rank and file? A Democratic "moderate" wonders about some of these questions:

This whole matter of discipline poses a serious problem. You have to decide what a party should be in order to determine how much discipline it should exercise. In the long run, I think the best policy is to let every man be his own agent and to have no reprisals, but occasionally that is difficult to adhere to. On the _____bill two committee chairmen and an Appropriations Committee member deserted the party. That was a situation in which the party really needed their support. The question arises whether they should be divested of their power since they seem to acknowledge no responsibility to their party on a crucial vote. Yet there are those who say the party has no business to interfere in such a case.

A somewhat more liberal colleague commented independently on the situation referred to above:

Yesterday's performance was nothing short of a disgrace. All we needed was six or seven more votes and that should have been no problem. Two [Democratic] committee chairmen supported the [Republican] President, going against the party leadership on such an important measure. If I were running the show they would live to regret it. Tomorrow morning_____would find himself presiding over an expanded committee, and he'd find that the people who had been added were people who had hated him for twenty years. Something must be done to force these people into line. If they are going to hold positions of responsibility within the Democratic party they must support the party, [but] the leadership probably won't face up to the problem.

In separate interviews two rank and file Republicans, the second noted as a ruggedly independent conservative, difficult to budge from his personal convictions, agreed that pressure was sometimes justified. When a clear-cut party position has been drawn, they observed, and the issue is an important one, the leadership is justified in bringing pressure to bear on members reluctant to follow their party.[8]

While we cannot deny that there was a lot of pressure put on in the labor bill, that was a party vote calling for teamwork. I believe in teamwork. You can do all the discussing you want, but when the die is cast you should do everything possible to carry out the party position. If I were a leader, there would be a lot of discipline because I think people should be pushed into line. I don't think you should do it where the issue is so important to a person's district that he may lose the next election if he goes along with the party. But I do think more of an attempt should be made to get a higher party vote.

*

There hasn't been too much effort to discipline members for failing to go along with the party position. Attempts are made to shore up members of the doubtful list. The most effective way to do this is not for the leadership to bring pressure but rather to get people back in the district to express their views to their congressmen. Pressure on the labor bill was somewhat justified since I think it was the key vote in the Congress. Unless someone had a good reason and was prepared to explain fully his refusal to cooperate, he should have gone along. A member shouldn't make political decisions which will prove harmful in the district, but there are times when an issue becomes such an important party issue that he should go along even though he has some doubts. There has never been

[8] Note, however, that his party's leadership made no attempt to dissuade the second speaker from voting contrary to an important party position, that of sustaining the President's veto of a public works bill, although the vote was to be close and a serious effort was being made to preserve intact the President's record of having all of his vetoes sustained. There is every indication that the member would have resented any attempt to influence his vote.

much effort to get me to change my vote, but that may be because they know I
am not susceptible to that sort of thing. On the Public Works bill, for example,
I was sitting next to a man and both of us intended to vote to override the President's veto. Halleck came by and asked the other man to change his vote, but
he didn't say anything to me.

"*We Don't But They Do.*" Serious and persistent attempts by party
leadership to influence voting in the House normally are restricted to a
few highly controversial legislative proposals of major importance. Although there was little disposition at the Brookings Round Table discussions to identify instances where pressure had been applied to members of
their own party, private discussions with individual participants revealed
extensive member knowledge of such cases and a willingness to talk about
them.

Even though few members spoke of pressure being exerted on their
side of the aisle, nearly everyone was convinced that such tactics were
frequently and harshly used by the opposition; specific instances were
identified. Where pressures within their own party were referred to or
admitted, they were characterized as relatively rare, and not vigorously
pursued. If pressure and threats were invoked by one's party, the action
was justified on one of several grounds: (1) the importance of the issue or
its central position in the party's legislative program; (2) a majority had a
responsibility to carry out its program and must take steps to ensure
legislative success; or (3) a minority, to have any effect, must stand together. On the latter point one Republican spoke of "the sense of unity
which develops from being a member of such a small group" and another,
after stressing that little discipline had been exerted, explained that what
efforts had been made were "due as much as anything to the fact that
Republicans are so few in Congress this year. That tends to make for
unity and for an increased effort to keep this little band together as much
as possible."

Patronage Essential to Discipline. Members of both parties emphasized
that the exercise of discipline depends largely on the availability of patronage. Depending on their party affiliation, they either pointed to the
paucity of the patronage open to them or spoke of the ineptness with
which national party leadership used the patronage at their disposal as a
means of securing cooperation. The Republican discussion reported below

was unusual not only in that two participants insisted that their own party was guilty of exerting pressure but because it focused on the patronage issue.

When we discussed pressure, I don't think anybody felt he had received any, depending on the exact definition, of course.

*

I said there was pressure on our side. I have had it brought on me. I suggest that a lot of it does exist, but I don't think it is as widespread as in the Democratic party.

*

Don't you agree Republicans are more individualistic in their voting and less inclined to go with the party and team than the Democrats are.

*

No, not really. For many years the Southern Democrats have fought the party line and voted with the majority on our side to get a lot of things done. That shows independence. On some issues, the southerners are probably whipped around. When a real issue arises where their votes really make a difference, though, they can be pretty well lined up. But look at the way we lined up on the tax bill in the Eighty-third. We even got _____ to change his vote.

*

Last session the _____ issue came up in our committee. Two Democrats voted with the Republicans to tie it up in committee. I happen to know that one of them wanted to go on Ways and Means, and he was told in no uncertain terms that unless he got "right" on that issue he wasn't going to go on, and he didn't. He was even called by Harry Truman. I don't think we are subjected to that type of pressure. The pressure on that bill was the most shocking experience I have ever had in the House.

*

I think one reason we are not pressured as much as the Democrats, and it is a weakness of our party, is that nobody in the Republican administration knows anything about patronage. The only reason you can have any control over a member of Congress is by means of persuasion or some sort of club, and the best club you can have is patronage. But our people have never chosen to play it that way, and therefore the club isn't there. I have gotten calls from the White House or the departments asking me if I would vote this way or that on certain things, but there has been no pressure or threats. They can't do a thing to me as long as they don't have any patronage to dish out. They don't give me any campaign money so they can't take that away.

A Democrat who, during the Eisenhower administration, stressed the need for a stronger party organization in the House regretfully noted that lack of patronage was one reason it was not likely to be forthcoming.

There isn't much discipline in the Democratic party because we need patronage in order to make it effective. We really have nothing with which to whip people into line. The patronage jobs we have here are practically meaningless. Unless you can do something downtown for somebody you really don't have the means for hurting them if they fail to go along.

In a discussion of the same topic several Democrats emphasized the petty nature of the patronage available to the party lacking the Presidency, the reluctance to enforce discipline, and indeed, the occasional willingness of party leaders to aid a member to get a project for his district, even though he often bolted the party on legislative issues.

In a party like ours, which embraces so many different groups and sections, there has to be wide latitude for individual freedom. Party discipline must necessarily be lightly borne by each of us, or we would never keep the party together. Even though we may never say it, our behavior shows we all understand this.

*

What has the Democratic party available to use as leverage to enforce party discipline? You can be named to joint committees, selected for trips, get some of the patronage around here.

*

That doesn't amount to much. To what extent does the leadership use sanctions? To what extent can the party say, "This fellow didn't go along, and we won't let him have this public works project in his district?"

*

I have never seen that used. I do recall when the House got behind one of our colleagues and gave him just what he wanted, even though he seldom went along with the party.

*

In that particular instance I can cite you two or three examples of where he has changed his position since then [and become more cooperative].

Members of both parties agree that the Kennedy administration has been far more knowledgeable in the use of patronage than was the Eisenhower administration, and much more disposed to employ it.

"*Our Opponents Are Robots.*" The image of party responsibility within their own party is essentially the same for both Democrats and Republicans: the reins of leadership are lightly held and sanctions are seldom invoked. Republican members mention, however, that Halleck is considerably more difficult for the independent to deal with than his predecessor, Joe Martin.

The situation existing in the opposition party is usually described in quite different terms. Individual members are robots, blindly following their leaders, unwilling or unable to exercise independent judgment and subject to the firm pressures of an autocratic leadership. Some excerpts from statements of Democrats reflecting their views on Republican practices follow:

I would not have beaten my opponent had he not been forced to go down the line with Republican policy. After the President vetoed the farm bill, he shifted position and voted against the bill. It was party pressure that did it. That was the kind of thing that defeated him. It is one reason we have a big majority in Congress now, and the Republicans have had great losses. We vote our conscience.

*

No Democrat has ever told me how to vote on any single issue. There is, of course, some group pressure, but I think the Republicans are much more serious about this than we are. I understand they are threatening to provide primary opposition for people who haven't gone along.

*

On the labor issue Republicans were exerting all sorts of pressure. Administration leaders came down and cajoled Republican congressmen to go along with them. Post Office patronage was certainly held out to these members. They control the purse strings. If a man goes along, he gets money for his campaign; if he doesn't go along he gets nothing. It's that simple.

Republicans are equally critical of Democrats:

It amazes me that the Democrats can't recognize they are regimented. It sounds like a Czechoslovakian saying, "We have all the freedom in the world here," or a man behind bars saying, "You can't put me in jail."

*

The Speaker has gotten just about what he has wanted during the time I've been here, no matter what has been involved. He's got an unusual chain of command to help him. Look at the record roll calls on the key issues; the Democrats go down the line. The leadership speaks to them through Walter Reuther on labor matters, Jim Patton when it comes to agriculture, and Clyde Ellis on REA.[9]

*

There is a sharp contrast between the way we operate and the way the Democracts operate. Rayburn is the boss; he sets the policy. We have a policy committee, a minority leader, and a whip, all with important responsibilities. We are less regimented than the Democrats are, and we have more democracy in our organization. They seem to thrive under complete dictatorial leadership. That is the kind of leadership they want, and I don't think we stand for it.

*

[9] Reuther is Vice President of the AFL-CIO; Patton is Director of the National Farmers Union; Ellis is General Manager of the Rural Electrification Association.

Bills have come to our committee about which individual Democrats have expressed opposition to me; yet on the committee roll call every Democrat has voted to put the bills out. That would never happen on our side where an individual had a different personal position. Yet the Democratic leadership has sufficient power to whack every one of those boys in line.

*

Last session there was a teller vote on an issue in which Mr. Sam was much interested. He stood right in front of the line on the Democratic side. Any Democrat who went through the line against his position had to pass him right up. Only one man did so.

The Blocs

There are many different groupings within the House, the majority of them organized along special interest lines and inactive except when those interests are threatened. Two large, somewhat loosely organized blocs are often also identified; these are the Conservative Coalition and the Democratic Liberal Bloc. Both are somewhat fluid groups, the latter somewhat more formally organized, the core of the identifiable members being associated with the Democratic Study Group. The blocs can simplify or complicate the job of the leadership. Strategy is often prepared with their leaders specifically in mind.

The Conservative Coalition. The Conservative Coalition is perhaps the most discussed grouping in the House. An informal alliance of Republicans and Southern Democrats, there is much conjecture but little of substance regarding the way in which the coalition functions. Some representatives assert it rests largely on the natural voting inclinations of certain members of Congress, with little formal effort exerted to weld it into an effective group; other legislators are convinced that close cooperation and frequent consultation characterize the relationship between the acknowledged leaders of the group, Democratic Representative Howard W. Smith, chairman of the Rules Committee, and Charles Halleck, the Republican leader.

All agree that the coalition, however organized, constitutes a force that must be reckoned with in estimating prospects and strategies for legislative victories, though there is evidence that the election of a Democratic president in 1960 weakened it. Discussions with legislators even prior to the 1960 election revealed that congressmen, regardless of philosophical or political persuasion, believed that the number of conservative (as opposed to moderate or liberal) Southern Democrats in the House who could be relied on to support the coalition side of important public issues was gradually dwindling. Yet the number remains significant. Even among opponents there is widespread admiration for the skill with which the leaders of this group maximize their strength. Much of the success of the coalition is credited to the canny, practical thinking of a leadership which recognizes that there are definite limitations to what can be accomplished and proceeds to operate within those boundaries, seldom making a concerted effort for a losing cause. Careful selection of those issues on which to make a stand and skillful designation of floor managers and active participants are important elements of the formula for success.

Among House Democrats in the Eighty-sixth Congress, there was some feeling that should the civil rights issue decline in importance in the South, or should the vote become crucial to success at the polls, some conservative Democrats who owed their elections to their strong stands on that issue would fall, to be succeeded by more liberal candidates. But one leader of the liberals emphasized that a sizable group of southerners were already liberal on economic matters and that it was their support that made possible the passage of any liberal legislation. The following is an excerpt from a discussion of the problem by Democrats:

> The disappearance of the civil rights issue would introduce more unity among Democrats in Congress. Of the one hundred or so Democrats who don't go along with civil rights proponents, a full seventy would make common cause with their fellow Democrats on almost all other issues, foreign and domestic.
>
> *
>
> That is a little high. It might eventually get to seventy, of course, because some men would have trouble getting re-elected if the civil rights issue were not a factor.
>
> *
>
> I agree that civil rights has been a very divisive issue. But people who are liberal on economic matters generally vote that way regardless of the civil rights issue and the difficulties. If we want a count in any Congress, it is obvious that the north-east-west liberals could never pass anything. We don't have the votes. The only way we can pass legislation that is liberal in economics, whether it be education, housing, or airports is by a substantial attrition of southern votes.

Another discussion illuminates the thinking of liberals with respect to the nature of the coalition, its leadership, and the reasons for its success.

How many votes does Judge Smith [acknowledged leader of the Southern conservatives] control, would you say, when he really wants to put his foot down?

*

There is just no way to define his control. It depends on the issue. If it involves something on which there is a natural inclination to agree with his position, he can get more support. He is a realistic leader. He confessed he couldn't do anything with votes on the farm issue—he can't sway more than four or five there. On a bill about which there is no great interest or knowledge in the South, he could probably change thirty or forty votes.

*

He takes his position in relation to the realities of what he can do rather than on his conviction about what should be done. Smith and Halleck clearly are the intellectual leaders of the conservative coalition. They are the idea men, the people who check to see how many votes they have and prepare their ground on that basis. They work out what is a practical position and take few losses that can be avoided. The conservative coalition is a very bright group.

*

When he [Smith] goes to the well of the House to make a motion to recommit in a heated controversial debate, he doesn't do it on the spur of the moment. The groundwork has been laid and the coalition is coming into being. I have seen it happen again and again.

*

Would you say that _____ [a committee chairman] is a member of this conservative coalition?

*

I think that gets to the point: he is in and he is out. That is the way most of them are. He is very very liberal on REA and things like that and very very conservative on many other things. He is an individualist and not a bloc member. He will take his groups as he finds them.

Conservative Republicans are likely to deny that anything in the nature of an alliance exists between them and the Southern Democrats, although they are prone to speak with respect and admiration about many Southern congressmen. They do point out that the two groups often "think the same way" even though the seniority system and other features of congressional organization eliminate the possibility of a party realignment. The Republican members of the round table, for example, identified spending issues, labor legislation, "the extension of the hand of the federal government," and loyalty-security issues as areas of cooperation.

Some of the Republicans were fearful, however, that a new type of Southerner is replacing the conservative ally of old, making cooperation less likely in the future. Consider the following discussion:

The average Southern member is susceptible to influences from business groups —the real estate people, the banks, the building and loan people in small towns. Most Southern members come from smaller communities and naturally line up with those opposed to public housing, for example, because they are persuaded to believe it is a form of socialism, and they have generally been strongly opposed to anything with socialistic tendencies. That group is dwindling though. With labor unions going into the South, the number of Democrats supporting the conservative position is decreasing year by year.

*

There are a group of Southerners I call TVA Southerners. Those in the TVA area don't vote with their Southern colleagues; they vote with the Northern Democrats. They are pretty liberal all the way.

*

There are some people from Georgia and North Carolina who are slipping. Almost every year you can see them voting a little bit less conservatively. I don't think we can count on the Southerners as permanent allies. I think it is about a 50-50 proposition.

The Democratic Liberal Bloc. The Democratic Study Group includes the majority of the junior, younger, non-Southern Democrats. Organized first by a handful of liberals who believed that the party leadership did not pursue sufficiently the liberal tenets of the party platform but was too much disposed to compromise and accommodation, and moderation if not conservatism, the group has sought formal organization—with officers, an executive committee, and a whip cadre—in an effort to maximize liberal strength. Some liberals who for one reason or another prefer not to be associated directly with an organized unofficial group of that kind have nonetheless maintained liaison with it.

House liberals sympathetic to the goals of the Study Group but detached from it are unhappy, if not resentful, that there is a tendency to regard the Study Group and liberal Democrats as one and the same. There is criticism, too, of the tendency to identify a liberal position on civil rights questions as the primary requisite for inclusion in the ranks of the "liberals." Indeed, within the Study Group itself, there is some concern that liberalism is often carelessly defined. At a meeting of Democratic congressmen, attended mostly by members of liberal persuasion, regret was expressed that "the many good liberal Democrats" from the South were often not recognized as such and that the popular image of a liberal was often sectionally based, centering around the civil rights question. One Southern liberal on economic matters who expressed resentment that one's civil rights stand was equated with his general philosophical position on the conservative-liberal spectrum said:

Let's take a situation we had in committee today, a critical vote on the TVA power program. A couple of votes cast against it came from people who by all the accepted definitions are liberal Northern Democrats. Two or three of the other northern congressmen didn't want to go along but did so because they thought we'd get even with them. I think this power issue is a definitive one in determining liberalism in economic matters. The New York liberals are all for civil rights and immigration. _____is a great liberal. When he was in the House he was one of its most conservative members, but he did protect his record on civil rights and immigration. That is all the reputation you have to have to be a liberal in New York.

This statement led participants to emphasize the importance of distinguishing between issues and of recognizing that a person could be "conservative" on one issue but "liberal" on most others. It was suggested that a distinction be made between liberalism on economic issues and liberalism on civil rights matters. This led to an enumeration of some areas to which one could apply the liberal-conservative yardstick: foreign policy, human rights, natural resources, attitude toward the Supreme Court. As the list grew longer, one congressman said, "I think your categories are a blind alley. I think you are going to end up with as many categories as you have issues." "Basically in the House we vote our district," stated one liberal leader, "and that defines our blocs." The following discussion then ensued:

You just can't fit the term "liberal" into any logical framework, except in this way: You find people voting together, and guys going up to each other in the House because they have an affinity of philosophy in terms of issues.

*

We can argue forever on what is a liberal. The other question is whether there is presently a bloc in the House in some state of identifiable organization which is referred to as the "liberal bloc" by some people. The answer is yes, there is. It is the group formed largely by Eugene McCarthy,[10] and some others. Its articles of faith were largely the 1956 Democratic party platform which included a civil rights plank and a set of rather progressive-minded economic issues. While this group is no great shakes, it is a source of internal power and an identifiable group. It gets out papers once in awhile, it meets—sort of—and it has a kind of internal organization. Its basic cement is some rising above the purely

[10] Elected to the Senate in 1958.

local interest, such as voting for foreign aid when actually few districts in the country would give you a majority by referendum to spend money for foreign aid.

*

There is a question, however, of long-term versus short-term self-interest. It doesn't necessarily represent a purist position to take a position against your district. It may be long-term self-interest.

Although they make up a rather solid core of the Democratic representatives in the House, the liberal Democrats have often found it difficult to advance their program effectively. One of the more militant of the liberal Democrats speculates about the reasons:

There seems to be a great inability to exercise a collective will. A lot of that is due to the nature of the Democratic party beast—it is a pretty iconoclastic beast. Many of the new Democrats here this year are here by accident as people realize. Therefore they are likely to be rebels. A good example is _____. He keeps complaining that he wants leadership, a leader of the liberal bloc. Yet he is the type of person who wouldn't follow anyone's leadership. Organizing a liberal bloc just isn't going to happen. Ten of us liberals have been meeting together occasionally. We met recently on the _____ bill and discovered we couldn't even agree on that. We are people of good will, friendly to one another, but really we are all prima donnas. We can't accept authority from others. I think liberals will founder on the rocks of their own independence. They will also founder on the rocks of the internal organizations of Congress. For example, _____ is one of the really good new House members. The other day I said to him, "We have got to get busy and show those Southerners that we are going to get our revenge for their failure to support us on _____. We intend to vote against bills of importance to the South." Will you go along? My colleague replied, "Well, yes. You know I am with you and I'll begin voting with you pretty soon. But the fact is that I have a bill before Bonner's committee on Merchant Marine and Fisheries. As soon as I get it past Bonner [a Southerner] you can count on my vote." I told him we needed him before, not after, Bonner.

A moderately conservative colleague who enjoys a pleasant, friendly working relationship with the liberals offers his analysis:

The liberal Democrats are more organized and unified than other House groups but not necessarily more effective. They are more partisan and often self-defeating. Conservatives tend to put things on a broader base. Liberals resist compromise more strongly and make such partisan statements they often alienate unnecessarily possible sources of support. Thus they are not as effective as their numerical strength might lead one to expect they would be.

Although there is likely to be continuing disagreement within House liberal ranks, as within many groups, regarding how best to function, the schism between the militant, unyielding liberals and those possessing more political realism was especially apparent in the closing days of the 1959 session. In that session the liberals found themselves frustrated on several important issues. In the wake of substantial liberal gains in the most recent congressional elections, the failure of liberal programs to win congressional approval was particularly aggravating, and considerable criticism of the leadership was voiced. Resentment flared at the lack of support from Southern colleagues and some liberals sought to fight back, lending strength to the observations of the congressman quoted above. The plan of these members was to defeat legislation that would be beneficial to those members of the party who had helped sink the liberal program; two bills coming before the House were special targets, even though other liberal members regarded the bills as meritorious. Two of the active participants in the effort to defeat the proposals explain their thinking:

We decided yesterday we would unite and vote against a bill because it was of particular interest to Southern members. But what happened? Once we got over to the floor some of our people began coming up and saying, "But this is a good bill. How can we oppose it? This isn't the issue we should choose for the showdown." Our reply was that it might be a good bill, but we had to defeat the South, to show them they would have to take their consequences for deserting the Democratic party. When the vote was taken, more than 300 supported the bill and only 50 voted against it. That is the way our group is going to function. If they keep waiting for a perfect issue, they may never find it. We have got to show the South that we mean business or we're not going to have any effect.

*

I am getting a little impatient with some people who call themselves liberals but hesitate to vote with us when there is a showdown. We had a situation the other day when _____ who never supports us had a bill he wanted, a reclamation bill designed to help his district. Some of us decided we would do a job on him. But the liberals divided again. Some thought it a good bill. Whether it is a good bill or a bad one is immaterial. The important thing is that it offers a chance to do a job on those who have been doing a job on us for so long.

Other liberals regarded such tactics as most unfortunate and short-sighted. One veteran congressman said he thought his colleagues "pretty much upset by earlier actions" were "on a momentary emotional jag." Added he, "I think we have to pick our issues, and I think we have to support good legislation when it does come before the House." A Southern moderate often included in the liberal group commented:

I think those liberals were short-sighted in attempting to vote against good legislation in order to penalize individuals or sections. The fact is that as far as the first bill is concerned they were penalizing most two people who had supported them. That doesn't make much sense, and I don't think it is the way to legislate.

And another liberal member urged increased efforts to make liberal legislation attractive to the House rather than attempts to retaliate against legislators who withheld support.

I don't think we should attempt to solve our difficulties in that way. You can't solve problems such as we have by opposing legislation. That is vindictive rather than thoughtful. I think we can do a lot, however, to gain increased support for policies in which we are interested. For example, the food stamp plan gave us the support of many other groups. A stepped up school lunch program can be made attractive to people from many areas and in many kinds of districts. With a little careful planning we can dress up our legislation so that other groups will find it attractive.

Unquestionably, the liberal bloc was despondent during the final hours of the first session of the Eighty-sixth Congress. Yet this dejection was not without its rewards. The election to the Senate of the bloc's designated leader had weakened the organizational aspects of the group's activities. The session's failures focused attention on the need for reviving more formal procedures. Looking back on the session, one charter member said, "We haven't had any program; we have no real liaison with ourselves." A first term member commented:

Many of us are pretty discouraged at this point. One of the great lessons we have learned is that joint action pays off. We have seen that when it has been used by others. There is no reason we shouldn't use it ourselves. The record of this session makes it clear that a loose, informal, sketchy approach is inadequate to get more than occasional close victories.

There is evidence that this bloc has learned from its mistakes and that its role in party councils is increasing. Its improved cohesiveness makes it a force to be reckoned with and leads to consultation. The leadership can advance the bloc's strength as a reason for pursuing a course of action it desires to pursue, in the face of opposition from other influential party members.

The Liberal Republicans and Other Blocs. In recent years there has been no significant, organized Republican liberal bloc in the House. As one GOP stalwart said:

> I mean no offense to anyone, but the Republicans don't have a liberal bloc. It is more a splinter than a bloc. It is smaller and it sticks together less. The liberal Republicans are not as clear-cut a group as some other groups here. I don't classify myself as a liberal, but I certainly vote for a lot of liberal programs. I think Republicans are a little more inclined to divide their vote than Democrats. We don't buy all the liberal program or all the conservative program.

If a liberal bloc faces problems of organization and agreement on a plan of procedure, it is evident that other clusters of congressmen have their problems also. Many temporary groups are established to advance particular legislative proposals; when their goal is achieved, they fade into oblivion. Area groups such as the New England members may unite temporarily, too, to promote legislation of mutual interest. There is a loose organization known as the Western Conference, which meets rarely, when waging common cause seems important. Often, however, partisan divisions within the group are sharp, limiting severely the range of subjects on which joint action is possible. Blocs with homogeneous membership may be more effective. When trade policy is before Congress, members favoring a protective tariff have banded together, held frequent meetings and planned bipartisan strategy. In recent years, members from textile areas have waged common cause.

The farm bloc, once a potent force in the House, seems less effective of late, partly because of divergent intragroup interest. "The farm bloc is split into wheat blocs and cotton blocs that don't work together. The peanut bloc is split up into the runner, the southwest spanish, and the Virginias. The wheat bloc is splitting up by classes of wheat. The cotton people are split between the old cotton growing part of the South, the Texas group, and the California group, and the three can never get together any more. The Texas group is even split—one area is in the new part, and central Texas is all for the old South."

Indeed, many of the traditionally cohesive blocs show signs of losing their unity. Yet, for all their problems, the blocs cannot be ignored, particularly when they are bipartisan and not confined to one geographic area. They constitute both a potential threat and source of support to the leadership. And legislative strategists keep them firmly in mind as they seek to maximize their own strength on legislative proposals.

The individualism that characterizes the House bears significantly on the nature of party leadership there. For the leadership is preoccupied with accommodation and consensus within the party if not within the House itself, and relies heavily on personal influence to achieve this. At the same time, it is reluctant to use tools that might restrict its freedom of action but that would convey simultaneously a greater sense of participation to rank and file members. Though House leaders are prepared to act quickly to meet emergencies and threats to their power, they are disposed to tolerate the imperfections of a system they have come to understand if not manipulate. Uncertain regarding the effects of change, they resist reform. They might prefer stronger party discipline, but they stop short of an all-out attack on the quasi-anarchy that interferes with party effectiveness and attainment of legislative goals.

The result is that the House of Representatives strikes some observers as a world where, just below the top layer of leadership, there are interlocking circles of personal influence and interests, each centering in an individual who has learned how far he can go and is prepared, if necessary, to go that far. These powerful figures stand between a leadership that is too permissive or hesitant to rule firmly, and a rank and file that, though it may resist coercion, is too amorphous to maximize its strength or to make its collective influence felt. These men are respectful of one another and seek no overt clash with the elected leaders. But they are largely free of direction by the leadership and from accountability to anyone except their own constituents. Power is personal as well as institutional and individualism is king. To an amazing degree the legislative parties are subordinated to the interests of their individual members. The House is a society in which every legislator may win influence and respect by mastery of its ways; to all it holds out the promise of increasing power with the passage of time.

VIII

The Problem of Being Returned

" A CONGRESSMAN IS THE SHORTEST DISTANCE between two years," complain many members of the House. Attributed to various colleagues and former colleagues, the statement reflects the widely held congressional opinion that the election process is virtually continual for House members. They cannot afford to ignore this fact in their activities: elections are always upon them, and they are running for office all the time, some more subtly than others. As one representative stated, "You should say 'perennial' election rather than 'biennial.' It is with us every day."

A Two-Year Term

Although most congressmen probably would agree with one colleague that "the two-year term really complicates the business of being a U. S. congressman," there is relatively little serious agitation within the House for quadrennial elections. In part this is because some members have dismissed the possibility as remote and therefore not worth their serious attention; in part it rests on an expressed belief that the shorter term is valuable in providing the nation with an opportunity to register quickly widespread changes in sentiment. Several House Democrats discuss the matter:

We will never get a four-year term. The Senate will never go along with the idea because senators will not want to have congressmen free to run against them without having to relinquish their House seats should they lose. As it now stands, congressmen hesitate to risk everything by challenging a senator.

*

A four-year term would simplify our problem, and I think the people would favor it. At first I thought the two-year term was fine but I have changed my mind. In theory it sounds fine to have a great democratic response every two years, but after you have been here awhile you see the problems.

*

330

I disagree with the idea of the longer term. I think it is clear we are not going to have a parliamentary system in the United States and the only real flexibility we have—on the chance that sometime we might get a terrible president—is in the House. Only one-third of the Senate seats are up every two years. Only the two-year House term permits real turnover. I think you could quite easily get into a situation where a four-year term would put firmly into place a government that people want to turn out.

*

I recall hearing a member growling about the two-year term and a constituent stopped him very well by saying: "No one twisted your arm to take the job." We all knew the situation when we came to the House. This country has been functioning for a long time under the present system, and I would rule out the four-year term as nothing more than a wild pipe dream.

The Advantages of Incumbency

Although members of Congress are inclined to talk about re-election campaigns in terms of the problems involved, they agree that as incumbents they possess extraordinary advantages over their opponents. There is a tendency to believe that, aside from isolated instances where an overriding issue is present, there is little excuse for defeat. At the beginning of a new Congress legislators often discuss the defeat of former colleagues in terms of failure to make full use of the many perquisites of incumbency.

"Elections are Won in the Off-Year." Virtually everyone on Capitol Hill agrees that nonelection year activities traditionally not associated with elections probably provide the most effective means of strengthening support and promoting re-election. As one representative put it: "You can slip up on the blind side of people during an off-year and get in much more effective campaigning than you can when you are in the actual campaign." No matter how significant the achievements during an election year, motives are often suspect: the congressman is motivated, skeptics will say, primarily by his desire for victory at the polls rather than by a sincere desire to make an important contribution to constituent, district, state, or nation.

The forum which is available to congressmen, the many opportunities to build good will and achieve publicity, the assistance of a trained staff, being in a position to speak knowledgeably about issues—all are factors promoting the continued electoral success of incumbents. Prompt attention to the mail is especially heralded as providing a strong base for re-election efforts as is member-initiated communication with constituents. As one representative was told by his father, who had preceded him in the House: "Son, I have three pieces of advice for you if you want to stay in Congress. One, use the frank. Two, use the frank. Three, use the frank." This opportunity to mail materials free is very helpful.

Frequent appearances in the district—speaking before community groups, participating in community programs, perhaps touring the district in a mobile office when Congress is not in session—are also stressed, as are "educational" activities such as television and radio clips of a public service nature.

One of the most effective and able women to serve in the Congress relates:

> I have the feeling that the most effective campaigning is done when no election is near. During the interval between elections you have to establish every personal contact you can, and you accomplish this through your mail as much as you do it by means of anything else. At the end of each session I take all the letters which have been received on legislative matters and write each person telling him how the legislative proposal in which he was interested stands.
>
> Personally, I will speak on any subject. I am not nonpartisan, but I talk on everything whether it deals with politics or not. Generally I speak at nonpolitical meetings. I read 48 weekly newspapers and clip every one of them myself. Whenever there is a particularly interesting item about anyone, that person gets a note from me. We also keep a complete list of the change of officers in every organization in our district. Then when I am going into a town I know exactly who I would like to have at the meeting. I learned early that you had to make your way with Democrats as well as with Republicans. And you cannot let the matter of election go until the last minute. I budget 17 trips home each session and somehow I've never managed to go less than 21 times.

Commented one congressman at the revelation of the frequency of the trips to the district, "Good God!"

Limits to the Advantage. It is also recognized, however, that there are circumstances when careful attention to duty, the maintenance of favorable political alliances, and maximum use of publicity opportunities are insufficient to bring about re-election. As one Democrat observed, following his party's gains in the 1958 congressional elections:

There is no question but that an incumbent has strong advantages. He has a forum by virtue of being a congressman, and of course he also has the frank. These are two very important items. At the same time I would point out that sometimes you cannot fight the trend. A good example is 1958. Some representatives got caught in that trend and were replaced by men far inferior.

Financing the Campaign

It is difficult to state just how much is spent in a "typical" congressional campaign. Strength of the opposition, the geography and population of the district, the situation with respect to the presence or absence—and location—of communication media, and funds available are all determinants. But whatever the expenditure, congressmen believe campaigning is too expensive. Some of them don't know how much money is expended in their behalf—and in many cases they don't want to know.

Ineffective Legal Limitations. State and national limitations on spending are so unrealistic that nearly all candidates are conditioned to violating the spirit of the law though well versed in remaining technically within it. Relatively little concern is expressed within the Congress for modification of election laws primarily because they are not taken seriously, not because those on the books possess merit. In many congressional districts, it would be impossible to conduct a satisfactory yet minimal campaign within the statutory limitations. Just as national party organizations have responded to the unrealistic $3 million maximum placed on expenditures of the Democratic and Republican national committees by encouraging the creation of many other committees, congressional candidates have stimulated the development of special committees within their own districts—committees whose activities are coordinated usually with the personal committees of the candidate, but whose receipts and expenditures are filed separately and need not be included in the candidate's totals.

The Federal Corrupt Practices Act of 1925 is archaic. It provides that House candidates may spend up to $2,500 unless state law establishes a lower figure. The amount may be increased to $5,000 depending on the number of votes cast in the district in the preceding election, the total being figured on the basis of three cents a vote. Each House candidate is required to file reports with the clerk of the House listing contributions and expenditures handled by him personally or by someone for him "with his knowledge and consent" in support of his candidacy. One weakness of federal law is that no official has been designated to compel submission of the reports, to examine them, or to report violations. Another weakness is that primary elections are not covered by the federal act. Nor are committees working within a single state in behalf of any congressional candidate required to report at the federal level.

Though a majority of the states provide for expenditure ceilings of some kind, they are ineffective. Most laws apply only to expenditures by the candidate, ignoring campaign committees organized in his behalf; where the ceilings include expenditures by the candidate and those made on his behalf with his "knowledge and consent," the loophole is obvious. Where committees are also subject to limitation, there is little attempt to include all a candidate's committees under a single ceiling. Even where the law seems to provide for central responsibility, a careful reading reveals ways to avoid it. It should be noted that certain kinds of expenditures are specifically excluded from the computation. These include assessments or filing fees levied by state law; necessary traveling or subsistence expenses; stationery, postage, writing, or printing—other than for use in billboards or newspapers; distribution of letters, circulars, or posters; and telephone or telegraph service.

Because of the obvious ineffectiveness of present statutes, various reforms have been advanced with respect to campaign contributions and expenditures. These range from complete abolition of ceilings to enforcement of strict limitations, and include providing incentives to giving in the form of tax credits or deductions. But the politicians have learned to live with the present system and are aware of its flexibility. Though some might prefer change, few feel strongly enough about it to pursue a reform program vigorously.

Despite the obvious weaknesses in the law, many candidates prefer to leave knowledge of the over-all expense involved to their subordinates and could not tell you accurately about the total campaign effort, even if they wished to do so. Some preface discussions about money with disclaimers that they are directly involved, as did one midwesterner, "from what I hear the campaign organization talk about, I think it cost me about $18,000 in the last campaign."

Of one thing nearly all congressmen are certain, regardless of their political affiliation: their opponents spend far more than they. It is reasonable, of course, to expect that a less publicized challenger might have to spend more money than his better known opponent. But the firmness and frequency with which congressmen assert that the campaigns of rivals reached exorbitant proportions while remaining somewhat uncertain and vague as to costs incurred in their own efforts give cause for some skepticism.

Variation in Costs. Some of the problems that state and federal statutes create for the legislators are revealed in the discussion presented below. The group was asked how much their most recent campaign had cost. The first to respond was a midwestern congressman, whose low expenditure aroused the envy of colleagues. They were, however, appalled to learn that he had contributed about 40 percent of the total.

I believe it was $4,872 I spent in the last election. I paid my own traveling expenses in the district; I didn't count that in the total.

*

How about committee expenditures? What about the party?

*

The party helped to the extent that my name appeared in the same ads with the county and state tickets.

*

Did the party take care of precinct workers?

*

So far as I know there isn't a paid precinct worker in my district with the exception of those in the city of _____. Those are paid $10 on election day.

*

But the party organizations provide precinct workers.

*

They don't work for me; they work for the ticket. I put almost $2,000 of my own money in the campaign last time. The rest was raised by finance committees in the various counties, mostly in one county.

Next to speak was an urban congressman whose district was "marginal" politically. His story differed sharply from that of the previous speaker and led to a discussion of the legal limitations on expenditures.

Campaigns are a lot more costly in a metropolitan area where you have television and the mass media methods. We don't have much of a party organization in my area. My organization has to carry the whole ticket and so, in effect, I have to raise the money. To be candid, in my district it costs a lot more to run a campaign than you can legitimately spend.

*

Is that honest?

*

That is a proper question and one that disturbs me because I don't believe you can be elected in some of these districts, mine included, within the spirit of the law. You can do it within the technicalities. What we had to do was technically legal—we created a whole slew of committees, each one of which would take over a portion of the campaign. I honestly didn't have control of that, and if anyone asked me to take an oath and testify to that effect I could do so. But it would not be true to say that is within the spirit of the limitation on expenditures. The laws are impossible to adhere to in a metropolitan area.

*

How much does it really cost?

*

I had to run the campaign for the party in my area. My campaign last time ran over $60,000. It is a big district, of course, but that is a lot of money. The fact that the two important newspapers in my district refused to support me added to my expenses as I had to spend more money to publicize my candidacy. When the campaign is underway, I usually have about four direct mailings, and you can figure that costs plenty.

An eastern congressman from a "safe" district spoke next. Though he is in a better position than most members to contribute personally to his own campaign, he expressed the resentment of many colleagues that this seemed essential.

The differences in campaign costs always puzzle me. I assume by the stunned silence when our colleague mentioned he spent less than $5,000, that it was thought to be very small. I only spent about $2,000 in my campaign, though my opponent spent much more. The party organization puts out county literature and supplies precinct workers, but it also needs a little bit more from me as an individual. It pained me to spend that $2,000 because most of it comes out of three or four pockets. I have no widespread fund-raising campaign. There must be something wrong with our system. It seems to me congressional campaigns get short-changed. Someone else's campaign is always more important.

Another representative of an urban area in the West revealed his costs approximated those of the big city congressman who had already spoken. It should be noted that both represent districts in which their party is heavily outnumbered by the opposition.

My district is large and similar to that of _____. If you include the costs of the primary I too spent about $60,000 last time. I know that one of the senators in my state spent at least $1 million in his campaign. Legally speaking, he would be limited to somewhere around $30,000. Now it is obvious that you cannot cover a large state like ours in the various media for $30,000. Something should be done to make election costs more realistic. You couldn't put on an advertising campaign for selling dog food in one city for that amount.

These remarks led his colleague to add:

One reason my campaign costs so much is that when you buy television time in my area you take in the whole population of [a major city] even though I am only trying to reach the one-third who live in my district. The same is true when you use the metropolitan newspapers. We reported the $60,000 in the newspapers. I wanted people to see just what it does cost to run a campaign in an area like mine under the situation that prevailed.

An eastern representative whose district contains an urban-rural balance contributed these comments:

We spent $28,000 for our campaign, but we had no paid precinct or poll workers. They were all volunteers. We did have three paid workers in the headquarters. We didn't use television much because we couldn't afford it. Contributions by about three different families in my district raised $5,000. All the rest of the money was raised by means of banquets, cake sales, and parties. Most of the money went into newspaper ads and the campaign pamphlet. We couldn't afford any mailings; had we gone into that, the costs would have gone to $60,000 easily.

In sharp contrast to most of the expenditures previously noted, were those of a rural legislator whose district normally returns him with a heavy majority.

I spend about $1,200 and my opponent spends even less. In my state the primary is far more important than the election. When I first ran there were eight of us in the primary and I spent about $25,000. In my area the most effective type of campaign is one of personal contact, getting around into the towns, meeting people, getting into the shops, shaking hands up and down the street.

A western incumbent who also represents a rural constituency, but one much larger geographically, explained that all such districts were not the same.

In the sparsely settled area I represent you run into other problems. We have about thirty papers in which we have to advertise and we have four TV stations. I would estimate that something close to $24,000 or $25,000 is spent in my behalf. That is for a minimum cost campaign including a two-column six-inch ad in the papers. Last time we had no radio spots until the final four days, and then we used only three a day, building up to five daily before election. I know the opposition spent a great deal more.

It is obvious that wide divergences exist in campaign expenditures for congressional seats. It is clear, too, that except for the "safe" districts, campaigns tend to be expensive affairs of which only a portion of the total costs ever come to light. To add to the confusion, some representatives when asked about the costs respond in terms of the expenditures of their campaign committee while others include outlays of various groups working in their behalf.

A discussion of campaign expenses with another group of congressmen further substantiated the fact that costs vary significantly. When asked how much money was necessary replies such as these were made: "$19,500 approximately;" "It could vary from $3,000 to $30,000;" "The only time I had a problem it cost about $17,000;" "The first time I ran I spent a total of $2,200. I lucked in. I have never claimed to be anything but a political freak in that, but it is the fact."

The media pose a special problem in many districts and in some ways they dictate approximate expenditures. There may be so many newspapers in a district, for example, that it becomes impossible for the candidate to place ads in all of them and thus obtain full coverage. At the same time he may fear to antagonize editors by choosing between papers. Different sections of a district may receive different television and radio programs, increasing costs sharply. In other situations, the networks reaching a member's district may also reach those of several other congressmen. In such cases he must forego television or radio or pay for coverage that will do him no good. Consider this discussion:

I have 47 weeklies and they constitute a problem because of the expense involved in full coverage. I wait until the last week and then send every editor a letter thanking him for his kindness and saying I am sure he knows how much I would like to take a big ad but with 47 weeklies of course I can't because of the expense limitations imposed on me. I mention I am sending a little material and if he hasn't any space for it that is all right, but I am sending everybody in the district $25, and they can give me what space they wish. I don't have literature and I don't have billboards and I don't have radio.

*

The techniques of getting around vary tremendously. I don't use radio or television because my congressional district is about six miles square and just a small piece of the city of _____. It would not make sense for me to spend money on radio and television, but many colleagues have districts that extend tremendous distances and should be covered by these media.

*

I must have at least one mailing. Radio and television costs are more expensive than mailing. One general mailing costs about $4,000, but I will get a complete and total coverage that way which I am not sure of with the broadcasts.

*

You have a small territory to cover. I have 66,660 square miles.

*

The problem in my district is to campaign vertically, rather than horizontally, because I have some very tall buildings. The only way to get into many of those places is with a piece of mail. We try to make use of neighborhood newspapers for campaigning purposes also.

*

The amount spent depends a good deal on the efficiency of the media. If, for instance, you happen to be in a district about 50 miles in diameter which is covered by one television station everyone watches, you probably could use television very effectively and relatively cheaply. If, on the other hand, you are in a community where there are five or six television stations but also ten or twelve congressmen, you obviously can't use television or you would be splattered all over the lot.

*

There are 50 weekly papers and 7 dailies in my district, plus 10 radio stations and 3 TV stations. It is too expensive to attempt frequent coverage so I used 126 billboards last time.

As illustrated below, it may be misleading to characterize one-party districts as low campaign cost areas. Members from such constituencies warn that the absence of serious opposition in the general election does not necessarily mean campaign costs are negligible. An expensive primary may replace it:

In a one-party state in the South you don't have to spend as much money as we do in a two-party state.

*

The cost in a primary fight in the South is as great or greater than that of any campaign anywhere. In a two-party state you almost always are part of a general election where more than one campaign is going on. That is expensive to you, of course, but at least people know there is an election. In a congressional primary fight in the South, the only elections that take place along with it are a few isolated county jobs and getting out the vote has to be done entirely by the congressional candidates. In one much publicized primary contest a few years ago in my state, I'd estimate the successful challenger spent $30,000 or $40,000 to oust the incumbent.

A major asset to a candidate, and one which reduces his costs, may be the existence of a strong party organization which can ensure victory:

Those of us coming from cities which send several people to Congress often have the benefit of a strong city organization which is very helpful and becomes the backbone of our election campaign.

*

That is the understatement of the evening.

*

Our problem is to supplement the official organization in order to bring other groups into our camp.

*

Your election problem is to get the Mayor's support.

In 1962, the treasurer of the Democratic National Congressional Committee gave this estimate of campaign costs:[1]

The average campaign in a big city district against stiff opposition will run somewhere between $25,000 and $50,000 for a liberal candidate. In a suburban or small city-rural district the cost for such a candidate will average between $15,000 and $25,000.
The range, of course, is wide. An Indiana congressman was elected in 1958 with total expenses of $4,500. Two years later he spent $13,000 and was defeated. This year one prospective liberal candidate for a tough California seat estimates $75,000 will have to be spent to elect him."

Reporting Expenses. The care that some members take to remain technically within the law is evident when they discuss the reporting provisions of campaign statutes. Their comments reveal how flexible the law really is. Two representatives, the second of whom had been critical of expenditures of $60,000 by a colleague, discuss a recent campaign, distinguishing between expenses included within the federal ceiling and those excluded:

So far as money is concerned I reported and certified to about $8,500. But I was very careful to stay within the three cents per vote limitation on the specified items. In my case it came to $4,000 for television, radio, and newspaper advertis-

[1] *The Machinist*, April 26, 1962, p. 4.

ing. That accounted for about half of the expenditures. The other things—stamps, letters, etc., don't count in the reporting.

*

My campaign last year cost about $9,500 and I was, just as _____ was, careful to stay within the $2,500 limit! [laughter] Now that happens to be a fact. Several weeks before the election I canceled over $600 worth of spot announcements which would exceed the $2,500 limit. I did so not only because of my great respect for the law but because I was afraid my opponent would challenge me if I didn't do it.

It was obvious that many members were surprised to hear that one of their fellows had expended in excess of $60,000 to gain re-election. Soon their questions turned attention back to him:

How did you report your $60,000?

*

The various committees reported their expenditures, and we added it together in one nice item so people could see just what the total was.

*

When you are filing your return and you come to the point which says, "I know of no other money spent in my behalf" what do you do?

*

Maybe your laws are different, but all I have to state is what I spent through my official committees. The others are citizens committees, lawyers committees, and doctors.

*

You said that the practice you follow in connection with committees might violate the spirit of the law. It not only violates the spirit, it violates the letter of the law. The Federal Corrupt Practices Act requires that you report not only what you spend yourself but everything that was spent in your behalf to your knowledge.

*

There is the answer. It isn't to my knowledge because I don't know. I have no control over the independent committees.

*

You mentioned television a moment ago. If you appear on a television broadcast you are bound to know about that.

*

. . . but not about the cost.

*

He is right! I was a guest on many of the television shows. That is the kind of thing which would be included in my campaign expenditures. But there was a series of radio talks by various people about my views. I didn't know who did that, but they cost quite a bit of money. And other people were speaking in my behalf on radio and television, and it was beyond my control. Billboards went up, but I had nothing to do with putting them up or financing them or even in selecting the material that went on them.

*

But you are required to report that.

*

There are certain exemptions.

*

I was about to name them. There are two things. One is an unlimited group of expenditures and the other is limited. You have a ceiling of $2,500 in the latter group, which includes expenditures for television, radio, newspaper advertisement, billboards, and precinct work.

*

I have a different interpretation of the law. My interpretation of "your knowledge" means you would have to have knowledge of the specific funds spent. If you go on a television program and some committee pays for it and you don't know what they have paid for it, I don't think you violate the law.

*

Let's face it. The law is so screwy any one of us could probably get in trouble if someone was in a position to give us trouble. Everybody is just about equally guilty, if anyone is guilty.

*

On the statement we are required to turn in to the clerk of the House I always put a declaration above my signature saying, "while I know there were other funds collected and spent by committees in my behalf, I have no specific knowledge of these receipts or expenditures." You are not required under federal law to report what a committee spends.

*

Yes you are.

*

All I know is that a group of lawyers handles this matter for me. They said we were technically within the law. I want to say that though I spent more than $60,000, there is no question my opponent spent even more. He didn't report it because he had union manpower and their treasuries. He ran a lavish campaign.

Only one congressman mentioned that his state had taken steps to provide for full disclosure of expenses; in that situation a "realistic" ceiling made evasion unnecessary. The exclusion of expenditures of official party organizations provided a loophole, however, should unusual circumstances seem to require it.

We have a very rigid state law with regard to expenditures. It is spelled right out that no money can be spent on your behalf without your knowledge. If that provision is violated, both the person who spends the money and the candidate are subject to a fine and may be declared ineligible for holding office. But we have a very realistic limitation in the state which includes primary and election. It does not, however, include expenditures of the regular party organization.

Opponents' Spending. Virtually every congressman with whom campaign expenditure was discussed emphasized that, whatever the costs of his campaign, his opponent had exceeded them. Some of them wondered what could be done about excessive spending by opponents, as did this midwesterner:

I would like to have the record show my opponent spent at least three times as much money as I did. He obviously is violating the state law and going way beyond the limit. He reported what the law allowed, but we knew that his signboards alone called for more than was legal. What should we do? Should we press charges? Even if committees did pay for it, it is a violation of our state law.

One congressman related that huge expenditures by his opponent served to stimulate his own supporters to exert more strenuous efforts in his behalf. Said he:

I spent nearly $60,000, but my opponent spent about twice that. He had a daily fifteen-minute radio program on our best station which probably cost $40,000 for the time he was on. He was doing such a good job of publicizing himself that my supporters realized we were in a serious situation, and they formed various committees and raised funds. The labor unions financed his radio program.

Many members stress the fact that though their opponent may not have spent much more than they, groups friendly to him added substantially to his total campaign effort. Said one of these congressmen:

About $6,000 was spent in my campaign and I would say my opponent spent about the same. However, in addition to that, unions paid $20 a day throughout my district to precinct workers, drivers, and other workers of the other party. They had a fabulous crew. I know that in one city alone they spent $6,000 to get their vote out. I have no way of knowing the grand total.

So strong is the conviction that opponents are the "spenders" in elections that there was no objection, and much agreement, when one representative set forth the following rule of thumb: "In my own district I simply assume that if I spend let's say $15,000 in a campaign, my opponent will probably spend $50,000 or $60,000. Is that pretty much the pattern for the rest of you?" One or two congressmen even insisted the speaker had been too conservative in estimating the difference.

Sources of Funds. Campaigns are expensive and raising the money is not always an easy task. Some congressmen are fortunate in that the party organization handles fund raising problems. But those members are few in number. There are problems involved in heavy dependence on the official organization, as the following comment illustrates: "I've never had a finance committee before, having relied on the local organization. But I am thinking about organizing one because of all the criticism back home from the party about my vote on the labor bill." If the organization disapproves of an incumbent's voting record, it may be more reluctant to provide him with adequate funds. Even if it is sympathetic, it may not be able to allocate an amount the congressman regards as minimal.

Party committees—from national to local levels—generally are less generous than candidates feel they should be. Said one congressman:

> The whole matter of financing says a great deal about the attitude of American party organizations toward members of Congress. They just don't think we amount to very much. The sheriff in my county has seventy or eighty jobs to pass out, and everyone is interested in who is sheriff. No one cares about us.

An aggressive candidate, it is true, may succeed in wresting from the national or congressional committee, a sum in excess of that provided to colleagues in his particular category of need (as established by the committee involved), but that is not an easy task. In those rare instances, it is more than likely that the committee, rather than supplementing its original contribution from the treasury, will suggest to a potential contributor that his contribution be sent directly to the candidate. In that way other candidates may not realize their colleague is receiving extra assistance.

Inadequate support from the party organization emphasizes the importance of enlisting the aid of a vigorous finance committee; in many instances, despite such support, a congressman will be required to become— some of them choose to become—his own chief fund raiser. This is a time-consuming and difficult task. Complained one congressman:

> In a district where I have half a dozen radio stations, three TV stations, and about thirty-five weekly papers, I can run a pretty good campaign on about

$15,000 which is not a lot of money. But I have to spend so much of my own time the first couple of months as a fund raiser—time which I could far more effectively put into straightforward politicking.

Another disadvantage is that if a legislator solicits funds for his own cause, he may find it difficult later to deny a contributor's request for help. And, in view of the laws regarding ceilings on campaign expenditures, it may be preferable for him to remain apart from the fund-raising ventures.

As the earlier discussion of campaign costs illustrates, many candidates are required to contribute generously to their own campaigns, and must turn to relatives for help, too. A surprising number of congressmen appear to have decided to run for the office without the encouragement of party leaders in their district and thus in early contests are more likely to have depended on personal funds than on organizational support. Veteran legislators are more likely to begrudge personal expenditures.

Often congressional candidates appoint finance committees, composed whenever possible of respected bankers, lawyers, businessmen, and union officials, and rely on them to tap available sources in the district.[2] It is not uncommon for these committees to incur the wrath and resentment of county and local party leaders since the official organization is often seeking funds from the same sources.

Other independent groups supporting the candidate are encouraged to be self-sustaining and, where possible, to provide financial support for some of the candidate's campaign activities. "Friendly" national organizations may be of appreciable assistance by providing fees and honoraria for speeches and talks. The head of one such group interested in congressional elections views this form of indirect financial assistance as of nearly as great significance as the direct campaign contributions made by his organization.

Representatives of both parties seem to agree that of the organized

[2] One Democrat from California, where politics remains somewhat unorthodox, found Republicans to be much better fund raisers than Democrats and now selects Republican dominated finance committees to raise his money. Says he:

"I have never had a campaign successfully financed by my Democratic workers. I find that my Democratic group will tell me money can't be raised, and they won't try. But my Republican groups have an entirely different attitude. They will go out and try. They have been primarily responsible for financing my last three campaigns, not with big contributions but with a lot of effort."

nonparty groups, labor helps the most. Republicans who receive relatively little labor support frequently mention that labor not only contributes substantial sums to Democratic coffers but provides paid election
day workers in support of Democratic candidates. And one Democratic
legislator expressed the view of many Democrats when he said: "Labor
is the only group I am aware of that is conscious of congressional elections and looks upon them as important." One of his liberal colleagues expressed the view that labor's financial support, while appreciated by
candidates, has not always been favorably regarded by party officials. "In
some northern urban districts," he said, "labor contributions have created
tensions between them and the party people. Some party people are beginning to say that if they don't provide financial assistance to candidates
and labor does, allegiance may turn to labor rather than party. In some
areas, it has resulted in more financial assistance from the party."

While labor union support for Democratic congressional candidates
is widespread, its recipients state that much, if not the bulk of their financial support, comes from small business and professional people. Nor are
all of them entirely satisfied with what they receive. Three liberal Democrats, one representing an eastern urban area, another a sparsely settled
western district, and the third a midwestern industrial area, gave their
views:

I've heard that the unions have made contributions to pro-labor men in marginal districts. I thought some of you on the labor committee would benefit from
that since I know of contributions of $1,000 and better to some candidates. One
labor leader told me they couldn't make a contribution to me but suggested that I
give them my printing bill, and they would take care of it. The bill came to a
little more than $3,000 and I submitted it to them. Then they said they had run
out of funds, so I had to pay it myself. I had another bad experience. I had an
argument with a labor leader. Labor had offered to contribute $1,000 to my cam-
paign and had the check ready when a labor leader from whom I wouldn't take
any guff called the union and told them not to give it to me. The union official
showed me the check and said he had been told to countermand it. I couldn't get
the money because another labor union not in my district said, "We don't want
you to give it to him."

*

I got a contribution from labor last time, the only contribution I have ever
received from them. But when Senator Goldwater was kind enough to put all the
labor reports in the *Congressional Record*, I went down the list and discovered that
even though I was a member of the labor committee and from a marginal district,

the contribution to me was small in comparison to some sent to anti-labor congressmen—some even Republicans—in other areas. In my state at least, contributions of the labor people to their own political organization, COPE, don't come back to the state. They are used elsewhere.

*

I have found it important to build up a close personal link with the top labor people in my area so they feel a sense of personal responsibility to raise funds for my campaign. They feel they are letting me down unless they go out and push the right button here in the capital to take care of me back home. I think it is a splendid attitude for them to have.

One freshman Democrat interviewed at the time a controversial labor bill was before the House spoke out sharply against the charge that he was a "labor" congressman. Said he:

> Some people say those of us who oppose this legislation are controlled by labor. That is nonsense. Labor made a contribution to my campaign last time and I appreciated it. I got $3,100 from them. That was helpful, but it amounted to only 12 percent of my campaign budget. That means, relatively speaking, it was not much noticed. Who is going to sell out for $3,100?

As the following discussion indicates, leading industries of a state or congressional district do not always contribute heavily, or as anticipated, to congressional campaigns.

> There is no rule of thumb you can apply to where funds will come from once you have counted the labor group. There is no industry in our state that has more reason to be interested in what happens in Congress than the oil industry. Yet they are tight as far as contributing to a congressional campaign is concerned. Individual oilmen who should be interested in what kind of legislation is passed with respect to depletion allowance or imports are notorious in their refusal to get interested in congressional campaigns in a financial way—and that goes for contributions to either party. On the other hand, you will find small businessmen or lawyers or dentists taking a pretty substantial financial interest, generally on the grounds that they know the man and are interested in seeing him go to Congress.

*

Is this an unkind suggestion to make: It is pretty difficult for congressmen from certain states to vote against the predominant industry in their states, so there is no need for the industry to use any leverage.

*

That is true if you are going to put it only on the basis of votes, but everyone here knows that your vote is not the point at which you exert the most influence for something that is of interest to your district or state. If you confined your activities in behalf of your district to voting, you would not be much of a factor in Congress.

*

There is a large lumbering industry in my state and year after year they give money to the Republican candidate. My predecessor voted against every housing bill that came along, and yet they consistently supported him because he was a Republican. I could do a lot more for them.

Special Fund Raising Activities. Members of Congress and their supporters often develop special ways of raising money. Card games, a portion of the pot being turned over to the campaign committee, membership in "_____ for Congress" Clubs, testimonial dinners, and auctions in a candidate's behalf are some of the methods used to raise money.

Congressmen are mixed in their reactions to the value of a mass fund raising campaign directed to small contributions from a large number of people. All are convinced, however, that once you have gained a contributor, you are assured of a vote and possibly a campaign worker. As one legislator put it, "It is like betting money on a horse. If they will put money on you, they will root you home. That is the big advantage of the dollar contribution." Some representatives favor door-to-door solicitation of small contributions but mention the difficulty of recruiting interested and capable solicitors. Others feel that the results do not justify the work involved. One man who no longer uses that type of appeal spoke of mailing letters to 25,000 union members in his district whom he expected to be especially sympathetic to his cause. They were invited to a rally to be addressed by a prominent United States senator, and they were urged to enclose a dollar in an enclosed envelope to be returned to campaign headquarters. Receipts were insufficient to pay for the cost of the mailing. The consensus was that the value of the general appeal was less the financial gain to be realized for the campaign treasury than stimulating interest in the campaign and providing a sense of participation and commitment to those who contributed.

Much more successful than a general request for funds, members agree, is the special mailing directed at special groups in society by recognized leaders within those groups or sent to constituents who are personal friends of the candidate or who have received assistance of some sort from him. Many congressmen maintain a special list of people to whom such appeals can be made, adding to it as the congressional office performs helpful service to other district residents. So successful are appeals to such constituents that some congressmen report that from one third to one half of their campaign funds can be raised in this manner. One representative stated:

We have two mailing lists in my office, one a contributor list, the other a general mailing list. We have never used the general mailing list for funds because we never felt we were in a situation where that was necessary, but we get about a 50 percent response from the contributor list in requests for financial contributions. The letter will get about 25 percent and follow-up phone calls get another 25 to 30 percent.

Often contributors, in addition to receiving a letter of appreciation from the congressman, will be sent periodic reports of his activities and other materials not normally provided to most other district voters.

Importance of Timing of Contributions. Experienced politicians stress the importance of raising their campaign funds early in order to be able to make firm commitments for choice radio and television time and to plan their over-all campaign strategy more accurately. While contributions are gratefully received at any time—last minute contributions may be valuable in paying off accumulated bills and in reducing the personal expenditures of candidates—to be of maximum assistance, supporters should forward checks at an early stage of the campaign. One congressman spoke of a generous offer of assistance which, he lamented, came too late to be effective.

On election eve I had a final television debate with my opponent. I had hardly arrived home from the station, when I had a long distance call from a friend doing volunteer work in my campaign. A businessman, who had a visitor from New York staying at his home, had called him. The New Yorker had watched the debate and was so incensed with my opponent's tactics that he wanted to spend $2,500 on election day to purchase spot announcements in my behalf on all the radio stations in _____. Did I have objections? I said I had already spent all the money I could spend and was not going to authorize anyone to spend more for television, radio, or newspaper advertising. I had no objections, but I said I thought it was wasted money. If I had $2,500 I could put it to much better advantage on election day than buying spots. Our conversation ended that way, but I later heard that the man had phoned an advertising agency and authorized them to spend that much money. It was so late that he couldn't even buy that much time and was able to spend only about $1,200 or $1,300. If only I could have gotten together with him even a week before the election I could have used that money to much better advantage.

"There Is Never Enough Money." Concern about money is so central a problem in most election campaigns and so many congressmen are so vocal about the failure of interested individuals and groups to contribute adequately to the campaign effort that little thought is directed to the possibility that some candidates do not face a "money problem." At one Democratic discussion a midwesterner asked, "What can be said about the law of diminishing returns in election expenditures? Certainly that has never applied to any of us. Is there anyone here who feels he couldn't have spent considerably more than he has had available?" To his surprise several participants answered the question in the affirmative. Added one: "There are certain techniques that I have used which I won't use again because I don't think they were valuable. I think the money could have been saved."

In suggesting that research be undertaken on effective use of campaign funds, the President's Commission on Campaign Costs substantiates the view of congressmen who believe that there is a limit to the sum that can be used effectively. The 1962 commission report states: "Most politicians agree that half of campaign expenditures are wasted, but none knows which half. Less money would be spent on campaigns if the wasteful half could be identified."

One veteran campaigner who represents a "switch" district and has lost two congressional elections is among those who believe that money is less important than many of his colleagues assert:

I've never believed money is the factor some people think it is. Anyone who claims he was beaten because his opponent spent too much money is just looking for an excuse. You can run only so many radio spots, newspaper ads, and television spots, and use just so many billboards. When I hear of some of the fantastic sums which are said to have been spent in campaigns, I just don't know how they have been able to get rid of so much money in so short a time. I certainly don't believe they can use it effectively.

Yet, despite these views, which are shared by some colleagues, money is for many legislators the number one problem—funds for elections and extra funds for special projects such as newsletters and questionnaires throughout the term. One enterprising junior congressman has suggested cooperative action of a group of ideologically compatible colleagues:

I don't know what the answer is to the chief problem all of us have—money. When the congressional committee calls me after election and asks what help I need I always say, "Money—that is all I want from you people." I think some of us ought to consider combining forces and hiring a man at $25,000 a year to act as fund raiser for us. His sole function would be to raise funds which would be divided among whatever group decided to contribute to his salary. It seems to me that we have not given enough serious thought to this matter. We are all going off running our own show; it would be much more sensible for a group of us to sit down and say, "Look, we have a common problem here."

The Role of Official Party Organizations

Congressional recognition that perhaps the best way to woo many voters is by means of activities not directly related to the election campaign does not result in minimizing campaign efforts. Waging an effective campaign is, understandably, a major concern of congressmen, and they are constantly searching for new techniques. Many informal discussions are held with colleagues on the matter, and there is much adapting of undertakings which have been used successfully in other districts. Countless hours are spent reviewing campaign ads and literature, posters, automobile bumper stickers, and billboard suggestions in the search for effective materials; additional time is spent with layout artists and editorial assistants worrying about wording and position placement problems. Where an election is concerned, no task seems too small, no detail too insignificant to attract the attention and concern of some of the campaigners.

For some members campaigning is an ordeal; for others it is strenuous but enjoyable. A few even approach the contest with enthusiasm and relish. But whatever the attitude toward running for office, there is considerable congressional sentiment that members are required too often to "go it alone" in the endeavor.

The feeling is strong that local, state, and national party organizations are indifferent and/or ineffective in lending support. Said one Republican, "If we depended on the party organization to get elected, none of us would be here. Because the organization is not too helpful, it doesn't have very much influence with us." Except for the rare member who is the beneficiary of a strong city organization, the statement appears to reflect general House opinion. There are indications that in some areas congressional contests are becoming more fully integrated into state and local campaigns, but even there the effort is unlikely to be sufficient to alter congressional views appreciably. As one politically experienced Democrat observed philosophically:

I don't think there is any element of the party that is particularly interested in or concerned with the election of members of Congress. The National Committee is preoccupied with the White House. The state committee has its eyes on the state house and the county committee is interested only in the court house. The congressman is just sort of a fifth wheel on the whole wagon.

A colleague agreed:

That is the experience in my state, too—congressmen are just orphans. The past election was the first time in memory that congressional candidates had their names on state billboards of the party. It was also the first time we were mentioned in radio and television spot advertising done in behalf of the party—and that was an afterthought.

State and Local Organization. For the most part, state party organizations are relatively unimportant in the campaign plans of members of Congress, though it appears that the congressional races are receiving somewhat more attention than formerly from state chairmen and state central committees. In a few states, central finance committees are beginning to contribute funds to congressional campaigns, and, as noted, there are areas where the local organization is so strong that they select the congressional candidate and conduct and bear the expenses of the major part of the campaign effort.

But more often one hears congressmen maintain that not only is it unusual to receive financial assistance from local official party organizations, but, indeed, congressional candidates may be expected to contribute to the support of such groups. Representative of this situation are the following comments:

I was rather amused by the question about support from county and district organizations because we always contribute to the county organizations and help subsidize them in our district. In our state their activities are pretty well confined to getting out the vote on election day.

*

In my state the state committee asks for contributions from the candidates and the congressional candidate is expected to contribute approximately $300.

*

I have to subsidize my county organization. Our state had a $100 dinner in the last campaign and raised $700,000 in one evening, and I didn't get a penny of it. When I asked the national and congressional campaign committees for help, they said they were having trouble raising money, and if they could raise it, they couldn't send it to my state. "You raise $700,000 there in one evening," they said, "We don't even think about that kind of money down here." So I get nothing from the national, nothing from the state, and have to give some to each of my three county organizations.

On the other hand, there was some testimony of this kind: "As far as fund raising is concerned in my own district, the county committee had a fund raising subcommittee which does a large portion of the fund raising for the district."

Criticism that state and local groups do not concern themselves with congressional elections is widespread. A frequently expressed comment is that of a first term Republican:

There wasn't one congressional candidate in my section of our state who had even one inquiry from headquarters as to how we were doing in our campaign. Even _____, who was having the fight of his life, heard nothing from the state committee. Most of us felt we were operating in a complete vacuum as far as any liaison with the state campaign committee went.

In some areas the local group is hostile rather than indifferent. Said one Democrat, "My county committee is never any problem because it is so inactive it is difficult to find. When I have found it, it usually has opposed me." Added another Democrat from a section of the country where strong party organization is much more customary: "When I first ran for the House, our district leader favored my opponent. In order to be protected back home, I had to become district leader the next time around. Thus I have to double in brass. I am the congressman and the district leader." While examples of such hostility seem relatively rare, the different goals of incumbent congressmen and state and local party leaders tend to promote a working relationship which, though often pleasant, is loose and informal and perhaps a little distant. It is especially difficult for congressmen whose districts are geographically distant from Washington to maintain the close associations with local officials that promote full confidence.

A few states are organized on congressional district lines, but this is not common practice. As one representative indicates, this fact points up a problem that is likely to cause some degree of continuing difficulty:

> One reason we have to do so much ourselves is that most of us do not represent a natural political subdivision. Our districts may cut across city or county lines. Few states are organized along congressional district lines. To representatives of other political entities congressmen are boobs who think only of their district's political problems rather than local or state or over-all national problems. Before I came to Congress I was active in politics at the county and state committee level, and I couldn't understand why congressmen were so hard to get along with. But after being elected to Congress, I attended a state central committee meeting and I could see what was wrong. The party is not organized to be of maximum benefit to us, and we are forced to rely on our own organizations.

One reflection of the lack of interest on the part of state party leaders in things congressional is the fact that they seldom seek to exert influence on House members, especially with respect to legislation. In the experience of one House leader: "Our national committeeman and the state chairman have called me occasionally about something, but I suspect they were calling because the White House had asked them to do so. They have never been too effective because they didn't know too much about the subject of their call."

The National Party Organizations. Although it is suggested occasionally that the national and congressional campaign committees of both parties should exert a more positive role in the selection of congressional candidates, few congressmen regard such a proposal as feasible or realistic. Even where genuine concern is expressed regarding the ability of local party groups to designate high calibre candidates, hope for improvement is directed toward the state rather than the national party leaders. The legislators are sensitive to local pride and prejudice and are convinced that national intervention would be resented. As one member of Congress said: "These committees just can't be more active in seeking candidates for congressional seats. Even though they might do a better job than some of the people at the local level, they are in no position to do it. You know the old saying—he's an SOB, but he's our SOB." Nor does one solon who headed his state party organization for a time believe it generally desirable to draft candidates. Says he:

> Unless the candidate is sufficiently interested to seek the job himself, it may not

work out well. I am inclined to feel some of the people who are drafted are not particularly interested or effective. Local pressure on potential candidates is to be preferred to national pressure, but the best procedure is to have good candidates seek office on their own initiative.

While reluctant for the national party to participate directly in the selection of congressional candidates, many congressmen believe the national groups have a positive obligation to provide direct assistance in the form of money, materials, and practical advice once the candidate has been chosen. An obligation exists too, it is felt, to stimulate interest in the contest and to arouse and maintain local enthusiasm for the candidate and the importance of the race. As one member stated:

> I think the national and congressional campaign committees can and should perform valuable services in a congressional race. They shouldn't attempt to select the candidate, but once he is selected, they can give a great deal of assistance from an organizational point of view and can also provide tips with regard to publicity. You have to go slowly in terms of interfering in the local district. We may all worship the same God, but we want to do it in our own way.

Another legislator believes it is the function of the national and congressional committees to develop an organization "to get at the grass roots and provide for the screening of candidates. Of course they can't select candidates for local areas, but they could help set up machinery and in other ways make it more likely better candidates would be forthcoming." Evidence is slight that, at the House level, national party groups do much more. Occasionally, one hears that overtures are made to attractive prospective candidates, but for the most part reliance seems to be placed on attempting to impress local organizations with the necessity of obtaining high quality nominees.

The national committee is relied upon by very few members of Congress for contributions—financial, informational, or services. Contacts between the individual legislator and the national committee are infrequent and, regardless of which party acts as initiator, tend to consist of requests for assistance of some sort. Republicans tend to be somewhat more critical of their national committee than Democrats, but little enthusiasm is evident anywhere in Congress for the top party committee.

Republicans have the benefit of a well-developed congressional campaign committee created specifically to meet their needs and focused directly on ensuring as large a Republican congressional representation as possible. Since in the absence of a strong congressional committee, these functions would be performed by the national committee, their transfer to the congressional scene deprives the parent body of an important means of strengthening its relationship with congressmen. Democratic legislators, lacking a congressional service organization of the magnitude of their Republican counterparts—marked differences exist in budget, staffing, and activities—are somewhat more dependent on their national committee. Though they are not happy with the services they receive from party headquarters or the attention they believe is given there to problems at the congressional level, they are more likely to be critical of the inadequacies of their congressional committee, which many contrast unfavorably with the Republican committee.

The Republican tendency to downgrade their national committee is no doubt influenced in part by the natural rivalry and antagonism which exists between the congressional committee, whose services to them are many and tangible, and the national committee itself. What is often forgotten, however, is that the congressional campaign committee is almost entirely dependent for operating funds on the national committee. Campaign committee personnel criticize the national committee for failing to provide them with sufficient funds to do an effective job,[3] and since the congressional committee budget determines in part how helpful the committee can be to individual legislators, it is not difficult to convince congressmen of the correctness of this position. This somewhat uneasy relationship increases the reluctance of national committee officials and staff to approach congressmen directly since such action might be regarded as an attempt to usurp congressional committee prerogatives. Thus, the natural affinity of the legislator for his benefactor, the congressional committee, is increased by the aloofness of the national committee, which creates an impression of lack of interest.

Both national committees are negligent about providing legislators with information regarding their activities as well as the nature of their potential services. Thus, one Republican, the only member of his party holding a statewide office in his state, was irate when the Republican national chairman entered the state on a speaking tour without informing the con-

---

[3] In 1962 the National Committee made this distribution of its receipts: national committee 56 percent; senatorial committee 11 percent; congressional committee 33 percent. In 1963, its $2,980,000 budget included $850,000 for the congressional committee and $200,000 for the senatorial committee.

gressman that such a trip was contemplated. To politicians, alert to the political implications of such a visit and the prestige factors attached to participating in the arrangements, negligence of that kind is unpardonable.

One legislator who has also seen extended service as a national committee member discussed the uneasy situation existing between Republican congressmen and their national committee:

As a member of Congress and at the same time a member of the Republican National Committee I've been a little disturbed about the tensions and frictions which exist between the National Committee and the Congress. I think much of it is unnecessary, although some of it is understandable when you consider the personalities involved at both levels. The National Committee has not done an adequate job of publicizing the services they can perform for members of Congress. As a result many congressmen think they do nothing over there. I think each group unnecessarily antagonizes the other. It just never crosses people's minds to use the National Committee for many things. They have a fine research division, and there are any number of ways they could help.

At that point, another legislator commented, "They don't take the trouble to tell us what they can do for us." To that statement, the lawmaker with service in both bodies replied:

I have suggested that to them. Someone from the National Committee should come up at the beginning of the session and call on all congressmen, establish a relationship, and tell them what the committee has to offer, and of its interest. Also, the Congressional and Senatorial Campaign Committees are saying, "We are the boys who do things for you and they won't give us enough money." It is the National Committee which raises the money for the national party. The Congressional Committee couldn't perform any services if the National Committee didn't get the money and make it available.

But running through discussions of the National Committee were comments such as these: "What I would like to know is what they do. Does anyone get any benefit from them in his district?" "We are all agreed the National Committee should be abolished, aren't we?" "It does more harm than good."

To criticism that the National Committee should be doing far more for the party, one defender responded:

Their activity depends on how much money is available. If they had the money they would expand their services. If they don't raise enough, then they have to telescope down and do the best they can with what they have. They have done a pretty good job of keeping the party alive, of sending out materials and information. They ought to get 'E' for effort.

Though legislators are agreed that the National Committee performs important and necessary functions during presidential campaigns, some think they should maintain only skeleton staffs between those contests as the following discussion points up:

The two Congressional Committees have not been operating very long. When you get three committees you will have a certain amount of rivalry.

*

There ought to be very close liaison among the three groups. Other than that, the National Committee ought to become almost dormant between presidential elections.

*

They are!

*

They sure spend a lot of money for a dormant organization!

A knowledgeable Democrat, in summarizing the major differences between the Democratic Congressional Campaign Committee and the Democratic National Committee, makes an important point about the nature of prepared materials distributed by such groups, which is often missed by congressmen and their staffs: no matter how high the quality of materials emanating from the committees, to be most useful to a congressman they should be adapted to the local situation. Some releases, speeches, fact books, or suggested advertising, can be used with little or no change; others are valuable primarily in suggesting ideas or possible approaches. Said the congressman:

The services of the National Committee are greater [than those of the Congressional Committee]. They are more likely to send you research material and information sheets. They have a larger staff than the Congressional Committee and are in a much better position to help, but they must necessarily prepare things of a general nature. Then the material has to be adapted if it is to be used effectively in an individual district. The committee is doing a fair job in an important situation. It sends you a great deal of stuff you cannot use, but on the positive side it does give you ideas.

In contrasting the two Democratic committees another congressman said:

The National Committee has been helpful, at least in my kind of district, in coming up with useful research material. The fact books they publish, and other material of that nature, contain much good ammunition. The Congressional Campaign Committee has come up with a moderate amount of money for me every time I've run. It has been my impression that there is more sound and fury coming out of that Congressional Campaign Committee than valuable material.

On the other hand, one influential congressman dryly described his relationship with the Democratic National Committee: "The national party organization has never provided any services to me. It has never provided any funds for me. After I get nominated each time, however, it does send me a telegram of congratulations which I am very happy to have."

There is evidence that at least occasionally the committee is lax in meeting its commitments about money. Said one legislator:

When I came to Congress—even before—I went to the National Committee and offered to be of assistance to the Democratic party. During a recent presidential campaign, they sent me out to make 26 speeches in five or six states, in the course of which I expended $680. After the campaign I decided it was reasonable to ask the committee to reimburse me for these expenses since it had insisted in the beginning that I would be reimbursed. I sent in my statement and said, "I am $680 in arrears," and they replied, "Well, what about it? We are $1,500,000 in arrears." Finally, after I raised a row I received a reply from an employee of the committee saying, "Congressman, don't you know that you should have collected your expenses from each place that you spoke?" Now, that was ridiculous. In the final days of the campaign I spoke in as many as five or six places some days. Usually I knew no one in the community.

There is general recognition that the chairman of the National Committee serves an important and necessary function in acting as a party spokesman and in offsetting and countering the claims of the opposition. Individual members of the National Committee are sometimes singled out for special praise also. Said one congresswoman: "In our state we have a national committeewoman who is a catalytic influence throughout the whole state. I couldn't get along without her during the period between elections. She solves every problem. We never could have accomplished what we did in our state without that kind of personality." Another House member attributes increased interest within the state organization in the fate of congressional candidates to the activities of his national committeeman:

In my state we decided to bring life into the party by getting a new national committeeman. He makes special trips down here with the state chairman and vice chairman and committeewoman and we have conferences. It has been very, very helpful. The relationship has been so good that the state organization has set up a special committee to help congressmen, financially and otherwise. This last campaign is the first time we had any real help from them.

But such testimonials are relatively rare. Members of Congress tend to be negative or, at best, neutral when speaking of their National Committee.

Criticism may rest partly on congressional belief that the more national orientation of the National Committee and the national party are not always especially consistent with the more parochial interests of the individual congressman and his district. In 1959 the chairman of the Republican Congressional Committee underscored this point by openly advising Republican congressmen to disassociate themselves from those policies of the Republican President with which they disagreed. He emphasized they were running in their own districts on their own platforms, and he made it clear that his committee would not discriminate in any way against congressmen with antiadministration records. His statement served to explain the legislators' preference for their own congressional committee as opposed to the national committee.

At the same time that one notes congressional grumbling that neither the National Committee nor the Congressional Committee helps sufficiently in the campaign itself, it should be pointed out that many congressmen really do not want committee representatives in their districts. They want money, but they do not care about advice. The following discussion touches on this point:

I didn't get any help from the National Committee, nor did I get much from the Congressional Committee. They had a coordinator for several states, but he didn't do much for me, and they sent me less money than ever before—practically none, in fact. You can understand that in a presidential year, but last year with no president to elect, all the focus was on the congressional race. Here is _____ with what he means to the party, in a very close race. Why wouldn't they be in there working like mad?

*

Did you call on the committees for help? Maybe they figured if you needed any help you would let them know.

*

Frankly I wouldn't want the Congressional Committee or the National Committee playing around in my district. They could not influence any voters in my favor. [This statement by a congressman in a district where the opposition party has a heavy majority.]

*

They have been thrown out of so many districts they don't go in unless there is some indication they are wanted.

House and Senate campaign committees are maintained by both parties. Only the House committees are referred to here. Both the Democratic National Congressional Committee and the National Republican Congressional Committee are located in close proximity to the congressmen they serve—the Democratic committee is housed in two rooms on the first floor of the Cannon House Office Building, and the Republicans occupy parts of two floors in the Congressional Hotel, which is located just across the street from the Cannon and Longworth buildings. This proximity contrasts favorably with the Democratic and Republican national committee offices, both of which are located in downtown Washington.

Each committee includes one representative from each state in which the party is represented in the House. In 1963, there are forty-one members of the Democratic National Congressional Committee plus three ex officio members and thirty-eight members of the National Republican Congressional Committee, including the chairman. The Democratic group is organized with a chairman, three vice chairmen, and a secretary, the other members being divided into four committees—executive, finance, research, and speakers. The Republicans have a chairman, six vice chairmen, a secretary, treasurer, an auditing committee, and an executive committee.

Actually, the power of the chairman is commanding in both instances. He, along with the top staff people, makes not only the day-to-day decisions but most of the policy decisions also. Both committees are large, unwieldy bodies that seldom meet. When they do meet, the sessions are largely perfunctory. Since the primary concern of most congressmen is re-election, some who serve on the campaign committees are occasionally puzzled and disturbed by the fact that little attention is given to getting their committees together for discussions of how best to grapple with the problem of making the group a more effective instrument of assistance to members of Congress. Although there is little evidence of widespread House dissatisfaction with the way the committees function, it is generally recognized that membership carries with it little power and few responsibilities. Comments of two members of the Republican committee will serve to illustrate the feelings of some participants and indicate a few of the problems involved in making such a committee a more active body:

> The committee is not as active as it should be. We don't have any meetings. I'd say one man has too much power, and there is no real effort to activate the group. It is not organized properly either.[4]

*

> I am on the executive committee. We meet occasionally but not regularly, and most of our meetings are about finances. By the nature of the situation it is a one man show, with the staff assisting. I'm afraid that situation cannot be corrected. Occasionally someone has a hot idea of something that should be done, but things move slowly, and pretty soon his congressional office requires his attention, and he forgets about pushing his idea any further.

Reorganization of the committee has led to a decline in criticism that it is a one-man operation. But even when the feeling prevailed that committee members did not sit down together in any serious discussion of methods and goals, Republicans were not very critical of the activities carried on by the committee itself. Some of the services provided, it is true, were not useful to individual members and were characterized as a waste of money, but others were regarded as beneficial. A Republican discussion touches on committee activities:

> The Congressional Campaign Committee does make available to us time for radio and television broadcasts and is willing to foot the bill up to a certain maximum each year. That has been genuinely helpful to me in my own area and also to many others from my state.

*

> The art department does a beautiful job of designing literature for you and suggesting effective displays. If you want flip charts they will prepare them. They will provide you with mats to send to newspapers, too. You can get twenty or more if you need them, and that helps tremendously in getting good coverage in the weeklies.

*

[4] Since the discussion, the chairmanship has changed hands. There is less criticism on this score now. The present chairman has encouraged, with some success, committee members to participate. Although few meetings of the full committee are held, the executive committee meets regularly.

The photographer will come to your office or meet you somewhere on very short notice and take a picture of you with a high school group, for example. They prepare postcards of the scene and provide you with a number sufficient to give several to each kid before he goes home. The school children mail them back to all their relatives.

*

The speech kit they put out is very good and has been very helpful to me.

The Republican organization, because of its size, is more departmentalized than its Democratic counterpart. An executive secretary is in charge of administration and handles matters relating to finance. Three main divisions have been established—field, public relations, and services.

Field staff personnel are assigned to specific regions where they work closely with state and local political leaders, providing information, materials, and know-how to assist in building party organization. The field director's office also makes available considerable voting information about each congressional district, including a precinct-by-precinct breakdown of the major party vote for President, senator, and congressional contests over a period of several years.

The publicity division has on its staff former newspapermen, radio and television personnel, and speech and research writers. Services of this division include the following, according to a release of the Republican Congressional Committee:

Press Relations—provides general advice and counsel on matters relating to newspaper and magazine publicity; prepares press releases and other publicity material on request; provides advice on the mechanics of wire service operations, newspaper deadlines, timing of stories, and similar matters; works with congressmen and staff on developing full news potential for such congressional activities as office mail, the member's committee work, floor speeches, record votes, etc.

Radio-Television—provides assistance in the writing and producing of radio and television programs for stations in the district, prepares and distributes each week a five minute script dealing with a subject current in news; provides five minute TV films of topical interest for use on congressman's regular program or as a separate show; produces campaign films on a wide variety of subjects; provides radio and television spots for use during campaign; has available for use a screening room and a film library from which prints may be ordered at cost for showing before groups in the district; has available a cameraman to film news clips in which the congressman is featured and to work in developing programs tailored to individual needs.

Speech-Research—prepares and distributes each week newsletter material which may be of assistance in preparation of congressman's newsletter; prepares speech material for use on special occasions, such as Lincoln's birthday and others; prepares an Easter recess speech kit and a campaign kit containing speeches on a wide range of subjects; provides research assistance on special projects, including the gathering, assembling, or preparation of material on any specific subject.

The campaign division includes experienced staff artists, layout men, printers, and photographers to work with members of Congress on their campaign service needs. Briefly, it includes the following services:

Art—provides art work for newsletters, campaign literature, and television programs; works with congressional office in developing the best type of promotional material for use in the campaign; is of assistance in dealing with printers and suppliers to obtain low bulk rates for campaign and other type materials; and provides general advice and counsel on any problems requiring the services of an artist.

Photo—provides a complete photo service which speedily makes and processes for daily newspapers in the congressman's home district, pictures in which he is featured; prepares mats at cost for use in the weekly newspapers; provides in quantity group-picture photo postcards of the member with his constituents ready to mail; provides a news service of color pictures to be used for hand cards and postcards; and offers general advice and counsel on photographic needs.

Printing and Reproduction—provides general advice and assistance on campaign printing and reproduction problems; and works with member on printing and reproduction needs as they arise.

The Republican Congressional Committee provides each Republican House member with an account against which he can draw for expenses connected with any of the foregoing activities. The sum varies from year to year depending on the financial resources of the committee, but in 1962 each congressman received $1,000 for this purpose as opposed to $1,500 in 1960.

The Democratic Congressional Committee has no money available for such purposes nor does it seek to duplicate the services offered throughout the session by the Republican committee. The present director of the Democratic committee, who succeeded his father in the position, shares his predecessor's view that it is not the function of such an organization to provide the "mass production" services provided by the Republicans. Though undoubtedly there are services he would like to be able to add to those presently available to Democratic congressmen, he prefers a smaller, more individual-oriented operation than that of the Republicans. During the campaign period there is little comparison between the volume of materials received by Republicans and Democrats from their respective organizations. The Democrats stress "ready-made" items such as reports of congressional committees on important public problems and the summaries of achievements of various legislative committees.

It has been suggested that the greater magnitude of Republican activity is dictated not only by its greater financial resources but also by the fact that the Republican party, because of its minority status in the country, needs to work harder to get votes for congressional candidates.

One valuable service provided by both the Democratic and Republican campaign committees is to furnish their party's nominees with the voting records of opponents if the latter are incumbent congressmen or have ever served in the Congress. On occasion, they have even been known to furnish information about teller (nonrecorded) votes. But the committees never supply voting records of members of their own party to anyone without the specific permission of the member concerned. Thus a candidate against an incumbent in the primary is denied the information by his party—though it is possible, of course, that in some circumstances the opposition party might be willing to provide it. One Democratic congressman told of his experience with the Democratic committee when he sought to oust an incumbent:

I agree that the best thing the congressional committee does is provide information. If your opponent is a congressman, you can get his voting record so that you can be better informed and attack him. But I had the unique experience of having to oust a Democrat who voted like a Republican and was in league with them. As a matter of fact, when I beat him in the Democratic primary, he had won the Republican nomination. Until I defeated him in the primary, I couldn't get any information regarding his voting record from the Democratic committee. But once I had won the primary, and was preparing to face him in a general election, I was able to get all the information I wanted.

During the campaign period itself, both the Democratic and Republican committees distribute funds to the party's congressional candidates, the extent of the aid being determined by the funds available and an estimate of the chances for victory of the party's candidate in the congressional district. The marginal districts, in which the outcome is in doubt, customarily get the most attention and the most funds. When possible, all party candidates receive some token assistance. Normally, a higher percentage of Republicans get such support than Democrats.

There is little feeling that favoritism or party loyalty is involved in determining the allocation. Congressmen seem unaware that some candidates from marginal districts get substantially more assistance than other candidates from marginal districts. The criticism is solely that the committees have so little money to dispense. It should be noted that within recent years the congressional committees, unhappy with the funds made available to them by the National Committee, have sought relief by sponsoring their own fund raising dinners.

A discussion between two Democrats, one of whom has served as a liaison between the Democratic National Committee and the party's congressional committee, reflects the views of many colleagues:

> The Congressional Campaign Committee is supposed to be sustained by the national committee and is supposed to be under wraps with respect to fund raising with the understanding that the national committee will finance its activities. The budget problem has been serious in both organizations. The money that has been sent out by the campaign committee to Democratic congressional candidates has been limited to peanuts simply because the money hasn't been there.

*

> I agree but I have seen no signs of any intelligent, intensive effort by the Congressional Campaign Committee to raise funds on a year round basis, at least in my three campaigns.

*

> At the root of that situation is the understanding that the Congressional Campaign Committee will limit its funds to what it gets from the National Committee and support National Committee efforts to raise money. There are some ethics involved in that. If the National Committee efforts were as successful as they should be, there would be substantial allocations to the Congressional Campaign Committee, which would be helpful to a lot of people.[5]

Volunteers and Personal Committees

In some areas, where the formal organization is not strong or has not been as helpful to the congressman as he feels it should be, legislators have developed rather effective personal organizations. These groups

---

[5] The first Democratic Congressional Campaign Committee dinner was held subsequent to this conversation, though the Republican committee had already sponsored such an affair. In 1961 Democrats adopted the Republican practice of merging financial operations of the national and congressional committees.

may function with a minimum of coordination and consultation with the official organization, or they may work with them harmoniously, adding important dimensions to the necessarily limited activities which the party conducts in behalf of its congressional candidate. The bulk of the volunteers and draftees are not sophisticated politically, but enthusiasm and a willingness to perform the everyday chores compensate, in part at least, for the lack of political acumen. Often, however, they include some remarkably skillful people. This type of organization shares with others problems of attrition, and faces too frequently the problem of what to do with the well-meaning but ineffective volunteer. On balance, however, congressmen find these amateur groups a source of tremendous assistance, without which the campaign effort would be greatly reduced. To many congressmen they are indispensable. Said one:

> Our sense of warm appreciation for the many good citizens who can't possibly get anything back from us for what they have done, except hope we will give them the best government of which we are capable is a note that we probably don't vocalize on very much. But at the end of each campaign, win or lose, I am sure we all have a tremendously warm feeling toward all the people in our own areas who have involved themselves so intimately in shaping our lives.

In one southern state where traditionally state and local party organization has been notoriously weak, the clusters of groups which gather around the congressional nominee are achieving significance. As the state has moved toward a two party system, the weak official organizations have sought to rally party standards around the more powerful independent structures. Reported one congressman, "Our state committee has found that by working through the congressman they can help build up their county organizations. Our organization gives us leverage, and we are beginning to get money and cooperation from the state group. They are finding we can help them in providing key people and getting good people interested in party organization and help build a party unit through our individual organizations."

Nonparty Groups

The role of nonparty groups in congressional elections is often substantial. Organizations such as the League of Women Voters do not endorse candidates or contribute financially to campaigns except as their membership may do so in an individual way. But by sponsoring nonpartisan forums for a discussion of the issues, they may be said to exercise some degree of influence.

Far more important—to congressional candidates at least—are the organizations that provide campaign funds and workers and endorse or "rate" candidates on the basis of their voting records. Some of these are well-established, continuing organizations. Others are temporary groups that are dissolved once an election is over, perhaps to be re-created when the next election approaches. The names of some groups provide no information as to the identity of their backers or the purpose for which contributions are made.[6] Of all the groups that regularly participate in election campaigns, those associated with labor are the best known and the most controversial.

Labor Groups. As noted earlier, friend and foe alike single out labor's activity for special comment. A sizable corps of election day workers are made available to candidates or, more likely, to a political party, the expenses being absorbed by labor itself. Even more significant, substantial sums of money are expended in direct contributions to candidates whom labor desires to encourage. These two concrete forms of assistance are those most appreciated by individuals who, confronted with limited budgets and manpower problems, are engaged in close contests.

Another activity in which labor is prominent is that designed to inform the laboring man and, indeed, all voters regarding the voting records of incumbent members of Congress. While various labor organizations participate in politics in one way or another, the best publicized is COPE, the AFL-CIO Committee on Political Education. As an "educational" endeavor, COPE distributes widely (about 10,000,000 copies in 1962) the voting records of congressmen on a selected number of issues, a black-

---

[6] Thus the *Congressional Quarterly* found that in 1962 a Committee on American Leadership was closely connected with the coal industry; the Committee for Economic Growth was established by restaurant owners to aid members of Congress who supported their position on the 1962 tax bill; the Nonpartisan Committee for National Betterment was identified with the lumber industry; and all contributions to "James H. Lum, a political committee for the November 6, 1962 elections," were executives of Monsanto Chemical Company. *Congressional Quarterly* Special Report, July 26, 1963, p. 1193.

faced "R" or a red-faced "W" indicating whether a representative voted "right" or "wrong" by COPE's standard of what action would be in the best interests of the great majority of Americans. Funds for this activity are provided by the AFL-CIO and member unions, and the voting records are forwarded to the unions to be given to their members. COPE also contributes to congressional campaigns, as do many other labor unions.

Some labor organizations, rather than use COPE's voting records, prepare their own computations for distribution to their members. The United Mine Workers of America includes in its newspaper votes marked "right" or "wrong" for those congressmen representing districts in which UMW workers are located. Endorsements are also published. The International Brotherhood of Teamsters and the International Association of Machinists (AFL-CIO) also furnish their membership with votes of the members of Congress on issues of special interest to the unions. The Teamsters Union has endorsed candidates and has sought to "purge" others.

In August 1959, five days after the Landrum-Griffin labor bill passed the House of Representatives, despite the opposition of labor, the President of the International Union of Electrical, Radio, and Machine Workers (AFL-CIO) wrote each congressman who had supported the legislation to assure him that "we shall do all in our power to prove to the working men and women in your district that you have cast your lot against them and that they should therefore take appropriate action at the ballot box." This letter, which was strongly worded, was regarded as a blessing by some congressmen. One of the most liberal southern Democrats explained in an interview that labor's support sometimes proved embarrassing in his district; it was helpful to have them criticize him. Said he:

Recently someone back home published the voting records of our delegation as set forth by COPE. There were headlines that I had voted 80 percent pro-labor whereas other congressmen from my state had very low support scores. Since I have few union people in my district this publicity will probably hurt me. The letter from James Carey, President of the Electrical, Radio, and Machine Workers, to those of us who supported the Landrum-Griffin bill on final passage will prove helpful to me because it indicates that labor will be out to get all of us. What it really does is give me ammunition to show I am not beholden to labor and that labor doesn't think I'm as great a guy as some of my opponents would like to make it appear.

Though on both sides of the aisle one hears that labor is often less subtle than other lobbying groups in advancing its cause, there is no doubt that its ability to deliver both money and campaign workers causes it to be both feared and respected as a force in elections. "It's just that sometimes they are not so smart in the way they operate," said one Democrat. "Sometimes they hurt people who are in general sympathy with them and that isn't very wise. It is a question of judgment."

On the other hand, one Republican who has never enjoyed labor support, while criticizing what he considered to be the "slant" of the voting records distributed by COPE, regarded that organization's attempt to focus the campaign on issues as both commendatory and effective. "I think most of us run into the ADA and CIO voting records. I am happy they have used that technique because even though they slant it and present phony issues at least they are directing their drive toward the issues."

Other Groups. As the Republican suggested, Americans for Democratic Action also distributes to its membership congressional voting records. Votes on selected measures are designated by plus or minus depending on correlation with the ADA position. This "guide for liberals" is careful to point out that voting records are incomplete in that they do not reflect a congressman's effectiveness in committee or his creativity. ADA also makes campaign contributions.

While the COPE and ADA voting records are the most publicized, farm organizations also prepare similar materials based on the measures they judge to be important. The American Farm Bureau Federation selects issues on which its members have taken a stand through voting at their county, state, and national meetings. The vote of each member of Congress on this is set forth in the organization's magazine as "yea" or "nay," votes favorable to the bureau's position being placed in bold-face capital letters; those unfavorable being listed in light-face lower case letters. The Farmer's Union, the more liberal of the two organizations, uses "plus" and "minus" or "X" or "0" to indicate approval or disapproval of members' stands on selected votes.

Other groups that are prominent in this kind of activity include Americans for Constitutional Action, a conservative group which publishes a "plus" and "minus" chart for congressmen, dividing issues into special categories (i.e., for individual liberty and against coercion; for economy and conservation and against waste) and also includes a "consistency index," which indicates the percentage of the time a congressman voted "FOR safeguarding the God-given right of the individual through strengthening constitutional government; AGAINST group morality, a socialized economy, and centralization of government power." At the end of each campaign, ACA presents distinguished service awards to members whose voting records indicate that they are in sympathy with the organization's principles. ACA endorses candidates and provides field assistance. In 1962, eighteen field representatives operated in sixteen states helping to organize campaigns, raise funds, and write speeches.

There are countless other groups that provide assistance or information. Among them are the American Medical Political Action Committee, which distributes campaign funds, and the Civic Affairs Association, which distributes voting record information to business firms and trade associations on legislation affecting business.

Another group, the National Committee for an Effective Congress, which seeks to aid in the election of liberals to Congress, does not publish voting records but does endorse candidates and contributes to campaigns, generally supporting liberal Democrats. The National Association for the Advancement of Colored People publishes in its magazine voting records of all members of Congress on key civil rights issues, marked plus or minus according to the NAACP position. A National Committee for a Representative Congress, formed in late 1959, also endorses candidates, not, it says, on the basis of political philosophy but on individual records, aiding members "who have clearly proven their courage and public usefulness."

A New Development. There has long been agitation within the ranks of business for a major organization that could counteract the influence of labor and liberal groups in elections. As an outgrowth of this sentiment, the Business-Industry Political Action Committee (BIPAC) was organized in 1963 as a political action arm for business. It is bipartisan in nature, intends to restrict its efforts to congressional races, and will provide financial aid for candidates who will support "sound fiscal policies and who uphold the free, private, and competitive system." It also plans to encourage citizens to be more active and effective in the political party of their choice.

Image versus Issues

Studies of voting behavior seem to substantiate the view that voters cast ballots without very much interest in, or factual knowledge of, the issues or a candidate's stand on them. Can one then assert that the "image" the voter has of the contestants, particularly of incumbents, is more important than the issues in determining congressional elections? Such would seem to be the view of a large majority of the members of Congress. There is little doubt that this view conditions the ways in which a congressman goes about his job and conducts his campaigns for re-election.

Interest in Issues. There is much thought among congressmen that voters possess little factual information on which to base electoral decisions. Nor do they believe there is much evidence of a desire to seek it. "Every once in awhile you get shocked by the lack of information people have about political events and candidates," said one congressman, "and you realize this is not the way they make up their minds." "It's appalling to realize how little people know about Congress and about issues," agreed a colleague. The legislators are distressed to find that voters don't know which party controls Congress, or even who their congressmen are. There is complaint, for example, that even those constituents who take the positive step of writing their representative sometimes are mistaken as to his identity. One congressman, disturbed by the state of public knowledge, exclaimed, "There are too many people in the United States who don't give a damn about government, and it is time we were concerned about it." Colleagues would tell him they have long been concerned about it. In view of the constant barrage of the electorate by congressional offices by means of television and radio programs, newsletters, questionnaires, and press releases, some members find the situation particularly distressing.

One result has been to focus congressional attention on the need to present the voter with a favorable picture of the person who represents him, without seeking to educate him extensively on the issues or to give him a beginner's course in American government. A representative expressed the situation succinctly:

The people back home don't know what's going on. Issues are not most important so far as the average voter is concerned. The image of the candidate plays a much greater role. If voters feel the candidate is conscientious and is trying hard to serve them, then that man has a good chance of coming back. Some people in marginal districts are able to hang on just because the public has this view of them.

One conservative and respected Republican congressman who firmly agrees that voters weigh a candidate's personality and image more heavily than his position on the issues thinks this fact explains, in part, his party's minority position in Congress. Said he:[7]

Personality is so important that it outweighs the issues in people's minds, and they tend to vote for candidates who have attractive personalities. I think that fact is one reason the Republicans in Congress are not as highly regarded as they might be. We have a lot of dead timber in our party here. We need more attractive and aggressive candidates. I would say this is really the problem the Republican party faces, at least so far as Congress is concerned. We lost some of the worst deadwood in the last election, but there are plenty of elder statesmen left who should step aside this time. They are not helping the party at all by staying here. We just have to do something about bringing a more active, aggressive, younger, intelligent type into the Congress.

There are people in the Congress who are so convinced that the image is what counts that they think there are no restrictions on how they can vote and still retain the favor of the voters. Said one able and ambitious representative of that group:

Too many politicians, whether they are in state legislatures or in Congress, run away from a vote because they are afraid of the consequences when they get back to the hustings. I don't think votes mean a thing. It is the image the politician creates in his district. In my district they think I am a fighter. I can do anything I want down here and they will say, "He is the greatest fighter we ever had down there." No one pays attention to the votes.

While no member of Congress with whom the matter was discussed took the position that issues were more important than image in determining election results, a substantial proportion cautioned that issues were important, too, and that, in unusual circumstances, they could even be decisive. Comments such as the following reflect that opinion:

[7] In 1959. There have been many changes on the Republican side since then which have made the observation less valid. At the opening of Congress in 1963, 83 of the 176 House Republicans had been elected within the previous four years.

The personality of the individual is extremely important but, particularly in marginal economic areas, issues are very important, too.

*

Issues are quite important. Of course economic conditions create the climate in which they are significant. At the same time I'd point out that the personality factor is at least as important as anything. Voters have to like you if they are going to vote for you and they form these opinions quickly. The feeling they get about you determines how far they will go along with you.

It was clear that the members canvassed do not think elections involve a full debate of the issues. This they usually attribute to lack of voter interest in such matters, or to the reluctance or refusal of the opponent to wage such a campaign. There was only one enthusiastic testimonial about a contest in which the rivals fought it out on the basis of their stand on the important problems of the day. Related one congressman:

In 1956, I had a very sharp lawyer for an opponent. We appeared together 18 or 20 times and he took out after my voting record. He even rapped me with a teller vote! In that session of Congress, his party had people watching folks they thought were in marginal districts, and they did everything they could to give him ammunition. He did a really good job. I doubled my majority, but for the first time people were really interested in issues, because that is what we were talking about.

Far more typical experiences were the following:

The only issue in my campaign was "clean up the corruption in Washington." I voted against citing that man Goldfine for contempt and my opponent followed me around saying, "Why did he do it?" Needless to say he didn't wait for an answer. There was no issue of substance involved in the campaign.

*

In my campaign last year I had ten or twelve joint appearances with my opponent and in not a one of them did he criticize a vote I cast. Most of the time he talked about state issues. And the people didn't seem to know which was the state issue and which was the federal issue.

One reason for the reluctance of some challengers to seek a full-scale debate on issues may be revealed in the testimony of one congressman who entered the House after extensive and distinguished service in his state legislature. Explained the freshman:

I had a very able opponent, a college professor who chased me around a good bit. He wanted to debate foreign policy. I will be very frank; at that time I knew nothing about foreign policy. My career had been geared to the state legislature. I wasn't about to debate him on that issue because he was well versed. During the campaign I prepared myself, and about a week before election I said I would debate him. Had I debated him about eight weeks earlier he would have led me all around the district debating this issue and I couldn't have gotten to the public to present my program. I campaigned strictly on my record in the state legislature. I ignored my opponent completely and that about killed him.

Sometimes, it is true, the personal desire of a candidate to conduct his campaign on the issues may have to be subordinated to the strategy developed by those entrusted with responsibility for the campaign. One forthright congressman who normally functions as his own campaign manager and who is unusually issue-oriented had some regrets about delegating the task to others in a recent election:

I was much disappointed in my last campaign. I have always run my own campaigns before, but this last time I had no enthusiasm for the race and said I would run but that others would have to do the work I had done before. I know now what my services must have been worth because they hired professionals to do everything, and they sold a cake of soap rather than a candidate. I tried to talk issues, but with all that stuff on billboards and so much literature around, it was clear they weren't thinking in terms of issues or discussing them.

When two legislators who have been returned to Congress several times despite the fact that registration in their districts is heavily in favor of the other political party were asked how they continued to survive in the face of such odds, their responses differed in emphasis. Both statements, however, pointed up the importance in their ultimate success of qualities of independence and concern for the district:

Basically I think my success is due to the fact I'm not afraid to take a position on matters about which I feel strongly. I'm frank and open, and I think the people of my district and my associates here like that approach. The real problem, of course, is to get enough people to know you are that way and to appreciate those qualities.

*

I try to keep my people informed as to my actions and try to be conscientious in carrying out my responsibilities to them. In voting on legislation, the interests of the country and the congressional district come before the interests of my party. I think people have come to realize that and to respect it. The other party has a registration edge of more than 60,000 in my district, and they know I am not a rubber stamp for my own party.

One well expressed and representative cross section of congressional opinion on the issues-image controversy was that made by a freshman legislator:

> To a portion of the public, issues are far more important than the personality of the candidate. In some circumstances it may well be that a certain issue is over-riding. But the fact is that everything is important. People vote for you for an infinite variety of reasons. No one action you take will make or break you, but too many wrong actions are likely to prove costly. What I am saying is that you can be independent to a point, but if you continually vote against what you are expected to vote for, you will have a lot of trouble staying here. But important as issues are, they are not more important than the character and image of the candidate.

Effect on a Congressman's Vote. If it is true, as many members of Congress believe, that the image the voters possess of their legislator is primarily what determines his fate at the polls, what are the implications for congressional voting on legislative proposals? Must a representative, in order to create a favorable image, follow the preferences of his district, where those preferences are known, or does he have unusual latitude in voting? One first-term congressman from the midwest who was interviewed shortly after the debate on controversial labor legislation that resulted in passage of the Landrum-Griffin bill wondered about the answer:

> I have been wondering to what extent constituents will return to Congress members who reach their own decisions about legislation in the face of mail which leans the other way. I am referring to the recent voting on labor legislation—Landrum-Griffin in particular. I represent a rural area and I share most of the feelings of the area regarding labor, but I was determined not to be stampeded into uninformed voting and finally decided to support the committee bill in the hope of making changes in that rather than to go along with the Landrum bill. I estimate 75 percent of my district would have preferred me to support the Landrum-Griffin bill. Whether I can vote the other way and survive is a matter only time can tell.

Another congressman who was interviewed the same week thought he knew the answer:

> I think you can vote pretty nearly the way you want to vote on issues. The people don't expect you to agree with them on every issue, and they respect you for arriving at your independent judgment. You must demonstrate that you are

conscientious, however, and that you are able to arrive at a reasonable and intelligent judgment. As soon as Congress adjourns I have a lot of explaining to do on Landrum-Griffin. I think I can persuade my people that I did the right thing. The important thing is that you state your position clearly and defend it before them.

The overwhelming view of those included in the Round Table Conference on Congress and others interviewed separately was that there are few limitations on the ability of a legislator to vote counter to his district's position and survive. Many made the point that such votes, if defended properly, can be turned to advantage. The voters, the argument runs, like to be represented by a man of conviction who is not afraid of standing up to be counted. They are not unduly disturbed that such a representative sometimes casts votes contrary to their personal views. But some lawmakers are more reluctant than others to test their constituents on some of the "big" issues; there is a feeling that on certain proposals a member would do well not to express too much independence. The following discussion reflects these views:

The personality and general impression of the candidate through his service to constituents and his campaigning, his helpfulness and his conscientious nature, ordinarily dominate in an election. This is not to say issues are not also important. You cannot buck district sentiment on certain issues. In my area, oil, coal, and mining are extremely important, and if you are "right" on these things you have a much easier time of it. But you are opening yourself to criticism if you vote against the district often.

*

I think you can vote as you wish on any issue, as long as you vote from conviction. You can go back to a district inclined to be very hostile to your vote and win them over completely. I did that on the Tideland Oil bill in my first term. Historically, my district and state have been very strong for return of the tidelands. I ended up the only member of either party from an oil producing state to vote against it. It caused an uproar in the district, but it was one of the most effective things I've done.

*

I had a different experience. I got myself on both sides of a critical and important issue: I voted for a bill that passed Congress and then voted to sustain the veto. I thought it would defeat me because I was in a ridiculous position. It was my first campaign for re-election and that is all my opponent talked about. Finally, though, I made hay out of it. I bought some radio time and said, "I want to talk about a very serious issue. This is one I am expert on because I am one of the few people who have been on both sides of it." That was the opening gun and I exploited it.

A discussion among members of the other party revealed somewhat more hesitancy on the part of some members to vote contrary to district sentiment. Running through the discussion was the implicit assumption that it could be dangerous to cast such votes. Since a legislator is more valuable to his party in office than out of it, he can justify casting occasional votes against his personal preferences and in line with what he believes to be the preference of his constituency. Whatever the merits, it is clear from the discussion that this is indeed the expressed basis for some votes. Sam Rayburn's frequently quoted advice to colleagues to "vote your district first" strengthens that view. And the point is made that occasionally an effort is made to avoid a roll-call vote because it might be awkward for a member to have to explain his vote back home. Consider the following discussion:

You are not just down here getting yourself re-elected; you are here standing for a party which is supposed to have a definite philosophy.

*

I take the position that "a politician's first duty is to get re-elected" and I think this sometimes requires casting votes you might prefer not to cast. The alternative to your re-election in most cases is the election of someone who would be diametrically opposed in conviction to what you stand for.

*

I couldn't disagree with anything more. That is how too many people approach legislation. Everyone here has heard time and again "my district just won't permit me to do that," or "after all, I have to get re-elected." My answer is, what good is it to be re-elected if you are not willing to stand up on issues which are important. I think you have to court defeat, really court defeat, if you are going to be a good congressman.

*

You are basing your argument solely on the basis of votes. But voting is only part of the duties of a congressman.

*

The only way the people have of knowing what you are doing when the chips are down is what the record votes are. You know how often it is said in the House "Let's not have a record vote on this because some of the boys will be hurt if we do." I don't agree with that philosophy. I think that on those things there ought to be record votes. If the parties are going to stand for anything and if representative government is going to mean anything, people have to know what their representatives and the parties stand for. I think you will agree that many a person says, "I have to vote this way if I am going to get re-elected." Those who accept your philosophy of casting a vote contrary to what they believe simply to get re-elected . . .

*

The first duty is to get re-elected.

*

Could it be you are arguing not only that you must court defeat but that taking a courageous and forthright and active position is actually in your view a way to get re-elected?

*

You may get elected, but you may get defeated, too. But those are the things I think you should risk, if this form of government is going to work.

*

You will have to admit you are somewhat of a political phenomenon. No one else could vote as you do and continue to represent your district as a member of our party. The whole point is whether it is important to have more members of our party in Congress or an AFL-CIO candidate in your spot. This is a decision you make, and you stand up and fight firmly for it. But there are too many other examples of people who have tried to do as you have done and have been defeated. In my opinion the other party has taken this country down the drain, and it is very important that we get people who are willing to stand up for the things we believe in but who are, if necessary, willing to be expedient in order to be here representing the party we believe in.

*

May I disagree somewhat? Some who have lost in the midwest have not stood up and been counted at all. I think a lot of them went down the drain because they wouldn't stand up and be counted. It depends on the district and the personalities and the individual. I don't think there is any pat formula you can develop for it.

Campaign Techniques

In the course of campaigning, nearly every congressman develops several approaches he regards as particularly effective. Willing—sometimes eager—to discuss his own favorite techniques of winning the favor of his constituents, he is often just as willing to hear his colleagues relate their own successful methods. Politicians seldom take elections for granted, and many are constantly seeking new means by which to strengthen their hold on their constituency.

Campaigning, then, is a favorite subject for conversation among the legislators, and the Brookings round table sessions that were devoted to this topic were among the most spirited of the series. Campaign strategy depends heavily, of course, on the personality and preferences of the candidate but is also influenced by such factors as the role and position of the party organization, the urban-rural complexion of the district represented, available funds, and the situation with respect to the mass media. The candidate's relationship with the press may be a very important element in the determination of the allocation of time, energy, and money in the campaign effort.

Personal Appearances. Some legislators assert they run primarily on the issues; others say privately they ignore issues and concentrate on projecting a favorable personal image; still others run against the Congress no matter which party is in control. There are many different avenues to electoral success, as congressmen are well aware, but whatever the elements in the candidate's bag of campaign tricks, emphasis nearly always is on the personal appearance technique. When asked to indicate the essence of success, two congressmen—one representing a rural district, the other an urban district—gave the same answer, one with which their colleagues readily agreed: "The most important thing in campaigning in my [midwestern] state is to shake hands. Get out and meet the public. Let them know you are not afraid to talk to them." "That is true in New York City, too. Spend less time making speeches before groups and get out and pump hands."

Invitations to speak before community organizations are seldom declined, whatever the time of year, if it is at all possible to be present. Sometimes these invitations are actively sought. Said one congressman: "I try to get before all the service clubs, the merchants' associations, trade union groups, and any organization that will take me as a speaker." Opportunities to officiate or speak at ground-breaking ceremonies, or the dedication of a new post office, or merely to be seen at important or well-attended community events are seldom missed. Touring the district annually in a trailer or mobile office to "report to the people" is another important means of reaching the voter and of creating the image of an active legislator, deeply interested in the welfare of his constituents. In addition to facilitating being of service to district residents, the congressman finds such tours valuable in informing him as to what people are thinking about. As one member put it:

The mobile office can be a good way of covering a district, particularly one which includes many small communities. It is very effective in the nonelection year and a very good activity in election years during the first month after adjournment. It is too early then to get an active campaign underway and you can get a lot of attention and publicity while being nonpolitical. We develop an elaborate schedule designed to cover virtually every town in the district. Where the towns are very small, we try to hit two in one day. Since the trailer is parked in a prominent spot on the main street, even when the office is closed, it provides excellent publicity and tangible evidence that their congressman is around. The important thing is that people know their congressman cares enough about them to come to their community whatever its size. There always is much newspaper publicity regarding the visit and radio announcements, too. Mats of the trailer are sent to the weeklies along with some copy and the schedule for nearby towns.

In another form of the same activity, some congressmen regularly visit all the post offices in their districts in nonelection years (it is not permissible to campaign there during election periods) greeting individuals and representatives of various groups to discuss any problems they may have. While such activity is widely heralded among the congressional group, one veteran member said that he had abandoned such visits. "I found," he said, "that I got all the difficult, unsolvable cases that had been before other congressmen and senators and I just gave up. People came from other counties."

Many congressmen are avid followers of the county fair circuit. Typical of the activities of many of his colleagues, one House member regularly distributes football schedules at these events, the schedules containing his picture, of course, and, in election years, a request for support. The same legislator speaks of having distributed 25,000 sun shades with "_____ for Congress" printed on the visor during one tour of the fairs. Others prefer the shopping bag or key ring:

> The shopping bag is the best gimmick in the world. People fight for the shopping bags and you see them later with walking billboards plugging your candidacy. You know, "Don't shop around; vote for Congressman _____." You can get rid of 15,000 in a couple of hours if you want to do so. Just remember to have your name printed on both sides so it will be sure to show.

*

> I use shopping bags and find them very good for a particular campaign. But I like this key ring shaped like my district with my name on it, too. Tens of thousands of them, costing a fraction of a penny apiece, were distributed six years ago and they are still around.

One congressman who believes strongly in the value of the handshake and devotes as much time as possible during campaign periods walking down the streets in business districts, relates that one community he represents has forty taverns. He sets aside two afternoons to cover those taverns, entering every one of them, without taking a drink. "The word gets out among the working people," he testifies, "and I have a reputation in that community."

Coffees at the homes of supporters, door to door canvasses, and visiting the supermarkets and main streets of small towns are common forms of congressional activity, particularly in election years. Often, on such occasions, various items are distributed by the congressman. One representative received national attention for his door to door distribution of pot holders to residents of his district. Another congressman makes good use of his time in his tours of his area:

As I go through the many small towns in my district, I carry a little pad of paper with me. When a fellow comes up and says he wants to do something for me I scratch him out a little ad and say, "Put that in the paper for me if you want to." In my last campaign it got to the point that I had more ads scattered all through the campaign period than I really needed—a $2 ad here and a $2 ad there.

The following discussion, on the personal appearances techniques, touches on these activities:

There is nothing like going home after the session and making personal reports to the people. Last time I made 173 personal appearances. I go before anybody who will listen to me, before groups of one hundred to seven hundred, to a candy pulling or a county fair. I have been doing that for ten years and in that time have made over 1,200 reports to the people. It is by far the most effective thing I do.

*

That approach is virtually impossible in our city districts because you can't figure out how to get a series going. We have tried every known campaign technique and I finally decided the most effective thing to do was go out and walk in the district. I find it difficult to get people out to rallies. The biggest political show we ever put on was a heavily subsidized affair with strong support from labor organizations and other groups. The chief attractions were a then sitting president and all the party brass we could possibly get. The timing of the event was good, yet we only got 3,000 people out.

*

Think of all the thousands of women's clubs in your city district and all the coffees you can have. Even in a rural district like mine we tried the coffee break idea one time. We had about thirty in three days, and it worked beautifully. Have fifteen to twenty ladies at each meeting, stay thirty minutes or so, and move on.

*

I find you waste a whole day. At the very most you might meet 75 ladies. It is far better to go down the streets where you can meet three or four hundred people in their places of business or on the street.

*

The trick with the coffees is scheduling. You have to have a good organizer who will line up fifteen or twenty separate appearances a day. I don't believe your walking can beat that.

*

Efficient scheduling is important but the real trick is in scheduling unusual times. If you can get people to talk about your being somewhere it accomplishes a lot more than just meeting a group of people. A predecessor of mine pulled a good gimmick once when he was out in a sound car and had a little time. He went by a field where there were a half dozen men baling hay. He stopped his car and made a full-scale thirty minute speech for those six men. It spread all over the district that he was taking his campaign into the hayfields.

*

There is another element here—publicity. That kind of thing is particularly effective if by coincidence a newspaperman happens to be along and will write of the event in a paper read by 300,000 people. If you aren't so fortunate, you can go around giving a lot of good speeches to people in wheat fields and not make much of an impact.

*

Another very good gimmick is that of going to the factories at the midnight and six a.m. changes of shift. One stop at a factory for a shift change at an unusual hour will do more good than fifteen or twenty stops at ordinary hours. The average guy thinks, "well, here is a fellow interested enough in me to get out at this outlandish hour. He must be a pretty good fellow."

*

These activities have to be efficient in order to work. We started out with the coffee hour, but we ran into two difficulties. One was that even when scheduling them as sensibly as possible you got into a lot of cross-hauling and back-tracking. Secondly, and perhaps worse, the darlings who held the coffee hours tended to invite their friends who were likely to be favorably disposed anyway. You spent an hour in pleasant conversation dosing yourself with coffee but the number of converts probably was limited. You simply can't tell a woman who is nice enough to put on a coffee klatch in her own home, "Look, you must invite all the people in your block whether they are friend or foe or whether you know them or not."

*

We had a coffee caravan which consisted of a station wagon with an urn of coffee, doughnuts, and so on, a loud speaker and a series of automobiles with car-top signs, and at least eight volunteer women who were willing to give their morning to the project. We would stop at a carefully reconnoitered street cross-ing, and the women would fan out two to a block and cover the area saying Con-gressman _____ is down at the corner with his coffee wagon. Wouldn't you like to come out and have a cup of coffee and chat with him? We would also announce our presence over the public address system. If no one was home in a household we left a "sorry you were out, I'll call again," message signed by me. A few men came, but most of the group consisted of women. It was very easy to start a good political discussion by getting one of my own friends to ask a question or two. This was helpful because it gets people to talk. Second, it had a multiplier effect because everyone in the neighborhood talked about it.

*

One of the best things that _____ did last year was to eat lunch sitting out on the curb in small towns. He'd go into a store, buy some crackers and some cheese and have the folks come around and join him for lunch. The fortunate thing, of course, was that a photographer was there to take a picture of him sitting there with a group eating crackers and cheese. The impression created was a hard one to tear down.

*

He walks with emperors and never loses the common touch!

The Opponent—Mention him? Debate him? Answer his attacks? The ques-tion of how to deal with one's opponent and the kind of campaign he wages is a subject of much serious discussion among congressmen. Some refuse to mention their opponent by name and will not meet him on the same platform on the grounds that the incumbent is the better known of the adversaries and will provide the opponent with an audience he could not obtain himself. Some members feel, too, that since only the incumbent has a record, he is the more vulnerable in debate. Others believe that because of their work in Congress, they are much better informed on the issues than the contender could possibly be. They view an encounter as an opportunity to expose the latter's inexperience and lack of information. Certainly a skilled and articulate performer in a district heavily weighted in his favor can afford more readily to be magnanimous and meet his op-ponent than some of his less able and statistically more insecure associ-ates. But sometimes decisions such as these are not within the discretion of the incumbents; circumstances may reluctantly force a politician into activities he might wish to avoid.

The trend in many areas for organizations such as the League of Women Voters, the Business and Professional Women, various church groups, and labor unions to sponsor nonpartisan meetings where candidates develop their positions more fully have caused serious dilemmas for incumbents reluctant to meet their rivals in joint debate. Few congressmen look forward to such invitations. Many would readily decline them were it not for the unfavorable publicity likely to result. At the very least the forums are regarded as restrictions on the freedom of the incumbent to wage the battle on his own terms. Most, sometimes after seeking to impose certain ground rules as a condition of appearing, finally consent to appear. One legislator who dislikes such appearances seeks to avoid them. Failing that, he makes his presentation and departs prior to the question period. Asked how the question period could be avoided, the member replied, "I have always gone on to another meeting by that time."

There is much complaint in congressional circles that such forums often are "rigged," that questions are "planted" in the audience. One congressman said that at one such meeting his opponent's brother and campaign manager went through the audience distributing typed questions. Other members speak of appearing in a series of debates with their opponents and discovering groups of hecklers were making the debate circuit, sometimes even asking the same questions. Some incumbents will not accept speaking engagements before groups they regard as hostile. A few welcome the opportunity as a challenge, but nearly all complain they are not treated fairly on such occasions.

One legislator who refuses to appear even before civic groups like the League of Women Voters explained how he does so:

I just tell them I have a record I am running on and my opponent has no record. I say, and it is true, that my campaign committee is opposed to my participating in such debates, that they don't think we should help build an audience for my opponent. I tell them that if they want to have him on a program, fine. I will be glad to appear at some later time or I will appear first.

A frequent observation is that if only the opponent were honest and willing to discuss the issues on their merits, then of course there would be no objection to joint meetings. Alas, according to incumbents, he seldom is! The following discussion points up some of the factors involved in decisions to debate or not to debate opponents:

I challenge my opponent before he has a chance to challenge me, and we always wind up with a series of planned debates.

*

I don't intend to go out and draw a crowd to come and hear what my opponent has to say against me. I wouldn't go through the kind of district I have and let the kind of opponent I had last year confuse constituents. There was no truth in the things he was saying. He went so far beyond the truth that even the district recognized it.

*

I wouldn't be seen on the platform with my opponent. I was caught once this past session, though, when someone got to an organization which was so close to me I couldn't afford to offend it. They developed the noble idea of a joint meeting. It was a very edifying evening. There wasn't one thing you could say wasn't true, and yet not one word of truth was in it. I finished by saying I knew he would be surprised to know how much I agreed with him. That floored him. He went into federal aid to education on which I have strong convictions so I just turned around and asked him questions. I didn't argue but exposed him as an ignoramus.

*

I have had to engage in debate with opponents on three occasions because I was challenged and I always respond to that. It really is unfair to the incumbent because he is the only one with a record, and it is easy to shoot some holes through anybody's record. It is more difficult to defend than to attack in such a case. You are debating your own record, and you don't have an opportunity to debate his because he doesn't have one.

*

That is not always so. When my opponent started objecting to my record I said, "All right, what would you have done? Here is the bill. How would you have voted and why?" They don't know why; they just know you voted this way, and they don't think that is right. An incumbent has a terrific advantage because he knows the issues. He has been through them.

*

An incumbent has to be careful he doesn't end up just being on the defensive. I don't believe in answering all the miscellaneous charges an opponent may spread. I usually watch what he does and see where he is weak.

*

In my first election I had an able opponent who was a school teacher and had quite a following, and I went around and debated with him everywhere. Last time my opponent wasn't that kind and I just ignored him.

*

I don't pay any attention to the candidate, but I have to pay attention to my real opponent, the CIO.

*

I also have been opposed to participating in debates with my opponent because I don't want to build an audience for him, but last time the Farm Bureau Federation arranged a meeting in which the two House candidates and the two rivals for the Senate seat appeared. The decorum was excellent. The Farm Bureau picked the issues, allowed each candidate five minutes to state his general philosophy, and then asked some specific questions allowing one minute for the response. Then questions were asked from the floor. Leaders came from all over the state, everyone was courteous, no one was put on the spot. They just developed what the true position was. Prior to adjournment each candidate was allowed two minutes to close. That kind of meeting is the greatest undressing for someone who doesn't know what he is talking about that you will ever run into.

*

Doesn't this discussion substantiate what everybody has been saying that campaigns don't prove very much and prove even less when you have an irresponsible opponent, which often happens? If you only could get an opponent who would squarely face up to what you stand for and get him honestly to put the question to the voters in terms of "wouldn't you rather have me than him?" But that isn't what happens and you spend your time wondering whether or not to respond to full page ads which distort the voting record, and if so, how best to do it.

*

It seems to me an exercise in futility. The campaigns I have been through have proved nothing. I resent spending my own money on them, and I resent any part of the effort of responding to what my opponent is saying. I don't mind meeting the people and I don't mind discussing what I have been doing and my position on things but if I could only eliminate my opponent. . . .

While there is no uniformity with respect to methods of answering attacks on a candidate's record or personal integrity, there is much sentiment that it is usually better not to try to do so. To seek to respond fully puts one on the defensive, permits the opponent to gain the campaign initiative, and sometimes arouses suspicion that the charge has some merit. Yet to ignore attacks may also be taken as an admission of their veracity and hurts the pride of the candidate at the very least. The following discussion of the problem by several Republicans touches on some of these points:

How do you answer a full page newspaper ad listing fifteen to twenty votes you cast, all of which are offensive to certain groups of people? There is no debate or discussion of the issues. They just say, "Cong. X voted as follows on these important issues."

*

I had a similar situation. The ADA-CIO voting list was circulated by mail to every voter in my district, so I prepared an answer in which I discussed these voting lists. I was planning a complete mailing anyway, and I just included my answer in it. I discussed voting lists like the ADA-CIO one, and I praised them because they have some merit. But I said, "In each session of Congress you have about 200 votes and they pick eight or ten out of 200. Somebody has to do the selecting. What caused them to pick the ones they did and were they fair selections?" Then I went on and discussed other voting lists.

*

It is a common—and effective—technique to take some very minute or unimportant votes in a man's record and blow them up to cover a general major area. By taking an unimportant vote, for example, you could say a man voted against teachers, retired workers, etc., and list the bill or amendment and the day of the vote. It is very impressive, and it seems authentic. A candidate could spend all his time trying to explain the actual situation.

*

The best advice is not to try to answer at all. Get them to talking about something else. Attack on another angle.

The Value of Publicity. Although in discussing campaign techniques, attention has been focused primarily on those prominent during the campaign period, it is clear that many on-going activities of a congressional office are undertaken with an eye on election day and the electorate. In many instances, the same activities that are effective throughout the term are merely accelerated during the campaign period. Examination of a congressman's calendar would show, for example, an increase in the number of trips taken to his district during the months prior to adjournment in an election year.

Perhaps the most important goal of many House members is to develop in the voter the image of an active, dedicated representative. It is toward this end that many of their activities are geared. Activity is the key word, and in many instances it is creating the illusion of activity that is important rather than the reality itself. One congressman who flies home to his district twice monthly always schedules office hours on each occasion in his home city and one or more of the many small towns. He represents a compact district which a few newspapers cover, and each time he is home he places a small ad in all these newspapers. The ad displays his picture and says, "On (date) at (time) I will be in (city or town) at the courthouse to see residents on any problem they may care to discuss." All that is involved may be a two-hour stop in a small town, but by running the ad in all newspapers in the district, voters become aware of the time he spends on district problems.

The Press. Congressmen are aware of the role of the press in lightening or increasing their own burdens. Though many blame the press for the poor public image of the typical member of Congress and complain that reporters distort the record and fail to emphasize the important things, few express their unhappiness publicly. Newsmen whom the congressman may despise and fear are given a cordial greeting when they stop by the office. Reporters probably have easier access to the congressman's time than any other group, largely because, despite their shortcomings, they possess the power to advance—or hinder—the congressman's cause. As one western Democrat said in evaluating his standing in his district:

> One thing working for me is the amount of publicity I am given in the local press. Ninety percent of the press give me good support. When I go home in an off-year I have my campaign manager try to arrange a schedule showing fifty to a hundred appearances. I get prominent coverage on that schedule, and people start talking about how very active you are when you get home. This is very helpful and would not be possible without the friendly attitude of the newspapers.

Comments a midwestern Republican: "The news media do a great deal in determining how a person gets along with his district. The way they present you to the voters can make your task either easy or more difficult. Of course, this is all supplemented by your own public relations activities."

Complained one Democrat:

> Unless I put an ad in the paper they never mention my name. The _____ company owns all the dailies and all the radio stations and all but one of the TV stations. They like my colleague and print the stuff he sends out. If I send out a news release they say, " _____ [referring to another member, not the speaker] and the rest of the delegation have introduced so and so or done so and so."

And a Republican expresses the feeling of many members of his party when he says the Republicans do not have a monopoly on press support:

> The press certainly isn't in the pocket of the Republicans as some people seem to say. As a matter of fact they're more likely to support the Democrats. I've had a terrible time in my own district because I just can't get the coverage. The _____ is a Democratic organ, although I must say they have endorsed me a

couple of times. Last time they didn't come out and endorse me, but they did say that if the reader happened to be a Republican then he should support me. It was a sort of left-handed compliment.

Two Democrats discussed their relationships with the press:

The first time I ran, a political science student made a survey of the coverage, given by the largest paper in the district, to the two congressional candidates in the last five weeks of the campaign. In terms of column inches my recollection is that my opponent had 620 and I had 50. I lost the election by half a percent that year.

*

We have two dominant dailies in the state both of which are important in my district. I have thirty weeklies, but the dailies are the ones that feed the up-to-date news. They were giving me no coverage so I talked to the editor. I showed him the releases I had been sending him and the coverage I had been getting. I said, "I don't know how many releases my opponent has been sending you, but you have been giving him this coverage." Although they are political opponents of mine, the paper had a sense of fair play, and from then on I got equal coverage with my opponent. If you can get that kind of coverage you don't have to spend much money.

Although congressmen as a group are publicity minded, many of them are forced to extraordinary lengths and expense to supplement normal news release procedures to ensure their district is aware of their activity. And some metropolitan representatives regard newspaper endorsement of their re-election as more important than any amount of advertising they might place, on the assumption that many readers watch for, and adhere to, the paper's recommendations. While newspaper publicity is regarded as valuable, placing political advertising in a newspaper is not considered as an important element in many campaigns today. Rural newspapers obviously are a better source for congressional releases and stories since the small staff is likely to welcome "news from outside" more readily and since there is less competition for coverage. For essentially the same reasons, they may also be a more effective means of getting through to the voter. As one rural district congressman put it: "I have twenty or thirty weekly newspapers, and I really use them. Rural people take those weekly papers and pass them around among themselves. People will go from one house to the other and borrow them. Because the newspaper is so important in the life of those people, I try to get my newsletters and things of that sort published there." As has been suggested elsewhere, some congressmen place ads at campaign time to ensure adequate publicity throughout their term rather than because of their belief in its effectiveness.

Radio and Television. Though extensive use is made of radio and tele-vision by candidates for Congress, these media rank well below the personal appearance so far as congressmen are concerned. They are par ticularly useful in that frequent brief appearances can be made with a saturation effect. Candidates of the party occupying the White House have found it helpful to get statements of endorsement from cabinet mem-bers and other high government officials and party leaders for use on these media. Usually, these are preceded and followed by statements of the candidates themselves, hopefully providing an association that will further their campaign. Television is regarded as especially helpful but too expensive to be used as often as candidates would like. One skilled legislator believes television is not only effective as a campaign tool but also regards it as a constructive force in elections:

TV is the very best of techniques. It is by far the most effective medium and I think it is good for the country, too. Unless a person is a consummate actor, folks can tell whether he is sincere and deserving. I am fairly convinced that TV has had and will continue to have a very good effect on improving candidates and their quality.

But one of the leaders of the House finds television less useful. In com-paring the effectiveness of television, radio, and newspaper advertising he says:

Television is virtually useless in a congressional campaign unless you are an extraordinarily good performer, and there is little competition for television time which is not the case in a commercial television situation where there are three or more stations. We use radio spots almost to a saturation point. We don't find our newspaper advertising worth a damn. Six years ago we had a polling group do some checking on some of our ads and discovered they weren't getting any re-sponse. The survey was not thorough enough to be truly scientific, but it was thorough enough to convince us.

This statement evoked a defense of television from another congressman:

I don't agree with you about television. I have found it to be pretty helpful particularly in areas where there is just one station and you have pretty much a captive audience. Of course, I have an area covered by _____ stations [a city not in his district], and it is too expensive to use except for an occasional spot an-nouncement. In other parts of the district where there is less competition I have found it very effective. People do watch it, and when I go around campaigning they say, "Oh, yes, I saw you on TV." I don't think it wise to spend too much time on TV—just enough to get your name across to the voters.

Literature, Billboards, Bumper Stickers. Campaign literature is distributed widely and in great quantity, though few people would assert it could match most other campaign techniques in effect. One very good campaign piece which technically is not a campaign piece at all is the end of session "report to the people," which many congressmen now use. As the campaign approaches, legislators are reluctant to frank mail that can be characterized as political—franking of newsletters, for example, has in some instances been subject to sharp criticism—but a report of accomplishments is regarded as legitimate and appropriate—and certainly effective. Especially good for rural areas, these reports have been mailed out within two or three weeks of the election. Said one congressman, "I think it the best single thing you can do."

Billboards are somewhat more controversial—there are congressmen who regard extensive billboard coverage as a central element in their campaign while others attach little importance to them. Increasingly, however, candidates are sensitive to the dangers of arousing special community groups with excessive billboards, signboards, and posters.

> We use very effectively what I call "baby billboards," . . . a plywood or masonite board three by four feet. We have them made in groups of 100 or more in order to get a good price and get them out on vacant lots and lawns and near heavily traveled streets. They are effective as a billboard. For instance, we use luminous paint and a bright orange background with blue lettering. It is very inexpensive. You get all the impact from the traffic going by.

*

> Of late the opposition has begun to write letters to the newspapers signed by "Garden Club Member" and so on, protesting against this abuse of the landscape. So I, as an old "Day-Glo" user, see the end of the road.

The problem of being returned to office is a continuing one which pervades and affects nearly every aspect of congressional activity. Though members work toward the re-election goal in different ways, some appearing to be almost indifferent to the outcome, nearly all are constantly on the alert for new techniques with which to win voter support. Some of the most effective are not readily understood by constituents to be closely allied to campaigning at all. Incumbents concede they possess an advantage but stress high campaigning costs and complain official party groups do not help enough in congressional races.

IX

Congressional Wives and Congressional Life

THE TWENTY-ONE CONGRESSIONAL WIVES[1] who accepted the Brookings Institution's invitation to meet and talk about their role and problems in connection with their husbands' work constituted an interesting and talented group. Of widely diverse interests and accomplishments, they could be characterized as sensible, self-reliant, and possessing a lively curiosity. They were quite different one from the other in many respects—just as their husbands differed from one another—and yet they clearly were unusually resourceful and able women, capable of meeting the challenges of the exacting demands made on them. As one of the group expressed it:

> I like congressional wives for their great ability to adjust to changes of pace. All my life I have been a person who rather enjoys a change of pace, but I admit I have found political life a terrific challenge. Every once in awhile I wake up and say to myself "you just aren't handling this at all. You can't cope." Yet I do think that congressional wives do a very good job. To the extent that *anyone* can cope, they do. I guess I should like to say that I gave up being the cherished violet long ago, but sometimes I long for the past. Congressional wives have to do too much all by themselves—handling the children, dealing with the banker, realtor, the contractor, or the garage man.

Attitudes Toward Politics

As might be expected, congressional wives' attitudes toward politics and the extent of their involvement in it differ noticeably. The majority

[1] They were: Mrs. Robert Perkins Bass, Mrs. Richard Bolling, Mrs. Frank M. Coffin, Mrs. Silvio O. Conte, Mrs. Ed Edmondson, Mrs. Gerald R. Ford, Jr., Mrs. Peter Freylinghuysen, Jr., Mrs. Robert P. Griffin, Mrs. Byron L. Johnson, Mrs. Charles Raper Jonas, Mrs. John V. Lindsay, Mrs. George S. McGovern, Mrs. Lee Metcalf, Mrs. Albert H. Quie, Mrs. James M. Quigley, Mrs. Henry S. Reuss, Mrs. John J. Rhodes, Mrs. Keith Thomson, Mrs. Al Ullman, Mrs. Bob Wilson, and Mrs. Sidney R. Yates. Mrs. John R. Baldwin, who was unable to be present at the luncheon, sent a thoughtful and helpful letter, which covered many of the points raised in the discussion.

are interested in politics, but only in a highly selective and personal way. Many possess no deep interest in, or understanding of, everyday political events or legislative issues. They are deeply committed, of course, to their husbands' success; virtually all congressional wives are. Events that are likely to be significant in determining their husbands' future or that place their spouses in a special role are those most likely to arouse them. Because of their close friendships with other congressional wives, they may also be interested in developments that involve certain of their husbands' colleagues. But most of the wives don't concern themselves with the day-to-day details of their husbands' work or expect to have political problems discussed with them.

There are exceptions. Some wives are obviously very astute politically, rivaling their husbands in interest and acumen and sharing with them many of the activities and decisions. They want to know about current political developments, and they are fully competent to give sound advice. At the other pole, a few congressional wives obviously don't care for politics and would prefer not to participate personally in political activities of any kind. They may even mildly resent or regret their husbands' participation. For them, campaigning is painful, to be endured only because the husband and the public all but require it.

It is evident that most wives of congressmen are immersed much more fully in the game of politics than they would have thought possible some years ago, and that their activities have altered their attitudes substantially. Some confess that initially they were reluctant participants who found themselves pressed into service with little alternative. Gradually, however, many of them have come to enjoy their role, and nearly all have come to accept it philosophically; one hears occasionally of wives who have not. Some who have become reconciled to the many and sometimes unpredictable demands of politics would, nonetheless, willingly relinquish their political activities if they could do so without injury to their husband's careers. Nearly always, however, they are pleasantly surprised by the cordial reception they receive as they carry out their political assignments. One wife of a freshman congressman who would herself prefer not to participate in the campaigning process was pleased to make that discovery in connection with routine precinct work:

People seemed surprised that I was campaigning for my husband. They would say, "Do you mean you are out campaigning for him?" I thought, "Well, if I am not willing to push doorbells, why should anybody else?" But it was a very rewarding experience for me to do that in the middle of that cold, forbidding community which turned out to be a group of small towns. I had never done it, and if I had a choice I would just as soon not have to do it. You know, you resist anything like that. But the surprising thing is that people are really glad to see you.

The testimony of one midwesterner illustrates the transformation in attitude which often occurs:

If I had known how much work was involved in being a politician's wife, I don't think I would have let my husband run that first time. But since being in politics I have decided it is the most frustrating, exciting, exhilarating, wonderful life. You just can't help but be thrilled to be part of this whole experience and you have to be part of it. You think you can't do many of the things you are called upon to do, but you find that you can do them when you have to. I had to substitute on a television show once, and it scared me silly even to think about it. But I managed to live through it. I have had to ring doorbells, to organize cities precinct by precinct, and call people to ask them to donate time on election day, things I thought I never would be able to do. I even speak before groups when I have to. I limit my talks to a very informal discussion of the role of the congressman; I find people don't know too much about how Congress operates.

Some wives have always been thrilled by politics and have moved quite easily into many of the responsibilities thrust on them. One of the most versatile and respected of these was asked to summarize the rewards and costs of having a husband in politics. Said she:

The rewards for me are having a husband doing exactly what he most enjoys doing in all the world. Also I think it is very fascinating and stimulating to be able to do it with him. He was a member of our state legislature when we became engaged and took me up to the capital to a session and introduced the legislature to me. Then I could make my choice: "Love me, love my cigars," or whatever the saying is. I have always enjoyed political life. It is as interesting to me as it is to him.

The cost, which I am sure would be the same for anyone with a large family, is the ghastly problem of schools and switching the children from home to Washington in January, or coming down into exile with them in September while the congressman stays home campaigning or mending fences. If you come down here you lead that delightfully frustrating life of the adult with children month after month while you know lots of exciting things are going on at home.

The Home and Family Life

Prominently mentioned by congressmen when they speak of the aspects of their job that most disturb them is the frequent separation from their families. Some observe, too, that it is almost impossible for a congressman to take a vacation with his school-age children: the average adjournment time for Congress since 1950 has been the first week in September, just about the time schools open.

Their wives share the view that a congressman's responsibilities pose special obstacles to normal family living. In the discussions at Brookings they were preoccupied with the special problems of the congressional family unit—the separations, the effects on the children of having no roots and having to change schools, the necessity and expense of maintaining two homes, and the heavy costs involved in the extensive traveling which appeared to be built into the job of the congressman. This emphasis was not surprising since the panel included a large proportion of families with children of school age. It was evident that a major concern about congressional life centered about its potential effects on these children.

Togetherness, Schooling, and Primary Residence. A basic problem to resolve for each family with school-age children is the determination of the primary place of residence, a decision in which the necessities of political life weigh heavily. The congressman's job requires him to make the Washington area his headquarters from January through July or August, or later, though there are congressional "recess" periods within that time, and current legislative scheduling practices make it possible for the representative to return to his district for long week ends.

Once Congress adjourns, the legislator normally considers it important to spend considerable time in his district, reporting to his constituents and strengthening his base of support; much of the period from the end of the session to January is generally so allocated. And the likelihood is greater than it used to be that the congressman will go abroad during the adjournment period, in connection with committee responsibilities or possibly as a reservist on active duty. The conflicts between his schedule and the September-June school year of his children are readily apparent. When the congressman's time is most flexible, his children are in school; when his youngsters are on vacation, the legislative work load often is at its peak as Congress moves towards adjournment. The wives at the meeting clearly were concerned about the problems created by this situation. There was considerable agreement with the statement of one mother of three children:

I think all congressional wives with children of school age would agree that 90 percent of these [separation] problems would be solved if Congress would just recess for a couple of months in the summer the way the Supreme Court does, so that the session would coincide more nearly with the school year. Two years ago a bill was introduced in the Senate to provide for that. With so many young people with large families coming to Congress now I still have hopes that such a bill will pass some day.[2]

Annual efforts by congressional wives to promote a summer vacation period have not been seriously considered by the leadership, although hearings have occasionally been held on the subject. In 1961, Speaker Rayburn, commenting on a petition circulated by the wives urging such a vacation, said, "the greatest nonsense I ever heard of, and I wouldn't mind being quoted on that." This attitude of the leadership led one congressional wife to say that "Congress shows a cheerful contempt for the younger members and their families because the decisions are made by people who don't feel this as a personal concern." (Speaker Rayburn and Speaker Martin were both bachelors, and Speaker and Mrs. McCormack have no children.) And another wife doubted that the problem would ever be solved:

I don't think we will ever get any relief on this conflict of vacation time until we elect a Speaker who is a young family man. This probably isn't possible because you don't get to be Speaker when you are that young, and by the time you have no children in school, the problem isn't important to you any more.

The congressional schedule also poses a serious dilemma for the congressional family in terms of the education of the children. When the congressman returns to his duties in Washington each January, will his wife and children move from the district with him, transferring the children from one school to another? Will they stay in the home state? Or will they remain in Washington most of the year so that the children's education may proceed uninterrupted by shifts from one place to another?

Many mothers are disturbed about the psychological effects of changing from school to school; in view of the rising academic requirements for

[2] A poll of members of Congress taken by *Congressional Quarterly*, in the spring of 1961 reported that 175 of the 294 respondents thought Congress should remain in session each year until its work is finished rather than adjourn for a summer recess. One hundred nine favored a summer recess, and ten members made alternative suggestions.

admission to college, some emphasize "continuous schooling is terribly important." While the broadening effects on their children of exposure to different groups of youngsters are noted by parents, concern is expressed at the same time that, by dividing their time between Washington and the district, their offspring will not be fully accepted in the home community.

I think it is difficult for the children to have two sets of friends, although down here they meet children from other states and countries and that is very interesting for them. They learn to accept other people and realize they are not so important themselves. I think they feel a little out of things when they do go home, though. I feel the same way.

Different families have resolved the problem in different ways, but virtually everyone agrees there is no perfect solution. Considerable separation from the husband and father seems virtually inevitable regardless of the decision. As congressmen gain seniority, or as they establish more firm control over their districts, there seems to be a tendency for families with children to spend the entire school year in Washington, although if the district is not too distant from Washington, the family may remain at home. Particularly during the first term, some members of Congress are reluctant to move their families out of the district which elected them. One wife of a freshman congressman explained:

Our election was a close one, and where my husband is concerned you don't have the case of a man who disappears down to Washington. He'll be in the district often, and I can be of more use to him by staying there retaining the contacts. Rather than move the whole family here, I come to Washington during the week whenever possible. My husband gets home every weekend; we have found that most political functions he should attend take place then. Fortunately we live close to Washington so not too much traveling time is involved, though it is expensive. Sunday is a very special time, and I put my foot down and try to save it. We try to disappear somewhere where people can't find us.

There is much experimentation in the search for a satisfactory resolution of the dilemma in which congressmen with children find themselves. Although many congressional families eventually become Washington based, a few firmly resist the trend. In such instances, the wives and children rarely get to Washington. More common is the practice of dividing their residency between the district and the nation's capital, spending part of each year in each place. There are families, too, in which the wife and children join the congressman in Washington only for the seven or eight months of nonelection years. Commented one wife:

I think you have to be separated from your husband whichever way you solve your problem. Even if you decide to live here year round, the congressman has to spend a certain amount of time in the district no matter where it is. Often he spends much time there. If you go back to the district with your husband in the fall and put the children in school there, then you are away from him when he returns to Congress in January. Let's face it, we just can't live like most people do.

We tried everything when my husband first came to Congress. We rented our house in the state, moved the furniture up here and rented a place. Moving the furniture back and forth was so expensive we decided it was cheaper in the long run to have two sets. The way it finally has worked out, I spend eighteen months in the state and six months in Washington. During the campaign year, I am home with all four children. Then in the second semester of school in the nonelection year, we rent our home, come up here, get the furniture out of storage and rent a house. My children range from five to fourteen in age—they don't like all the travel, but they want to be with their dad, and there isn't any other way to do it.

When I am staying in the state, my husband tries to come home at least every other week. It is expensive, but he does it anyway. Even when we are back here, we often don't have him on week ends. Home life is nil for congressional familes, but it is one of the things you have to face. If your husband is happy and is doing what he wants to do, that is what is important. I don't mean to sound like a Pollyanna, but there you are. He tries to keep Sundays free. We know that we are going to have Sundays together as a family, and there isn't any point in fussing about the rest of it. I think the quality of a man's company sometimes outweighs quantity.

One Home or Two? Since congressional families normally spend at least part of each term in the Washington area, questions about housing immediately arise. Owning a home in the congressional district is virtually required and, as one wife commented, "even if it were not a requirement I think it would be desirable to return to the same place for the sake of the children and the friends they have there." The question whether one should seek to purchase a second home in Washington depends in part on family finances and how much time is spent there. But there is a conscious effort to provide as much stability for the children as possible in a situation unordered in so many of its aspects. Eventually, congressional families, however reluctantly, usually decide to accept the financial burdens of a second home:

We bought a house. I checked with other wives and found that some families were moving around two or three times a term, changing children from one school to another. When we first made the move back here, we lived in a furnished, rented house for eight months, and we decided—I did—that we were much too unsettled. The children did not feel at home in school or in Washington. So I said: "The first thing we must do is make the children happy in school here." We decided to buy a house and get what furniture we could afford—we couldn't ship ours 3,000 miles. This year we are much happier. We have a home and we have roots, just as we have a home when we go back to the state. Why feel like we are just camping here when, after all, we are here eight months of the year?

Time and again congressional wives return to the subject of the expense as well as the inconvenience of their family's bipolar existence. Housing costs figure prominently in their discussions.

When you maintain two homes, a good part of the year you are living in both of them. Either that or when I am not in the state my husband maintains a small apartment there because he has to go back frequently. Whichever way it is done, there are two establishments going, and that is rather expensive. The transportation back and forth for my husband—and occasionally for the whole family—is also very costly.

Some families who find purchase of a Washington home impossible seek as much permanence as they can get: "We are renting because we don't have money to buy a place, but we did get a two-year lease so that we would have that much stability."

Many families seek to rent out their home in the district for the period of their absence, the congressman staying with relatives, friends, or at a hotel during his visits back there. Some who at first determined to keep their hometown residence available for their own use eventually found it necessary, for financial reasons, to find tenants for the period of their absence if not year round. As one wife explained:

Housing is one of our big problems. We do own a home in our district but we have to rent it. We can't afford to just turn the key and come back here. We own a house here that we live in about eight or nine months of the year. When we are home we usually take a place at the beach or stay with relatives.

When asked how many years have to elapse before they come to regard Washington as their home rather than the district from which their husbands were elected, congressional wives respond quickly and almost unanimously that that will never happen. Most of them also state that their children retain their allegiance to the district even though they spend much of the year away from it. A few mention a gradual shift in outlook, however. Many of the children have actually been born in the Washington area and that complicates the situation; as one wife said, "We have a Washington family and a district family now."

The number of years spent in Washington and the age of the children are regarded as important factors in determining preference, although there are statements that even older children long to return to the district.

We have been here seven years and the fifteen year-old is the hardest to break away from home.

*

What do you do when you have a thirteen year-old who won't come back here?

*

Mine wouldn't come if there was any way he could avoid it.

*

All of our children were born here in Washington, but I think they still consider that their home is in the district. They want to go there and live. I think it has great appeal for them because Grandpa and Grandma are there, and their memories are of the summer when we go to the cottage at the beach and the winter when we take them skiing.

On the other hand, the hometown loses its appeal for some children as they make new friends and spend more time elsewhere:

My children believe that you can't go home again. In a discussion the other day I said I would hate to sell my house back home. Both of my teen-age children said, "We are not going back there to live." There is your problem: Their lack of interest in our home area is the hardest thing my husband and I have had to face.

*

So far as our family is concerned, we are thinking of Washington as home more and more. My husband has been in Congress seven years now, and the children come back in September to complete the school year here. They are really growing up here, and most of their friends are here. They are losing touch with their old friends at home, and it is a problem. For my husband's sake that isn't good.

Although nearly all congressional wives at the luncheon session insisted that they would always regard the district as their real home, many of them expressed pleasure at being able to spend at least part of the year in Washington. "It's nice to come to Washington and be anonymous," said one. There was immediate agreement. "At home we have no privacy at all," said another congressional wife. "My husband represents the entire state and no matter where we go he is called on at all hours of the day and night and expected to be every place at once. This is where we have family life; we don't have it in the state at all." Said a third, "I feel a little out of things when I go home. I'm not too active in club work there or in the PTA or neighborhood house, or whatever it is. But that's one good feature of the life we lead. When you are away from home so much you don't have to do certain things you'd be required to do otherwise."

The wives agreed that they had to participate in too many activities when they were back home and that opportunities to be together as a family were fewer. And though some of them found neighbors and friends to be much interested in what was going on in Washington, others felt they had to be careful not to discuss their Washington activities too often. Said one:

I have made a conscious effort when I have gone home not to talk too much about my life here because I have found that people there are not as interested as you think they are. Whether that is due to a little jealousy or envy, or whether they just don't want to know I cannot say, but it is true. I have heard other wives say the same thing.

A Conscious Effort to Compensate. The congressional wives spoke of the fact that their husbands' work required them to be away from home more often than most fathers and mentioned the difficulties this fact was likely to create for the children. Although it was pointed out that "there are people who are worse off than we are—families of traveling salesmen who hardly ever get home, for example," some discussants persisted in the point that family life was complicated by their husbands' schedule. There was much testimony that the children resented the situation.

The separations were not without certain advantages, however, as some participants noted. Congressional families are more likely than most others to be appreciative of the time they have together, and the parents make conscious attempts to compensate for the somewhat un-usual family life pattern.

I think we work harder at being good parents than the average family does. An average family which lives a so-called normal life knows it is going to have night after night and weekend after weekend together, whereas we know we will not. For at least four or five months during the year we are not even a family. I do think that as a result we wives work harder at being good parents and spend more time with the children than we would if we were living a so-called normal life.

*

I think everyone in the family appreciates all the more the time we do spend together because we just don't have as much of it as some other people.

Involvement of Children in Politics

The children of members of Congress tend to become active participants in the political process at an early age. They quickly become sophisticated about the mechanics of politics though they may lack information about the subtleties. There was testimony from the congressional wives that some make use of the information they have acquired by participating later in college campus politics. Many of their fathers had a similar beginning: growing up in a political household where politics was discussed regularly at the dinner table and in the living room, where plans were made to organize precincts and rallies, where the children attended political gatherings with their parents and were introduced to political personalities, or where they were photographed with their politician parent for campaign purposes.

Some children of congressmen work in their fathers' offices doing simple, often tedious chores. Later, as they grow older, the complexity of the tasks may increase. Whatever the assignment, they are proud to be participating in something so important. Though they may protest to their parents that the work is uninteresting, descriptions provided to friends convey the impression it is exciting and significant. As one mother related: "My husband paid our daughter $10 out of his own pocket for work she did in his office. She filed and clipped and pasted and hated it, but when she got out with her own friends, you would have thought she had the most glamorous job on earth."

Press stories about nepotism in congressional offices may conceivably affect the extent of involvement of some of the youngsters in office activities. Commented one parent:

We have a fifteen year-old boy who is pretty alert. He was keenly interested in the campaign and hated to go to bed at night because he didn't want to miss the conversation. He is very much interested in what is going on in Congress and in Washington and looks forward to the time when he might work in my husband's office. Yet because of all the nepotism charges it probably wouldn't be advisable. It isn't fair. His interest is stimulated and then he faces a blockade.

Only one parent at the Brookings meeting expressed disapproval of the tendency to expose children to at least some form of political activity. She was one of the few wives who was reluctant to participate in campaigns herself. Said she:

It is awfully hard for children to evaluate what is going on around them. So often they let their hearts rule their heads and can feel very bitter. My children have been here in school ever since my husband has been in Congress, and they haven't become involved in politics. I wouldn't want them involved. I don't think a child understands very often what is involved in a campaign, and I wouldn't want mine disillusioned as some people are. I never permit the use of my children's pictures because I don't want them exploited. My husband is up for election instead of me and the children.

One discussant pointed out that children are not always interested in politics; when young they may actually be embarrassed about their fathers' position.

When children are young, they are sometimes embarrassed by politics. They go to school in an automobile with campaign stickers on it and are just mortified. They are embarrassed to hear their father get up and speak, and they hope he isn't going to make a mistake. They feel they are different from the other children, and I think that at a certain age they want to be just like everybody else.

There was general agreement, however, that for most sons and daughters of congressmen exposure to political life is a maturing experience that helps them in their adjustments to various groups and situations and in developing poise. At the same time, parents are aware that some risks are involved. A distorted emphasis on matters of procedure and technique rather than on personal qualities or principles may develop.

I think one problem of teen-age children in politics is that they are likely to become very proficient in and very familiar with the mechanics of politics— that is what we discuss a great deal at home—and not realize that the real ingredients of a successful politician are other things altogether than just how to organize a campaign—the judgment, experience, and all the rest. They become very slick campaigners.

*

They develop into public relations experts.

Some fear was also expressed that children might come to regard a career in politics as the logical pursuit for them just because their fathers had been successful, or that they might become too politically oriented.

One thing that disturbs me occasionally is the children's great involvement in campaigns, and seeing signs that the boys think it will be the normal thing for them to continue in politics. I don't know how you feel about politics; I think it is the best of lives. I love it, but I don't think any child should think he can step into something his father, or mother for that matter, has created. I don't think that because a father has been a congressman, the son should be a congressman. Youngsters should think in terms of a professional career and then politics as the further expression of that, but not of just politics straight off.

That there are real rewards for the child, however, parents readily attest. After the risks had been enumerated, discussion returned to the values received.

One thing I feel as much as the children is the relationship which develops between you and your community in the course of campaigning. If you come to an area as an utter stranger as I did, campaigning quickly makes it more your home than the area where you were born. The children feel this way too. Instead of being the children of a neighborhood or a suburb, leading an isolated life, the whole community is theirs. If they have paraded the streets, gone into clubs or union halls, participated in door to door canvasses or seen their parents do it, their roots become very widespread and deep. Even though they leave the area and come down here—whatever community they go to—I think they will meet things in a different way later in life because of this rich experience at home.

*

Our children are six and nine. We went through a tough primary last summer, and when it was over, everybody heaved a sigh of relief and felt we could settle down. Not at all. We had a two week breather and started in again. By the end, the children were pretty fed up, but they were also very wise. It is a good experience for any child no matter how young. They get used to people coming and going and, they fit in with all sorts of people. They have learned a lot.

Some children are drawn into political campaigns because the voters in the district represented by their father seem to expect the congressman's family to campaign as a unit. A number of the discussants believed that their husbands' constituents looked favorably on the team approach. They regarded the children as important assets, worth many votes. "Districts may differ," said the most politically experienced of the wives, "but in some the voters get to feel it is a family they are voting for." "That's our situation," affirmed another. "They want to see the congressman's family and they regard the election as a family proposition. If they didn't like me or the children, they wouldn't vote for my husband. So we are all in the race together. Your community determines that. Our district is largely rural with more than a dozen counties."

Although there was no dissent to the notion that if constituents come to feel they know a congressman's family, political advantages will accrue, several conference participants were reluctant to respond to this knowledge by injecting the entire family into the campaign. One whose reluctance to have her children involved has already been noted, declared she did not believe wives should play too active a role either.

I may belong to the wrong generation. I have always felt that only my husband was running for office. I have absolutely refused to speak in public myself. In the first place, I don't think I am qualified; in the second place I am apt to express an opinion that would be completely opposite from what my husband believes.

Whatever the decision regarding the extent to which the children of congressmen should be exposed to politics, one fact is certain: their mothers are alert to the dangers involved as well as aware of the potential benefits. Their concern is evident and, as one of them commented, "makes it likely that the kids aren't going to get too far out of hand just because their father happens to be a congressman."

Wives' Role in Campaigns

All congressional wives are directly involved in their husbands' political campaigns to some extent, but marked differences are apparent. These differences are attributable to many factors and combinations of factors, such as the personal inclinations of the wife and the desires of her spouse, the nature and expectations of the district, the political division within the constituency and the strength and role of the party organization there (a close contest and/or a weak party organization may increase the need for participation by the wife), and the size of the congressman's family and the ages of his children.

Few of the wives probably would have had much interest in politics were it not for their husbands' careers. Some have had to work hard at developing interest and political awareness; for many of these, there is little interest beyond the immediate range of their spouses' political world. ("I am not especially interested in politics as such, and I have never been able to throw myself into a campaign with any real enthusiasm.") But the exigencies of the situation have forced them to apply themselves to mastery of at least some basic facts and practices, and many, starting at best from an essentially neutral position toward politics, have been surprised to discover they have come to enjoy certain of the campaign roles assigned to them. Some who "enjoy" politics get their sense of excitement about it from their husbands' political successes rather than from an appreciable personal involvement; others are not content with a passive role: by experience and preference they are equipped to play a major role, and they participate fully in the campaign itself. Most wives desire to remain in the background and restrict their activities in the campaign period to perfunctory appearances.

Virtually all of the wives believe that the voters like to meet or see them. For that reason, whatever their private attitude, they appear frequently at meetings whether they do anything beyond that. ("I do think people like to meet the candidate's wife." "I never speak if I can possibly avoid it. But people like to see you around." "Our district doesn't expect the wife to be too forward, but they are always glad to see you. They don't expect you to take on major speeches, but they welcome you in very informal situations to speak to small groups of women.") Nearly all congressional wives are skilled in meeting people and exchanging pleasantries; even those who are reticent by nature have trained themselves to do that much.

The luncheon panel considered participation by the wife more essential in a rural type district than in a densely populated, compact urban one, although some discussants from large cities regarded their activities as helpful. One woman from an urban district did not believe her presence in the campaign would make much difference, however. She said:

Our area is concentrated. The organization is important, and I don't think they particularly care whether the wife is around or not. I help some in the office, but as far as speaking or going around is concerned, that is taboo. I didn't go to one coffee party, and my opponent's wife went to about 200; I am not sure of the value of it. I think they vote for the man, particularly in a concentrated area like ours.

A very attractive wife of a representative confessed that she just could not bring herself to engage in any of the political activities which were carried on by other conferees.

I don't enter into politics at all. I just show up at evening meetings. I really don't admire myself, but it is just a matter of temperament. I think you have a lot more fun if you enter into it and know what everything is all about. I know I would be happier if I did. But I would hate ringing doorbells, for example. I think I would freeze on the spot.

Another discussant, who now plays an active role in campaigns, was quick to express sympathy: "Maybe some of us can help you. I think we were all extremely miserable when we first had to undertake this."

Although it is evident that few wives of legislators are as fearful about undertaking campaign activities as the wife quoted above, the enthusiasm with which they approach even minimal campaign responsibilities varies tremendously.

I don't campaign with my husband as much as I used to because now I am down here with the children in the fall. I will go home for a week or so at a time, however, and go with him to various meetings, particularly the coffee things. I never speak. Sometimes I go to a meeting which he can't attend, but I just shake hands with everybody and perhaps am introduced. We have a very good campaign organization and I must admit I don't participate any more than I really have to. I am not like some of you; I don't think campaigning is marvelous fun. But you feel very mean if you don't help because you want them to win. So you have to sort of grit your teeth and go ahead and participate.

*

When my husband first ran, he and I and his campaign manager were the only three in the state who thought he would win. That year I typed, mailed out materials, arranged schedules, and did everything. There was no one else to help. Since then I have felt a little bit out of it because quite an organization has developed. If we can just avoid taking this too seriously, it saves us all. I think politics is loads of fun. I love to go with my husband. I don't speak or make public appearances except when absolutely necessary, but I do love it.

Family responsibilities are unquestionably a major consideration in relegating many wives to peripheral campaign duties. As one conferee said, "I think this is one of the big conflicts the wife of a candidate faces: Should she go with her husband, or give the children at least one parent at home most of the time? During the summer I stayed home pretty much; when school started, I began attending political functions with my husband." Many attempt to resolve the problem in that way, by remaining at home with the family during most of the campaign and enlisting the services of a relative or friend to take care of the children during the two or three weeks immediately preceding the election so that the wife can join the candidate on the campaign circuit. Another fairly common procedure, if the wife and children remain in the Washington area, is for the wife to make several short trips to the district during the course of the campaign.

My feeling is that if you can campaign with your husband and manage your family, well fine, but I think a woman's place is first with her family. I stay here with the children and go home for four or five brief trips during the election period. I worked with my husband in his first campaign, and I must say that was most exciting and exhilarating. No campaign ever comes up to the experience of the first one. I worked in headquarters handling all the little chores someone has to take over, such as folding and stuffing envelopes and getting people together to work. I also went around to meetings with him a great deal. Right up until I was pregnant with our first child, I spoke informally before women's groups. Now I confine myself to helping out occasionally in the Washington office during the busy part of the campaign period.

Not all wives with families are able to confine themselves to so sporadic a campaign schedule, however. One conferee who clearly relishes politics and assumes important responsibilities in her husband's campaigns persuaded a school teacher from her state to move to Washington for three months to take care of her children and then hastened back home to campaign with her husband. Another westerner who does not particularly like politics also joined her husband on the campaign trail though her role was that of companion rather than political assistant. As she described it:

The children are in school during the campaign. Their grandmother comes to take care of them, and I travel with my husband for three months. Our district covers three-fourths of the state, and we get home once every two weeks. I just go along as a companion, to give a little moral support, check his clothes, and do the little things I do at home. I just like to be good company. I always remain in the background. The voters are making a decision on the candidate. That is the way I feel about it as a voter myself. The wife is not the one who will be making the decisions in Congress.

Sometimes, if there is a primary contest or if the November election appears likely to be closely contested, the wife will return to the congressional district in advance of her husband to help get the campaign under way. This is especially likely if the prospects for an early adjournment of Congress are remote. Again, some wives who precede their husbands home tend to be more directly involved in political activities than others. One may return to the district with a sound film prepared by her husband and show it at various coffee meetings, as did one participant. Since Congress was in session at the time she undertook the project, her appearance as a substitute for her husband's presence was readily accepted. Another wife, who had entered politics before her husband, regularly returns to the district by the first of June when there is an August primary and remains until after the November election. Her campaign responsibilities are heavy.

Usually I write the publicity and send it out. It was very difficult at first in a one paper town with the paper against you. Now the paper is more friendly, and the task is easier; the paper sends its reporters over to get the news. I don't ever make speeches, but I still do campaign organization work. If there is a precinct that doesn't look good, I go into it and try to build it up since I have the know-how and am used to the technique. I see that every house is canvassed and try to arrange for a poll. Then I always do spot-checking at the polls on election day. I usually work as an inside challenger and select a precinct I am not sure of but which I have worked on. Then I see how effective I have been. I always have a poll book and get quite a bang out of comparing them over the years. We always do a strenuous analyzing job after election. We take every precinct and break it down, get the figures from each of our workers in the precinct, compare it with his poll book, and talk with him to see how we can do better there next time.

There are several broad categories of participation by congressional wives in campaigns. There are those wives who are involved in the sense of being on display, of accompanying their husbands to political meetings, and attending coffee meetings. Wives in this group normally do not give speeches, nor do they help to arrange meetings or participate directly in the core work of the campaign. Another group supplements these activities by working more actively, although in a subordinate way, in the organization, perhaps at party headquarters, handling necessary but often unexciting tasks. They may organize coffee hours, recruit women as drivers to take voters to the polls or for general precinct work, or themselves assist in the mailings and routine office work. A smaller group of wives could be described as professional campaigners. They may have official and first rank campaign responsibilities such as accepting speaking engagements, directing precinct activities, or preparing advertising copy, brochures, and general publicity.

Whatever their intended role, it is likely that all wives find themselves with more activities than they had expected to perform. The following statements of the experiences of several of the wives indicate something of the diversity of activity that exists.

Out west we have to do our campaigning with a rather informally organized group. There the wife is more involved with the mechanics of politics than the ideas, although I like to think I am involved in the policies and ideas too. A good deal of my time is spent being a chauffeur and in helping keep things organized. When we started in political life I wrote brochures, not because I had any great ability but because I was the only person available. I don't do much writing now. I speak when it is necessary but I don't seek speaking engagements. I travel with my husband, and when he cannot travel, if there is need for it, I travel for him.

*

Our district is a rural one where everybody knows everybody else, and the wives are expected to be with their husbands or have a good reason not to be. People expect to know you and your family and love to hear all about what you doing. That interests them much more than the issues in Washington. As far as actual campaign work is concerned, our primary is the important thing, and that means that the campaign takes place in the summer when the whole family can take part. There are no professionals up our way; we all get out and do our bit. Our first campaign was the hardest; my husband had six primary opponents. I spent several days in the most antagonistic sections of each of several cities going from door to door. It was a liberal education. Last year there were times when I had to take my husband's place at political rallies when he had made double engagments. He would choose one and leave me with the other. I often got the hardest one because he feels a wife can stand up and smile and everything will be all right. In fact, I have always been sent out to do just that sort of job. The hardest nuts to crack are the best ones on which to try the sunshine technique.

*

My husband represents a fairly concentrated area of more than 700,000 people where the voter registration figures heavily favor the opposition. We really have to work to win. Last time we used a mobile office. At first we tried having someone take the office from one location to another, but that didn't work out too well, so finally I learned to drive it myself. I drove it all over the city and county. It had big pictures and signs like "meet your congressman." My husband tried to be at that office as much as possible, but I found I could be helpful there too. People came with their problems or gripes and wanted to talk to their congressman. Since he couldn't see everyone even when he was there, many of them would talk to me instead.

*

In our state everybody loves politics, and the big race is in the primary. I don't have to campaign much anymore, but there were more than a dozen candidates when my husband first ran. We could see that the contest was going to be between him and another man. The state had just redistricted, and there were sixteen counties instead of the old eight with which we had been pretty familiar. My husband took the new ones, and I took the old ones, and it was do or die. Every candidate for every office made the truckline on the back of a pick-up truck with a microphone. You had three minutes, and you made your speech. That went on every night in one little town after another. It hasn't been so rough since.

*

This is my husband's first term. His predecessor had retired, and our opponent started his campaign early, but my husband was in the state legislature which ran very late. In September we got a housekeeper, and I organized campaign headquarters. At first we just used volunteers, but then we hired a couple of secretaries and did a lot of mailing. In our city I organized a group of 150 to cover every ward and precinct on election day. We had them checking at the polls and handing out literature, and we had drivers. We had every factory covered with people to give voters a ride to the polls. I also went into two other cities and set up coffee hours and attempted to establish an election day organization. My husband's district includes 93 cities and towns, and since he had represented only one small county when he was a state senator, he was not well known. Therefore I went out every day too. I'd take fourteen to twenty people with me, and we'd cover a town until every house was contacted and then move on to another one. We spent three weeks in one Democratic city working very hard and getting a really wonderful reception. My husband got a better vote there than any Republican had ever received.

Other Activities

Campaigning, of course, is but a small part of the lives of wives of members of Congress. Inevitably they are drawn into community activities, partly because of genuine interest and partly because they are conscious of the special demands of their position as wives of congressmen. Because they spend so much of the year in the Washington area, most of them are active there rather than in the district. They prefer this not only because they are less in the spotlight but also because in the positions of leadership they might have to assume at home they would be vulnerable to misunderstandings and animosities that could conceivably be detrimental to their husbands' future. Even those wives who spend most of their time in Washington, however, find it wise to retain their district club affiliations and to attend meetings when they are at home. Said one of them:

> I still maintain my membership in all of the organizations back home—the League of Women Voters, the American Association of University Women, and groups like that. When you count up the dues it makes a sizable sum, but my husband tells me to maintain my membership. When I am home I try to go to all the meetings because it is a good way to see again people I have known and worked with in the past. I become a clubwoman to end all club-women.

For some wives, however, the necessity for moving to and fro between Washington and the home district removes the opportunity to participate effectively in many worthy organizations which in the words of one, "really get at the meat of living." As she explains it,

> I know several wives who really live the "great lady" role. They are extremely conscious of their position and live it to the hilt. I think they are probably the happiest wives in Washington. For my part, I feel I am missing a great deal by not being able to participate in what I consider to be the basic activities that support the best in our culture—American Association of University Women, PTA, Scouts, Camp Fire Girls, League of Women Voters—all the organizations that really get at the meat of living. The reason for the lack of active participation is the obvious one of not being in any one place long enough to be worth anything to an organization.

Many Washington-based congressional wives do find time to participate in activities of their church, the PTA, scouts, and such groups, however. Since there is less pressure than would exist in the district, participation may be more enjoyable.

The Brookings conferees were especially active in church work and in settlement house work. Most of them also participated in various activities of the Congressional Wives Club. This organization sponsors an ambitious program, which goes far beyond social functions. There is an extensive "educational" program, for example, which includes current events groups and language study classes. International clubs have been organized that extend membership to wives of foreign diplomats and are devoted to developing international understanding. Work with underprivileged groups in the Washington area is encouraged, with excellent results.

Red Cross units of the congressional wives meet regularly to sew and roll bandages. There are classes, too, in public speaking, bridge, art, and flower arrangement. There are trips to historic landmarks, regular teas, and many special events. There is even a bowling club. The Congressional Wives Club, then, is a busy organization that provides a variety of activities—some service, some educational, some social—to meet the needs and interests of its clientele. It offers an excellent opportunity for wives of new members of congress to make friends quickly with their peers. Congressmen frequently comment that the participation of their wives in such activities has proved beneficial to them since close friendships between wives of members often have led to the development of close ties between the members themselves.

Entertaining People from Home. Because their circle of acquaintants in the home district is large, the possibility always exists that congressional families will be called on frequently to entertain people from home who are visiting Washington; for some congressional wives this constitutes a heavy burden. A few families even open their homes to a designated number of students from their congressional districts each year and treat them as members of the family as they seek to gain a better understanding of the way Congress functions by "observing" in the congressman's office. Some wives who are particularly interested in the workings of Congress frequently attend sessions of the House, especially when their husbands are going to participate in debate. Many find this is a good way to entertain constituents, and at the same time add to their own understanding.

Working in the Congressional Office. A number of wives participate in one way or another in the work of their husbands' congressional offices, a few even serving as principal assistant. More common is part-time or occasional work in the office, particularly during "rush periods." Wives may assist in the reading and tabulation of annual questionnaires to constituents, in the addressing of the often extensive Christmas card mailings, or they may handle specific kinds of "case" mail problems.

Reports to the District. Some of them—in their own name—substitute occasionally for their husbands in writing newsletters to be sent to district residents, giving them a woman's slant on Washington. There is much testimony to indicate that these distaff-written newsletters are often more favorably received than those prepared by their husbands. Related one congressman, "Ordinarily I don't get too many comments on my newsletter, but whenever my wife writes it, we get a lot of favorable letters, some of them suggesting that I stop writing the report and let her do it all the time."

Despite impressive evidence that the wives' writing efforts have been well received, not all legislators are willing to permit their spouses to undertake the responsibility for an issue. Reported one wife, "Occasionally my husband will say he doesn't know what to put in his newsletter. I tell him I will write one about visiting the White House, or attending a reception, or touring Washington, or something like that. He doesn't even answer me."

A few congressional wives prepare regular reports for the people back home, although the vast majority who try their hand at writing newsletters or columns limit their efforts to one or two a year. Generally, the reports are not issue-oriented but seek rather to describe Washington and its personalities to constituents. One wife who prepares many of her husband's campaign materials also writes a weekly column, which is distributed widely throughout her home state. The mother of several children, she writes the column at home. As she explains her experience:

I write a weekly newspaper column from Washington, which is used by fourteen newspapers in our state as well as by two television stations. I don't comment on politics at all. The leased wire services and television networks provide good coverage on that—they know things the minute you know them in Washington. It would be pretentious of me to try to write better columns on politics than the professional political columnists. I find that whatever I can tell the people back home about the nation's capital in terms of the personalities, the glamour, the little personal things that happen, is very well received. Just like everyone else, they like to read about "names," in the news.

I had to learn this. At first I did "think" pieces. At Easter time I would write a column about religion in the nation's capital for which I would do a great deal of research. I learned a lot, but the readers were bored. So I began to say that in church at Easter we sat beside so and so, talked with cabinet member so and so, and saw so and so. If something clever or amusing happens somewhere when I am present, I mention that too. I really try to write good newspaper copy; I don't attempt to send a message. I try not to mention our own family except very casually. Oh, I mention little personal things about the children or my husband occasionally, but the column is not designed to toot our own horn. I am sure I would lose a lot of readers if I did that.

I receive a great deal of mail from the column and my husband reports that he gets many favorable comments as he travels around the district. The other day I said to him, "You know, I would like to see if I could write something a little more serious. I'd like to try something else now." And he said, "You stick to that column."

The Wives' Mail. Even wives who have little direct association with politics and almost none with the congressional office receive mail from individuals and organizations attempting to persuade them to influence their husbands on certain legislative proposals. Such mail is sometimes marked "personal," and the envelope carries no indication of its source— the sender wants to be certain the letter is not thrown away unopened. Few of these letters are answered. Most congressional wives will reply to none coming from outside their own congressional district; within that area, only letters from friends and acquaintances are likely to receive attention. Generally, if any reply is made, the response is to the effect that the congressman is the legislator in the family.

Constituents' Misconceptions

Congressmen feel that the public possesses many misconceptions about the job of the congressman, and this sentiment is shared by their wives. The latter stress that people are particularly uninformed about the financial aspects of congressional life. Many wives consider the salary and perquisites inadequate in view of the demands made on congressmen, and they believe constituents tend to feel the legislator is well paid. They assert that there is a widespread belief that the government pays the entertainment expenses of congressmen—that Washington visitors, for example, think that if their representative takes them to lunch, the Congress takes care of the bill. In truth, the wives point out, such personal expenses place a heavy burden on legislators. And every organized group in a congressional district seems to expect a congressman to become a dues paying member or at least to purchase tickets for dinners or benefits sponsored by the group. There is little appreciation that other organizations are making similar requests and that it is impossible for the congressman to accommodate many of them. Each organization is convinced that its activities are worthy of support and is not understanding about failure to contribute to that support.

Again, frequent travel between Washington and the district is necessary for most congressmen, yet the public does not realize that only three round trips per year are paid for by the government, the rest of the financial burden being assumed by the legislator. In addition to imposing limits on the congressman's visits, these costs influence considerably the number of trips to the district which the rest of the congressman's family can take. Explained one wife:

> We would like to go back to the district often, but it is just too expensive. There are five in our family. We try to get back there every Christmas and it costs us $1,000 each time. My husband makes six to eight trips a year—he just has to do that—but the rest of us can't move around like that.

The wives regret, too, that most voters have no understanding of how busy congressmen really are. Nor do they realize that a congressman's responsibilities do not end with the adjournment of Congress; that, in fact, he often is extremely busy back in the district during the adjournment period or on special committee assignments. "They think," protested one conferee, "that when Congress adjourns in August you have until January for a vacation." "'How are you enjoying your vacation?' they'll say," added another discussant. "It always seems too petulant to try to stop and explain the true situation. Unless I think it is someone who would benefit from such an explanation I just say I am enjoying it." Some dismay was also expressed because "most people don't know when Congress adjourns or convenes or why." Thus, when members of Congress and their families return to the district "people ask 'what are you doing here?' Half the time people just don't know what is going on."

Lack of information about how Congress works leads to other misunderstandings. One wife who works part-time in her husband's office said:

> Most people don't know anything about the way Congress functions. Many people phone long distance and want to talk to the congressman. When you tell them he is on the House floor, they say, "*What*, he is not in his office?" When he is in committee they don't get the picture either. Now I just go through a regular spiel telling them that committees go into session at 10:00 or 10:30 a.m. and that they must phone earlier if they want to talk to the congressman.

The wives agreed that, in the words of one of their number, "the telephone has worked a great hardship." Not only are constituents finding it increasingly convenient to phone their congressman about their problems or their reactions, rather than writing him, but they are not sensitive to the time changes between regions, or capable of making judgments as to what is really important. As the wives analyze the situation,

A two or three hour time change can make quite a difference. They don't realize that when it is 11 p.m. at home it is two in the morning here. They have a serious problem, they have explored it thoroughly, and now they have a message for their congressman. At one or two o'clock in the morning our phone rings and they want to talk to him.

*

I have had the press call at two in the morning. When you protest it is late and you were awakened they say "it is very important. It is vital." It never is vital, and press people should know better. They are just suiting their own convenience.

Another difficulty observed by the wives was that many constituents seem to think their representatives can solve all problems effortlessly, that their power to obtain quick and favorable action is practically unlimited. Unfortunately, congressional wives believe, both the expectations and attitudes of voters are often unreasonable. Failure to obtain prompt satisfaction leads to sharp, unjustified criticism of the legislators, which their wives resent.

An Interesting, Stimulating, and Varied Life

Despite its many drawbacks, congressional life has important compensations, which for most congressional wives far outweigh the disadvantages. They are glad their husbands are doing "something important," that the legislators enjoy their work and are set apart from their fellow citizens. If they resent the carping to which a member of Congress is exposed, they also note with satisfaction evidence that his efforts in behalf of constituents are often appreciated.

From a personal point of view the wives enjoy the associations that being part of the congressional milieu facilitates, "the occasional witnessing of an historic event, the privilege of being invited to the White House, the satisfaction of meeting interesting people." They may derive much personal satisfaction from politics and thus be pleased to be "at the center of things." For most of them the life is a far more stimulating, interesting, and varied one than would have been their lot if their husbands had not entered politics. They emphasize that their main concern is to help their husbands in their careers: since the life of a congressman is strenuous and tension packed, he needs the cooperation and sympathetic understanding of his spouse. Even if they do not assist in political activities, the role of the wives may be central. As one wife stressed: "The wives carry a great responsibility and a great burden. Many a politician has gone very far because of the type of wife he had behind him. Often she is the silent kind who because of personality or time does not participate actively in the political life her husband leads." But some congressional wives, stressing the unique opportunities afforded them, would deny that their problems are any greater than those facing wives whose husbands are in other occupations. Said one:

I don't think congressional wives are really any different from wives in any other line of work. Our job, as I see it, is to backstop our husbands. It takes all kinds of wives just as it takes all kinds of wives in any group. In some instances, you can see that the wife is the driving force, and in other instances, the man couldn't possibly be married to a woman like that. The particular problem of congressional wives is mostly a matter of being physically in the wrong part of of the country at the wrong time, but the real problems of living aren't too different from those of any other family.

It is clear that, if asked to describe their lives, congressional wives would echo the words of Ellen Maury Slayden, wife of a member of the Texas delegation, about a half century ago: "Oh, what a mixture of sweet and bitter this congressional life is!"[3]

[3] *Washington Wife: Journal of Ellen Maury Slayden* (Harper, 1963), p. 86.

X

Is It Worth While?

My father served in Congress from 1909 to 1919 from the State of Texas. During his last term I was one of his clerks. Congress sat for six months the first session and three months the second session. A representative got about fifteen letters a week. Only at rare intervals would a constituent come to see him. He had no pressure groups to contend with. Because Congress enacted only a few bills each session, legislation got the deliberative attention it deserved. Every member had plenty of time to study bills in committee before they came on the floor. Debate was important in the consideration of every bill. A member did not take the floor until he had carefully got together as many facts as were available. When he spoke, he knew his subject. A good debater had no trouble getting a large audience in the chamber. Most of the member's time was spent on legislation. There was little else for him to do.[1]

Thus wrote Representative Martin Dies in 1954, recalling a relaxed and orderly pattern of congressional life, which would not be recognized by the congressmen of today. Though many members thrive amidst the turmoil, the uncertainties, and the fast pace that now characterize their life, others would prefer the more leisurely, less fretful existence of their predecessors.

The Price of Congressional Life

The life of a current member of the House is not an easy one. He works long hours yet virtually never can meet the many demands on his time. No matter how effective he is and how much he accomplishes, he can never satisfy all of his friends and constituents. He can seldom fully anticipate his schedule, being constantly subject to the whims of others. His job will not make him rich, and the position he holds is not accorded

[1] "Truth about Congressmen," *Saturday Evening Post*, Oct. 30, 1954, Vol. 227, p. 31.

the respect and deference by the public to which he thinks it is entitled. Tension, if not conflict, is a dominant element in his life.

Sources of Tension. The sources of tension are many and varied. The complexity, diversity, and volume of legislative proposals tax severely his industry, knowledge, and self-confidence and require that he cast votes on issues he does not fully understand. To compensate for his inability to master many of the issues himself, he relies on the judgment of colleagues presumed to have the necessary expertise. Yet this dependence on others, though necessary, is in itself a source of unrest and uneasiness. A clear-cut party position, especially on matters of less than paramount importance to his constituents, might ease his task and conscience significantly, but the party takes few official stands.

There are persistent demands from constituents, some of them patently outrageous, others legitimate, many impossible to evaluate, which draw the legislator into unpleasant or prolonged encounters with the executive. Whatever the merit of the constituent request, the member's dependence on voter support usually dictates that he and his staff expend precious time and energy in an effort to satisfy it, or at least to determine that the constituent is not entitled to redress. Most congressmen do like people and enjoy being of service to them; indeed that is one of the greatest sources of satisfaction with the job. Yet the most tolerant are at times dismayed by the thoughtlessness and ingratitude of some of their constituents. Letters and phone calls at home at all hours of day and night, demands rather than requests, and frequent slights or insults add to the member's irritation with voters. And the belligerence of some constituents' dissatisfaction with the results of his endeavors are distressing and difficult to accept with equanimity, especially when an earnest effort has been made to exhaust all avenues of approach. The legislator takes far more abuse from people than he would wish. And it bothers him.

His life is not only exhausting and exacting, it is uncertain. His future is precarious, dependent on the whim of inadequately informed voters from whom he seldom gets definite instructions. His insecure tenure leads to concentration on the problem of re-election and dictates attention to the types of activities believed essential to this. His problem is complicated by the fact that even on important issues the mandate from his constituents is frequently not clear, and on less controversial ones it usually is not even observable. This does not mean he will not be held accountable for errors of judgment. He knows that public sentiment is capable of shifting or firming suddenly and that his foresight may need to match the public's hindsight. He is constantly vulnerable, then, to forces that he may neither be able to anticipate nor control. Frequently, too, conflicting demands are made on him, and there is no sure way to resolve them.

In the House, the member is part of a system he does not fully comprehend and may never master. Its mysteries are often difficult to unravel, a source of considerable dissatisfaction. Sometimes he is exasperated by the inaction, the cumbersome traditions, and his inability to obtain a significant role. The latter plight is made more serious by his strong desire to secure a status with which he can impress constituents. His apprenticeship period may be particularly trying since he discovers that he is not immediately accepted as a full-fledged member of the group. Failure of House veterans and leaders to solicit his views increases his sensitivity and occasionally leads to bitterness. Commented one frustrated representative, "Sometimes you get the idea that everything is managed at the top and that the decisions are none of your business. Or that the leaders feel they don't have time to keep you informed."

There are many other unappealing aspects of the job, some of them closely related to the tension-producing situations referred to above. For many serious members one of the most disturbing features of congressional life is the little time available for meditation and contemplation, for systematic study of important problems. An allied complaint is that "there are so few opportunities to sit down together and talk over mutual problems." One member in discussing some of the shortcomings of House practice commented: "There is so little opportunity to change things. What we really need to do is stop and take a good look at ourselves, but the prospects are not good that we will." Much of the work, though it serves some parochial purpose, seems unimportant, yet the legislator fears to ignore or shed it.

The necessity of "shooting from the hip" on occasion and the difficulties inherent in surmounting successfully the stern competition for the attention of the public give rise to actions that lead critics to assert the member is shallow. Observed one former academician serving in the House, "Politics *demands* gross simplification to the point of over-simplification. Statements run the risk of being little more than slogans."

The disruption of a normal family pattern, the moderate salary with which to meet the high built-in costs of the job, the long sessions, which the congressman is not always persuaded are necessary, the exhausting and continuing pace that permits relatively little time for relaxation—all of these constitute serious disadvantages. And campaigning, an enjoyable exercise for some legislators, is much dreaded by others. The member wonders why he subjects himself to the strains, and he worries about his role. Commented one hardworking representative: "Sometimes the frustration of the job seems overwhelming. You get the feeling you are not contributing as much as you would like to legislative policy."

Sometimes a member may obtain release for his frustration by lashing out at "the system." Thus one liberal Democrat, angered by the defeat of several proposals he thought could have been passed, blamed the moderate leadership of his party in the House. In a reference to the influential position of southern members in party councils including the speakership and committee chairmanships, he asked, "How do you expect to win when you have a union army led by confederate generals?" And a liberal colleague evidenced a similar frustration: "Here we have a majority of 130 and yet have accomplished much less than we did in previous congresses when our majority was slimmer. Something definitely has to be wrong in such a situation. The answer is the lack of leadership."

For members of the minority the frustrations may be even greater, particularly if they have remained relegated to minority status for extended periods of time. They become despondent about their inability to "stem the tide." If they firmly believe that the policies of the opposition are injurious to the nation, the despondency deepens. They may ask colleagues as one member did, "How long can you keep on feeling you have to continue to fight for your country if you are fighting virtually alone?"

But all minority members do not share that view. As one said: "I feel there is altogether too much defeatism among Republicans. It distresses me. All I hear is, 'well, if things don't get any better, I am going to pull out and let somebody else do the worrying.' It doesn't bother me at all that our cause may not prevail immediately. Just because we are 153 compared to 282 doesn't make it impossible for us to write a pretty good record this session."

Disruption of Family Life. Representatives often refer to the disruption of family life. In fact this may well be the disadvantage most frequently mentioned in connection with a job which, on balance, is generally satis-fying.[2] He is often separated from his family for the better part of several months a year. A typical lament was expressed in late August when Con-gress was still in session that "we are separated nearly half the year and that is a pretty bad situation."

And some legislators say that congressional life is even more difficult for the family of the member than for the member himself since he may be thoroughly engrossed in his work: "My wife has said bluntly more than once that politics is for bachelors and grandfathers. It is not for fathers." Problems associated with the education of their children are especially difficult. As one congressman said: "I think it is very hard on the family, particularly if you have school age children, and they move back and forth from one school to another. It is a good experience for one or two years, but after that it is a great sacrifice on their part." Another member summed congressional thinking when he said: "One of the really underestimated problems in a congressional life is that Congress, like war, is always harder on the women and children than it is on the men."

The Financial Burden. Originally paid $6 a day during attendance, mem-bers of the House today receive an annual salary of $22,500[3] of which, for income tax purposes, up to $3,000 is deductible for living expenses. They are permitted three paid round trip visits to their district each session, but prior to 1963 they were allowed only one.

Personal expenses are heavy, heavier than most citizens realize. Com-plained one member bitterly: "Being a congressman is an unusually costly operation. The average person thinks we are making a killing here, that we are rolling in money. As a result we get requests for contributions from everyone." The two-year term means that election is always just around the corner and in most districts campaign costs are high. Many members maintain two homes, one in the district and one in the Washing-ton area, make frequent trips to their constituency (some go home

---

[2] It was the item most frequently expressed by congressmen interviewed in con-nection with the preparation of this volume. But it should be noted that most opinions were solicited at the conclusion of a long session when the disadvantages would naturally be most apparent.

[3] The Speaker receives $35,000 yearly plus a $10,000 expense allowance.

weekly), and have heavy entertainment expenses. Although most congressmen seem to accept the situation philosophically, it is a fairly common observation that frequently visitors to Washington are under the delusion that congressmen have generous expense accounts, when in fact they have none at all, and therefore are in a position to entertain them. And some visitors mistakenly believe that meals in the House Restaurant are free to members of Congress. With respect to the frequency of requests for contributions to district organizations one member said:

> When I get to the district I have to attend all sorts of banquets and other functions. All of this increases the out of pocket expenses. Then there are various other contributions. For example, a women's club sent me ten $1 tickets to a function it was sponsoring. I returned the tickets. The head of the organization told me the ladies were very upset. I explained I had more than 1,200 organizations in my district, a large percentage of whom called on me for contributions and that I just couldn't afford to do it. She explained that her organization was different. They all think their group is different!

Office expenses for activities such as the newsletter or questionnaire frequently exceed allowances, and the legislator sometimes is forced to draw on personal funds for these undertakings. While many congressmen assert they are foregoing higher salaries to serve in the House, even those who are making more money than they might receive in other occupations are concerned about the high costs of the job. Less money would go much further back in the district. Some members seek to supplement their incomes by writing articles or scheduling paid speaking engagements, although they are not as successful in these endeavors as Senators. Other members may retain their interest in a business back in the district. For many solons, however, the obstacles associated with such undertakings are serious if not overwhelming. Being a congressman is a full-time job. Said one legislator: "This is not only a job where you don't make any money, it has become a full-time job. Some years ago it was possible to be a congressman and maintain an active and remunerative business. The fact that it is a full-time job means that some congressmen just can't afford to stay here."

Congressmen representing districts close to Washington are especially vulnerable to constituent and party organization demands on their time, thus obviating the advantages that proximity to the district might appear to have for members desiring to maintain an interest in a law practice or business. Qualms about possible conflict of interest aside, few solons believe they are in a position to participate actively in another occupation. As one stated: "It is a matter of principle, but even if it were not, there would be no time. Between sessions I am very busy on congressional matters."

The Inside Versus the Outside View

Although many members of Congress are quick to identify things about their job and the workings of the House that differ substantially from their precongressional expectations, a large number of congressmen, notably freshmen, seem reluctant to state that the realities depart much from what they had anticipated. Yet even those who profess to have found few surprises often reveal by their remarks that their "outside" view did indeed differ markedly from what they have experienced as members of the House. It is likely that even the more sophisticated of the congressmen had considerable adjusting to do when they first entered Congress.

Prior Misconceptions of Members. The near absence of party discipline or instruction regarding voting, the inadequate system of communication, the importance of tradition, and the complex nature of the lines of authority and action are all subjects for comment by even the more knowledgeable of legislators. Congressmen are shocked by the "utter and complete lack of party discipline. I thought the lines of authority and action were simpler than they actually are. On what seemed to be issues of importance, there has been no line of communication from anybody on how you should vote." Many congressmen also expected to share more fully and quickly in the drafting of legislation, and others did not foresee how busy they would be, or how their time would be allocated. They failed to anticipate the extent of the nonlegislative as opposed to legislative aspects of the job. The following comments indicate these reactions:

I came here thinking I would immediately share in the drafting of legislation. As all of us soon discover, the likelihood of first or second termers, and particularly minority members, doing any major drafting of legislation that passes is slim if not completely unknown. And I campaigned on the issue of how few bills my predecessor got enacted into law! Now I know that if we had been here, there is little chance that we would have done more.

*

From the outside, we felt that there was some relationship between the number of times a person spoke and what he did, or between the publicity he got and what he did. When we read that he spoke in the House, we envisaged 435 people listening in rapt attention.

*

I had supposed most of a congressman's time would be devoted to the consideration of legislation. Ideally, I think it should be. Practically, it is not and probably cannnot be.

*

I had visions of coming here and finding it sort of a lark. Now I find I am in a position where percentagewise the men work longer hours and with greater dedication than in any other phase of our life anywhere.

Representatives confess they were pleasantly surprised by the high calibre of their colleagues. They had entered Congress prepared to believe themselves superior to the majority of the legislators, but respect for their peers developed quickly. In the words of one member:

I came here expecting that I was lowering myself a little bit to be associated with some of the people I had read about in the press, some of the characters in Congress who make the headlines. I looked down my nose just a bit. But after I got here I became very much impressed by the number of dedicated people in the Congress who work harder and longer and take more guff than they ever would take in private life, in order to serve their people.

And another stated:

One of the pleasant surprises to me was the special competence of a great many members of the Congress. The first few months I was here, I was amazed as I watched subcommittee chairmen handle bills on the floor and display their expert knowledge on problems that really covered a rather broad area. The capabilities of a good majority of the Congress are really impressive.

Misconceptions of the Public. Whether they admit to having held erroneous ideas about the legislative process or the duties of a congressman prior to their election, legislators are united in believing that the public is poorly informed about Congress. They insist that the views held by the public do not do justice to elected representatives, their job, or the legislative process. Ignoring the fact that they and their colleagues lacked proper perspective regarding Congress prior to election, some members severely indict the voters for the misconceptions they possess. Public disparagement of congressmen and lack of appreciation of their tasks and the way they perform them are among the most discouraging and disturbing features of the job. Yet they see no remedy for the situation.

Understandably, representatives are particularly sensitive to assertions that congressmen generally are not of high calibre, that they are un informed, narrow in outlook and range of interest, lazy, greedy, and possibly dishonest. Such charges are challenged by House members. Although they readily admit, privately at least, that there are people in the House who should not be there, there is no doubt that they are impressed with the resourcefulness and ability of the average member. They regret that disclosures regarding activities of a few of their associates are often used to indict the Congress as a whole: for this they blame the affinity of certain elements of the press for "sensationalism." The failure of the press to present a balanced view of the Congress is frequently scored.

Congressmen believe that not only does the public tend to underestimate the intelligence and versatility of legislators, but it also mistakenly thinks the job of the congressman to be substantially less demanding than it is. Thus solons insist the public is not aware of the long hours they spend in discharging their congressional duties, and of the little opportunity for vacation. Said one of the most idealistic, noted for his straightforward honesty and independence: "The general public thinks congressmen are more corrupt and less hardworking than they actually are. It fails to give congressmen credit for what they do. It doesn't realize how much work, and how much diverse work, is involved in being a congressman."

Although members resent being dismissed as lazy, many of them are not surprised that citizens fail to appreciate the congressional workload, since they themselves were astounded to discover how onerous it is. Said a member:

> Our constituents think that congressmen have a soft easy job. They think we are on vacation when Congress is out of session. I wish we were, but of course it is closer to the fact to say we don't get any vacation at all. The average citizen has no conception of how hard we work. The mortality rate of congressmen shows very clearly what the real situation is.

Many congressmen attribute the failure of people to appreciate the congressman and the work he does to widespread ignorance regarding the

IS IT WORTH WHILE?

mechanics of the congressional operation. The public, it is said, tends to oversimplify the process and is incapable of grasping its intricacies. It does not understand that legislation itself is complicated and often not easy to appraise. As one congressman said: "This government is so complicated and people just don't realize it. They tend to equate legislation as being either good or bad. They oversimplify the problem. All legislation has some good and some bad in it, and it is a matter of determining where the balance is."

The American people know little of the important role of the committee system or its implications for public policy, do not realize that there are firmly established ways of doing things in the House that are not easily avoided, and are impatient for results. "The public feels that if you understand a problem exists and is acute you can solve it quickly by introducing corrective legislation," stated one member. "People don't understand the parliamentary situation or how things get passed. They think the minute you see the light you can achieve your goal. That just isn't true."

During the period when there was a Republican President and a Democratic congress, legislators of both parties complained about the public's lack of understanding of the situation. Republicans said their party was erroneously held responsible for mistakes because the President was Republican, citizens failing to appreciate that the President's freedom to enact his program was severely hampered by a Democratic congressional majority. Democrats contended that because they controlled the Congress, the public charged them with responsibility for the program, ignoring the fact that what Congress could accomplish was limited by threats of a presidential veto.

One representative expressed the view that the most serious error made about Congress is that "the public thinks a congressman can do far more for them than he actually can do, and so they make all kinds of demands. Some of these things just cannot be accomplished."

In one expression of this view, there is also widespread feeling within the House that constituents exaggerate the ability of members to intervene successfully in their behalf in disputes with the executive branch. "The public thinks congressmen are endowed with great powers to straighten out administrative decisions," observed another member. "As a result they call upon us for practically everything." Complained one congressman: "Anybody who has any problems with the federal government thinks the solution occurs just as soon as he calls his congressman about it. They must think we have a magic wand which can solve all of their problems."

Congressmen share the view that many constituents are unreasonable regarding failures to achieve results. Though the legislators deeply appreciate the gratitude of many individuals whom they have assisted, the ingratitude of the few stands out clearly in their minds. Since some people anticipate a favorable result as a matter of course, they are not properly appreciative even in the face of a completely satisfactory resolution of the problem. If results fall short of constituent hopes or expectations, the congressman may feel the voter's wrath.

The Satisfactions of the Job

After complaints about the job have been aired, however, the fact remains that there are important compensations that lead legislators to seek voluntarily continued exposure to the demanding, strenuous, and insecure existence that characterizes the world of the congressman. They could make more money elsewhere and escape some of the frustrations, disappointments, and indignities as well as enjoy a more normal and relaxed schedule. Yet as one freshman member put it:

I think we all want to come back. I know I do, even though I have a good practice in my home community. My wife says that there should be a politicians anonymous similar to the alcoholics anonymous, that politics gets in your blood and you just can't seem to get it out, that we wouldn't be happy anywhere else.

A third term congressman concurred: "I think the tensions here become a part of a person's life and existence. They call it 'Potomac Fever' and a lot of things, but once you are here and it gets in your blood, there is no turning back." Other members speak of being similarly gripped by politics; discussions about their job are replete with analogies to the alcoholic or the dope addict:

I have never taken dope but I imagine the politician is rather like a dope addict. It [politics] gets on your back and you can't shake it.

*

There is an emotional excitement in being here. It is like alcoholism. At one time or another most of us no doubt have been beset with the frustrations of the thing and have thought "What am I doing this for?" Then we reflect on it; for about two weeks it would be fine and then we would be like the alcoholic without his drink.

It is this fascination for politics that caused a much respected legislator to confess, "I love the job and worry that when the time comes for me to pass off the stage, I may not have the balance to accept it with the grace I hope I might." What are the attractions which make the job so irresistible?

Excitement and Challenge. With all its drawbacks, the job of the congressman is exciting, stimulating, and challenging. There is a tremendous variety in the work, and little of a routine nature that cannot be delegated to someone else. And as one congressman observed: "It is always different even when we are dealing with the same problems." Another member expressed part of the appeal for him when he said, "You are on the Board of Directors of a $100 billion a year corporation." Even legislators who initially viewed election to Congress as a transitory thing often find themselves captivated by the opportunities and rewards it provides. One successful businessman relates his own experience:

I came here with the idea I would spend one term; there was agreement with my partners that I would be gone two years. I was a desperation candidate. They couldn't find anyone else to run and I agreed to be the sacrificial lamb. After I got elected and saw the type of work it was, my whole life was changed by it. I could earn more money in my business I know, and my family would be better off. Yet there is such an intriguing challenge for me here that I can see no other future for myself.

Fashioning the Paths of History. Members feel they are doing something important ("political decisions are among the most crucial of all"), that they have an unusual opportunity to "deal with issues that are fashioning the paths of history." Explained one congressman: "It is a sense of not only having a ringside seat at the greatest show on earth but also having a chance to say a line in it every once in a while, and perhaps influencing the course of the play a little bit too."

This theme is a recurring one in expositions by members on why they remain in Congress. It is advanced as a primary justification for making the sacrifices that many members assert are involved in congressional service. Seldom expressed is the sense of power and influence that comes from participating in matters of moment, but this is recognized too. Congressmen know that large segments of the public do not think well of representatives or of politicians as a group; they are also aware that in other circles the congressman is an important figure. By helping to determine national policy and by being in a position to influence many diverse kinds of decisions, the legislator considers he occupies a remarkably strategic and significant position in our national life. That eases adjustment to unpleasant tasks. As one veteran member described it:

> Occasionally, perhaps just once or twice a session, you sit there on the floor and are able to think of yourself as one tiny particle in the whole stream of history. The hard work falls away, and the tension is relaxed, and you have a sense of purpose that I don't think you find in any other profession.

A colleague described his position similarly:

> Each of us as he looks back at any given year or period in this job sees a measure which was strengthened because of his activities. He knows that as he gains seniority his opportunities to make a still greater contribution will grow. It is not just the votes he casts or the cases he processes, or the administrative decisions he works for or against. It is the little amendments in bills, the little twists here, the little holding actions there, that give him a sense of permanent satisfaction. He can say, "because I was there at the time, possibly the decision was altered ever so slightly in a constructive direction." And, looking back, each congress does produce significant additions to the corpus of law in the United States and each of us has some part to play in that. I, for one, take a certain vicarious thrill in having been a member of the congress that admitted Hawaii to the Union. That will be an historic event after everything else passes away. It finished a long piece of unfinished business.

Helping Others. Another major attraction of the job as congressmen see it is that they are in a position to be of assistance to other people. To many individuals, congressmen represent the only, or perhaps final, source of help. The knowledge that people depend on them and that they alone may be able to ensure that a wrong action is corrected is tremendously satisfying to the legislator. For many of them it represents the most important single advantage of the job; to nearly all of them it is a most important feature. As one member said:

Some of the greatest satisfactions have come not in what would be regarded as major legislative accomplishments. This job provides the greatest opportunity for a person to help people who are faced with a blank wall and have been unable to get help from anyone else. You have the great power of the federal government to assist you in helping them. You are able to serve your fellow men better [than in other occupations] and more effectively.

Service to constituents may be measured in other terms than intervention to seek satisfactory resolution of their difficulties with agencies of the federal government. It may involve informational and educational functions. Solons often express pleasure with the opportunities available to them to "educate" residents of their districts regarding the issues of the day or merely to disseminate factual information that might otherwise escape the average citizen. Many feel a responsibility to exert a positive role in this respect.

A Sense of Duty. A number of congressmen assert they remain in the House "to fulfill life's purpose." Related one midwestern legislator:

Sometimes I think about how much I would rather be back on the farm. But then I realize there were people who had enough confidence and faith in me to send me down here again. I never pushed hard to get into politics, but it seems I keep moving further along in it. So I am here for two reasons. I think there must be some purpose to my life and, second, people have confidence in me. I look around me and see men of much more ability. Yet perhaps I can do something for my people and add something to this total cause.

Other members mention as an important element in their decision to remain in the Congress their desire to advance certain principles to which they are dedicated. ("We may pass over these things lightly or with a spirit of levity, but essentially a person has to have a dedication to certain principles that he thinks important in order to stay around here.") Or they may regard congressional service as a duty: "This is a job that somebody has got to do, and I am very much imbued with the idea that right now the government needs people who think as our party does."

To a protest that it is difficult to remain in the House fighting for principles that have little chance of being adopted one member retorted, "You can be a rock in the midst of the current, though." This sense of obligation to continue the struggle for the goals in which one believes, despite poor prospects for success, is evident in the following excerpts from a discussion of minority members of the House:

I wonder if we can stop this trend which we believe is dangerous by throwing ourselves right in front of the runaway car. That would just kill us. Rather we have to jump in and try to steer the car back into the direction it should go. The one reason I am here is the perhaps futile hope that maybe the tide can be stemmed, maybe you can get in that car and stop it. Maybe somewhere you can get a message across. But it is one of the most discouraging things I have ever experienced.

*

The battle we are fighting is similar to the role of the stern parent as opposed to the parent who gives the child everything he wants. In the long run, I am sure it is not good for the child to have everything he wants. But you get awfully tired of being the stern parent, subject to abuse and accused of not being interested in your fellow human beings.

*

Of all the things Sherman Adams said in defending the budget, the thing I liked least was: "We are just giving the people the kind of government they want." I can't subscribe to that, for the same reason you have mentioned. What people want is not necessarily the kind of government they ought to have.

Getting an Education. For other congressmen the attraction of the House lies in the fact that it represents an unusual learning experience, one in which the member can constantly grow, developing new understanding and insights. This they find exciting. Congressional service "is the greatest educational opportunity a man can have," and this fact alone makes it possible to endure the disadvantages and irritations of the job. One of the most able men in the House says:

The life of a congressman is more frustrating than being a private in World War II. I despise it a great deal of the time and spend a ridiculous amount of time thinking about how nice it would be to get out of it. But the thing that will keep me in the job until I get defeated is that I cannot conceive of any place on earth where you can learn more about more different things. To me it is the most fascinating educational institution on all subjects with, curiously enough, a fair amount of opportunity for the individual to decide what he is going to specialize in next in terms of learning.

This view is corroborated by the testimony of another serious-minded conscientious representative who said: "There is a constant intellectual challenge. I have two degrees in government and I learned more my first year in Congress than I did in six years of college. You have that practical everyday brush with the facts of American life."

Members of Congress may feel, too, that the job is attractive because it provides an unusual opportunity to pursue personal goals. One representative explained, in advancing that view:

> My principal interests for a long time have been politics and government and law. In Congress you have a unique opportunity to engage full time in all three. Conceding there are a lot of frustrations and disappointments, I think it is about as satisfying an outlet for my interests as I can find.

Another source of interest to many House members is "the interplay of human relations." They enjoy watching, and participating in, the struggles for power, the maneuverings involved in the passage or defeat of legislation, the impact of forceful personalities on legislative results. They study their colleagues, seeking to determine what makes them perform as they do, and their excitement grows with the increasing accuracy of their powers to predict behavior and results. The House actually is a very subtly constructed and complex social structure; many members recognize this, and it is a fascinating challenge to them. "What makes Sammy Run? With 435 versions it is difficult to figure out" observes a man noted for his ability to gauge the interests and actions of his colleagues. Commented one representative:

> What makes this thing so fascinating is that it is a human panorama. Tremendous psychological forces are working all the time and human relations are in play constantly. It is so complex you couldn't actually draw the lines of interrelationship. There is the element of friendship, there is every degree of respect and relationship. What makes one man follow another man's lead? That is what makes it so fascinating.

The Despondency of the Few

Individual and group discussions with members of Congress lead to the firm conclusion that the vast majority would desert the House only reluctantly, unless some higher political office were in sight. But, inevitably, there are some members who are less fascinated by the legislative process than their colleagues. Said one much respected House Democrat:

I don't know why I am here. I haven't found anything to give me satisfaction in the time I have been in Congress, and I don't find the business of being a congressman stimulating or as interesting as the practice of law. I had more control over my time when I was in law practice. There are so many frustrations, especially in this Congress, that I don't think the job is worth it. I agree it is bad unless you have some main achievement that you can look back upon. But I don't have any of those feelings. I haven't won anything or accomplished anything in my service here.

And an equally conscientious and respected Republican stated:

I think the period of adventure and enthusiasm has worn off somewhat in my case. I sit in a committee room from 10 to 4 every day from the middle of January until about the last of July. That gets pretty tiresome when you have to go back to the office and do a full day's work. And I have an adverse party registration situation in my district. I begin to wonder whether it is worth continuing the fight. Instead of being thrilled and excited, when I see the votes that are cast and the direction in which we are headed, I become alarmed. I don't know whether I want to be a part of this history we are making right now or not. I have my doubts about whether we can look back on it favorably.

Special situations may of course explain the despondency of some members. Thus one man who responded most reluctantly to the entreaties of his party's leadership that he move from one committee on which he was an acknowledged expert to another key committee for which he possessed little background reacted sharply to the change. At the first opportunity, he followed the course he had suggested he might take: he left the House and ran for another office. Shortly after he had changed committees he said: "It will be years before I get the experience to know as much about anything as the field I just left. I am at a dead end in this Congress. Sure there is a way out. That is not to run the next time or to run for some other office that might provide more stimulation."

Even among congressmen who enjoy their work, there is much variation in the extent of their commitment to legislative service. Some may not gain the feeling of exhilaration and satisfaction that other colleagues receive; they may take a more detached attitude toward the job and believe themselves capable of being equally happy in another vocation. Commented one House leader to his colleagues as they discussed the satisfactions of the job, "I don't mind telling you there are about five other things I would rather be doing than what I am doing right now."

On Balance the Vote is "Aye"

Yet there is something about congressional service that captivates most incumbents and makes them reluctant to yield their seats. One midwestern member summarized the views of a majority of the representatives when he said:

Winston Churchill said it all when he said that happy is he whose means of livelihood turns out to be a career that is stimulating and challenging and that is certainly what this is. I feel very happy to be here. You have a chance to educate your electors, and if you don't succeed in that and find their views different from your own, you frequently can get a little credit with them by voting your conscience.

One House member with much reason to feel disillusioned and frustrated about his congressional service displayed in a newsletter to his constituents that he was far from regretful that he had entered the House. After asking what factors led a man to run for Congress and to want to stay there once elected, the representative went on to give his opinion:

Money is not the explanation because many, if not most, congressmen could earn a larger income in other fields. A desire for security is certainly not the answer since there is little security for a congressman who must run for re-election every two years. Certainly it is not the working conditions. Most members work far longer hours than they would be forced to put in were they in business. Furthermore, a congressman like a doctor is always on call. A congressman must attend a great many more social functions than the average citizen, thus leaving him little time for a normal family life.

What is it which attracts a man to this type of life? Some would say it is the desire for power. Some the desire for prestige. Both are partial answers, but they do not present a full explanation. The chief interest in holding a congressional office lies in the satisfaction one can gain from feeling he is actively participating in the important decisions of government. Furthermore, the office of representative has a great potential. A congressman has a great opportunity to assist in the dialogue between the people and their representatives. A representative must lead as well as follow. He must help interpret the government's policies to the people. He must help educate them concerning their responsibilities. Last but not least is [his] vote. It should not be taken lightly.

Thus the fascination of congress lies in the nature of the office and the real opportunities it offers the incumbent to contribute to the welfare of the American people. Its very operations and procedures make the life interesting. An additional important factor is the friends we make in the process of our work.

The life of a congressman though it has its agonizing, depressing periods; though it is filled with annoyances large and small, real and imagined; though it is uncertain and tenuous and filled with tension does, in fact, seem worth the disadvantages. For at the same time it has meaning, challenge, interest, and prestige. It provides enduring, if sometimes strained, satisfactions. In seeking to explain the motivations of members of Congress, one is reminded of the words of Daniel Webster, which appear above the Speaker's rostrum in the House of Representatives:

LET US DEVELOPE THE RESOURCES OF OUR LAND, CALL FORTH ITS POWERS, BUILD UP ITS INSTITUTIONS, PROMOTE ALL ITS GREAT INTERESTS AND SEE WHETHER WE ALSO IN OUR DAY AND GENERATION MAY NOT PERFORM SOMETHING WORTHY TO BE REMEMBERED.

Index